ANNALS OF COMMUNISM

Each volume in the series Annals of Communism will publish selected and previously inaccessible documents from former Soviet state and party archives in a narrative that develops a particular topic in the history of Soviet and international communism. Separate English and Russian editions will be prepared. Russian and Western scholars work together prepare the documents for volume. Documents are chosen not for their support of any single interpretation but for their particular historical importance or their general value in deepening understanding and facilitating discussion. The volumes are designed to be useful to students, scholars, and interested general readers.

# The KGB File of
# Andrei Sakharov

*Edited and annotated by*

Joshua Rubenstein and Alexander Gribanov

*With an introduction by Joshua Rubenstein*

*Documents translated by*

Ella Shmulevich, Efrem Yankelevich, and Alla Zeide

Yale University Press

New Haven & London

This volume was prepared with the cooperation and support of the Andrei Sakharov Archives and Human Rights Center at Brandeis University. The archive, now called the Andrei Sakharov Archive, was transferred to the Houghton Library, Harvard University, in the summer of 2004. The documents and the photographs from the archive are reproduced by permission.

Introduction copyright © 2005 by Joshua Rubenstein.
Copyright © 2005 by Yale University.

Designed by James J. Johnson and set in
Sabon Roman type by The Composing Room of Michigan, Inc.
Printed in the United States of America by Vail-Ballou Press.

*Library of Congress Cataloging-in-Publication Data*

The KGB file of Andrei Sakharov / edited by Joshua Rubenstein and Alexander Gribanov.
p.   cm.   —   (Annals of Communism)
Includes bibliographical references and index.
ISBN 0-300-10681-5 (alk. paper)
1. Sakharov, Andrei, 1921–   2. Human rights workers—Soviet Union.   3. Dissenters—Soviet Union.   4. Soviet Union. Komitet gosudarstvennoi bezopasnosti—Archives.
I. Rubenstein, Joshua.   II. Gribanov, Alexander, 1945–   III. Series.
JC599.S58K43   2005
323′.092—dc22
2005002061

A catalogue record for this book is available from the British Library.

The paper in this book meets the guidelines for permanence and durability of the Committee on Production Guidelines for Book Longevity of the Council on Library Resources.

10   9   8   7   6   5   4   3   2   1

Yale University Press gratefully acknowledges the financial support given for this publication by the Daphne Seybolt Culpeper Foundation, the David Woods Kemper Memorial Foundation, Joseph W. Donner, the Edward H. Andrews Foundation, the Historical Research Foundation, the John M. Olin Foundation, the Lynde and Harry Bradley Foundation, Jeremiah Milbank, Roger Milliken, the Milton V. Brown Foundation, Lloyd H. Smith, the William H. Donner Foundation, and Keith Young.

If a man speaks out, it does not mean that he hopes necessarily to achieve something. He may hope for nothing but nonetheless speak because he cannot remain silent.

ANDREI SAKHAROV, 1973

# Contents

*Illustrations follow page 166*

# Preface

More than four years after the death of Andrei Sakharov in December 1989, the Federal Counterintelligence Service (FCS) of the Russian Federation gave his widow, Elena Bonner, a collection of sixty-four reports from the Secretariat of the Committee of State Security (the notorious KGB, or Soviet secret police) to the Central Committee of the Communist Party. The FCS had inherited domestic functions from the KGB and also a considerable part (if not all) of the KGB archives. The associates of Sergei Stepashin, who was director of the FCS from March 3, 1994, until June 30, 1995, selected these documents and handed copies to Elena Bonner at a conference in May 1994 marking the anniversary of Sakharov's birth.

Bonner later obtained additional documents from the Archive of the President of the Russian Federation (APRF), which inherited materials from the Central Committee and its archives. Among the files from the presidential archive are political reports from the KGB. Copies of other KGB documents were provided by the Russian State Archive for Social and Political History (RGASPI), which was at one time the Central Party Archive. Several other documents appear through the courtesy of the human rights activist and former prisoner of conscience Vladimir Bukovsky, who obtained a copy of the files of the 1992 Constitutional Court trial of the Communist Party of the USSR. There is no doubt that the KGB archives contain many more than the 204 documents kindly placed at our disposal by Elena Bonner; 146 of these documents are collected in this volume. The vast majority appear here for the first time.

The title of this book indicates two opposing forces: the security apparatus and the physicist who dared to challenge the absolute authority of the Communist regime. The Soviet regime first came to know Andrei Sakharov as one of the country's leading physicists and the primary designer of the Soviet hydrogen bomb. But once Sakharov began openly to question Kremlin policies and campaign on behalf of imprisoned human rights activists, the KGB felt compelled to remove his security clearance and place him under constant surveillance. These top-secret reports about Sakharov's dissident activities were intended for members of the Politburo, the leading political figures in the country.

Sakharov has described his public activities and the government's response in his *Memoirs*. Today, reading these KGB reports, we can examine the Kremlin's side of the story—the mechanism of Central Committee decisions, the rationale for its actions, and perhaps an evaluation of the results. These documents are not an objective portrait of Andrei Sakharov or his colleagues in the human rights movement. They tell us much more about the organization that produced the reports. The dry, unemotional, bureaucratic language of the KGB material collected in this book will help us find answers to some obvious questions. How did this repressive machinery work? How did Soviet leaders understand their options in various situations? What operational procedures did KGB officials have at their disposal? To what extent did the KGB hold the initiative and to what extent was it a tool for Party bosses?

From time to time Politburo members wrote comments in the margins of these reports. In some cases they only affixed their signatures after reading the documents; in others they scribbled something more substantial. We shall comment on their responses, almost all of which were relevant to Andrei Sakharov's life. In addition, this collection also contains some letters from KGB chairmen, such as Yuri Andropov and Viktor Chebrikov, to other branches of the establishment, such as the Academy of Sciences.

The KGB Secretariat (specifically, the Office of the Chairman) had its own methods in issuing documentation. Every document has a mark in the top left corner of the first page or at the end of the text: a number, a dash, one or several letters and sometimes a suffix, such as

the code "1169-A/ov" that appears on the first document in our collection. The letter *A* stands for Andropov. Correspondingly we find the
letter *Ch* for Chebrikov on the documents issued under his name, *F* for
Fedorchuk, *Tsv* for Tsvigun, *Ts* for Tsinev, and *K* for Kryuchkov. This
system was established decades ago; after World War II Viktor Abakumov, the minister for state security, codified his documents in the same
way.[1]

The numbers preceding the letter or letters signify the document's
place among the documents issued through the KGB Secretariat in a
given year. In 1972, for example, document 42, with the code #1414-
A, was issued on May 26. Another document, issued in December of
the same year, bears the code 3085-A. It follows that during 1972 the
KGB Secretariat issued more than three thousand documents of this
type. One should note that for every year represented in our collection
(from 1968 to 1990) the total number of documents remained more or
less the same—over three thousand.

The copies we have were slightly altered as they were prepared for
declassification by FCS officials. The usual archival markings are absent and many marginal handwritten notes and signatures have been
removed. We can see the difference when we compare copies supplied
by the FCS with others received from the Presidential Archive. Among
the missing elements the most important are the obligatory locator
markings of the Russian archival system: f. (*fond*, collection), op.
(*opis'*, inventory), and d. *delo*, file). Moreover, small portions of the
text were removed from the copies provided by the FCS. Often the
missing portion contained the phrase "by operational means," since
any mention of operational procedures was taboo.

The authenticity of documents in this collection cannot be taken for
granted. Authorship is rather simple to confirm in the case of translations, where mistakes or distortions are easy to spot, but the situation
is more complicated when KGB officials used information recovered
from conversations, telephone calls, and other oral data. The issue of
authenticity is not related directly to the question of veracity. These
documents were not intended to be objective; their very language practically excludes the notion of truthfulness. This language evolved as an
instrument for constructing and maintaining a virtual reality: Communist "newspeak" attributed everything bad to imperialist intrigues,

---

1. See document no. 1392-A in *Neizvestnaia Rossiia. XX vek* [Unknown Russia:
The twentieth century] (Moscow, 1992), 1:136.

everything good to the efforts of the Communist leadership. Thus Sakharov won the Nobel Peace Prize through successful manipulation by "reactionary forces" and "secret services" of the West. These reactionary forces could even attempt to arrange a Nobel Prize in chemistry for Sakharov although he was a physicist (Document 35, October 2, 1971). The language of the KGB reports is difficult to reproduce in English. Since the KGB authors were sedulously avoiding the truth, they repeated the same lies over and over again. As is the case with the output of any bureaucracy, the KGB reports abound in clichés and formulaic combinations.

This collection does not contain all the data and files that the KGB amassed on Sakharov. For undisclosed reasons, the officials of the FCS and other state archives have withheld large numbers of documents. The gaps correspond to significant periods of time, in some cases to years. Since the KGB's surveillance over Andrei Sakharov undoubtedly continued unabated during those periods, they must have produced a great number of documents that are not now available to the public. Prominent among the withheld documents are all "operational documents," while the KGB reportedly burned 583 volumes in nine steps.[2] The entire auto-da-fé was evidently carried out between October 17, 1988, and September 6, 1989.

A file on Andrei Sakharov was obviously initiated long before he burst onto the world stage in the spring of 1968 with his first essay, "Progress, Coexistence, and Intellectual Freedom." More than likely, "operational research" against Sakharov was initiated in the late 1940s, when he was first screened for secret weapons research in preparation for his assignment to Arzamas-16 (the Installation, as he dubbed it in his *Memoirs*). It must have been updated periodically and then, in the 1960s, reactivated in earnest. Perhaps it was in the late

2. However, even an official statement by the KGB that documents have been destroyed cannot be considered proof of their disappearance. For one case in which officially shredded documents were mysteriously reborn and returned to their creator, see Mikhail Malinin, "Kak mozhno i nuzhno borotsa s KGB" [How it is possible and necessary to fight the KGB], in *Mezhdunarodnaia Konferentsiia KGB: Vchera, segodnia, zavtra* [International Conference on the KGB: Yesterday, today, tomorrow] (Moscow, 1994), 181–82. According to Vadim Bakatin's memoir, 550 volumes were burned; see his *Izbavlenie ot KGB* [To get rid of the KGB] (Moscow, 1992), 158–60. On the massive destruction of numerous files related to human rights and the dissident movement, see Amy Knight, *Spies without Cloaks: The KGB Successors* (Princeton, 1996), 194, indicating as her source an unpublished manuscript by Arsenii Roginskii and Nikita Okhotin titled "Arkhivy KGB: God posle putcha" [KGB archives: A year after the putsch] (Moscow, 1992), 7.

1960s that the file passed into the category of "operational investigation." Nevertheless, the documents under study here make no mention of operational data inherited from the 1940s and 1950s.

A full list of all 204 KGB documents about Andrei Sakharov that have been declassified can be found in the back of this volume. The editors also chose a title for each KGB report; most of the reports were sent without a title. The 146 documents included here are drawn from this larger collection of KGB reports, which are stored in the Andrei Sakharov Archive at Houghton Library, Harvard University. (The processing and arrangement of these papers were completed when the archive was located at the Andrei Sakharov Archives and Human Rights Center at Brandeis University. The materials were transferred to Harvard University in the summer of 2004.) Material from the included documents that was redundant or barely relevant to the KGB's surveillance, tactics, and strategy in dealing with Andrei Sakharov was cut by the American editor, Joshua Rubenstein, and is signaled by ellipses. The entire set of documents, in Russian and in English translation, can be found at the following Web site: www.yale.edu/annals/sakharov/

Before the FCS documents were released, they passed through the obligatory declassification procedure. The upper right corner of every first page has the stamp:

DECLASSIFIED
Central Archive of the Ministry of Security
Russian Federation
[Signed] Afanasieva
1994

It would be interesting to know what Mme Afanasieva was thinking when she removed the last formal strap securing these documents from public scrutiny.

*Alexander Gribanov*

# Acknowledgments

I would like to express my gratitude to many individuals and institutions. I am especially thankful to Elena Bonner, who donated a major portion of these documents to the Andrei Sakharov Archive and then helped the editors understand important details in the KGB reports. I am also grateful to Vladimir Bukovsky for generously donating documents from his magnificent collection.

I would also like to express my deep appreciation to several institutions in Moscow, including the Archives of the President of the Russian Federation, the Russian State Archive for Social and Political History (RGASPI), the Archives of the Federal Security Service of the Russian Federation, the Andrei Sakharov Museum and Archives, the Memorial Human Rights Society, and the State Archive of the Russian Federation (GARF). The Open Society Archives in Budapest were also helpful. All these institutions were sources of material and information.

I also thank Ella Shmulevich, Efrem Yankelevich, and Alla Zeide for translating these documents into English. I very much appreciate the advice and assistance of Yale Richmond, who served in the U.S. embassy in Moscow in the late 1960s, and of Gabriel Superfin, of the Forschungsstelle Osteuropa, University of Bremen, who helped with his comprehensive knowledge of the human rights movement both as an activist and as a researcher.

My deepest gratitude goes to colleagues who generously contributed to the English version of this book: Robert Szulkin, Gregory Freeze, and Edward Kline. Finally, I must thank my co-editor, Joshua Rubenstein, for his patience and generous help in acquainting me with the American practice of editing primary sources.

*Alexander Gribanov*


A number of colleagues and friends helped me to complete work on this volume. Most of all, I am grateful to Elena Bonner and her daughter, Tatiana Yankelevich, for asking me to edit this material. It was a privilege for me to work with them and to explore Sakharov's life as a human rights activist.

Alexander Gribanov of the Andrei Sakharov Archives and Human Rights Center at Brandeis University proved to be an astute, patient, and thorough-minded collaborator; his knowledge and understanding of Sakharov's career were an invaluable source of documents, facts, and inspiration.

In Moscow, Bella Koval and Katya Shikhanovich, of the staff of the Arkhiv Andreia Sakharova, provided valuable assistance during my visit in the fall of 2002. My discussions with Yuri Samodurov of the Andrei Sakharov Museum were also helpful, pointing my research in several useful directions. I also benefited from interviews with Ludmilla Alexeyeva and Alexander (Sanya) Daniel, who have been friends and co-conspirators for many years; Sanya was especially generous with his time and did not hesitate to share unpublished material with me. Boris Belenkin, Valentin Gefter, and Gennady Kuzovkin, Sanya's colleagues at the Memorial Human Rights Society, were also helpful. Anatoly Chernyaev did not hesitate to share his unique perspective as someone who worked closely with Mikhail Gorbachev during the heady years of glasnost and perestroika. Otto Latsis spoke with me about being a member of the Central Committee under Gorbachev. And Alexander Levada explained Sakharov's standing among the Soviet people on the basis of his superb and unprecedented polling data.

Yevgenia Albats, Boris Katz, Edward Kline, and Benjamin Nathans read parts of the volume; their editorial suggestions were consistently helpful. Mark Kuchment helped me to understand various Russian-language documents. And the astute observations of Stephen F. Cohen always inspired productive directions for my research and thinking about the meaning of dissent in the Soviet Union.

Staff members of the Harvard University Libraries also assisted me; I thank in particular Anna Arthur of Widener Library and Susan Gardos and Helen Repina of the library of the Davis Center for Russian and Eurasian Studies for helping me locate material. Mark Kramer of the Cold War History Project was also generous with his time and attention. As always, the support of the Davis Center, where I have enjoyed the privileges of an associate for many years, continued to make my work possible. David Peter Coppen of the Sibley Music Library of the Eastman School of Music at the University of Rochester kindly provided bibliographical assistance.

My agent, Robin Straus, encouraged me throughout. I am also grateful to my editors at Yale University Press, Jonathan Brent and Vadim Staklo, for entrusting this volume to me and continuing my connection to the Annals of Communism series. No student of Russian history could ask for a more discerning or committed editorial project. And my colleagues at Amnesty International have always supported my intellectual fascination with Russian history and shared my preoccupation with the fate of human rights activists and prisoners of conscience such as Andrei Sakharov.

As always, I am most grateful to my wife, Jill Janows, and to our son, Benjamin, for their unstinting patience and understanding during yet another labor of scholarly love.

Finally, Alexander Gribanov and I dedicate our work to the memory of Larisa Iosifovna Bogoraz. She was a remarkably brave and intelligent woman and an inspiration and friend to both of us, as she was to Andrei Sakharov. She died in Moscow in April 2004, just as this volume was nearing completion.

*Joshua Rubenstein*

# Chronology

1921  Andrei Dmitrievich Sakharov born in Moscow on May 21, the first child of Dmitri Sakharov and Ekaterina Sofiano

1938  Enrolls in Physics Department of Moscow State University

1941  Hitler invades the Soviet Union on June 22. Sakharov fails the army medical examination in July; with the Physics Department of Moscow State University, he is transferred to Ashkhabad

1942  Sakharov graduates with honors; he works at an armaments factory in Ulyanovsk from September 1942 until January 1945

1943  Soviet project to build an atom bomb initiated under the direction of Igor Kurchatov; Sakharov marries Klavdia Vikhireva on July 10

1945  Sakharov is accepted by Igor Tamm as a graduate student at the Theoretical Department of Moscow's Lebedev Physics Institute (FIAN) in January; his daughter Tatyana is born; Germany surrenders in May; the United States drops atom bombs on Hiroshima and Nagasaki before Japan surrenders in August

1947  Sakharov is awarded Candidate of Science degree after defense of his thesis, "Theory of 0−0 Nuclear Transitions"

1948  Sakharov is included in Tamm's research group, assigned to develop a thermonuclear (fusion) bomb

1949  First Soviet atom (fission) bomb is successfully tested on August 29; Sakharov's daughter Lyubov is born

1950  Sakharov is transferred to Arzamas-16, the secret facility for the development of nuclear weapons, located at Sarov

1951    Sakharov and Tamm develop the idea of realizing a controlled
        thermonuclear reaction by magnetic confinement of a high-tem-
        perature plasma
1951    The United States tests a "boosted" bomb on May 21; this is es-
        sentially a fission bomb whose explosive power is boosted by in-
        clusion of a thermonuclear component
1952    First U.S. thermonuclear "super" device tested on November 1
1953    Stalin dies on March 5; Sakharov is awarded Doctor of Science
        degree in June; the first Soviet thermonuclear bomb is success-
        fully tested on August 12; Sakharov is the principal author of its
        "layer-cake" design, similar to the 1951 U.S. boosted bomb, but
        more powerful; Sakharov is elected a full member of the USSR
        Academy of Sciences and receives his first Hero of Socialist Labor
        award and the Stalin Prize
1954    The United States tests a deliverable thermonuclear "superbomb"
        on March 1
1955    The Soviet Union tests thermonuclear superbomb on November
        22; Sakharov is primarily responsible for the "third idea," using
        radiation of a fission bomb to trigger the fusion reaction
1956    Sakharov receives second Hero of Socialist Labor award and
        Lenin Prize
1957    Sakharov's son, Dmitri, is born
1958    Sakharov publishes two articles on the danger of nuclear testing:
        "Radioactive Carbon in Nuclear Explosions and Nonthreshold
        Biological Effects" and a popular version, "Radiation Danger of
        Nuclear Tests"
1961    Khrushchev reprimands Sakharov for opposing unilateral deci-
        sion to resume nuclear weapons tests; his father, Dmitri Sakharov,
        dies in Moscow
1962    Khrushchev personally presents Sakharov with third Hero of So-
        cialist Labor award
1962    Sakharov campaigns to ban all nuclear tests except those con-
  −63   ducted underground; the Treaty Banning Nuclear Weapons Tests
        in the Atmosphere, in Outer Space, and Underwater is signed in
        Moscow on August 5, 1963; his mother, Ekaterina Sofiano, dies
        in Moscow
1964    Sakharov successfully opposes Nikolai Nuzhdin's election to full
        membership in Academy of Sciences on the grounds that
        Nuzhdin supports Lysenko's rejection of modern genetics; meets
        the dissident biologist Zhores Medvedev; Brezhnev replaces
        Khrushchev as general secretary of Communist Party
1965    Sakharov writes his first paper on cosmology; the writers Andrei
        Sinyavsky and Yuli Daniel are arrested in Moscow for publishing

their stories abroad under pseudonyms; the Soviet human rights movement begins to emerge

1966   Sakharov signs two appeals—against the possible rehabilitation of Stalin and against the introduction of Articles 190-1 and 190-3 into the Criminal Code, which are aimed at further restricting freedom of expression

1967   Joins committee to save Lake Baikal; writes letter to Brezhnev in defense of young imprisoned dissidents; as a result loses his post as a department head at Arzamas-16, but remains deputy scientific director; publishes paper on the baryon asymmetry of the universe

1968   *A Chronicle of Current Events* begins to appear in Moscow. Sakharov circulates his essay "Progress, Coexistence, and Intellectual Freedom"; he loses his security clearance; Warsaw Pact forces invade Czechoslovakia to end Prague Spring; Sakharov meets Alexander Solzhenitsyn for the first time

1969   His wife, Klavdia Vikhireva, dies of cancer; he returns to Theoretical Department of FIAN as a senior scientist

1970   Together with the mathematician Valentin Turchin and the historian Roy Medvedev, Sakharov writes a letter to the Central Committee calling for democratization of the Soviet Union; with Valery Chalidze and Andrei Tverdokhlebov he establishes the Moscow Human Rights Committee; he attends his first political trial in Kaluga; he meets Elena Bonner, who is active in defense of prisoners; Solzhenitsyn is awarded the Nobel Prize for literature

1972   Sakharov and Bonner register their marriage on January 7; his first interview with a Western journalist appears in *Newsweek* on November 13

1973   Broadcast of Sakharov's interview in July with Swedish correspondent about Soviet problems sparks a warning from procurator and fierce attacks in the Soviet press; in September, Sakharov asks the U.S. Congress to support linking trade benefits to the Soviet Union's emigration policy

1974   Solzhenitsyn is expelled from the Soviet Union in February

1975   Sakharov writes *My Country and the World;* the Helsinki Final Act is signed on August 1; Elena Bonner is permitted to travel to the West for medical treatment; Sakharov is awarded the Nobel Prize for peace

1976   The Moscow Helsinki Watch Group is founded in May; Sakharov sends appeal to Amnesty International calling for the release of political prisoners throughout the world

1977   Sakharov writes to President Jimmy Carter urging him to defend human rights activists; Carter responds that "human rights is a

central concern of my administration"; Sakharov writes to
Amnesty International on the abolition of the death penalty

1978    Sakharov begins to write his memoirs

1979    Soviet forces invade Afghanistan

1980    Sakharov denounces the Soviet invasion and calls for a boycott of
the Moscow Summer Olympics; he is banished to Gorky without a
trial; publishes two articles on elementary particles and one on cosmology

1981    He endures 17-day hunger strike to win a visa for Elena Bonner's
son's wife, Liza Alexeyeva, to join him in America

1982    Leonid Brezhnev dies on November 10; he is succeeded by Yuri
Andropov, former head of the KGB

1983    Sakharov's article "The Danger of Thermonuclear War" appears
in *Foreign Affairs*

1984    Andropov dies on February 9 and is succeeded by Konstantin
Chernenko; Elena Bonner is detained at the Gorky airport on
May 2; Sakharov declares a hunger strike to gain her permission
to travel for medical treatment; she is convicted of "anti-Soviet
slander" on August 10 and sentenced to exile in Gorky

1985    Chernenko dies on March 10 and is succeeded by Mikhail Gorbachev; Elena Bonner is permitted to travel to the United States
for heart surgery

1986    In February Sakharov appeals to Gorbachev for the release of
prisoners of conscience; in April there is a catastrophic meltdown
at the Chernobyl nuclear reactor; Sakharov and Bonner are permitted to return to Moscow in December

1987    In February Sakharov argues against Soviet linkage of nuclear
weapons reduction to termination of U.S. Strategic Defense Initiative; Gorbachev begins campaign of glasnost and perestroika;
political prisoners begin to be released

1988    In June Sakharov's article "The Inevitability of Perestroika" appears in Moscow; in August he helps to establish Moscow Tribune, a discussion club of the liberal intelligentsia; Sakharov
makes his first visit to the United States, where he meets President
Ronald Reagan, President-Elect George H. W. Bush, and Edward
Teller; in December he visits Azerbaijan and Armenia in attempt
to resolve their differences over Nagorno-Karabakh

1989    Sakharov is elected to the Congress of People's Deputies; visits
Tbilisi to investigate the April 9 clash, in which Soviet troops attacked and killed twenty-one demonstrators; Sakharov speaks
out frequently at the First Congress of People's Deputies and calls
for the repeal of Article 6 of the Soviet Constitution, which grants
monopoly of power to the Communist Party; he dies of a heart

attack in Moscow on December 14; after four days of public
mourning and funeral services attended by tens of thousands of
Soviet citizens, Sakharov is buried in Moscow's Vostryakovskoe
Cemetery

1990   Sakharov's *Memoirs* are published
1991   The second volume of the memoirs, *Moscow and Beyond, 1986–
       1989,* is published

# Abbreviations

| | |
|---|---|
| APRF | Archive of the President of the Russian Federation |
| AS | Arkhiv Samizdata |
| CDU | Christian Democratic Union (Federal Republic of Germany) |
| CPSU | Communist Party of the Soviet Union |
| CSCE | Commission on Security and Cooperation in Europe |
| CSU | Christian Socialist Union (Federal Republic of Germany) |
| FCS | Federal Counterintelligence Service |
| FIAN | Physics Institute of the Academy of Sciences |
| FSB | Federal Security Bureau (successor to KGB) |
| KGB | Committee for State Security |
| KOR | Committee for the Defense of Workers (Poland) |
| NTS | Popular Labor Alliance |
| RGASPI | Russian State Archive for Social and Political History; formerly Central Party Archive |
| RSFSR | Russian Soviet Federative Socialist Republic |
| SA | The Andrei Sakharov Archive at Houghton Library, Harvard University |
| UDHR | Universal Declaration of Human Rights |

The KGB File of Andrei Sakharov

# Introduction
## Andrei Sakharov, the KGB, and the Legacy of Soviet Dissent

### Joshua Rubenstein

O N JULY 11, 1968, the *New York Times* carried a startling piece of news on the front page. Under the headline "Soviet Expert Asks Intellectual Liberty," the article described how a distinguished Soviet physicist had "issued a plea for full intellectual freedom, Soviet–United States cooperation and a worldwide rejection of 'demagogic myths' in an urgent program to avert nuclear war and famine." The physicist's essay was now circulating inside the Soviet Union. Its author was identified as Andrei Sakharov, and according to the article, Sakharov had helped design his country's hydrogen bomb. Over the next few days the *Times* elaborated on the story, praising him in an editorial as "a very brave man. In the present repressive, almost Stalinist, atmosphere in Moscow, it took great courage for even a distinguished nuclear physicist to write and circulate his remarkable manifesto." The editors presciently concluded: "It would be an insult to the intelligence of the Soviet people to assume that Academician Sakharov is alone in his views."[1]

Other major news outlets quickly carried stories of their own. *Newsweek* congratulated Sakharov for "thinking the unthinkable." *Time* called the essay "a thunderbolt," and the *Christian Science Monitor* declared the essay to be "extraordinary," an attack on "the very foundations of the Soviet state." By the end of July, the *New York Times* so believed in the significance of Sakharov's essay that it published a complete translation covering three full pages in the first section.[2]

For most Western observers, this unexpected essay marked the beginning of Andrei Sakharov's career as a dissident. Coming at a dramatic moment, when Czech Communist reformers had captured the world's attention with their attempt to create "socialism with a human face," Sakharov's essay reinforced the exhilarating hope that genuine democratic reform could take hold in Eastern Europe and the Soviet Union. But Sakharov's daring initiative and the broader experiment in Prague were crushed when Warsaw Pact forces invaded Czechoslovakia. Alexander Dubcek, who led the Czech Communist Party in its noble failed attempt at liberalization, was taken away to Moscow, where he and his reform-minded colleagues were compelled to reverse the liberal changes they had introduced. After Dubcek's return to Prague a few days later, he was permitted to retain the formal leadership of the Communist Party temporarily, but in April 1969 he was demoted and expelled from the Party; later he was sent to a remote location to work as a forestry official. He was not allowed to talk with anyone outside his family without official permission. Andrei Sakharov endured a less onerous punishment. Although the KGB (the Soviet secret police) withdrew his security clearance and he was no longer permitted to work inside a secret weapons laboratory, he was invited to resume his physics research a year later at a prestigious institute in Moscow.

The KGB had learned about Sakharov's essay in May 1968. Almost immediately its chairman, Yuri Andropov, passed along a copy to the Politburo, characterizing the document as "anti-Marxist."[3] By June, Andropov was growing concerned about "demagogic attempts [by other dissidents] . . . to exploit the name of the well-known Soviet scientist Academician Sakharov by systematically asking him to endorse documents of politically harmful content." Nonetheless, Andropov remained cautious and suggested that "it would make sense for one of the secretaries of the Central Committee to receive Sakharov and conduct an appropriate conversation with him."[4] The KGB remained mindful of Sakharov's unique status and the secretive nature of his work as a physicist; in many of Andropov's initial reports, Sakharov's name, at times the names of people associated with him, and even some of the issues raised in the reports, such as his work on nuclear weapons, were written in by hand so that KGB typists would not know his identity or learn about sensitive information.

At the same time, the KGB initiated close surveillance of Sakharov himself. Still, because of his high standing in the *nomenklatura,* the KGB did not install listening devices in his apartment until the spring of 1970, and then only after receiving explicit permission from the Politburo. From the spring of 1968 until Sakharov's death in December 1989, the KGB kept the Politburo up to date on his defiant behavior, sending hundreds of reports to the political leadership of the Soviet Union. A few years after Sakharov's death, his widow, Elena Bonner, was given more than two hundred of these memorandums. One hundred forty-six are collected here.*

The reports, though, portray reality through a distorted lens. After looking over these formerly top-secret documents, the veteran activist Ludmilla Alexeyeva was struck by the language the KGB employed. "They sounded exactly like the newspaper articles they used to denounce us," she recalled. "We always thought that among themselves, Soviet officials used plain language about what we were trying to do. Who would have guessed that they talked about us in private in the same way they did in public."[5] These reports, in fact, present a distorted picture of Andrei Sakharov's career as a dissident and the intellectual, political, religious, and nationalist dissent that captured the world's attention at a time when Sakharov was moving beyond his role as a scientist to become a voice for democratic reform and respect for human rights. They also provide important insight into official attitudes and actions.

The evolution of his dissident activity did not unfold in a political vacuum. By 1968, a steadily expanding group of audacious young people, intellectuals, and Communist Party veterans had been holding public vigils and circulating appeals on behalf of imprisoned human rights activists. One case in particular had provoked the initial protests. In September 1965, two Moscow writers, Andrei Sinyavsky and Yuli Daniel, were arrested for sending their stories and essays to the West, where their work was published under pseudonyms. Their friends refused to accept their arrests quietly. They organized petitions on behalf of Sinyavsky and Daniel and even held a demonstration in Moscow's Pushkin Square on December 5, 1965, Soviet Constitution Day, de-

---

* The KGB reports to the Central Committee made up only a modest portion of its files on Sakharov and Bonner. In 1991 the KGB informed Bonner that it had destroyed 583 volumes of operational reports; these were raw materials based on information from KGB informers and surveillance teams that watched and intruded upon their lives for nearly two decades. See Elena Bonner, "My Secret Past: The KGB File," *New York Review of Books,* June 25, 1992, 46.

manding respect for Soviet laws and that the trial of the two defendants
be open. This demonstration is often considered the beginning of the
Soviet human rights movement. Sinyavsky and Daniel were convicted
in February 1966 under the notorious Article 70 of the Criminal Code,
which forbade "anti-Soviet agitation and propaganda," and were sentenced to labor camps in Mordovia, east of Moscow.[6]

   This cycle of arrest, trial, and protest was repeated for two years. By
1968, more than fifteen hundred people had signed appeals protesting
various cases, evoking the kind of attention in the West "that a fish
would have for an ichthyologist if it suddenly began to talk," in the
words of the dissident writer and activist Andrei Amalrik.[7] These activists were challenging long-held constraints. One emblematic moment occurred in the fall of 1967 when the KGB warned Pavel Litvinov, a physics teacher and the grandson of the famous Soviet diplomat
and commissar for foreign affairs Maxim Litvinov, that he would be
better off if he destroyed a collection of documents he was putting together about the trials of two young activists, Viktor Khaustov and
Vladimir Bukovsky; they had been convicted earlier in the year for participating in a demonstration in January 1967 in defense of political
prisoners. Litvinov was not intimidated. To everyone's surprise, he
wrote an account of his conversation with the KGB, sent copies to several Soviet newspapers and three Western Communist newspapers,
and circulated it in samizdat. The BBC prepared a dramatized version
of his account for broadcast to the Soviet Union. Amalrik caught the
uniquely brazen quality of Litvinov's action: "It was not only the conversation itself, of course, since there had been plenty of such conversations and warnings, but the fact that Pavel had recorded it and made
it public. In so doing, he had thrown out a challenge not only to the
KGB, but to one of the most important unpublished laws of Soviet society: a kind of agreement between cat and mouse to the effect that the
mouse will not squeak if the cat starts to eat it."[8]

   Amalrik himself was heavily involved as a liaison between the dissidents and the Western press. Thanks to him and others, appeals were
handed to foreign correspondents and often broadcast in Russian to
the Soviet Union over the BBC, Deutsche Welle, Radio Liberty, and the
Voice of America. Such broadcasts spread the word about political arrests and often provoked further protests, even visits to Moscow from
people all over the country who wanted to help the defendants or share
their own stories of injustice with activists whose names and addresses
they had learned from Western radio programs.

But the trials and ensuing protests made up only one worrisome pattern for the regime. At the same time, more and more uncensored literature was circulating, bringing news of political arrests, violations of judicial procedure, conditions in prisons and labor camps, anti-Semitic incidents, and the suppression of ethnic minorities, along with independent-minded essays, short stories, even entire novels. All this activity was more than just an affront to the regime's painstaking system of censorship. It was also a signal to the Kremlin that a growing number of citizens were finding their own voices and were discussing aspects of life in the Soviet Union without censorship.

In the spring of 1967, no less a figure than Alexander Solzhenitsyn—whose novella *One Day in the Life of Ivan Denisovich*, about a labor camp inmate, had created a sensation in 1962 but whose subsequent major novels were now banned in the Soviet Union—appealed directly to the Writers' Union to abolish censorship for works of fiction and turn the Writers' Union itself into a defender of artistic creativity rather than a repressive tool of the regime. The country, Solzhenitsyn wrote, needed its writers "to express their considered judgment about the moral life of man and society, or to explain . . . the social problems and historical experience that have been so deeply felt in our country."[9] Solzhenitsyn's "Letter to the Writers' Union Congress" joined the flood of samizdat literature.

Other dissidents had even broader ambitions for samizdat. For two years, ever since the petition campaign had begun on behalf of Sinyavsky, Daniel, and other prisoners, news had reached Moscow activists of reprisals against the signers: loss of employment, expulsions from the Party, "chats" with the KGB, threats of arrest, and incarceration in psychiatric hospitals. "Accused of breaking [its] own laws," the activist Boris Shragin observed, "[the regime] answered by breaking them again."[10] Each incident deserved to be recorded. For months there was an ongoing discussion among several of the dissidents over how to collect and circulate this information. Finally, on April 30, 1968, the first issue of *A Chronicle of Current Events* appeared. It soon proved to be among the preeminent achievements of the human rights movement. By its final issue, number 64, which came out in 1983, the *Chronicle* had reported on the full range of nonconformist activity in the country, from outlying regions, from all the national republics, from prisons and labor camps, and the proceedings of ostensibly closed political trials. For fifteen years it survived the arrest of editors, countless searches, and threats of hostage-taking. Sakharov

believed *A Chronicle of Current Events* embodied "the best in the human rights movement, its principles and highest achievements—the
defense of human rights using objective information, and with a principled rejection of violence. The very fact of the almost uninterrupted
publication of the *Chronicle* for more than 15 years is a miracle of self-
sacrifice, of wisdom, of courage and intellectual integrity."[11] Its comprehensive information, dispassionate tone, and regular appearance
reinforced its appeal. And the activists quickly understood its usefulness as a vital record of their struggle with the regime. Material circulating in samizdat was now touching on so many specific episodes of
injustice that it was all but inevitable that more general criticism of the
regime would emerge to place all of these problems in perspective. The
most startling and comprehensive of these early critiques was Andrei
Sakharov's long essay "Progress, Coexistence, and Intellectual Freedom."

   Sakharov was not one of the young, disaffected intellectuals or idealistic Party members who had joined the ranks of active dissidents, as
they would later come to be called. He was among the country's most
honored scientists. Born in 1921, he came from a long line of eminent social and intellectual figures. His paternal grandfather, Ivan
Sakharov, was a respected defense attorney in tsarist Russia who
edited a collection of essays against capital punishment. "While still a
child, I read with horror the remarkable collection of essays *Against
the Death Penalty* published in Russia with the participation of my
grandfather . . . during the wave of executions following the 1905 revolution," Sakharov recalled in a statement to Amnesty International in
1977.[12] "My grandfather's work on this book was an act of conscience and, to an extent, civic courage."[13] His father, Dmitri Sakharov,
was a talented pianist, but it was his career as a teacher of physics that
most influenced the young Andrei. Dmitri Sakharov wrote textbooks
and popular science books, including an introduction to physics and a
history of lighting devices. On his mother's side, Sakharov's ancestors
included a Greek family named Sofiano, who had come to Russia in
the eighteenth century. Many Sofiano men distinguished themselves as
military officers in Russia's wars. Their careers and their ethnic background made them vulnerable in the 1930s, and two of Sakharov's
Sofiano relatives disappeared in the purges.[14] He also lost an uncle on
his father's side of the family.

   At Moscow University, Sakharov made an immediate impression on
his teachers and classmates. He had an unconventional and unex-

pected way of solving scientific problems. A colleague, the physicist Yakov Zeldovich, said of him many years later, "I don't understand how Sakharov thinks."[15] He also had two unusual and dramatic talents that set him apart: he could write in mirror script, after the fashion of Leonardo da Vinci, and he could write simultaneously and equally well with both hands. The first talent may have been little more than a parlor trick, but Sakharov's ability to write with either hand made a vivid impression on his colleagues as he filled a broad blackboard with extensive and complicated formulas.

After the German invasion in June 1941, he was deferred from military duty because of a chronic heart condition and was able to complete his undergraduate studies. For the duration of the war, Sakharov was assigned to a cartridge factory, where he made a substantial contribution to the reliable production of 14.5-millimeter armor-piercing bullets by inventing a magnetic device to test their cores. He began graduate work after the war under Igor Tamm, the leading theoretical physicist at the prestigious Physics Institute of the Academy of Sciences in Moscow, known by its acronym, FIAN.* As he finished his graduate training, Sakharov also published several scientific papers until abruptly, in 1949, his name ceased to appear in print; it did not appear again until 1957.

The explanation was simple enough, but it would not be publicly acknowledged for years: Sakharov was drafted into the program to develop nuclear weapons. By 1950, he was directed to work in a secret facility devoted exclusively to their design and production. Known as Arzamas-16, it was located three hundred miles east of Moscow, and incorporated the monastery and old city of Sarov, which had ceased to appear on any Soviet map. (It was also not far from Gorky, where Sakharov would be exiled many years later.) Arzamas-16—or the Installation, as Sakharov calls it in his memoirs—was a military facility, surrounded by rows of barbed wire and heavy security. It had been built by prison laborers, many of whom were still working there when he first arrived. "Every morning long gray lines of men in quilted jackets, guard dogs at their heels, passed by our curtained windows," he wrote many years later.[16] Sakharov joined legendary physicists, most notably Igor Tamm, Yakov Zeldovich, and the scientific director of the

* Tamm was not initially disposed to accept Sakharov. He is reported to have told him, "You know, young man, it's hardly likely that you will make a physicist. You have a sort of humanistic mind." Tamm was both wrong and acutely prescient. See *New York Times*, December 20, 1986, 8.

Installation, Yuli Khariton, in a concentrated effort to build a thermo-nuclear weapon before the Americans could do so.

He did not accept the assignment willingly. Blessed with a coveted research position, Sakharov "twice rejected attempts to entice [him] away from FIAN and the frontiers of theoretical physics." But the third time, in 1948, he recalled, "nobody bothered to ask my consent." By order of the Council of Ministers and the Party Central Committee, he was assigned to a special research group "to investigate the possi-bility of building a hydrogen bomb."[17] Despite his earlier reluctance, Sakharov threw himself into the work. He turned out to be unusually talented, not only as a theoretical physicist but also as an engineer. "I understood, of course, the terrifying, inhuman nature of the weapons we were building," he acknowledged decades later.

> But the recent war had also been an exercise in barbarity; and although I hadn't fought in that conflict, I regarded myself as a soldier in this new scientific war. . . .
>
> Over the course of time we devised or borrowed a number of princi-ples, including strategic parity and nuclear deterrence, which even now seem to justify intellectually, at least to some extent, the creation of thermonuclear weapons and our role in the process. Our initial zeal, however, was inspired more by emotion than by intellect. The mon-strous destructive force, the scale of our enterprise and the price paid for it by our poor, hungry, war-torn country, the casualties resulting from the neglect of safety standards and the use of forced labor in our mining and manufacturing activities, all these things inflamed our sense of drama and inspired us to make a maximum effort so that the sacrifices—which we accepted as inevitable—would not be in vain. We were possessed by a true war psychology, which became still more overpowering after our transfer to the Installation.[18]

Their efforts proved to be immensely effective. Five years after Sakharov joined the team of scientists, on August 12, 1953, the Soviet Union successfully tested a thermonuclear device, which Sakharov had principally designed.* For this work and involvement in other, related projects, he received in secret three Hero of Socialist Labor awards (the highest civilian honor in the USSR), the Stalin Prize, and the Lenin Prize (awards that carried staggering amounts of money by Soviet standards), as well as a high salary, special housing, a chauffeur on

---

* The first Soviet atomic bomb was detonated on August 29, 1949, and shocked the United States, which had assumed that the Kremlin would require years to develop such a weapon. Sakharov had not worked on this device.

call, restricted consumer goods, and a bodyguard for a time who even went swimming and skiing with him. Moreover, he was rarely permitted to fly because, as he recalled in his memoirs, he was "considered too valuable to risk in a plane crash."[19] In 1953, at the age of thirty-two, he was also elected a full member in the Soviet Academy of Sciences, one of the youngest scientists ever so honored. Igor Kurchatov said of him that day, "This man has done more for the defense of Russia than all of us present here today."[20] But only his colleagues in the highest ranks of scientific research and leading government officials knew of his importance.

After Stalin's death on March 5, 1953, Sakharov gradually became involved in broader social and scientific questions. As he remarked in "Progress, Coexistence, and Intellectual Freedom," his views "were formed in the milieu of the scientific and technical intelligentsia."[21] For years, in fact, his friendships with other scientists, in particular with Igor Tamm, helped to broaden his thinking about Soviet society and the responsibility of scientists to address the country's problems. Their isolated community at the Installation was a haven of relatively free intellectual and political discussion within Stalin's highly controlled kingdom. The scientists could read Western journals and thus had broader and more informed access to the world than almost anyone else in the Soviet Union had ever enjoyed.*

They knew, for example, how the fields of biology and genetics had been devastated by ideological constraints; with Stalin's support, the followers of Trofim Lysenko, a charlatan biologist, had thoroughly stifled research into modern genetics and plant biology. Lysenko claimed that he could transform one species of plant into another—turn rye into wheat, say—by altering its environment. Perhaps the most notorious consequence of Lysenko's influence was the arrest of one of the world's leading plant geneticists, Nikolai Vavilov, in 1940 and his death in prison in 1943. After the war, Lysenko renewed his ideological offensive. By 1948 he was able to announce the support of the Central Committee for his assertion that genes did not exist, thereby preventing any Soviet scientific research based on modern-day understanding of heredity. Work in the field came to a halt as hundreds of

---

* The famous dissident Yuri Orlov studied physics at Moscow State University after World War II. His department enjoyed a similar kind of autonomy and was relatively free of ideological constraints. As Orlov once recalled, it was "a wildly un-Soviet regime." See Yuri Orlov, *Dangerous Thoughts: Memoirs of a Russian Life*, trans. Thomas P. Whitney (New York, 1991), 98.

genuine researchers and experimental agronomists were fired. Lysenko and his followers had triumphed. As Nikolai Nuzhdin, one of Lysenko's principal associates, proclaimed, "Mendelism-Morganism has been condemned. It has no place in Soviet science."[22]

Other branches of science, including physics, were threatened with similar ideological measures. In 1948, while Soviet physicists were frantically working to design an atomic bomb, articles critical of Einstein's theory of relativity appeared in Moscow journals. And then in June 1952, a corresponding member of the Academy of Sciences named A. A. Maximov published an inflammatory article called "Against the Reactionary Einstein-Mania in Physics," in which he claimed that the "Theory of Relativity without a doubt propagandizes antiscientific attitudes concerning fundamental questions of contemporary physics." According to Maximov, "the camp of idealism, running through Einstein, Bohr, and Heisenberg, has directed the development of physics into a dead end." Maximov went on to denounce quantum theory as well.[23]

Sakharov and his colleagues did not let this article pass unnoticed. In December 1952, eleven of them, including Tamm, Lev Landau, Mikhail Leontovich, and Sakharov, took the extraordinary step of sending a collective letter to the administrative head of the hydrogen bomb project, none other than Lavrenti Beria, Stalin's former (and feared) security chief. The letter made it clear that Maximov's article and several earlier pieces from 1948 could lead to an "abnormal situation in Soviet physics. With all our experience, we know what enormous damage such articles can cause. They orient our scientific workers and engineers in an incorrect direction, and they have a malicious effect on the teaching of physics."[24]

In effect, they were warning Beria that if the party wanted to develop atomic and thermonuclear weapons, it had no choice but to leave physics and physicists alone. Beria passed their letter along to Georgy Malenkov (who was regarded as second in command after Stalin) and there were no more attacks on the integrity of Soviet physics. It was spared the fate of biology. Sakharov and his colleagues demonstrated their usefulness eight months later, when the first Soviet thermonuclear device was detonated.

Given Sakharov's subsequent career as a dissident, it is startling to learn how affected he was by Stalin's death in March 1953. By then he knew "quite enough about the horrible crimes that had been committed—the arrests of innocent people, the torture, the deliberate starvation, and all the violence,"[25] but he was not immune to the widespread mourning that overtook the country. Years later Alexei Adzhubei, one-time editor in chief of *Izvestia* and Khrushchev's son-in-law, noted that after Stalin's death there was "a widespread feeling of vulnerability, a sort of bereavement. For most people the name of Stalin was linked with the place of our country in the world arenas, with assurance that difficulties, obstacles, disasters would be overcome. 'He can do every-thing, he will find the one correct solution'; that was how people thought, that is how this personality was regarded—higher than God, closer than father and mother, unique."[26] While some independent-minded people quietly celebrated Stalin's death, Sakharov shared the grief around him. "I am under the influence of a great man's death," he wrote to his wife. "I am thinking of his humanity."[27]

Nonetheless, Sakharov soon understood, as did many other people in the country, that the death of Stalin and the grudging relaxation in cultural life that Khrushchev permitted—the famous "thaw"—needed to be defended and broadened. At the urging of Zeldovich, Sakharov wrote a letter to Nikita Khrushchev in 1954 in defense of a new play that challenged "the highhanded greed and selfishness" of Party bureaucrats. *The Guests,* by Leonid Zorin, was among the inde-pendent-minded works that animated Soviet culture in those years and inevitably became a target for conservative critics. Sakharov was re-sponding to the organized press campaign against it; although his let-ter was "undramatic and unproductive," he noted that it was "the first step I had taken outside my own field."[28]

Soon, however, he was outpacing his colleagues with new initiatives. He made a point of defending a colleague's father who had been ar-rested for telling a lewd joke about Khrushchev. After sending his ap-peal to Khrushchev, Sakharov was summoned to see Mikhail Suslov in his Kremlin office. A long-time member of the Politburo, Suslov was a veteran Stalinist and a strict guardian of Soviet ideology. But Sakharov was not intimidated and spoke up for his friend's father. The fellow was eventually sentenced to two and a half years of confinement, but was released after one year; Sakharov liked to think that his inter-vention "played some part in this relatively mild treatment." It would not be Sakharov's last attempt to help a prisoner.[29]

Under Khrushchev, Sakharov's most telling confrontations with of-ficials came over the issue of nuclear fallout and nuclear testing. In 1955, after the successful atmospheric test of a new and extremely powerful thermonuclear device that he was credited with designing,

Sakharov learned that the shock wave from the explosion had been so unexpectedly severe that it had killed two people, a young soldier and a child. Their deaths and other related casualties "heightened my sense of foreboding," he recalled in his memoirs; he "could not escape a feeling of complicity." When he was invited to propose the first toast at a banquet to celebrate the successful test, he said, "May all our devices explode as successfully as today's, but always over test sites and never over cities." His words stunned the other guests, "as if I had said something indecent." The presiding army marshal quickly offered a vulgar joke to make clear who would decide on the actual use of nuclear weapons. Sakharov came away feeling "as if I had been lashed by a whip. We, the inventors, scientists, engineers, and craftsmen, had created a terrible weapon . . . , but its use would be entirely outside our control. . . . The ideas and emotions kindled at that moment have not diminished to this day, and they completely altered my thinking."[30]

That same year, on August 16, 1955, two administrators at Arzamas-16 drew up an enigmatic letter for Sakharov's personnel file. At the outset, they acknowledged his substantial contribution to the design of the Soviet hydrogen bomb, referring to it with the standard euphemism *izdelie,* or "gadget." And they went on to emphasize that he had earned a place of "authority and respect" among his colleagues. But then they turned to his "shortcomings": his lack of ideological commitment, his "inappropriate refusal to be considered as a candidate to the city council, and similarly incorrect remarks (during the selection of personnel) about the ability and capacity of certain nationalities to do theoretical work." This last rebuke was based on the fact that Sakharov was surrounded by Jews in his laboratory.* These shortcomings, the authors asserted, could be blamed on "comrade Sakharov's easy susceptibility to other people's influence and [the fact] that the party organization of the institute and the political department have not worked enough with him."[31]

One cannot help speculating on the tone of this letter. If Sakharov

---

* His supervisors in the government were always nervous about Arzamas-16 because so many of its leading figures were Jews, among them Khariton and Zeldovich. When a second secret Installation was created, with the hope "that competition between the two organizations would generate new ideas . . . and spur an overall expansion of research," the ministry made a point of having "few Jews in its leadership." Sakharov wryly observed, "In private, ministry officials nicknamed the second Installation 'Egypt' (implying that ours was 'Israel'), and referred to our dining room as 'the synagogue'" (Andrei Sakharov, *Memoirs* [New York, 1990], 84).

continued to act in a politically independent manner, they were hoping not to be held accountable. And if he continued to make outstanding contributions to weapons research—as he would do for another thirteen years—they could point to their enthusiasm for his work. Sakharov did not disappoint them on either count.

In 1957 he wrote about the harmful genetic effects of nuclear testing; the article appeared in 1958 and, with Khrushchev's approval, was translated for magazines and distributed by "Soviet embassies and propaganda agencies" in the West.[32] At that time the Kremlin was looking for ways to inhibit further Western development of nuclear weapons and had declared a unilateral halt to nuclear testing; Sakharov's warnings about radioactive fallout fitted into the regime's propaganda plans. But Sakharov was determined to stop Soviet atmospheric tests of nuclear weapons altogether. Knowing how advanced Soviet weapons research had become, Sakharov did not think atmospheric tests were scientifically necessary, and he feared they could aggravate the arms race and increase the dangers of nuclear fallout. Although he managed to relay his message to Khrushchev, the Politburo rejected his advice and Soviet testing resumed in 1958.

But Sakharov did not retreat into silence. "No nuclear tests were conducted by the USSR, the United States, or Great Britain in 1959, 1960, or the first half of 1961," Sakharov wrote in his memoirs.[33] Khrushchev, though, abruptly decided to break this moratorium and resume testing. In July 1961 Sakharov and other scientists were summoned to a meeting with Party leaders, where Khrushchev announced his decision to resume testing in the fall. He was not asking for the scientists' endorsement and did not expect any criticism.

Sakharov was not deterred. First orally and then in a scribbled note to the general secretary, Sakharov "volunteered the opinion that we had little to gain from a resumption of testing." Moreover, he feared that "new tests will seriously jeopardize the test ban negotiations, the cause of disarmament, and world peace." Khrushchev reacted with sharp impatience, berating Sakharov before a roomful of Party leaders and fellow scientists.* A year later, after the atmospheric testing of two similar devices, which Sakharov argued was unnecessary and likely to result in hundreds of thousands of casualties from nuclear fallout, he

---

* Khrushchev did admire Sakharov. He remembered him as "an extremely talented and impressive man" and "a crystal of morality among our scientists." See Nikita Khrushchev, *Khrushchev Remembers: The Last Testament,* trans. and ed. Strobe Talbot (Boston, 1974), 68–71.

broke down under the strain of his futile efforts. "It was the ultimate defeat for me. A terrible crime was about to be committed, and I could do nothing to prevent it. I was overcome by my impotence, unbearable bitterness, shame, and humiliation. I put my face down on my desk and wept." Years later, in a conversation with Hedrick Smith of the *New York Times,* Sakharov vividly recalled the importance of these events in his life. "I could not stop something I knew was wrong and unnecessary. It was terrible. I had an awful sense of powerlessness. After that I was a different man. I broke with my surroundings. It was a basic break. . . . The atomic question was always half science, half politics. . . . It was a natural path into political issues. What matters is that I left conformism. It is not important on what question. After that first break, everything was natural." This episode marked the beginning of his rupture with the Soviet establishment and his decision "to speak out, to act out, to put everything else aside."[34]

For a time Sakharov's focus remained within the framework of Soviet science. He was heartened by his contribution to the partial nuclear test ban treaty in 1963. When talks between the United States and the Soviet Union broke down, Sakharov reminded Soviet officials of an American fall-back position put forward by President Dwight Eisenhower in 1959. The Soviets revived the proposal, and the treaty, which halted tests in the atmosphere, in space, and underwater, was concluded.

In 1964 he helped defend the integrity of scientific research against Lysenkoism. Even after Stalin's death, Lysenko and his supporters retained some influence. But by the 1960s, at the initiative of the biologist Zhores Medvedev, a group of Soviet scientists began to expose the disastrous effect of Lysenkoism on the country's agriculture.

Andrei Sakharov joined these efforts. In June 1964 the nomination of Lysenko's associate Nikolai Nuzhdin for full membership in the Academy of Sciences was scheduled for a vote. It would be a major step to challenge Lysenko in his presence. As Sakharov recounted in his memoirs, he did not look for allies but resolved on his own, in an "impulsive but fateful decision," to take the lead against Nuzhdin. Sakharov was unaware that several physicists and biologists, including Tamm and Leontovich, were planning "a concerted attack on Nuzhdin" as well.[35]

When the debate over the nomination began, Sakharov was granted the floor before the other opponents and denounced Lysenko and all he represented. He urged "all those present to vote so that the only

yeas will be by those who, together with Nuzhdin, together with Lysenko, bear the responsibility for the infamous, painful pages in the development of Soviet science, the collapse of Soviet genetics, and the
physical destruction of scientists, which fortunately are now coming to
an end." When he finished, he could hear Lysenko threaten him in typical fashion, loudly proclaiming that "people like Sakharov belong in
prison." Lysenko continued to interject himself into the debate, accus-
ing Sakharov of "slander" and "creating a disgraceful scene." There
were twenty-nine candidates that day for full membership in the Academy, and only Nuzhdin was turned away, on a vote of 23 in his favor
and 114 opposed, an overwhelming rejection.[36]

Sakharov was not easily forgiven for his intervention. In August, in
an article headed "Against Misinformation and Slander," Mikhail Ol-
shansky, the president of the All-Union Academy of Agricultural Sciences, called Sakharov "incompetent and naive" and demanded that
he answer for his slanderous outspokenness "before a court."[37] Such
attacks did not frighten Sakharov. In a letter to Khrushchev dated August 3, 1964, he made clear that he "could not be silent about the abnormal and tragic situation in Soviet biology." He urged Khrushchev
to permit "an open discussion of problems in the history of biological
sciences in the USSR. . . . The demagoguery of Lysenkoism will not
fool anyone who is familiar with its shameful history." And he concluded by recommending that Khrushchev read a manuscript by the
young scientist Zhores Medvedev that thoroughly exposed the history
and impact of Lysenkoism on the country.[38]

In October Khrushchev was removed from power and replaced by a
group of Party officials led by Leonid Brezhnev. Brezhnev had once
been in awe of Sakharov. In March 1962, after Sakharov received his
third Hero of Socialist Labor medal in the Kremlin, "Brezhnev darted
out of a side corridor and greeted me effusively," Sakharov remembered, "taking both my hands in his and shaking them without letting
go for several seconds." Even in 1965, after he assumed power, Brezhnev remained solicitous of Sakharov. Through others, he tried to encourage him to join the Communist Party. And knowing of Sakharov's
misgivings about Kremlin policies, Brezhnev told a colleague that
"Sakharov has some doubts and inner conflicts. We ought to try to understand and do all we can to help him."[39] But whatever action Brezhnev authorized, it did not assuage Sakharov's doubts.

In fact, the new leadership's reactionary initiatives soon dismayed
him. The arrest of Sinyavsky and Daniel in September 1965, rumors of

more arrests to come, the suppression of books that might have appeared under Khrushchev, and persistent reports of Stalin's rehabilitation at the forthcoming Twenty-third Party Congress in March 1966 suffused the intellectual community with a sense of foreboding. Sakharov shared in this anxiety. Before the Party Congress convened, a group of leading scientists, artists, writers, and other intellectuals sent a petition directly to Brezhnev, voicing their opposition to Stalin's rehabilitation. This was not a group to be easily dismissed. Among the signers were the physicists Igor Tamm, Pyotr Kapitsa, and Andrei Sakharov; the dancer Maya Plisetskaya; and the veteran writer Ilya Ehrenburg. Tamm had received the Nobel Prize in physics in 1958; Kapitsa would receive the same recognition in 1978. This petition, in February 1966, was Sakharov's first public expression of dissent. The petition did not mince words. It warned Brezhnev that neither the Soviet public nor Western Communist parties would support the rehabilitation of Stalin, and that such a move "would be a great disaster." When the Party Congress met a few weeks later, it did not contradict the condemnation of Stalin that Khrushchev had organized at the congress in 1961. Stalin's name, in fact, was not even mentioned.

Sakharov added his signature to another petition in the fall. This time, he and twenty other prominent figures protested the introduction of two new articles in the Criminal Code: Articles 190-1, which made it illegal to circulate false statements about the regime, and 190-3, which forbade violations of public order by a group, in effect forbidding unauthorized demonstrations. Both changes were in direct response to the Sinyavsky and Daniel case and their unconvincing prosecution under Article 70, which forbade "agitation and propaganda" against the regime. At their trial the prosecutor claimed that the defendants had intended to subvert the government with false statements. This charge was required for prosecution under Article 70, but it was never clear how the court could determine their anti-Soviet motives when the defendants claimed to be loyal citizens who wanted to strengthen the Soviet Union by eliminating remnants of Stalinist abuses.

For the dissidents the introduction of Article 190-1 meant two significant changes. The new article called for a sentence of up to three years in a labor camp rather than the maximum of ten years plus five years of exile provided under Article 70. On the one hand, Article 190-1 was a less severe law that the regime could invoke if the nature of a defendant's protest or the attention of the West made it expedient to do so. On the other hand, persons convicted under Article 190-1 could be sent to labor camps for ordinary criminals, where political activists, particularly Jewish ones, faced a great deal of hostility from the inmates, whereas those convicted under Article 70 were generally confined with other political prisoners.

Sakharov signed the petition along with his fellow physicists Vitaly Ginzburg, Yakov Zeldovich, Mikhail Leontovich, and Igor Tamm, as well as the writers Vladimir Voinovich, Veniamin Kaverin, and Viktor Nekrasov and the composer Dmitri Shostakovich. The regime did not retreat and soon found it useful to invoke both articles in response to dissent. But the participation of such luminaries inspired hope in many younger activists. The nature of dissent seemed to be changing: "Professors, academicians, writers—not to be compared with us striplings of the early 1960s," the dissident Vladimir Bukovsky once recalled.[40]

In those years, a significant proportion of scientists were among the petition signers. Andrei Amalrik confirmed that a majority of those who protested against a major political trial in January 1968 were scientists.[41] Many scientists had been drawn to their fields because other intellectual pursuits involved more substantial concessions to communist ideology. Fruitful scientific research had to employ classical logic and genuine methods of investigation as opposed to dialectical materialism. But once the regime began its harsh response to this initial campaign of petitions, it became increasingly rare for a scientist to take on a public role. Many remained behind-the-scenes supporters, circulating samizdat or raising money for the families of political prisoners. They were among the "most vulnerable to the simplest forms of repression: dismissal from work or, in the case of students, denial of work in the area of specialization."[42] Sakharov was the only prominent scientist to sign several of the movement's initial petitions and then not only refuse to withdraw but actually deepen his commitment.

By the close of 1966, Sakharov was slowly building momentum for a more daring and dramatic statement. On December 5, 1966, Soviet Constitution Day, he joined a small vigil next to Moscow's landmark statue of Alexander Pushkin, doffing his hat at 6 P.M. in a brief, silent gesture of defiance "as a sign of respect for the Constitution and support for political prisoners."[43] None of the dozen or so other participants recognized him. Two months later, he sent a private letter to Leonid Brezhnev, appealing on behalf of the imprisoned writers Andrei Sinyavsky and Yuli Daniel, as well as several young people who had been arrested for coming to their defense. This page-and-a-half letter, for all its brevity, presaged the countless appeals he would later address: a focus on specific cases, concern over psychiatric abuse, violations of Soviet constitutional and criminal procedures, with the soon-to-be-familiar rebuke that such actions would "unavoidably have the most undesirable international and internal consequences." Moreover, Sakharov did not hesitate to declare that "democratic transformation of our country, de-Stalinization of government and party structures make up the most urgent necessity," yet there is "strong dissatisfaction with the slow pace of this process." Tellingly, under his signature Sakharov added in his own handwriting that he was a three-time Hero of Socialist Labor, an academician, and a recipient of a Lenin Prize and other government awards. The signatures of several Politburo members are visible on the first page of the letter, indicating they had received and read it, and there is an added handwritten note assigning the letter to the archives.[44] Sakharov did not lose interest in the case of Yuli Daniel. In the summer of 1967, when he learned about the deplorable conditions that Daniel faced in a Mordovian labor camp, he called Yuri Andropov directly to ask that the KGB look into the situation. Sakharov was later told that Daniel would soon be released, a claim that proved to be false.*

That same month he prepared an article about the role of the intelligentsia and the danger of a thermonuclear war with the long-time journalist and veteran intelligence officer Ernst Henry. Sakharov voiced his opposition to any kind of antimissile defense and invoked the names of the French physicist Frédéric Joliot-Curie and the American chemist Linus Pauling, both of whom had supported a nuclear test ban and restraints on Western development of nuclear weapons. On the surface, there did not seem to be anything "anti-Soviet" in the piece. Sakharov congratulated the Soviet government on its insistence that a "moratorium on antimissile defense systems . . . must be studied not in isolation from the problem of disarmament but as part of the whole question of universal disarmament." He went on to express his fears that an exchange of nuclear weapons would destroy civilization

---

* A year later, in August 1968, Sakharov called Andropov for a second and last time. Once again he was calling on behalf of imprisoned activists: the arrested demonstrators who had gone to Red Square to protest the Warsaw Pact invasion of Czechoslovakia. Sakharov expressed concern over their fate, reminding Andropov that "Communist Parties are following developments [in Czechoslovakia], and it will make matters worse if the demonstrators are tried and sentenced." Andropov told him that he "did not think the sentences would be severe." See Sakharov, *Memoirs*, 293–94.

and concluded with the observation—no doubt sincere but also to be expected for an article that he hoped to see appear in the Soviet press— that "American scientists . . . understand the total senselessness, cruelty, and criminality of the Vietnam War."[45]

Sakharov and Henry wanted to place the article in *Literaturnaya Gazeta* (Literary gazette) but in the end did not succeed in persuading the editor in chief, the notorious reactionary Alexander Chakovsky, to publish it. Sakharov even appealed directly to Mikhail Suslov to review the decision, but Suslov did not want to see it appear in the Soviet press "since its ideas might be interpreted incorrectly." Sakharov himself later admitted that his "answers were more radical than he had anticipated."[46] (The article subsequently appeared in Roy Medvedev's unofficial journal *Politichesky Dnevnik* [Political diary].) Sakharov's loyalties remained intact. Later that year he joined another group of 125 cultural and scientific figures in an appeal to Brezhnev to end censorship. Here again, although the language of the appeal challenged official Soviet attitudes, it was addressed in a respectful manner and was not circulated in a way that would embarrass or discomfit Kremlin officials.[47] Sakharov still hoped for a genuine dialogue with them.

The regime, however, was not pleased with his persistent forays into politics. "As a politician he's muddleheaded," one official declared at a meeting. In an attempt to discipline him, the regime reduced Sakharov's salary by almost half and removed him from his position as department head at the Installation, although he remained its "deputy scientific director."[48]

By 1968, Sakharov was ready to be more outspoken and defiant. That January another notorious political trial was held in Moscow, the Trial of the Four, as it was called. Alexander Ginzburg, Yuri Galanskov, Alexei Dobrovolsky, and Vera Lashkova were young people who had collected information on earlier political trials and tried to aid the defendants with petitions and appeals. Their trial and attendant publicity in the West proved to be more than a minor irritant to the regime and helped to embolden other activists.[49] At the same time, the Prague Spring began to unfold in Czechoslovakia, provoking a host of expectations that Communist rule could be reformed without violence. Written in a voice that was "fresh, utopian, and hopeful," Sakharov's essay "Progress, Coexistence, and Intellectual Freedom" encouraged such optimism.[50] While he summarized his concern over the fundamental dilemmas of modern industrial society—military expenditures, environmental pollution, the role of scientific and technological

progress—he also described the continuing legacy of Stalinist dictatorship in Soviet society.

Two ideas in particular startled readers in the West. First, Sakharov
outlined his belief in the convergence of the Western and socialist systems of government. "Convergence" was not a new idea in the West,
but Sakharov's essay signaled that Soviet scientists shared the idea that
"the rapprochement of the socialist and capitalist systems, accompanied by democratization, demilitarization, and social and technological progress, is the only alternative to the ruin of mankind." And second, Sakharov insisted that the challenges before modern society
could be effectively addressed only within a democratic society, with
the participation of a country's citizens and respect for human rights.*

So many years have passed since Sakharov's first essay appeared and
so many events have overtaken the drama of that time, most spectacu-
larly the collapse of the Soviet Union itself, that it is hard to recreate
the breathless feelings his essay aroused. Alexander Solzhenitsyn took
exception to many of Sakharov's ideas, but he still expressed the admiration that so many people shared in response to his first essay.

> We so rejoice in every little word of truth, so utterly suppressed until
> recent years, that we forgive those who first voice it for us all their near
> misses, all their inexactitudes, even a portion of error greater than the
> portion of truth, simply because "something at least, something at last
> has been said!"
>
> All this we experienced as we read Academician Sakharov's article
> and listened to comments on it at home and from abroad. Our hearts
> beat faster as we realized that at last someone had broken out of the
> deep, untroubled, cozy torpor in which Soviet scientists get on with
> their scientific work, are rewarded with a life of plenty and pay for it
> by keeping their thoughts at the level of their test tubes.[51]

The KGB was not so pleased. Until the appearance of "Progress, Coexistence, and Intellectual Freedom," Sakharov had not crossed an ill-

---

* This is a bitter message for any dictatorship to accept. In China, the late reformer
and Communist Party leader Deng Xiaoping issued a famous declaration in 1978 calling for economic reform based on "Four Modernizations": of agriculture, industry, science and technology, and defense. After the young dissident Wei Jingsheng composed a
wall poster demanding that democratization be added to these four goals, he was arrested and sentenced to eighteen years' imprisonment. "Without democracy," Wei
Jingsheng proclaimed, "society will become stagnant and economic growth will face
insurmountable obstacles." For the text of the wall poster, see "The Fifth Moderniza-
tion" in Wei Jingsheng, *The Courage to Stand Alone: Letters from Prison and Other
Writings*, ed. and trans. Kristina M. Torgeson (New York, 1997), 210.

defined boundary that separated tolerable nonconformity from out-right disloyalty. Certainly the regime was keeping track of his written appeals, his participation in the vigil at Pushkin Square, his meetings with the independent-minded historian Roy Medvedev, whose book *Let History Judge* was among the first from within dissident circles to document Stalin's crimes. No doubt the KGB was wondering how far Sakharov would go and if he would dare to jeopardize his august position in Soviet society. The answer became clear in the spring of 1968.

As it happened, the KGB learned of the essay when a secretary he had asked to type it passed a copy to the KGB. And the dissident activist Andrei Amalrik shared a copy with the Dutch correspondent Karl van het Reve. Van het Reve thought of an ingenious way to evade Soviet censors and inform his newspaper, *Het Parol* (The word), of Sakharov's essay: he called his editor in Amsterdam on a Saturday, when he guessed that his own office telephone would not be monitored by a Dutch-speaking KGB agent, and dictated a translation. From that moment on, Sakharov's life would be turned upside down.

Over the next twelve years, until his exile to Gorky in January 1980, Andrei Sakharov assumed the role of a widely recognized and open dissident in Moscow. If in the West (and in the eyes of the KGB) he came to be considered the leader of the human rights movement, in reality he was fitting himself into a network of activists. "I understand that because of my fate and because of my past and my position, I occupy a special place among dissidents," Sakharov once explained. "But it is not the place of a leader or head. I am not the commander of an army."[52] As Ludmilla Alexeyeva once observed, "There [was] no formal structure. . . . There [were] neither leaders, nor subordinates; no one [assigned] tasks to others; instead each [was] prepared to do what [was] necessary if other volunteers [could] not be found. No one [had] obligations other than those of conscience."[53] Sakharov was among the three founding members of the Moscow Human Rights Committee, which was the subject of many KGB reports. His involvement with the Human Rights Committee was an important stage in his evolution as a dissident and helped to shape the KGB's attitude toward him. Andropov grew increasingly wary of Sakharov's meetings with other activists and his growing awareness of the tragic gap between the professed guarantees of Soviet law and legal procedure and the actual practices of Soviet courts. Over the next two decades, Sakharov stood vigil outside of closed courtrooms, wrote appeals on behalf of more than two hundred individual prisoners, and continued to write carefully composed essays about the need for democratization. By 1973 he was meeting regularly with Western correspondents. He would receive them in his apartment, one correspondent recalled years later, "wearing a tattered sweater, workman's short and baggy trousers . . . [then] describe his latest thinking in a quiet, direct voice that left an impression of enormous inner strength."[54]

Such meetings concerned the KGB. "Because Sakharov is in constant contact with foreigners and because some of them express interest in his past scientific activity," Andropov informed the Central Committee in March 1974, "we deem it useful to create a special commission to determine whether the information he obtained during his work in the Ministry of Medium Machine Building* still constitutes a state secret."[55] Sakharov, in fact, was well aware of his unique status and was always careful never to give the KGB a pretext to claim that he was abusing his one-time security clearance. Even one of Andropov's successors at the KGB acknowledged at a Politburo meeting in the fall of 1986 that there was never "any reason to charge Sakharov for divulging secrets."[56]

His views also evolved. If in 1968 he was willing to call for a return to "Leninist principles"—as if such a policy guideline could lead to genuine reform—within a short time he explicitly endorsed the establishment of a Western-style liberal democracy and the need for a market-oriented economy. These statements and more ambitious essays circulated as samizdat inside the Soviet Union as well as in countless translations around the world. (In his memoirs Sakharov proudly pointed out that "the International Publishers Association released statistics showing that in 1968–1969 more than eighteen million copies of 'Progress, Coexistence, and Intellectual Freedom' were published around the world, in third place after Mao Zedong and Lenin, and ahead of Georges Simenon and Agatha Christie.")[57] Sakharov became the most recognized figure among the dissidents, embodying for the West a spirit of liberal tolerance and a stubborn, principled commitment to nonviolence that marked the entire history of the movement.

The KGB was quick to grasp the significance of his role even as its reports to the Central Committee frequently distorted Sakharov's behavior. There is a surreal quality to these communications. Here is Yuri

---

* The Ministry of Medium Machine Building was the euphemistic title for the Soviet Union's program to develop nuclear weapons.

Andropov, chairman of the KGB from 1967 to 1982, reporting to the Central Committee of the Communist Party about every move in Andrei Sakharov's dance of defiance: his major appeals and statements, meetings with disaffected religious believers, Jewish would-be émigrés, workers, and intellectual activists like himself, as well as visits to foreign embassies and interviews with foreign correspondents.

It seems farfetched to think that the fate of the Soviet empire depended on knowing how Sakharov and Solzhenitsyn got along when they met for the first time, what they discussed, and if their divergent approaches to Russian history would strain the inevitable respect they had for each other. Such questions, in fact, required the careful consideration of the most powerful people in the second most powerful country on earth. They understood how precarious their power really was, how much open dissent could be tolerated, before the system and its official ideology would be fatally challenged.

Andropov in particular was vigilant on this point. Writing to the Central Committee in December 1975, when the Kremlin's reliance on repression was under increasing scrutiny because of the Nobel Peace Prize awarded to Sakharov and pressure from Western Communist parties, Andropov reminded his colleagues that it would be "impossible at this time to renounce the criminal prosecution of people who oppose the Soviet system."[58] This document is one of the most candid and revealing in our collection, an explicit admission that Soviet leaders believed they had no choice but to rely on force and intimidation to sustain their hold on the country. But intimidation and threats were no longer silencing every manifestation of dissent.

The regime was particularly provoked by Sakharov's behavior in 1973 and 1974, when he began to meet frequently with Western reporters. In the spring of 1973, Sakharov gave an extensive television interview to the Swedish correspondent Olle Stenholm. In the course of it Sakharov explored the evolution of his thinking since the appearance of his first essay in 1968. He acknowledged to Stenholm that at that time he "was still very far from the basic problems facing the people and the whole country. I was still materially privileged and isolated." But his subsequent experiences confirmed for him the need for greater freedom, for competitive elections, and for an opening for private enterprise. He also wanted to expose the country's gross inequality and address the challenge posed by restless national and ethnic minorities in a democratic manner. When Stenholm asked if Sakharov did not feel hopeless in the face of the regime's intransigence, he summed up his philosophy of action in a striking and memorable phrase: "If a man speaks out, it does not mean that he hopes necessarily to achieve something. He may hope for nothing but nonetheless speak because he cannot remain silent."[59]

Over the next year, Sakharov outlined his misgivings about the process of détente. He did support the relaxation of military and political tensions between the Soviet Union and the United States. He warned the West, though, that it was dealing with a dangerous opponent and should not relax its commitment to human rights principles. He appealed to the U.S. Congress to approve the Jackson-Vanik Amendment to a trade bill, which intended to make extension of most favored nation status, and thus the lowest tariffs, dependent on the Kremlin's willingness to allow freer emigration. He also urged the West not to accept a détente defined by the Soviet Union alone. As he told Western reporters on the fifth anniversary of the Warsaw Pact invasion of Czechoslovakia,

> I mean rapprochement without democratization, rapprochement in which the West in effect accepts the Soviet Union rules of the game. Such a rapprochement would be dangerous in the sense that it would not really solve any of the world's problems and would simply mean capitulation in the face of real or exaggerated Soviet power. It would mean an attempt to trade with the Soviet Union, buying its gas and oil, while ignoring all other aspects. . . .
>
> It would mean cultivation and encouragement of a closed country, where everything that happens may be shielded from outside eyes, a country wearing a mask that hides its true face. I would not wish it on anyone to live next to such a neighbor, especially if he is at the same time armed to the teeth.[60]

It was statements of this sort that led to the avalanche of public denunciations of Sakharov in the fall of 1973. By 1976 Andropov was prepared to call Sakharov "Domestic Enemy Number One" before a group of KGB officers.[61]

From the outset of their surveillance, the KGB and the Politburo kept searching for an adequate explanation for Sakharov's apostasy. "Having made a great contribution to the creation of thermonuclear weapons, Sakharov felt his 'guilt' before mankind,"* Andropov spec-

---

\* Sakharov himself dismissed this explanation for his evolution into a dissident. "There are some in the West who think that I began to protest injustices as an atonement for working on the bomb. But this is not true," he told a Western reporter in November 1972. "I developed a moral consciousness gradually in the 1950s" (*Newsweek*, November 13, 1972, 13).

ulated to Brezhnev in January 1971.[62] No, it was the fault of that woman, that temptress Elena Bonner (whom he married in 1972), with her connections to Zionists and dissidents. (Gorbachev said this out loud at a Politburo meeting!)* Like Eve offering the apple to the hapless Adam, she exerted a sinister, subversive influence on Sakharov—"she draws him into active antisocial activity," Andropov warned his colleagues—and so led them both to be cast out of paradise.[63] (Sakharov once described the regime's portrayal of his wife's influence this way: "an imperious, vain, and self-serving woman manipulating a meek old man in an ivory tower, once a scientific genius, now senile.")[64] Or Sakharov must have lost his reason through some accident of personality or history. Within months after sending Sakharov to Gorky, Andropov claimed that "his psychological state has clearly taken a turn for the worse. Sakharov's behavior often does not correspond to accepted norms; his behavior is patently contrary to common sense."[65]

Vladimir Bukovsky examined thousands of KGB and Central Committee documents relating to the suppression of the human rights movement. As he read them, he could not help being impressed by the extraordinary amount of attention paid to the dissidents. "The KGB reported literally everything to the Central Committee," Bukovsky concluded, "and for each particular [incident] the Central Committee and then the Politburo had to reach a decision. Not only our arrests, trials, banishments, and searches, but even the smallest operational details required the attention of these fifteen very old and extremely busy people."[66] Furthermore, all KGB reports to the Politburo, including the memorandums about Sakharov in this volume, were considered sensitive state secrets. They were all mechanically stamped with the following admonition on the first page: "Comrades who receive completely confidential documents of the CPSU Central Committee are categorically forbidden to transmit them or make them known to anyone without the special permission of the Central Committee. It is ab-

---

* At a Politburo meeting on August 29, 1985, Gorbachev led a discussion on how to respond to a letter from Sakharov, who was still in Gorky, requesting that his wife be permitted to seek medical treatment in the West. In the end Soviet leaders decided to let her go, but their give-and-take had several crude moments. When KGB Chairman Viktor Chebrikov complained that Sakharov was being unduly influenced by Elena Bonner, Gorbachev immediately said, "That's what Zionism really is." Another Politburo member, Mikhail Zimyanin, called her "a beast in a skirt, a henchman of imperialism." A transcript of this Politburo discussion is in the collections of the Harvard Project on Cold War Studies, Case 89, 469:23.

solutely forbidden to copy the documents or to make excerpts from them. The comrade to whom this document is addressed must sign and date it after reading it."

Several years after the collapse of the Soviet Union, Ambassador Anatoly Dobrynin, who represented Moscow in Washington for twenty-six years, wrote in the mid-1990s what he could not acknowledge during his long tenure as ambassador: that in the eyes of the regime, "the dissident movement . . . caused considerable damage not only at home, but also to our relations with the rest of the world."[67] The dissidents exposed the country's problems and official crimes. They "accomplished something that was simple to the point of genius," Andrei Amalrik remarked. "In an unfree country they behaved like free men, thereby changing the moral atmosphere and the nation's governing traditions."[68] Such openness and lack of fear confounded the regime. It was not equipped to deal with a nonviolent movement. Soviet officials preferred to contend with conspiracies, slander, even violence, convinced as they were that all their enemies were mirror images of themselves. Even after Party leaders disavowed the outright terror of the Stalin years, they still relied on force and intimidation to keep the population in line. As Pavel Litvinov observed in the 1970s, "Even now the regime exists, perhaps not only, but mainly, on the interest from the capital of fear amassed [under Stalin]."[69]

It was the job of the KGB to exploit this "interest from the capital of fear" and prevent the emergence of an independent civil society that could challenge the political domination of the Communist Party. Sakharov's career as a dissident almost precisely coincided with the years Yuri Andropov served as chairman of the KGB. Leonid Brezhnev may have been general secretary, but it was Andropov who was Sakharov's and the dissidents' principal antagonist. His rise to power coincided with the emergence of the human rights movement, and his unprecedented term in office, from 1967 to 1982, accorded him the authority to fashion the regime's response.

Andropov was the most successful and durable security chief in Soviet history. Almost all his predecessors had been executed or removed in disgrace. For years an unfounded liberal image of Andropov circulated both inside and outside the Soviet Union: it was said, as *Newsweek* reported when he came to power, that "he spoke English, collected big band records and relaxed with American novels."[70] After Andropov died in February 1984, there was speculation that he would have carried out significant reforms if only his health had held up and he had lived longer. The historical record does not support such an understanding of his role. In 1956 Andropov orchestrated the Soviet invasion of Hungary and as Soviet ambassador in Budapest helped to direct Red Army movements. In 1965, when Solzhenitsyn was no longer in the regime's favor and his novel *The First Circle* was being banned, Andropov was pressing for harsher measures against him.* In 1968, although he was only a candidate member of the Politburo, he was among those who pushed the hardest for the Warsaw Pact invasion of Czechoslovakia and ending the Prague Spring by force. And in 1979 he was among the main proponents of the invasion of Afghanistan and a useless, destructive war.

Andropov played an equally repressive role inside the country. The entire Politburo and Central Committee supported the idea of suppressing the human rights movement and enforcing censorship of artistic, cultural, and political expression, but it was Andropov who consistently sought to expand the powers of the KGB, appealing again and again to the Politburo with initiatives of his own: to increase the use of psychiatry as a tool of intimidation; to exile Solzhenitsyn and Sakharov, if not to the West, then to a location inside the country where foreigners and domestic allies would not be able to talk with them or obtain their writings (as Andropov suggested in September 1973, "Sakharov could be offered the possibility to work in Novosibirsk, Obninsk, or some other city with a special regimen, in order to help him escape from his hostile surroundings and, above all, the Western press");[71] to organize periodic, systematic crackdowns on dissent until finally, by the early 1980s, when his political influence reached its peak and he was general secretary, there was hardly a human rights movement left.†

When we review Andropov's career as head of the KGB, it is easy to see his policies as clumsy and heavy-handed: there was no apparent subtlety in arresting people for their beliefs, consigning healthy activists to psychiatric hospitals, or sending others out of the country. But the pattern of these methods, the frequent compromises, and the

* See the Politburo discussion of January 7, 1974, which ultimately led to Solzhenitsyn's expulsion after publication of *The Gulag Archipelago* in the West; Andropov did not hesitate to remind his colleagues of his hard-line stance nine years earlier, when he was not yet a member of the Politburo (Michael Scammell, ed., *The Solzhenitsyn Files* [Chicago, 1995], 284).

† Alexander Yakovlev once said that Andropov "wanted to turn the county into a socialist barracks" (*Literaturnaia Gazeta*, May 15, 1991, 3).

ultimately drawn-out struggle against dissent reflected the realities of
the post-Stalin period, when the regime had to be concerned about
Western public opinion. Such concerns were frequently reflected in
Andropov's reports to Brezhnev and the Central Committee. In the
context of Soviet history, they showed both the reforms accepted by
the system after Stalin's death and substantial sensitivity to pressures
from Western governments and public opinion.

   The KGB did learn how to compromise. By the early 1980s, over a
quarter of a million Jews were permitted to emigrate to Israel and the
West, perhaps the most tangible achievement of any dissident group in
the country and very much the result of Western pressure and the internal support Jewish refuseniks received from the broader human
rights movement. After the trial of Sinyavsky and Daniel in 1966, the
regime preferred to send writers out of the country rather than arrest
them. The careers of Solzhenitsyn, Sinyavsky, Alexander Galich, Vladimir Voinovich, Georgy Vladimov, Joseph Brodsky, Andrei Amalrik,
Natalya Gorbanevskaya, and Vasily Aksyonov came to maturity
alongside the human rights movement and altered the contours of Soviet culture. All were compelled to emigrate, some after serving prison
terms. Other human rights activists, such as Pyotr Grigorenko, Valery
Chalidze, Pavel Litvinov, Ludmilla Alexeyeva, Alexander Ginzburg,
Kronid Lubarsky, Boris Shragin, Valentin Turchin, Alexander Esenin-
Volpin, Anatoly Shcharansky, and Yuri Orlov, to name the most
prominent, were also permitted to leave, compelled to emigrate, or
sent abroad in exchange for convicted Soviet spies who were prisoners
in the West.

   Sending dissidents and nonconforming artists and writers to the
West had both intended and unforeseen consequences. The regime was
happy to remove scores of such figures from Soviet society. Gradually,
though, the presence of such eloquent witnesses in Europe and Amer-
ica—Solzhenitsyn and Brodsky received Nobel Prizes in literature;
Pavel Litvinov, Valery Chalidze, and Ludmilla Alexeyeva lived in New
York; and Natalya Gorbanevskaya and Alexander Ginzburg worked
in Paris—helped to erode sympathy for the Soviet regime among
Western intellectuals. It is a curious historical paradox that under
Stalin, when the Kremlin was carrying out ruthless terror, many distin-
guished writers and intellectuals on the left, most notably Jean-Paul
Sartre and André Malraux, at various times and for various reasons
publicly defended the good name of the Soviet Union. But under
Brezhnev, when the regime was behaving with infinitely greater toler-

ance, in spite of its neo-Stalinist cast, very few Western intellectuals of any recognized standing were willing to defend it. In the 1970s, even Western Communist parties, especially in Italy, France, and Spain, were prepared to criticize the Kremlin's repressive policies, giving Eurocommunism an unexpected appeal. The writing and testimony of the dissidents, coming at a time when a universal human rights standard was gaining currency in the West, made all attempts by Kremlin representatives or Western sympathizers to defend Soviet behavior look like empty demagogic rhetoric. The regime was finally exposed for what it was: a dictatorship controlled by a single political party using the idealistic rhetoric of Marxism to camouflage its crimes.

As Andropov's reports to the Central Committee make clear, the KGB was always looking for ways to broaden the repression of dissenting voices. For nearly fifteen years, after each crackdown new activists took on the responsibilities of those who had been arrested or sent abroad. *A Chronicle of Current Events* resumed its appearance after a period of eighteen months, from the fall of 1972 until May 1974, when its editors gave in to threats from the regime that it would arrest someone for each new issue; this was essentially an exercise in blackmail, a threat to take hostages. During the period of suspension the editors continued to compile information, and in May 1974 three Moscow dissidents—Tatyana Velikanova, Sergei Kovalev, and Tatyana Khodorovich—held a press conference in Sakharov's apartment to announce the appearance of three issues of the *Chronicle,* which they promptly handed to Western correspondents. The regime could not ignore such brazen behavior. Kovalev was arrested at the end of December. His trial, which opened in Vilnius, Lithuania, a year later, took place on December 10, 1975, the very day that Sakharov was receiving the Nobel Peace Prize in absentia; Sakharov was not permitted to attend the ceremonies in Oslo, but Lithuania was Soviet territory, and he stood outside the Vilnius courthouse to show solidarity with his friend.

Despite stepped-up repression, the dissidents kept looking for new ways to challenge the regime. Events in Europe unexpectedly provided the groundwork. For many years the Kremlin had been pressing Western governments to recognize the territorial changes in Eastern Europe that it had imposed after World War II. Although the West had long relinquished any hope of reversing Soviet gains in Eastern Europe, several countries in Western Europe insisted that any such agreement had to include humanitarian provisions. Known as Basket 3, this section of the Helsinki Final Act concerned the reunification of families, greater freedom of communication, and a commitment to respect "freedom of thought, conscience, religion or belief," to "promote and encourage the effective exercise of civil, political . . . cultural and other rights," to accord ethnic minorities "equality before the law," and to "act in conformity" with international commitments on human rights.

In the summer of 1975, as the Conference on Security and Cooperation in Europe (CSCE) was about to convene in Helsinki, most observers in the West assumed that the Final Act would end up as just another international agreement on human rights that the Soviet bloc could blithely sign and then blithely ignore. The veteran activist Valery Chalidze vividly captured the Kremlin's cynical posturing: how it dismissed its obligations with a unique kind of dialectic, making "commitments to guarantee human rights on its own territory, while on the other hand [telling] those to whom the commitment was made that securing human rights is exclusively its internal affair."[72]

Western observers were well aware of such false promises and urged President Gerald Ford not to go to Helsinki to sign the Final Act. A *Wall Street Journal* editorial bluntly urged, "Jerry, Don't Go," and went on to argue that "It is hard to see any Western gain at Helsinki . . . [so there is] no reason to endow the whole project with the President's personal imprimatur." The *New York Times* shared this skepticism. "Nothing signed in Helsinki," the *Times* observed, "will in any way save courageous free thinkers in the Soviet empire from the prospect of incarceration in forced labor camps, or in insane asylums, or from being subjected to involuntary exile." In its news analysis, the *Times* even commented that the summit gathering in Helsinki was "a personal triumph for Mr. Brezhnev."[73]

Ironically, only Soviet officials went to Helsinki with substantial concerns about the summit's possible impact. Anatoly Dobrynin acknowledged that when members of the Politburo examined the actual text of the Final Act, "they were stunned" to see that foreign governments were being given a role in the way information could be controlled and dissent in the Soviet Union tolerated.[74] "It was not . . . an unambiguous endorsement of the status quo version of détente that they had agreed to pursue several years earlier," as Daniel C. Thomas noted in his comprehensive analysis *The Helsinki Effect*.[75] Dobrynin and others recognized the potential danger to the Soviet regime and expressed "grave doubts about assuming international commitments that could open the way to foreign interference in our political life." But such views were dismissed by the Kremlin's most senior diplomat, Foreign Minister Andrei Gromyko, who confidently reminded his colleagues that the Final Act also recognized the principle of nonintervention in internal affairs, a kind of escape clause that the Kremlin liked to cite whenever treatment of its citizens was questioned. "We are masters in our own house," Gromyko reassured Dobrynin at the time.[76]

Soviet and Western officials, American journalists, and many activists behind the Iron Curtain had every reason to agree that the Final Act would not help to bring about democratic reform or a letup in repression. Events turned out differently.

As negotiations over the Final Act proceeded, both American and Soviet officials found the intrusion of the human rights issue awkward. At that time, in the early 1970s, human rights were a relatively new issue in international affairs and in the eyes of many political leaders an unwelcome political nuisance. There is no indication that when President Lyndon Johnson met with Soviet Premier Alexei Kosygin in Glassboro, New Jersey, just a few years earlier, in 1967, the issue of human rights or the fate of individual prisoners of conscience or Jewish refuseniks ever came up. Within a handful of years, however, no American president or secretary of state could meet with his Soviet counterpart without being pressured by Congress or private organizations to seek the release of prisoners or the emigration of one family or another. "Cold war realists like Henry Kissinger sought to keep human rights issues off the agenda with the Soviets," Michael Ignatieff once noted, "arguing that they might jeopardize higher goals like détente."[77] Richard Nixon was no less hard-nosed. Speaking at Annapolis on June 5, 1972, Nixon made clear that he had no use for "eloquent speeches" and "appeals" for the United States to try to improve human rights conditions in other countries, including the Soviet Union. "We would not welcome the intervention of other countries in our domestic affairs," Nixon declared, "and we cannot expect them to be cooperative when we seek to intervene directly in theirs."[78]

The West Europeans nonetheless insisted on the humanitarian provisions of Basket 3. Human rights had become too important an international issue to be ignored. Soviet activists were the first to invoke international agreements as part of their appeals to the Kremlin and to Western governments. Anatoly Dobrynin, whose job as ambassador to Washington compelled him to gauge public opinion, was well aware that "famous dissidents were emerging" (Solzhenitsyn and Sakharov

among them) whose compelling example of civic courage, alongside
their eloquent appeals, was already compromising the moral legitimacy of the regime.[79] At the same time, events in Latin America were
making it all the harder for a coldhearted American administration to
talk about human rights in Eastern Europe when its role in the overthrow of Salvador Allende in Chile was suspected and General Au-
gusto Pinochet was directing his own orgy of violent repression without a word of protest from Nixon and Kissinger.

Finally, the Soviet regime helped to concentrate the attention of the
West by its relentless persecution of dissidents. Just when negotiations
over the Final Act were at their most serious, the Kremlin was cracking
down on *A Chronicle of Current Events* (1972–73), orchestrating an
ugly press campaign against Sakharov and Solzhenitsyn (1973), and
then in early 1974 deciding to arrest and expel Solzhenitsyn from the
Soviet Union in reprisal for publishing *The Gulag Archipelago*. Daniel
C. Thomas summarized the dilemma posed by the Solzhenitsyn affair
for all the CSCE delegations.

> "The Soviet author's plight was uniquely symbolic for the CSCE, and
> every diplomat in Geneva understood this," according to a member of
> the American delegation. For the Soviets, it symbolized the question
> of how much domestic liberalization the regime would accept in order
> to gain the benefits of détente. For Western delegations, it symbolized
> the question of what human rights concessions they could expect from
> the Soviets as part of détente. "Most delegates at the Conference real-
> ized that the trial and imprisonment of a man who for Western public
> opinion epitomized Soviet dissent would make a mockery of the ideals
> of human rights, fundamental freedoms, and the freer movement of
> people and ideas, which the West was seeking to have recognized at
> the CSCE." While the CSCE "held its collective breath," Soviet au-
> thorities weighed the political costs of imprisoning or releasing their
> well-known prisoner. They compromised on February 13, and ex-
> pelled Solzhenitsyn from the Soviet Union. Had he been imprisoned,
> "the Conference might not have concluded for a very long time, if
> ever."[80]

If human rights as a political and moral question had affected negotiations before the Final Act was actually signed, the issue gained even
greater relevance in the years that followed. Several factors contributed to this unexpected development. In the summer of 1975, isolated groups of activists—prisoners in a Soviet labor camp and church
leaders in East Germany—began to refer to the Final Act as a docu-

ment they could use for their own purposes. In Prague, Czech activists hoped to invoke the Final Act to revisit the Warsaw Pact invasion of 1968 and have it condemned as a violation of the principle of nonintervention. And in Poland, a group of intellectuals circulated an appeal with direct references to the Final Act; this was the initial step of the Committee for the Defense of Workers (or KOR), which later played a crucial role in the formation of Solidarity.

That summer as well, the Kremlin permitted Elena Bonner to travel to Italy for treatment of glaucoma. Sakharov had been pressing Soviet officials to let her go, and his threat to appeal to Western leaders meeting in Helsinki seemed to tilt the scales in his favor. Andropov warned the Central Committee that "Sakharov's entire behavior is overtly provocative," designed "to harm the prestige of the Soviet state on the eve of the European conference."[81] So the Politburo relented and Bonner left for Italy in the middle of August. Two months later, the Nobel Committee of the Norwegian Parliament named Sakharov the recipient of the Peace Prize for 1975. In its citation the committee emphasized Sakharov's determination to link the cause of peace with respect for human rights and individual freedom:

> In a convincing fashion Sakharov has emphasized that the individual rights of man can serve as the only sure foundation for a genuine and long-lasting system of international cooperation. In this manner he has succeeded very effectively, and under trying conditions, in reinforcing respect for such values as all true friends of peace are anxious to support. . . .
>
> Sakharov has warned against the dangers connected with a bogus détente based on wishful thinking and illusions. As a nuclear physicist he has, with his special insight and sense of responsibility, been able to speak out against the dangers inherent in the armaments race between the states. His aims are demilitarization, democratization of society in all countries and a more rapid pace of social progress.[82]

As the documents that follow make clear, the regime organized a broad campaign to counteract the award, enlisting members of the Academy of Sciences, major newspapers, and agents in Western Europe to denounce Sakharov as an enemy of peace and détente.* But Elena Bonner was already in the West, so in Oslo on December 11 she

---

* See Christopher Andrew and Vasili Mitrokhin, *The Sword and the Shield: The Mitrokhin Archive and the Secret History of the KGB* (New York, 1999), 322–33, for additional material about the harassment of Sakharov and Bonner at this time.

was able to read her husband's Nobel lecture, "Peace, Progress, and Human Rights." In it Sakharov reiterated themes that had animated his public career: an end to the arms race, greater respect for the environment, international cooperation on a host of social and economic challenges, and universal respect for human rights. As might be expected, he emphasized ongoing concerns in the Soviet Union—the rights of invalids, of Jewish and German would-be émigrés, of oppressed national minorities such as the Crimean Tatars—and he took the time to list dozens of Soviet prisoners of conscience, challenging the international community to come to their aid in the name of universal values and the Helsinki Final Act.

*Pravda* and *Izvestia* published the Helsinki Accords in their entirety, as the regime was required to do according to a preliminary agreement. In contrast, Stalin's government had abstained in 1948 when the United Nations adopted the Universal Declaration of Human Rights (UDHR). Copies of the UDHR remained hard to find in the Soviet Union, and any found in a dissident's home was likely to be confiscated. Andrei Sinyavsky once heard a labor camp guard cynically declare to the inmates, referring to the UDHR: "You don't understand. It's not for you. It's for negroes."[83] But now, after 1975, human rights activists would be operating within a framework endorsed by the regime itself.

And it was in the Soviet Union that activists mounted the most organized and telling challenge. Andrei Amalrik came up with the idea of having a group to monitor Soviet compliance with the human rights provisions of the Helsinki Final Act. When he was forced to emigrate in 1976, the initiative passed to Yuri Orlov, a war veteran and distinguished physicist who had been expelled from the Communist Party as far back as 1956 because of his appeal for greater democracy. Orlov picked the members carefully, wanting the group to reflect a broad variety of issues facing the country. Several veteran activists became core members: Alexander Ginzburg administered a fund to help the families of political prisoners; Ludmilla Alexeyeva knew the editors of the *Chronicle;* Malva Landa maintained contact with numerous prisoners; Sofia Kalistratova was the only lawyer in the group; and Elena Bonner had her own unique status, as well as her long-standing commitment to helping political prisoners. Orlov then recruited two Jewish refuseniks, Vitaly Rubin and Anatoly Shcharansky.

In spite of KGB pressure, Orlov publicly announced the formation of the group at a press conference in Sakharov's apartment in May

1976. Over the next eight months the Moscow Helsinki Watch Group issued reports on almost twenty issues, from the plight of Crimean Tatars, to the right of ordinary workers to emigrate to escape economic or political difficulties, to the exclusion of seven students from a school in Lithuania because they had been attending church services and visited the home of a prominent Catholic activist.

Orlov's vision provided an example of how to unite disparate groups of activists. Within a year of its birth, parallel Helsinki groups were formed in Ukraine (November 1976), Lithuania (November 1976), Georgia (January 1977), and Armenia (April 1977). They all kept in touch with Orlov's committee, often relying on members in Moscow to help distribute reports, even on occasion to translate them into Russian. And though the regime eventually carried out a concerted crackdown on the Helsinki groups—sixteen members were under arrest by the end of 1977—the Helsinki Watch groups marked a revival of the dissident movement and significantly reinforced the international standing of human rights just as Jimmy Carter became president of the United States and declared the promotion of human rights the cornerstone of his foreign policy. Over the next few years, under Presidents Carter and Reagan, follow-up meetings to review compliance with the Final Act were held in Belgrade and then Madrid. Sakharov hearings were also held in European cities. These meetings provided forums for exiled dissidents and representatives of nongovernmental organizations to present information on human rights abuses in Eastern Europe and the Soviet Union. The work of the Helsinki Watch groups inside the Soviet Union was not carried out in vain, despite the arrest of so many of its members. Their reports were presented at these follow-up conferences and further eroded support for the Kremlin in the West.

At the same time, there were increasing contacts among dissidents in Czechoslovakia, Poland, and the Soviet Union. Sakharov issued several statements in support of Czech and Polish activists and they tried to follow his activities as best they could. In January 1979, Zbigniew Romaszewski, a representative of the Polish opposition group KOR, was able to come to Moscow and visit Sakharov. They discussed the different challenges they faced; Sakharov was particularly impressed by the cooperation between members of the Polish intelligentsia and the working class. "In Poland," Sakharov was told, "the workers hold the intelligentsia in high esteem and are proud of them."[84] As Sakharov knew at firsthand, one weakness of the human rights movement in the USSR was its isolation from ordinary workers, an isolation the KGB worked hard to enforce.

Since the emergence of the human rights movement in the mid-1960s, the regime had made at least three concerted efforts to stifle dissent altogether: in 1968–69, between 1972 and 1974, and again in 1977–78. But in each case, the Kremlin decided to relent because of pressure and awkward publicity in the West. The trials of well-known members of the Moscow Helsinki Group in 1978—Orlov, Ginzburg, and Shcharansky—generated intense media coverage; Shcharansky was on the cover of *Time* on July 24, 1978, while his wife, Avital, who was based in Israel, campaigned on his behalf in Europe and the United States. Faced with this kind of pressure, the regime once again retreated.

By the fall of 1979, however, the KGB began to act with greater assertiveness and less concern for its image abroad. Sakharov's removal to Gorky in January1980 was the cornerstone to this pattern of stepped-up repression. Outspoken, defiant, and seemingly immune to arrest, Sakharov posed a unique challenge. No doubt Andropov wanted him outside the capital before the Olympics opened in the summer of 1980 to prevent his apartment from becoming a pilgrimage site for bothersome Western visitors with more than track and field on their minds.

In December 1979, just weeks after the Soviet invasion of Afghanistan, Andropov again insisted that the Politburo take action against Sakharov. Summing up his case, he reminded his colleagues that Sakharov "between 1972 and 1979 visited . . . [foreign] diplomatic offices eight times, . . . had over 600 meetings with other foreigners," and "conducted more than 150 so-called 'press conferences' for Western correspondents," which led to "about 1,200 anti-Soviet programs" broadcast on Western radio stations.[85] The figures may have been inflated, but the KGB's close surveillance never wavered. Andropov was about to have his way.

On January 3, 1980, Sakharov condemned the Soviet attack on Afghanistan in an interview with the *New York Times* and called for the withdrawal of Soviet troops. Two weeks later he again infuriated the Kremlin by calling for a boycott of the Olympic Games. "While the USSR is engaged in military hostilities in Afghanistan," Sakharov told ABC News, "the conduct of the Olympic Games in Moscow would contradict the Olympic charter."[86] The regime would no longer tolerate this kind of insolence. Five days later Sakharov was banished from Moscow and taken to Gorky.

Several factors contributed to this new and more determined policy. First, after the Soviet Union invaded Afghanistan to support a fragile pro-Soviet regime, the United States and many other countries condemned Soviet aggression. The United States embargoed grain shipments, boycotted the Summer Olympics, and gave overt military support to the Afghan resistance. Détente between the two superpowers was faltering. The U.S. Senate was refusing to ratify the SALT II agreements, which would have further limited the development of nuclear weapons. President Carter's support for Sakharov and other dissidents also angered Kremlin leaders. The West was losing what little political and economic leverage it once had. From the Kremlin's point of view, increased repression could not make matters worse.

Second, the regime was growing increasingly concerned over the sheer diversity of dissident voices. Dissent was no longer limited to urban intellectuals. Religious believers, national and ethnic minorities, even invalids were now adopting protest techniques they had learned from the human rights movement. A new group had been formed to monitor the abuse of psychiatry, while still another committee was dedicated to providing material assistance to political prisoners and their families. And much to the regime's annoyance, two small groups in the provinces were agitating among workers to form free trade unions and were even establishing ties to Moscow-based dissidents. The human rights movement was proving to be more than a nuisance. In March 1977 *A Chronicle of Current Events* reported that Novosti Press Agency was preparing a book on dissidents and "on how their activity hinders trade and increases economic difficulties."[87] The book failed to appear, but the Kremlin was now taking its message to heart. Enough was enough.

Third, the Jewish emigration movement continued to defy the Kremlin. Its activists welcomed foreign visitors, organized seminars on Jewish history and the Hebrew language, and sponsored discussion groups on scientific topics in efforts to sustain the morale of Jewish scientists who had been fired from their jobs after applying but failing to gain permission to emigrate. In 1979 more than 50,000 Jews would leave, the highest annual figure until that time. Their example was now inspiring Armenians, Germans, and Pentecostals, even ordinary Russians and Ukrainians to demand exit visas. By insisting on the right to leave, such groups were not seeking to reform Soviet society; they preferred to start their lives anew in another country. But their visible protests, including vigils in public squares and frequent contacts with journalists, diplomats, and foreign visitors, reflected the resolute non-violent resistance that the human rights movement sought to encourage.

This crackdown was the most systematic and far-reaching. Although *A Chronicle of Current Events* continued to appear until 1983, the KGB was able to dismantle most of the visible groups whose reporting had complicated life for the regime. Members of Helsinki Watch groups in Moscow and Ukraine, Christian activists, Crimean Tatar leaders, and editors of samizdat journals were among those arrested and brought to trial. The crackdown extended well into the 1980s and was designed to ensure that "each group . . . stopped its open, public activity and fell silent," as Peter Reddaway, the foremost scholar of Soviet dissent, reported in 1983.[88] Officials boasted of their broader powers in the presence of their dissident victims. One declared in August 1981: "Previously we brought people to trial only for their actions. But now we will try them for preparing to act, and for assisting others." Six weeks later, another agent boasted: "By the summer there won't be a single democrat or nationalist left in Moscow. We're making Moscow a communist city!"[89]

The Jewish emigration movement was severely affected by the new atmosphere. If in 1979 more than 50,000 Jews were able to emigrate, by 1980 the figure was down to just over 21,000. In 1981 it was further reduced to 9,400, in 1982 to 2,700, and in 1983 to only 1,315.

This prolonged crackdown was also connected to the failing health of Leonid Brezhnev and the growing influence of Yuri Andropov and the KGB. Andropov relinquished the post of KGB chief in the spring of 1982, after the death of Mikhail Suslov. He then took Suslov's place in the Politburo as the member in charge of ideological questions, a post that also made him next in line after Brezhnev. This was a half year before Brezhnev's death. Andropov was replaced by Vitaly Fedorchuk, head of the Ukrainian KGB, who came to Moscow with a reputation for brutality. Activists in Moscow soon discerned a new trend in the KGB's work—intimidation and frequent arrests of people who were not identified publicly as dissidents but who read and circulated samizdat. Soon after Fedorchuk's promotion, a KGB officer told an activist whose apartment had just been searched, "We've got a new leader now, and we're eliminating all samizdat and all the places where anti-Soviet literature is kept."[90]

But the regime made one miscalculation in its treatment of Sakharov in particular: it allowed Elena Bonner to travel freely between Moscow and Gorky, providing a means for Sakharov to send letters, statements, appeals, and essays to the West and remain an annoying thorn in the side of the Kremlin. Within days of their arrival in Gorky, she was back in Moscow with a statement from her husband. "I am prepared to stand public and open trial," Sakharov challenged Kremlin officials. "I do not need a gilded cage."[91] With Bonner's help, Sakharov remained highly visible. In spite of her own serious health concerns, she proved to be indefatigable; by the fall of 1982, Elena Bonner had made more than a hundred round trips between Gorky and Moscow.[92]

Between 1980 and 1984, Sakharov succeeded in publishing a great deal of material, including the following major statements:

- A long essay in the *New York Times Magazine* on June 8, 1980, explaining his views on the world situation, Soviet domestic problems, the human rights movement, and his life in Gorky.
- A statement on the Madrid conference to review the Helsinki Final Act, published in the *Los Angeles Times* on September 9, 1980. Sakharov expressed his hope that the Helsinki agreement would provide a forum to review the status of human rights in all the participating states.
- An article, "What Should the U.S.A. and the U.S.S.R. Do to Preserve Peace?" in *Parade* magazine on August 16, 1981.
- A letter in the British journal *Nature* in June 1982, addressed to his fellow scientists in the Soviet Union: "It is shameful that foreign scientists (our deepest gratitude to them!) show a greater concern for our affairs than we do ourselves." He recalled abuses from the Stalin era and implored his colleagues to defend fellow scientists and others who fell victim to injustice.
- A letter to participants in the Pugwash Conference held in Warsaw, Poland, in August 1982. Published in the *New York Times* on September 10, the letter explained Sakharov's views on détente, the arms race, and the need to defend prisoners of conscience.
- A major article, "The Danger of Thermonuclear War," in the American journal *Foreign Affairs* (Summer 1983), written as an open letter to Sidney Drell, deputy director of the Stanford Linear Accelerator Center and a friend of Sakharov. Sakharov discussed nuclear weapons as a means of deterring nuclear aggression only. He called for parity in conventional arms and cautioned against a nuclear freeze, an idea that was

gaining popularity in the West. He insisted on the need for serious arms control negotiations, but reluctantly agreed with the Reagan administration's plan to build one hundred MX missiles in order to restore nuclear parity. As always, he expressed support for human rights:

Finally, citizens have the right to control their national leaders' decision making in matters on which the fate of the world depends. But we don't even know how, or by whom, the decision to invade Afghanistan was made! People in our country do not have even a fraction of the information about events in the world and in their own country which the citizens of the West have at their disposal. The opportunity to criticize the policy of one's national leaders in matters of war and peace as you do freely is, in our country, entirely absent. Not only critical statements but those merely factual in nature, made on even much less important questions, often entail arrest and a long sentence of confinement or psychiatric prison.

- An article in the *New York Review of Books* of July 21, 1983, reviewing *The Anatomy of a Lie* by Samuil Zivs. Zivs was an official Soviet spokesman on human rights. His book, as might be expected, slandered human rights activists and other dissidents in the Soviet Union. Sakharov exposed its distortions and aspects of Ziv's career in his review.

Sakharov found the energy to work on physics as well. He wrote six scientific papers, with a primary focus on cosmology and the origins of the universe, which appeared in the Soviet publication *Journal of Experimental and Theoretical Physics* during his exile. From the Kremlin's point of view, it was useful to show that Sakharov continued to write scientific articles, that he was living a "normal," productive life in Gorky. For the same reason, physicists from FIAN were occasionally permitted to see him in Gorky. Sakharov enjoyed these visits, but he always understood they were "designed to muffle the campaign in my defense." In fact, only one physicist succeeded in seeing him in Gorky without official permission. That was Misha Levin, his former university classmate, who came to Gorky twice during Sakharov's exile and managed to meet him at the main post office or in a café according to a prearranged plan.[93]

At the same time, the Kremlin was always eager to discredit him. During Andropov's brief term as general secretary, official propaganda took an ugly turn. In 1983 the dissidents, Sakharov and Bonner in particular, were attacked in one of the most widely read Soviet magazines.

*Smena* (Shift), which had a circulation of well over a million readers. Written by Nikolai Yakovlev, this article (and there were others) claimed that the "CIA has turned to the services of international Zionism. . . . One of the victims of the CIA's Zionist agents is Academician A. D. Sakharov." The article went on to describe Elena Bonner as "a horrible woman [who] forced herself on the widower Sakharov." In June the president of the Academy of Sciences, Anatoly Alexandrov, told *Newsweek* that Sakharov had suffered a "serious psychic shift." Later that summer, Andropov himself informed a group of U.S. senators that Sakharov was "crazy." And in December another Soviet official called Sakharov "a talented but sick man," implying that he was mentally ill.[94]

Sakharov and Bonner remained in Gorky until December 1986. They endured relentless harassment throughout their six years in exile, harassment that was at times small-minded and at other times substantial. They had no telephone, and even public telephones on nearby streets were disabled. KGB agents stopped them from making calls from telephones in other parts of the city and from the central post office. Envelopes arrived filled with dead cockroaches. When Bonner was due to leave for medical treatment in Italy, they received disturbing photographs of mutilated faces. When Sakharov planted trees in a modest garden, the saplings were cut down. On the way to a concert, their taxi was stopped in order to ensure they would be late. Their car was periodically vandalized. "Whenever the authorities did not like something, it was our car that suffered," Elena Bonner recalled. "Either two tires would be punctured, or a window smashed or smeared with glue."[95]

Some incidents were more serious. Sakharov had hardly been in Gorky a week when two men came to the apartment, apparently drunk. One brandished a pistol and threatened "to turn their apartment into an Afghanistan." The police officers stationed outside his door failed to intervene and removed the intruders from the apartment only after Sakharov had alerted them twice to the unpleasantness.[96] On another occasion, Bonner slipped in the mud while getting out of her car, fell hard, and fractured her coccyx. But the KGB men in two surveillance cars not only refused to help her but "laughed and jeered at her" as she lay on the ground.[97] In September 1983, during one of her trips from Gorky to Moscow, other passengers abused and threatened her. "The shouting intensified and passengers from other compartments joined in. They filled the corridor, demanding that the train be stopped and I be thrown off. They shouted things about the war and about Jews." Elena Bonner always referred to the incident as a "pogrom." "I kept wishing I had a yellow star to sew onto my dress."[98]

To reinforce their isolation, a small jamming device was installed near the apartment to prevent their listening to foreign radio broadcasts; Sakharov had to carry his shortwave radio outside in order to pick up transmissions. When he and Bonner left the apartment, security agents would enter, rifle their papers, and vandalize the radio if they happened to leave it behind. Under such conditions, Sakharov was compelled to carry all his manuscripts, the shortwave radio, diaries, photographs, and personal notes when he left the apartment; the shoulder bag weighed as much as thirty pounds. Sakharov continued to work on his memoirs, and getting their hands on the manuscript became an overriding preoccupation for the KGB. Once the bag was taken when he left it in his dentist's waiting room. On another occasion, when Sakharov was sitting alone in his parked car, agents rendered him unconscious with some kind of narcotic and made off with the bag and all its contents from the back seat, including 900 handwritten pages and 500 typed pages of memoirs. Despite such setbacks, Sakharov always returned to his desk to write again, determined to resist the KGB.

And then there were harsher, more physical challenges to overcome. Living in Gorky, Sakharov did not forget how his life as a dissident affected members of his family. On several occasions he and sometimes Bonner went on hunger strikes to compel the regime to relent on a matter of principle. In 1981 he declared a hunger strike in order to help the wife of Bonner's son Alexei Semyonov gain permission to join him in the United States. Later he went on hunger strikes so that Bonner herself could go to the West for medical treatment.

By 1984 the regime had grown tired of Bonner's trips to Moscow; on May 2 she was detained at Gorky airport and charged with "anti-Soviet slander." Through the ensuing crisis, her children in the West received misleading reports. After Sakharov declared a hunger strike and was forcibly confined in a Gorky hospital on May 7, they were unable to confirm his whereabouts or the state of his health. It was reported that Bonner sent a telegram to his children in Moscow; but he had disappeared on May 7, the telegram was received on May 16, and it was not reported until May 20. Would Bonner not have tried to contact them earlier? Then she was reported to have made a telephone call to a journalist in Italy saying that Sakharov "is no longer with us." How could Bonner call Italy? There was no direct dialing to Italy from Gorky or anywhere else in the Soviet Union at that time. And why would she alert the world to his death, if that is what the caller meant, with an ambiguous phrase?

There was such a rush of anxiety and speculation over Sakharov and Bonner's fate that even President Reagan felt compelled to intervene and try to defuse the crisis. He called Ambassador Dobrynin at home "to make a personal and confidential request to Konstantin Chernenko [the new Soviet leader] to permit Bonner to leave for medical treatment." Reagan expostulated, "What if she dies in the Soviet Union?"[99] But his overture was rejected. Over the next three months, the regime released photographs purporting to show that Sakharov and Bonner were alive and well. A dubious telegram, supposedly signed by them both, arrived at the home of her daughter. Then there were further rumors that a Moscow psychiatrist and authority on hypnosis was treating Sakharov with mind-altering drugs to induce him to recant his views. It was not until August 27, after Bonner was convicted of anti-Soviet slander and exiled to Gorky for five years, that a film was released showing Sakharov eating and reading the July 16 issue of *Newsweek*. Only later did the full truth of what had happened come out: Sakharov did embark on a long, determined hunger strike to protest the treatment of his wife, and the doctors responded by painful force-feeding, assaulting Sakharov physically in order to shove food down his throat.

This prolonged and unsettling episode underscored the regime's dilemma in dealing with Sakharov. When the Kremlin removed him to Gorky, it resolved one problem and created another. He was no longer an activist but a prisoner. Only Nelson Mandela in South Africa commanded so much attention. As long as Sakharov was alive and in the Soviet Union, his situation reminded the world of the Kremlin's arbitrary and heartless treatment of dissidents. They knew his death in custody would provoke tremendous indignation, but they may have decided, in a realistically cruel, coldhearted calculation, that relations with the West were so poor that they had little more to lose. It should hardly be surprising that the regime was reluctant to reveal the truth about his treatment. Remember Andropov? He was said to be suffering from a bad cold and various infections until one day it turned out that he had died after months of a debilitating kidney condition. The Soviet government did not think it proper to tell the world about its leader's health. Why should it have behaved more openly with regard to its most famous prisoner?

Life in Gorky took an obvious toll on Sakharov's health. His heart condition grew worse, and he suffered at least one cerebral incident during a particularly torturous round of force-feeding. As for Bonner, she was not permitted to go to the West for medical treatment after he was exiled to Gorky until the fall of 1985, when she required multiple heart bypass surgery.* So their six years passed in Gorky, watching Brezhnev, Andropov, and Chernenko successively exercise power and then die before Gorbachev assumed the position of general secretary of the Communist Party in March 1985. The period of stagnation was over. Although life had not been dull under Brezhnev or his immediate successors, no one was prepared for the tumultuous years ahead.

Mikhail Gorbachev came to power at a time when the human rights movement was at its lowest point. Its groups had been disbanded, its publications severely curtailed, its visible presence in Moscow and other cities all but eliminated. Sakharov and Bonner were as isolated as they had been at any time since his removal from Moscow in January 1980. The system seemed altogether immune to change.

In April 1984, eleven months before Gorbachev reached power, Konstantin Chernenko initiated a discussion in the Politburo about re-instating Vyacheslav Molotov, Lazar Kaganovich, and Georgy Malen-kov in the Communist Party. Formerly close associates of Stalin, in 1957 they had been expelled from the Party after a failed attempt to re-move Khrushchev from the Party leadership. Now the neo-Stalinists had a chance to engage in discussions that must have made clear to Gorbachev the ideological obstacles he would have to overcome.

Archconservatives such as Dmitri Ustinov and KGB Chairman Vik-tor Chebrikov used the occasion to defend Stalin and condemn Khru-shchev. For Ustinov, "no single enemy did as much harm as Khrushchev caused with his attitude toward the Party's and the government's his-tory, and with regard to Stalin." Ustinov even suggested that the time had come to restore the name of Stalingrad, which had been changed to Volgograd. Chebrikov was more cynical. He acknowledged that they should expect to receive "not a small wave of letters from people who had been rehabilitated in the 1950s," who would oppose reviewing the case of Kaganovich in particular. Many of them, he added, had been "illegally rehabilitated." After all, "they had been punished in an alto-gether proper manner. Take, for example, Solzhenitsyn." (He had been

---

* She had traveled to the West for medical treatment in 1975, 1977, and 1979.

sentenced to eight years in the gulag after army censors read letters of his from the front that were critical of Stalin.) At that time, Chernenko was in his third month as general secretary; he was a painfully feeble man in his seventies whose physical limitations—he suffered from severe emphysema—symbolized the general condition of the country and its leadership. As Gorbachev sat at that table, it must have been clear to him that he might inherit power from people who feared change more than they regretted stagnation.[100]

Once Gorbachev was in power, his first public moves were not reassuring. He began by continuing the campaigns for greater discipline that Andropov had championed: efforts to curtail the consumption of alcohol, to target corruption, to improve management of the economy, and to create a more efficient system of planning.*

With regard to human rights as well, developments were not reassuring. In the labor camp for women in Mordovia, Tatiana Osipova was due to complete her term of five years and remain in exile for another five. (Osipova had been a member of the Moscow Helsinki Watch Group.) But then in April, just a month after Gorbachev's accession to power, her labor camp term was extended for another two years on the basis of the notorious Article 188, which had been added to the Criminal Code in 1983. Under its provisions, prisoners could have their sentences extended for up to five years for minor infractions of camp rules. As Yuri Orlov once explained, under this new law the "camp administration was both plaintiff and witness."[101] Osipova was the first prisoner to have her term prolonged under the new law. She was transferred to the Ishumbuv "severe regime" labor camp for women criminals in Bashkiria, where she became the only "political" among eight hundred women prisoners.† She remembers that camp officials in Mordovia and Bashkiria behaved more brutally toward their prisoners during Gorbachev's initial year in office.‡

Nonetheless, Gorbachev would have us believe that upon coming to

---

\* Andropov targeted "sloth, absenteeism and drunkenness" and urged "ordinary people [to expose] idleness, poor management, the squandering of state resources, an increasing crime rate and other common ills" (*New York Times*, January 4, 1983, 1).

† Soviet labor camps were classified by the harshness of their "regimens"; conditions varied with regard to housing, quantity of food, even the number of letters, food parcels, and family visits a prisoner could receive. From the least to the most harsh, the regimens were "ordinary," "intensified," "severe," and "special."

‡ Like Osipova, who shared her recollections with me in 2003, Orlov experienced tougher treatment in April 1985; he was beaten on the streets of a small Siberian town where he was living out his exile. See Orlov, *Dangerous Thoughts*, 282.

power he quietly announced a major departure from Kremlin policies that would have a profound impact on human rights throughout Eastern Europe. As he explained years later, "Immediately after the funeral of my predecessor, Chernenko, I called a conference of political leaders of the Warsaw Pact countries and told them clearly that now we were actually going to do what we had for a long time been declaring: we would adhere strictly to the principle of equality and independence, which also included the responsibility of each party for the development of its own country. This meant that we would not commit acts of intervention or interference in their internal affairs."[102] The effect of this change was not apparent until 1989, when one Communist regime after another collapsed, most of them to be replaced with far more democratic and more genuinely popular political leaders, including such men as Vaclav Havel and Lech Walesa, who had led the anticommunist movements in Czechoslovakia and Poland and had looked for inspiration to Sakharov and his colleagues in Moscow. Yet everyone familiar with history understood that "change in Eastern Europe could only be secure if it were preceded or at least accompanied by genuine change in Russia."[103] And genuine change in Russia was also about to take hold.

Gorbachev was ready to move more publicly and decisively. Sometime in 1986—it is hard to pinpoint exactly when without a definitive word from Gorbachev himself—his initial superficial moves to deal with corruption began to broaden into a more ambitious experiment to remake Soviet society altogether. Certainly the accident at the nuclear plant at Chernobyl on April 26, 1986, made the need for fundamental economic and political reform compellingly clear. An appeal from Sakharov may also have helped to initiate this fundamental shift in policy. That February, Sakharov sent a long letter to Gorbachev in response to the general secretary's interview in the French Communist Party's newspaper *L'Humanité,* in which he claimed that there were no political prisoners in the Soviet Union. "We do not put people on trial for their convictions," Gorbachev declared.[104] Sakharov knew better. He asked for a full-scale review of political imprisonment. As always, he took the time to focus on specific cases, citing the names and circumstances of twelve persons "whom he knew personally—Anatoly Marchenko headed the list—and called for the unconditional release of all prisoners of conscience."[105] The documents in this volume make it clear that Gorbachev shared the letter with his colleagues and even asked the KGB to respond to Sakharov's claims. Chebrikov's response on June 17 shows a somewhat chastened KGB chairman. On the surface, his report is straightforward and informative, conveying to the Politburo that just over 250 prisoners were being held under the principal political articles in the Criminal Code. But the memorandum is also significant for what it does not contain. While Andropov headed the KGB, his reports to the Politburo were as much policy directives—warnings of what might develop if the KGB's alerts were not heeded—as they were memorandums based on intelligence gathering and analysis. Throughout his tenure as KGB chairman, Andropov was seeking to use his position as a stepping-stone to ultimate power. Chebrikov had no such ambitions and did not play a political game against Gorbachev. Sakharov's letter, after all, must have been delivered through the KGB, which at least under Chebrikov could not withhold the letter from the general secretary. The KGB was no longer in the driver's seat.

Gorbachev, in fact, was beginning the process of allowing the population to stop being afraid. As he proclaimed in his book *Perestroika*: "Let's strictly observe the principle: everything which is not prohibited by law is allowed."[106] The Moscow-based human rights group Memorial has been able to document that by the middle of 1986 the regime had virtually stopped arresting prisoners of conscience. A decision had been reached, in other words, "to turn off the lever of repression."[107] This decision had profound implications. Just a decade before, in December 1975, less than three weeks after Sakharov was honored (in absentia) with the Nobel Peace Prize, Andropov made clear to his colleagues that it would be "impossible at this time to renounce the criminal prosecution of people who oppose the Soviet system, for this would entail an increase in especially dangerous state crimes and antisocial manifestations. . . . It is impossible to make concessions of principle on this question, since these would inevitably lead to further unacceptable demands on us."[108] Gorbachev, sensing the need to promote support for his initiatives "from below," understood that by renouncing the threat of political imprisonment, he would be inviting the kind of "antisocial manifestations" and "unacceptable demands" that Party leaders before him insisted on preventing. Still, neither Gorbachev nor the KGB announced a change in policy, but a series of actions soon caught the world's attention.

In February, Anatoly Shcharansky was released as part of an exchange of spies. News reports suggested that an elusive East German lawyer named Wolfgang Vogel had helped to arrange the swap; Shcharansky was brought to Potsdam and allowed to walk across the

Glienicke Bridge into West Berlin. There had always been a unique dimension to Shcharansky's case. His arrest and conviction for treason on the grounds that he had committed espionage for the United States severely strained relations with the Carter administration. It not only set a terrible precedent for the treatment of a prominent human rights figure but also raised the ugly specter of Stalinist anti-Semitism. Without disavowing the charges against Shcharansky, the regime released him after he had served nine years of his thirteen-year sentence.

Later that fall, the regime released a group of women political prisoners from Mordovia before their terms were officially over. One of them, the poet Irina Ratushinskaya, was well known in the West. Her release that October was taken as a gesture of goodwill toward the Reagan administration on the eve of the Reykjavik summit. At the same time, the "small zone," the only severe-regime labor camp specifically for women political prisoners—it was located in the town of Barashevo, near Potma, in the Mordovian Republic—was closed altogether.[109] By 1986, it held hardly more than a dozen prisoners. This was an unprecedented step and could have resulted only from a decision at the highest level. That same month, the Kremlin agreed to release Yuri Orlov, the founder of the Moscow Helsinki Watch Group, as part of a presummit exchange agreement in which yet another convicted Soviet spy would be traded for Nicholas Daniloff, an American journalist who was being held by the KGB on charges of espionage. As Orlov was brought from Siberian exile to Moscow and told of his impending departure for the West, a KGB official told him: "Know that changes are being prepared in our country such as you yourself once dreamed of."[110] This release too generated widespread publicity and was soon matched by a large-scale release of political prisoners in Poland. Jeri Laber, the long-time leader of Helsinki Watch, observed, "By releasing all the Solidarity activists, the Polish government was tacitly acknowledging that the attempt to crush Solidarity had failed."[111] History was beginning to speed up.

Nevertheless, such highly publicized releases were also accompanied by the tragic deaths of prisoners of conscience. From the outset the human rights movement suffered the worst kind of casualties; faced with harsh working conditions, indifferent medical care, and poor and inadequate food, many prisoners died. Political prisoners continued to succumb under Gorbachev, too: in September 1985 the prominent Ukrainian poet and activist Vasyl Stus died in Camp 36-1 in the Perm complex in Mordovia. There are conflicting reports of the circumstances surrounding his death. According to one, Stus died "while working the night shift of a forced labor detail." According to another, he succumbed during a hunger strike. When his family asked to have his body returned to Kiev, camp officials refused. He had died before his term was over, they explained, so his remains could not be released until they had served his entire sentence.[112] The death of Vasyl Stus failed to make much of an impression in the West. The *New York Times* carried a brief, obscure article; there were no angry editorials in major Western newspapers or questions about Gorbachev's standing as a reform-minded leader in the wake of Stus's murder, for that is what it essentially was.

In August 1986 another labor camp inmate named Mark Morozov died. He had originally been convicted of "anti-Soviet propaganda" for copying and distributing works by Solzhenitsyn and others, but after he expressed remorse for his actions his sentence was commuted to five years of exile. Within two years Morozov was arrested again and this time was sentenced to eight years in a labor camp, to be followed by five years of exile. He did not survive this new sentence. The circumstances surrounding his death remain unclear; it is possible he committed suicide. But if his mental stability was fragile before his arrest, as some veteran dissidents believe, the regime must be held responsible for holding him under conditions that could only have broken him further. Here again, the West failed to question Gorbachev's moral authority.

The death of Anatoly Marchenko in Chistopol prison in December 1986 could not so easily be ignored. Marchenko was one of the truly heroic figures in the human rights movement. The son of illiterate railroad workers, he spent six years in a camp for trying to cross the Soviet border into Iran. After his release in 1966, he headed for Moscow, where he struck up a friendship with Larisa Bogoraz, the estranged wife of Yuli Daniel, whom he had met in the labor camp. Marchenko told her of his determination to describe his experiences, to alert the world to the suffering of the prisoners at a time when most people, inside and outside the country, believed that the labor camp system had been dismantled. Working with Larisa Bogoraz, who eventually became his wife and the mother of his only child, Marchenko wrote *My Testimony*. The book circulated widely in samizdat and was soon published in eighteen languages. The regime never forgave him for exposing the moral degradation of prisoner and keeper alike as he chronicled episodes of hunger and self-mutilation. After its publication in

1968, Marchenko faced repeated arrests; he spent the next eighteen years in and out of prisons, camps, and Siberian exile. In August 1986, five years into his final sentence (when he still faced ten more years of confinement and exile), Marchenko declared an indefinite hunger strike, demanding to see his wife, who had not been allowed a visit for three years, and the punishment of the guards who had beaten him unconscious in 1983. It seemed unlikely the regime would accede to his demands, and Marchenko, who was famous for his stubborn defiance, appeared willing to sacrifice his life. Word of Marchenko's hunger strike reached the West almost immediately, but appeals and prominent articles—Marchenko's own appeal was published on the op-ed page of the *New York Times* on September 24, 1986—seemed to evoke little concern within the Kremlin. That, at least, was the impression in the West.

Officials in the KGB and the Party, in fact, were scrambling to resolve the matter. We now know that Larisa Bogoraz was approached on separate occasions by both KGB and Party representatives, each with a different proposal. Bogoraz initiated this process herself. Knowing her husband's stubborn nature, she wrote directly to Gorbachev to ask for Marchenko's release. In response, she was summoned to district Party headquarters and told that either she or Marchenko should make a formal request for commutation accompanied by a renunciation of his views. A short time later, the KGB dispatched a well-known agent, Bulat Imbayev, who had frequently interacted with dissidents, to offer her an altogether different way out: if she wanted to leave the country with Marchenko, the regime would allow them to go. Bogoraz responded that she would need to discuss the offer with Marchenko before reaching a decision, but when she asked for such a meeting, she was refused. Imbayev saw her at least two or three more times, but nothing resulted from their contacts. It is believed that Marchenko ended his hunger strike in early December. Documents that family members were permitted to see in Chistopol prison indicate that Marchenko received a visit from an official of some kind, and probably as a result of their discussion he called off his hunger strike. We know now that the Politburo had already approved of Sakharov's release from Gorky and that other political prisoners were being asked to sign statements disavowing their views as part of a plan to effect their release. Larisa Bogoraz even received a letter from Marchenko requesting a package of food and telling her that "we will see each other soon and it will not be in prison."[113] But then his family learned that he had died in Chistopol prison in the Tatar Republic on December 8.

Coming on the eve of Human Rights Day (December 10), when activists commemorate the adoption of the Universal Declaration of Human Rights, Marchenko's death brought headlines around the world.[114] It was suddenly and painfully clear that Gorbachev would have to do something to counteract the bad publicity. Soviet officials were still playing by the old rules; on December 12 the Soviet delegation to the Conference on Security and Cooperation in Europe, which was meeting in Vienna, walked out after the United States requested a minute of silence in memory of Anatoly Marchenko. In Moscow, though, the regime was moving to resolve the Sakharov problem once and for all and then deal with the broader problem of political prisoners.

Sakharov's release was not as sudden as it appeared to the West. His letter to Gorbachev in February 1986 had sparked a discussion within the Politburo over the question of political prisoners. And then on October 23, Sakharov wrote to Gorbachev again asking to be released from Gorky. He mentioned the health problems that he and his wife were facing and made clear that he wanted to devote himself to science and his family and to "make no more public statements apart from exceptional cases when, in the words of Tolstoy, 'I cannot remain silent.'"[115] That same month, journalists at *Literaturnaya Gazeta* and at *Novoye Vremya* (New times) approached the Kremlin—more than likely after receiving some kind of signal "from above"—with requests to interview Sakharov. They understood that "everyone stood to gain by a resolution of this problem."[116] Their requests were approved, an indication that Sakharov's exile would soon be ending.

Gorbachev had inherited a host of problems from his predecessors; he had also inherited their prisoners. Marchenko's death could have severely compromised Gorbachev's image in the West as a reformer. To chide the Kremlin, the *New York Times* noted that "[Marchenko] once wrote that words from prison are not heard. His words echo, forcefully and now poignantly. Does Mikhail Gorbachev who talks of change and openness hear them?"[117] It was time to do more than curtail the arrest of activists who remained at large; it was time to release all the country's prisoners of conscience and begin with Sakharov.

As we shall see, the Politburo had reached a decision on November 10 to end Sakharov's forced exile in Gorky and permit him and Bonner to return to Moscow. But the original plan was to dispatch Guri

Marchuk, the president of the Academy of Sciences, to Gorky to inform Sakharov of the decision. Gorbachev still faced opposition to this step. On December 2, at a meeting with nearly forty members of the Party apparat, Gorbachev explained the decision to release Sakharov. A prominent Central Committee member named Mikhail Zimyanin, who supervised ideological work, interjected with a sarcastic question, wondering if "Sakharov had said thank you" for the favor.[118] Gorbachev, disgusted, ignored the question. But Marchuk had still not been sent to Gorky. Something more dramatic was being devised.

On the evening of December 15, two electricians, accompanied by a KGB agent, entered Sakharov's apartment with orders to install a telephone. Before they left, they told him to expect a call at ten the next morning, but no one said exactly who would call or why. Sakharov and his wife "made all sorts of wild guesses," he later remembered. But Mikhail Gorbachev did not call until three that afternoon with the message that Sakharov and his wife were now free to return to Moscow. Sakharov thanked him, but then, to Gorbachev's annoyance, he appealed for the release of all prisoners of conscience, invoking the tragic death of Marchenko to reinforce his request. Still, Gorbachev could make only "a noncommittal reply."[119] Sakharov, it seemed, wanted to talk about one thing, Gorbachev another. When word of the call reached the outside world three days later, the Western media applauded Gorbachev's initiative and carried the news on the front page. But in reality, the important news was not that Gorbachev was calling Sakharov; Sakharov's appeal to the Kremlin in "Progress, Coexistence, and Intellectual Freedom" eighteen years earlier was finally being answered.[120]

After their talk, Gorbachev showed some deference to Sakharov. Three days after the telephone call, Sakharov was invited to a meeting with Guri Marchuk. They met at the Gorky Physics Institute. Among other topics, Marchuk brought Sakharov up to date on the status of disarmament negotiations, thereby recognizing Sakharov's competence in such matters. Four days later, on December 23, Sakharov made a triumphant return to Moscow, arriving by train at Yaroslavl Station.

Sakharov came back to a different Moscow from the one he had been summarily forced to leave. An entire scrum of journalists was waiting for him on the train platform when he arrived. With one or two exceptions, they were all foreign, and they hardly left him alone once he resumed life in Moscow. But what was a personal drama for Sakharov and his wife was a signal of enormous significance for the country as a whole. Sakharov recognized that "the question of my remaining in Gorky or returning to Moscow was something more than a purely personal matter: it was a yardstick by which the entire human rights situation in the USSR could be measured."[121] His presence in Moscow reinforced Gorbachev's image and legitimacy in the West. If Sakharov had been compelled to stay in Gorky, perestroika would have seemed artificial and a sham. Until that point, Gorbachev's initiatives formed a "revolution from above," a project conceived and promoted by leading officials who understood the country's stark need for change, if only to ensure that the Communist Party could sustain power. Unlike the "revolutions" in Czechoslovakia and Poland, where grassroots movements successfully challenged entrenched Communist parties, Gorbachev's program of perestroika was not forced on the government by anything other than Gorbachev's recognition that the Soviet Union had reached an impasse in its economic, social, political, and military development—the nuclear accident at Chernobyl in April 1986 and the ongoing war in Afghanistan were two of the country's critical problems—and only a complete shake-up could provide a way out.

The release of political prisoners highlighted the months that followed. Within weeks, the Kremlin expressed its intention to release all prisoners of conscience.[122] Nearly two hundred were sent home by the end of 1987. This was a serious concession on the part of Gorbachev. It enhanced his image in the West and distanced him from his predecessors and their legacy of repression. But the process involved was not without controversy and embroiled Sakharov as well. "It was not an *unconditional* release of prisoners of conscience," Sakharov noted. "Each case was reviewed individually, and each prisoner had to sign a statement that he would not in future indulge in 'illegal' behavior."[123] There were even indications that conditions grew worse in the labor camps in order to soften up the prisoners and make it easier to gain their cooperation. As Vladimir Bukovsky observed, prisoners "were released only after a prolonged, degrading campaign of pressure on them to recant."[124]

Faced with these pressures, Sakharov, Bonner, and the famous defense attorney Sofia Kalistratova tried to help political prisoners understand the options available to them. Sakharov may have been traumatized by Marchenko's death—he himself had endured several difficult hunger strikes—and believed it was necessary to get as many prisoners as possible safely home before more tragedies could take place. Nonetheless, in the eyes of other activists, it appeared as if Sakharov was extending too much support to perestroika and too much deference to a release process that suffered fundamental flaws.

At one point, no less a figure than Larisa Bogoraz, Marchenko's widow and a revered figure in her own right, argued with Sakharov, Bonner, and Kalistratova in a vain attempt to convince them that they were advocating "shameful concessions, . . . capitulations that could scar the prisoners for the rest of their lives."[125] Other activists were even more outspoken in their criticism. Writing in the weeks after Marchenko's death, Malva Landa and Valeria Novodvorskaya contrasted Marchenko's stubborn and principled stance with "the metamorphoses that have recently taken place with the Laureate of the Nobel Peace Prize." Marchenko demonstrated a steadfast refusal "to sink into self-deception, to any kind of naive, infantile optimism," in contrast to Sakharov, who, in their eyes, was willing to accept "unworthy compromises."[126] Sakharov was "upset" by such criticism, which "accused him of uncritical collaboration with the authorities,"[127] but he kept his own counsel. In April he met with the British Prime Minister Margaret Thatcher in Moscow and told her unequivocally that the West must back Gorbachev and his reform efforts. Such enthusiasm for Gorbachev "caused some disillusionment among dissidents who once regarded him as a hero of almost mythical size," Bill Keller of the *New York Times* observed. But Sakharov was convinced that he was only doing what he had always done: "I still say what I think," he insisted.[128]

This controversy took place within a broader debate among dissidents inside and outside the country over how to evaluate Gorbachev's initial reform efforts and the dramatic release of political prisoners. In France, one group of émigrés, including such well-known figures as Vladimir Bukovsky and Yuri Orlov, challenged Gorbachev to prove that the changes he was implementing were more than cosmetic and not merely a temporary tactic. Their letter first appeared in Western newspapers, but then, perhaps to their astonishment, it was reprinted in mass-circulation newspapers in the Soviet Union and discussed and criticized in *Pravda* itself.[129]

Such controversies aside, no one could ignore the dramatic changes around them. Journalists, writers, and activists of all stripes began to reinvent civil society. Ironically, it was the same regime that had once abolished freedom of the press that suddenly opened the floodgates and encouraged "a painful, frequently radical self-examination intended to build popular pressure for reform," in the words of the American scholar Thomas Remington.[130] Gorbachev himself acknowledged that "we needed glasnost to create the kind of atmosphere in society that would correspond to the needs of perestroika." As his initiatives for economic and political reform met stiff resistance from powerful elements within the Party, Gorbachev understood "that the same fate that had befallen Khrushchev awaited us if the efforts made from above were not reinforced by support from below."[131]

At Gorbachev's initiative, Soviet society was overwhelmed with information, documents, novels, and the public expression of historical and political opinions that made an entire country dizzy. By appointing a series of reform-minded editors to major journals and newspapers in the summer of 1986—Yegor Yakovlev to *Moskovskie Novosti* (Moscow news), Vitaly Korotich to *Ogonyok* (Little flame), Sergei Zalygin to *Novy Mir* (New world), and Grigory Baklanov to *Znamya* (Banner)—Gorbachev made a profound impact on the scope of glasnost and the psychology of the country. Like so many of the dissidents, these editors had come of age in the 1950s and 1960s. Several may well have shared the values, hopes, and disappointments of the human rights movement, but could not or chose not to cross over into open dissent. Others enjoyed typical Soviet careers and had not distinguished themselves in any particular way. Vitaly Korotich, for example, who turned *Ogonyok* into one of the most daring journals of the late 1980s, had enjoyed a conventional career as a government official in Ukraine. He had once visited the United States, then in 1984 published a typical piece of crude propaganda called *The Face of Hatred,* for which he received a government award. There seemed to be nothing to suggest that he would carry the banner of liberal reform. But when, thanks to Gorbachev, the opportunity arose to publish material that before could have appeared only in samizdat, editors such as Korotich took the lead in turning mass-circulation publications into serious forums to explore virtually every subject that once had been absolutely taboo.

Between 1987 and 1989 alone, the amount of formerly prohibited literature that appeared in the Soviet press was nothing short of astonishing: the novels of Boris Pasternak, Yevgeny Zamyatin, Andrei Platonov, Mikhail Bulgakov, Vladimir Nabokov, Vasily Grossman, and George Orwell; the short stories of Varlam Shalamov; Solzhenitsyn's *Gulag Archipelago* and the memoirs of Nadezhda Mandelstam and

Yevgeniya Ginzburg. Given access to Party records and KGB archives, journalists and historians were permitted to describe the full range of Stalin's crimes, including the torture and judicial murders of such figures as Isaac Babel, Vsevolod Meyerhold, and Nikolai Vavilov; the disastrous consequences of forced collectivization; the massacre of thousands of Polish officers at Katyn; the assassination of Leon Trotsky in Mexico; the persecution of the Russian Orthodox Church; systematic, violent anti-Semitism; and the forced deportation of several small ethnic groups. A more honest and comprehensive accounting of Soviet losses during World War II was also permitted, along with information about the secret protocols that accompanied the 1939 Nonaggression Pact with Hitler's Germany.

From the time of Khrushchev's removal from power in October 1964 until 1987, nonconformist writers and scholars could explore these subjects only in the most discreet manner, with hardly any access to documents and the ability to circulate what they had to say only within an underground culture of their own making, through samizdat or among a tight circle of friends. Now the country's most popular journals and magazines brought all this material to millions of readers. *Znamya* reached a circulation of 500,000; *Novy Mir*, 1 million; *Literaturnaya Gazeta*, 4 million; and *Argumenty i Fakty*, an astonishing 22 million subscribers.

Sakharov could not help being impressed by this outpouring of opinion and fact. "While we were still in Gorky, we began to notice astonishing changes in the press, the movies, and television," he recalled.[132] Within days of his return to Moscow in December 1986, well before the full flood of publications reached its peak, he told a Western reporter that "the word 'dissident' may be losing some of its resonance. People are now expressing their opinion more freely and this brings benefit to our society. The sort of articles that are now appearing read like some of the declarations from dissidents that were issued in the 1970s and for which many of my friends were jailed."[133] A few months later, he was even more enthusiastic. "I'm reading all the journals and magazines with great interest now. . . . I've been gulping down the journals. . . . Every day we're amazed because our standards and our points of reference are different. Total glasnost will come when we stop being astonished."[134]

At the same time, the country experienced the start of an economic and social revolution. Individual entrepreneurs were permitted to open small shops and restaurants outside of state control. And the founding of private organizations was permitted; as many as thirty thousand nonprofit organizations were established, giving voice to people who wished to protect the environment, defend human rights, or preserve architectural and national monuments. Religious communities could operate more fully on their own and without state interference. An independent civil society began to emerge, determined to move beyond the tight regulations that once governed all of Soviet life.

But as influential as the dissidents were in preparing the ground for Gorbachev's reforms, historians are likely to debate the role of the human rights movement in provoking Gorbachev's initiatives. Gorbachev himself has denied that the human rights movement had any discernible impact on the development of perestroika. Neither in his memoirs nor in those of his closest advisers is there more than a passing reference to Andrei Sakharov or the slightest acknowledgment of the dissidents' role in the post-Khrushchev period in promoting liberal democratic values. As recently as November 11, 2002, in a lecture at Harvard University, Gorbachev insisted that reforms could never have emerged from below primarily because virtually all the dissidents were either in jail or in exile by the mid-1980s. So how could they be credited with initiating change when they never had access to levers of power in the ordinary political sense?

Gorbachev and his advisers liked to claim that they found their inspiration within the very Communist system they were determined to reform. For them, the image of Vladimir Lenin as a tolerant political leader (in contrast to the murderous Stalin); the limited economic and cultural achievements of the New Economic Policy (NEP) of the 1920s; the political alternatives that Nikolai Bukharin offered the country; and most immediately the example of Nikita Khrushchev and the Twentieth and Twenty-second Party Congresses, when Stalin was denounced as a tyrant, offered a legitimate political legacy and the basis for a political program that included respect for fundamental rights and historical truth, economic reform, integration into the world economy, more open borders, unfettered debate within the Party itself, and an end to censorship in society at large.

Often referred to as "children of the Twentieth Congress," individual members of the Communist Party, in the words of Len Karpinsky, "did not entirely capitulate in the face of events but tried to fight the advance of conservative forces as best they could."[135] At one time Karpinsky himself had been a national leader of the Komsomol and a member of the editorial board of *Pravda*, only to be expelled from the

Communist Party in 1975 for an essay calling for democratic reform. Working quietly in academic institutes or on editorial boards of newspapers and journals, such liberal-minded Party members developed economic and political ideas that were not acceptable within the prevailing orthodoxy of the Brezhnev years. Later they became "ambassadors to Gorbachev of a larger liberal intelligentsia," as Anatoly Chernyaev, a foreign affairs adviser to Gorbachev, once described them, "one whose humanist, 'Westernizing' philosophical and practical orientation had been developing for over two decades" and "who kept alive the unfulfilled hopes of Khrushchev's 'thaw' for broader liberalization of Soviet society and integration with the international community."[136]

At times their work caught the attention of a wider public. The most famous such insider document was the "Zaslavskaya memorandum," leaked to Western correspondents in Moscow in 1983. As Stephen F. Cohen and Katrina vanden Heuvel have observed, "the professional life and political fortunes of Tatyana Ivanovna Zaslavskaya . . . reflect the long odyssey of reform-minded intellectuals in the Soviet Communist Party." Originally trained as an economist, Zaslavskaya became a sociologist at a time when sociology was barely tolerated as an intellectual discipline. She left Moscow for the Siberian city of Novosibirsk in 1963 and joined a unique institute whose leader, Abel Aganbegyan, welcomed independent-minded social scientists. The release of the Zaslavskaya memorandum, with its devastating critique of the economic system and its call for reform based on a close and honest examination of social classes within the country, provoked a political scandal; Aganbegyan's institute was officially reprimanded. But two years later, Aganbegyan became Gorbachev's chief economic adviser, while Zaslavskaya, who had first met Gorbachev in 1982, became a leading intellectual figure in Moscow. For her, staying within the system, albeit on the margins, provided the opportunity to have access to more open-minded political leaders who would eventually succeed the reactionary figures around Brezhnev. "But it was a very long wait," she once observed. "In the 1970s, Aganbegyan had a favorite toast: 'We will outlive them.' And if such people had not worked on all our country's problems for all those years, no political leadership could have started perestroika. People had to do the groundwork first."[137] It was Gorbachev who brought Aganbegyan, Zaslavskaya, and other liberal but not dissident voices into positions of influence and encouraged them to expound their views and contribute to his reform program.

Nonetheless, this revolution from above should not obscure the role of the human rights movement in shaping Gorbachev's priorities. It was the dissidents who first introduced the words *gulag, glasnost,* and *samizdat* into the world's vocabulary. (Vladimir Bukovsky once wrote that "Mr. Gorbachev did not invent glasnost—he borrowed it from the Soviet human rights movement.")[138] And it was their courage and sacrifice that helped to set the moral agenda for Gorbachev's reforms and the terms for his acceptance in the West. They may have been relatively few, but as Sakharov recognized during his exile in Gorky, what was important was "the qualitative fact of breaking through the psychological barrier of silence."[139] His own essays and memorandums, Amalrik's path-breaking book *Will the Soviet Union Survive until 1984?,* Valentin Turchin's *Inertia of Fear,* and many reports of the Helsinki Watch groups explored issues that affected all or a substantial number of Soviet citizens. The movement did focus on the defense of individual victims—a matter of principle that also served to raise legal consciousness—but it continually pointed to the country's economic and social problems and insisted that they could be adequately addressed only in a framework of open democratic reform.

This was essentially Gorbachev's program, and though an argument can be fashioned that any thoughtful person who took the time and energy to examine Soviet society would have reached the same conclusion that Gorbachev and Sakharov did, the fact is that the dissidents attempted to articulate it aloud at a time when the regime could respond only with arrests and other reprisals.

By 1987, though, the atmosphere had changed. Sakharov was caught up in the heady optimism of those years. Soon after his return to Moscow, he was able to closely review the status of negotiations between the United States and the Soviet Union over reducing the number of ballistic missile warheads and the controversy over President Reagan's Strategic Defense Initiative (SDI), or "Star Wars"—a project designed to intercept and destroy incoming ballistic missiles. The Kremlin saw SDI as a destabilizing factor in the nuclear balance of terror that theoretically, at least, could give the Americans the ability to defend themselves against a nuclear attack and thereby make it possible to consider a first strike of their own. Sakharov had always been skeptical that an effective system could ever be designed and constructed; as a weapons designer, he knew how many offensive options could be devised to overcome such a defensive shield. His argument helped to allay Kremlin anxieties and led to the delinkage of limits on

SDI and progress on other disarmament issues—what Sakharov called "untying the package." Just as his ideas had proved to be useful in 1963 when the Nuclear Test Ban Treaty was signed, Sakharov's contribution helped both sides reach an agreement to remove medium-range nuclear-armed missiles from Europe in the late 1980s.[140]

But domestic challenges and opportunities engaged Sakharov even more. With other liberal figures, he helped to organize a club called Moscow Tribune, "an embryonic legal opposition" that could promote "critical inquiry into different aspects of *perestroika*—economic, social, legal, ecological, and international."[141] Sakharov "was convinced of the absolute historical necessity of perestroika," as he wrote in 1988 in the last comprehensive statement of his views on major public issues. In some ways, his principal concerns remained as they had been in 1968, when his first essay stirred international attention: the release of prisoners of conscience and the connection between everyday freedom and economic and social development of the country. But by 1988, Sakharov's vocabulary was completely liberated of any Soviet jargon and he paid far more detailed attention to economic developments, to the point where he was not afraid to call for the repeal of laws forbidding so-called unearned income, for encouragement of entrepreneurial initiatives and the private ownership of land.[142] In 1968 he had not been ready to endorse these kinds of capitalist reforms.

He also traveled extensively. After nearly seven years of confinement in Gorky, he was eager to see for himself how the country was changing and to see something of the world. In November 1988 he made his first trip abroad, visiting Boston, New York, and Washington as a member of the International Foundation for the Survival and Development of Humanity. On the way back to Moscow, he stopped in Paris, at the invitation of President François Mitterrand, to help mark the fortieth anniversary of the adoption of the Universal Declaration of Human Rights. Sakharov went to Leningrad on several occasions for scientific conferences and to visit friends. As violence broke out between various ethnic and national minorities—the result of tensions that "earlier had been kept submerged by terror and censorship"[143]— he and Elena Bonner made a point of visiting crisis areas. In December 1988 they went to Armenia and Azerbaijan, along with Leonid Batkin and Galina Starovoitova (members of Moscow Tribune) and the historian Andrei Zubov, in a vain attempt to mediate a tragic interethnic and interreligious conflict that brought pogroms and warlike violence to Baku, to the small city of Sumgait, and to the Armenian enclave of Nagorno-Karabakh, within the borders of Azerbaijan. They each filed a separate report about their findings with Gorbachev's adviser Alexander Yakovlev. Sakharov and Bonner proposed going back to Armenia in January to help distribute aid to survivors of the devastating earthquake that had struck in early December, but Gorbachev opposed the trip. A few months later, after Soviet troops stormed a peaceful demonstration in Tbilisi, Georgia, in April 1989, killing more than twenty people with entrenching tools and poison gas, Sakharov and his wife visited the injured in a Tbilisi hospital, seeking to document the extent of the brutality and insist on a proper official investigation.

That spring, when elections were in progress for the Congress of People's Deputies, Sakharov lent his voice and prestige on behalf of friends and colleagues who were now candidates. He went to Komi, where Revolt Pimenov, a former prisoner of conscience, was a candidate. (Pimenov lost.) Sakharov also went to the Urals, and did not hesitate to speak his mind alongside other well-known liberal critics of Gorbachev and the Communist Party. In Chelyabinsk in September 1989, Sakharov appeared together with Galina Starovoitova, who had accompanied him to Armenia and Azerbaijan just months before. Speaking at a ceremony for victims of Stalinism, he used the occasion to challenge the preeminent role of the Communist Party. "I believe that the Party does not have the right to assign itself the leading role after what took place under its leadership."[144]

Sakharov never lost his moral compass or succumbed to wishful thinking; he had no illusions that Gorbachev's initiatives meant that the Soviet Union was now fundamentally a different country, that its misery was over, that a prosperous democracy would emerge out of the ruins of Russian despotism. Gorbachev's unexpected and startling reforms lulled Western leaders into complacency over the prospects for democracy in the Soviet Union; Sakharov never entertained such illusions.

Regrettably, several close advisers to Gorbachev and other government officials exhibited ugly condescension toward human rights activists of the Brezhnev era, an attitude that reflected a certain self-important arrogance. *They* were in charge, the levers of power were in *their* hands. For them, the sacrifice of so many dissidents was a mere footnote in the country's history.

When Sakharov was about to return to Moscow in December 1986, the regime's response was inadequate to the occasion. At a televised press conference at the Ministry of Foreign Affairs, an official could say only that "Academician Andrei Sakharov, currently living in Gorky, addressed the Soviet leadership with a request to move to Moscow. The relevant organizations, including the Academy of Sciences, have reviewed and approved his request, taking into consideration his long absence from Moscow. At the same time, the USSR Supreme Soviet adopted a decision to pardon Citizen Elena Bonner. Sakharov will have an opportunity to return to academic work, now within the framework of the Moscow facilities of the USSR Academy of Sciences." As Sakharov observed, "the style [of the statement] is priceless," a typical kind of bureaucratic doublespeak that presumed to congratulate itself for a generous gesture by denying responsibility for the harm its newfound generosity now sought to repair.[145]

In February 1987 Sakharov attended the Forum for a Nuclear-Free World and the Survival of Mankind, where Gorbachev was also present. They did not meet; when Sakharov appeared to be approaching him, KGB personnel intervened and prevented him from greeting Gorbachev or handing him a list of prisoners of conscience. They met a year later for the first time at a meeting of the International Foundation for the Survival and Development of Humanity. Both Sakharov and Gorbachev sat around a large oval table among a group of about thirty people. But when the time came for official photographs, Sakharov was asked to move to the other side of the table. Photographs of the meeting then could show Gorbachev without the need to show Sakharov present as well.

With glasnost and perestroika capturing the world's attention, Gorbachev tried to appropriate the term "human rights." In late 1987 the Kremlin created the Public Commission on Humanitarian Problems and Human Rights and assigned Fyodor Burlatsky to chair it. Burlatsky had been a speechwriter for Khrushchev and liked to brag to Westerners that he had lost jobs three times in his career for political reasons. But when it was time for Burlatsky to meet with Western human rights activists who had long championed imprisoned Soviet dissidents, he instantly became the typical Soviet bureaucrat, expressing reluctance to meet with former prisoners or to recognize what they could contribute to a discussion on human rights. His committee, after all, had been created as a substitute for the country's authentic human rights defenders; it would surely have been awkward for Burlatsky to face them.

When Jeri Laber of Helsinki Watch met with Burlatsky, she brought along such former prisoners and Moscow activists as Sergei Kovalev and Larisa Bogoraz in the vain hope that a dialogue between "Gorbachev liberals" and people close to Sakharov could prove fruitful, especially at a time (this was in January 1988) when prisoners of conscience were still waiting to be released. But Burlatsky could not conceal his disdain. Laber observed, "Burlatsky may have been a 'liberal' in the Soviet context but he had apparently absorbed the values of the Communist elite. He looked down on *zeks,* former political prisoners like Kovalev; they were tainted, in his eyes, by the indignities they had suffered in the camps. It is one thing to lose your job for being aligned with someone who falls out of favor; it is another to go to prison for acting on your ideals."[146] (There is an apocryphal story that one of Burlatsky's aides had the nerve to tell these former prisoners, "When you were enjoying yourselves in the camps, we were preparing the road for perestroika.")

In an interview with Stephen Cohen and Katrina vanden Heuvel, Burlatsky expressed the view that "individuals like Sakharov and Aleksandr Solzhenitsyn had a large impact on public opinion but not on political practice because they were rejected by the political system." Still, Burlatsky had to admit that "many dissident books published abroad were useful. They were read here, and people thought about their ideas." But then Burlatsky unashamedly expressed the opinion that the dissidents' outspokenness in defiance of official censorship hindered the work of people like himself, who remained within the system.[147]

Sakharov, in fact, had much greater access to the Western media than to the Soviet press. Immediately after his return to Moscow, the *New York Times,* the *Washington Post,* the Associated Press, CBS, and NBC carried interviews with him. Film studios were even made available for the first time to Western news agencies who wanted to interview a dissident. "There was absolutely no censorship," a CBS spokesman noted. "They wanted to demonstrate that there is a new attitude in the Soviet Union. Even three or five years ago this would have been a wild thought." The Voice of America also approached Sakharov for an interview; conducted by telephone on the morning of January 8, 1987, it was broadcast back to the Soviet Union. According to the *Washington Post,* this was the first time that the Voice of America had interviewed a well-known human rights activist in the Soviet Union and then broadcast the interview to the Soviet population.[148] But a long piece prepared by the Moscow journalists Oleg Moroz and Yuri

Rost for *Literaturnaya Gazeta*—which would have been Sakharov's debut interview in the Soviet press—was rejected by the editors.[149]

A half year had to pass before an article by Sakharov himself could appear. The occasion was unexpected: he was attending the premiere of a new production of Mikhail Bulgakov's 1925 satire on the Russian Revolution *The Heart of a Dog* when an editor of the monthly journal *Teatr* saw him and asked for a review. The subsequent article, which came out in the summer, was not only Sakharov's first appearance in the Soviet press since the 1960s but his first article on a nonscientific theme ever to appear in a Soviet publication.

Finally, it was not until November 1987, almost a full year after his return to Moscow, that an interview with him could be carried in the Soviet press. The reform-minded weekly *Moskovskie Novosti* asked Sakharov about the television documentary *Risk,* which explored Soviet and American rocket progress in surprising detail. While Sakharov admired the film and was grateful for its willingness to confront difficult truths, he expressed disappointment that it failed to mention that the 1962 missile crisis began with the Kremlin's decision to place nuclear missiles in Cuba. Sakharov remained outspoken: "The most terrible thing is a half-truth and keeping silent about something is also a lie." And he went on to conclude that "having in power the most outstanding personalities cannot be a reliable guarantee of peace if there is no glasnost, no openness of society and democracy."[150]

Of greater significance, Sakharov began to invest his energy and prestige in Moscow's now vibrant political scene. By the fall of 1987, a new movement was emerging that would capture the imagination of a significant portion of the Soviet public. Called Memorial, it was initially intended as an organization dedicated to the creation of a museum, a monument, and a comprehensive archive to commemorate the victims of Stalin's crimes. Sakharov became its honorary chairman and helped to broaden the original conception of Memorial into a dynamic organization that both conducted research into repression throughout the Soviet period—including compiling a full-scale documentary record of the Soviet human rights movement—and committed itself to campaign on behalf of human rights in contemporary Russia. Soviet officials made it difficult for Memorial activists to organize, but in just two years it became a large grassroots organization with chapters throughout the country, even though it was not yet established with full legal standing. Elena Bonner understood the significance of

Memorial's role in Soviet society; at a memorial service for Sakharov at the Academy of Sciences she asked Gorbachev to register Memorial as a suitable tribute to her late husband. Memorial was registered a few months later.

By the spring of 1989, the Soviet people were about to vote for the newly established Congress of People's Deputies. The process was complicated. The Congress would have 2,250 deputies. A third would come from territorial districts based on population; another third would represent Union republics and other constituent elements of the Soviet Union, leaving the final 750 seats from so-called public organizations, including the Communist Party (100 seats) and the Academy of Sciences (30 seats). Gorbachev arranged for a healthy block of seats for the Communist Party to make sure that important Party leaders would be included among the deputies. Additional seats were reserved for each of the unions of creative workers, such as writers, musicians, and cinematographers. Sakharov was nominated as a candidate from many electoral districts; he won election to the Congress as a representative of the Academy of Sciences only after pressure from rank-and-file members overcame the Presidium's attempt to exclude him from the ballot.

Sakharov's participation in the Congress of People's Deputies highlighted the final seven months of his life. The initial sessions "painted a merciless picture of what life is really like in our society," Sakharov recalled. "The Congress burned all bridges behind us. It became clear to everyone that we must go forward or we will be destroyed."[151] Sakharov was among those who urged Gorbachev to permit proceedings of the Congress to be carried live on television. Finally, the Soviet people had a genuine opportunity to see and hear Sakharov, to judge him for themselves, to listen to his arguments, and to watch him stand up for democratic principles in a legislature dominated by Gorbachev and his allies.

At times Gorbachev showed deference to Sakharov. Presiding over all the debates, he called on Sakharov twelve times, far more often than any other deputy. Sakharov was often defiant, playing "the role of Old Testament prophet, hectoring the resentful majority to assert its independence from the party and Government apparatus, and from Mr. Gorbachev."[152] Sakharov had recently denounced Soviet atrocities in Afghanistan. "A young Afghan war vet, who lived through the war in Afghanistan and lost both his legs, started to attack Sakharov" in a speech that was carried on national television.[153] Conservatives in

the Congress bitterly condemned Sakharov, claiming his remarks were
an insult to "the entire army, the entire nation, all our war dead." But
Sakharov refused to apologize and condemned the war itself as a
"criminal adventure."[154] The government confirmed the justice of
Sakharov's position when Soviet troops withdrew from Afghanistan in
February 1989, nine years after the intervention had begun.[155]

Gorbachev could also betray impatience with Sakharov and cut him
off. Near the close of the first session, Sakharov expressed frustration
over how little had been accomplished. Conservatives shouted at him,
and Gorbachev insisted he bring his remarks to a close or leave the
platform.

It was Sakharov and people like him, active as a loyal opposition,
who strove to expose Gorbachev's unwillingness to recognize the logic
of his own reforms and subject the Communist Party to democratic
imperatives. Perhaps if the Party had extended Khrushchev's legacy in
the late 1960s, if it had instituted Gorbachev-style changes then rather
than embarking on a program to repudiate Khrushchev's initiatives, it
could have made a persuasive claim to be a vehicle for democratic
change. In the mid-1990s, several years after losing power, Gorbachev
was willing to state the obvious. As he told his old friend Zdenek
Mlynár, "The suppression of the Prague Spring . . . engendered a very
harsh reaction in the Soviet Union, leading to a frontal assault against
all forms of free-thinking. The powerful ideological and political apparatus of the state acted decisively and uncompromisingly. This had
an affect on all domestic and foreign policy and the entire development
of Soviet society, which entered a stage of profound stagnation."[156]
The Party was responsible for this reversal and could not claim the
mantle of reform so easily. By 1986 the Moscow intelligentsia was far
more anticommunist and less willing to accept all the prerogatives of
power and prestige that the Party had assumed for itself. The Prague
Spring of 1968 could not be transformed into a Moscow Spring in
1986.

Gorbachev and his advisers were caught within this tension. They
genuinely believed they could fashion a more democratic society and
at the same time preserve the prerogatives of a one-party system. Time
and again in their interviews with Stephen Cohen and Katrina vanden
Heuvel, several of Gorbachev's advisers—people such as Alexander
Yakovlev and Fyodor Burlatsky—claimed that they could not imagine
a multiparty system for the Soviet Union, then went on to defend their
commitment to preserving the Party's "leading and guiding" role.

From the outset of Gorbachev's accession to power, Sakharov was impressed by him. "It seems to me that Gorbachev, like Khrushchev, is an extraordinary personality who has managed to break free of the limits customarily respected by Party officials," he commented. But he wondered "if Gorbachev and his close associates themselves may still not have completely thrown off the prejudices and dogmas of the system they inherited."[157] Sakharov grew increasingly impatient with Gorbachev and his continuing need to sustain personal control of both the government and the Communist Party. Sakharov understood that a legitimate democracy cannot exist if the country's highest political authority is not subject to the consent of the governed. Nonetheless, even as he saw no alternative to Gorbachev, he would vote for him only in the framework of a free, open, and competitive election. But Gorbachev felt the need to proceed in stages, ever mindful of the reactionary forces in the way of fundamental reform. For Sakharov, though, Gorbachev was proceeding too slowly.

Within months after Sakharov's death, Elena Bonner recalled a vivid example of Sakharov's independence before Gorbachev himself. "At the first Congress [of People's Deputies], when Gorbachev was being elected chair of the presidium without any alternative candidates on the ballot, Andrei Dmitrievich would not take part in the voting and even made a demonstrative exit from the hall. The next day Gorbachev asked him: 'Why did you walk out?' To which Andrei Dmitrievich replied: 'We have already had seventy years of elections without alternative candidates in this country and I don't intend to play this game any more.'"[158] It was this democratic legitimacy that Sakharov urged Gorbachev to seek and that, in his shortsighted lack of nerve, Gorbachev refused to pursue.* While Sakharov was alive and back in Moscow, both Gorbachev and Sakharov served as symbols of Russia's democratic opening. But after Sakharov's death in December 1989, Gorbachev lost a partner of equal standing, who could help him keep his political direction. When the enormous crowds surged through Moscow's streets and fields on the day of Sakharov's funeral, one of the most ubiquitous signs referred to Article 6 of the Soviet Constitution, which entitled the Communist Party to be the "leading and guiding force of Soviet society, the nucleus of its political system and of

---

* One cannot help wondering if such myopia contributed to Gorbachev's failure to see through the craven generals and ministers he assembled, who turned on him in August 1991. Gorbachev survived the coup but lost his political authority.

state and public organizations." The number 6 was displayed within a red circle with a bright red line through it, indicating the need to abolish it. One of Sakharov's principal demands in the months before his death was the elimination of this constitutional provision, but Gorbachev refused to go along. Sakharov was among the few people who dared to challenge Gorbachev publicly on this point. As David Remnick once observed about the two men, "Gorbachev would have preferred a compliant symbol; instead he was faced with a superior man who refused to let the powerful remain complacent."[159] If the party's undemocratic hold on power could not be compromised during a heady moment of liberal reform, then what kind of democracy could Gorbachev have in mind?

Sakharov knew what direction he wanted the country to go. He had begun to outline his thinking in the spring of 1989, when Gorbachev appointed him to serve on a commission to draft a new constitution. Some of his ideas would be familiar to an American audience: he envisioned a president elected for a five-year term by direct popular vote; a Union government with a bicameral Congress of People's Deputies; a Council of Ministers to serve as a cabinet; and an independent Supreme Court. Given that the new Union would be inheriting an economic system in which the state had exercised a complete monopoly, Sakharov wanted his constitution to ensure that individuals and corporations could own property and compete with state enterprises, many of which, he assumed, would remain in place. In Western terms, this would be a mixed market economy, but one in which the Union government would be required to provide a minimum standard of living for all its citizens.

Sakharov's innovative and substantial thinking focused on a structure for the "Union of Soviet Republics of Europe and Asia," as he proposed calling this new federation. According to this constitution, all the current Union republics and autonomous regions could choose to accept a new Union treaty or declare their independence; such a declaration could be made only by the appropriate legislative body. Republics that decided to join would have equal status and their existing borders would be guaranteed for at least ten years. Thereafter disputes over territory and borders could be resolved through a process of arbitration, which would adhere to the principle of self-determination for all peoples. As in other federal systems, the Union government would be responsible for defense, foreign policy, and nationwide currency, transportation, and communications systems. And all the rights associated with the Universal Declaration of Human Rights would be guaranteed throughout the country, with explicit prohibitions against discrimination on the basis of nationality, religious conviction, or political belief.

Sakharov intended his draft to serve as the basis for further discussion. He was not a revolutionary. He always advocated gradualist options, wanting to avoid political or economic dislocations that would disorient or harm large parts of the population. The Soviet people had already suffered more than enough from one grandiose experiment. He did not want to contribute to another. So he was against the breakup of the Soviet Union and hoped that a more flexible federal system, with the benefits of a common economy and security arrangements and with agreed-upon mechanisms for resolving conflicting territorial claims, would be attractive enough politically to sustain the support of the country's constituent republics.

Sakharov and Amalrik proved to be greater visionaries than Gorbachev. As long ago as 1969, Amalrik had described the possible breakup of the Soviet Union as a result of a political crisis or a war with China. "Party officials among the various nationalities . . . will aim for national separateness," hoping "to preserve their own privileged positions."[160] Even as the first session of the Congress of People's Deputies was set to open in the spring of 1989, Gorbachev had yet to propose how to reconstitute relations both among the republics and between them and the central authorities in Moscow. As he had to acknowledge in his memoirs, "In the matter of inter-ethnic relations, I must admit that at that time we were still not ready to put forward a real program of reform that would have included transformation of the unitary state into a truly federal one."[161]

By the final months of 1989, Sakharov was moving closer to direct opposition to Gorbachev. "The enormous gap between words and deeds in the economic, social, and political spheres" concerned him. He was unhappy about "Gorbachev's obvious desire to obtain unlimited personal power and his consistent orientation not toward the progressive forces favoring *perestroika* but toward compliant and controllable ones, even if they are reactionary."[162]

Sakharov, joined by other liberal deputies, called for a two-hour nationwide strike on December 11. They were borrowing a technique from Eastern Europe, hoping to organize a symbolic strike in the middle of the workday in order to pressure the Congress of People's Deputies, which was to reconvene the following day, to abolish Article 6 and thereby deprive the Communist Party of its monopoly of power.

When the Congress opened on December 12, Sakharov again seized the initiative, insisting that the pace of reform needed to be accelerated. But a visibly impatient and irritated Gorbachev turned off his microphone. His deference to Sakharov had reached its limit. Sakharov, too, was moving ever further away from his qualified support for Gorbachev. On December 14, the last day of his life, the Interregional Group held an open caucus at the Kremlin. Sakharov defended the strike call and urged his liberal colleagues to declare themselves a formal opposition. Although he looked exhausted, he had lost none of his moral energy for political action, as his speech to his hesitant allies made clear. "What is the meaning of political opposition?" he asked them.

> We simply cannot share responsibility for the actions of a government that is leading the nation to disaster and postponing the realization of *perestroika* for years to come. During that time the country will fall apart, collapse. . . . The only way, the only chance, for peaceful reform of the system is a radical quickening of *perestroika*. . . .
>
> And finally, I would like to respond to the accusation that the call for a two-hour political strike was a gift to the right wing, and that the gift would be augmented by our declaration of opposition to the government. I categorically reject this notion. Our appeal initiated a country-wide discussion this past week which has greatly expanded political participation. It's not a question of how many workers actually stopped work, although there were quite a few strikes in the Donets coal fields, in Vorkuta, in Lvov, and elsewhere. What matters is that the people have finally found a means to express their will and are ready to support us politically.[163]

This was Sakharov's last speech. In spite of his wavering health, he was determined to continue leading a challenge against Gorbachev and the Party. "Tomorrow there will be a battle," he told his wife that evening. But he would not take part in it. David Remnick remembered that during the final months of Sakharov's life, he "looked ten or fifteen years older [than sixty-eight]. His heart was worn down. He had trouble walking up more than seven or eight stairs before gasping for breath. His speech was a kind of low mumble."[164] Sakharov had asked his wife to wake him later that evening so he could prepare a speech for the next day's session of the Congress, but when she went downstairs she found him dead on the hallway floor.

While the government assigned Yevgeny Primakov, who was a member of Gorbachev's Presidential Council, to discuss funeral arrangements with Elena Bonner, "three medics in white smocks covered Andrei Sakharov's body with a pale green tarp and strapped it to a stretcher," Remnick reported. "Then they carried him down seven flights of stairs to an ancient humpbacked ambulance." Already that evening "there were the makings of a shrine: burning candles stuck in the snow, a heap of red carnations, a small photograph of Sakharov. Dozens of people wept. Others stood stunned by the sheer thought of what they had lost. There would be mourners on the sidewalk late into the night."[165]

Throughout Sakharov's career as a dissident and public figure, it was always an intriguing question just how widely known and respected he was in his own country. Long before it was possible to conduct a reliable public opinion poll, there was anecdotal evidence of his standing. Foreign correspondents were surprised to hear ordinary Soviet citizens ascribe exceptional powers to Sakharov. According to the *New York Times,* after he received the Nobel Peace Prize in 1975, "an elderly woman told her Russian employer, 'You know, they wanted to raise the price of vodka, but Sakharov would not let them.' Others have heard the same thing from cab drivers."[166]

*Literaturnaya Gazeta* published an article critical of Sakharov and his essay "Progress, Coexistence, and Intellectual Freedom" in February 1973, five years after it had initially appeared. This was the first article to attack Sakharov in the official press. Andropov immediately understood its potential to interest Soviet readers in what Sakharov was actually saying. "It can encourage the antisocial activities of Sakharov himself and increase an unhealthy interest on the part of hostile elements in the country," he wrote to the Central Committee four days after the article appeared. So Andropov insisted that Sakharov's name be banned "in official publications of the Soviet press." Andropov's recommendation was duly endorsed by the Central Committee, and Chebrikov, Andropov's assistant, was ordered to "see that it was done."[167]

By July, however, the regime backed away from its own policy. That spring, Sakharov gave his interview to the Swedish correspondent Olle Stenholm. The regime did not hold back. Within weeks an orchestrated campaign broke out in the Soviet press, with ugly articles and denunciations—sometimes linking Sakharov and Solzhenitsyn—by fellow academicians, prominent cultural figures (the names of Dmitri

Shostakovich and David Oistrakh appeared among the signatories),
and groups of workers.[168]

Such articles did not go unnoticed by Soviet readers. They were
among the first that sought to discredit Sakharov. In the West it was
long assumed that "most ordinary citizens . . . regard him as a traitor,"
the *Times* of London once observed.[169] But the regime knew better.
Later that fall, the Central Committee received a confidential report
about letters to the editors of *Pravda* and *Izvestia*. Apparently there
were too many "anonymous [letters], whose authors give a mistaken
evaluation of the harmful activity of A. Sakharov and A. Solzhenitsyn." One reader of *Pravda* expressed interest in reading "the original
text" of Sakharov's statements. Another, upon hearing Sakharov's
name for the first time, admitted that he "did not know his views and
that it was possible they contradicted [his] convictions." But this
reader insisted on defending "freedom of speech, freedom of thought,
freedom of the press." In one surprising note, a prosecutor from
Kochubievsky district, writing under his own name, called the press
campaign "deceitful." "In order to correct the situation," he went on,
"it is necessary to publish Sakharov's own article with an account from
his point of view. If he really went too far, then the people will condemn him." A second group of letters reached *Izvestia*. Of the 14,959
counted during that period, 809 dealt with Sakharov and Solzhenitsyn, of which 402 "had a negative, at times an anti-Soviet character,"
the Central Committee was informed. Andropov's earlier warning was
proving to be prescient; there were people in the country whose cu-
riosity and support for Sakharov were only encouraged by denunciations in the Soviet press.[170]

Seven years later, in the immediate aftermath of Sakharov's removal
to Gorky, the regime received further confirmation that at least some
Soviet citizens could respond sympathetically to his name. Natalya
Hesse of Leningrad was one of Elena Bonner's oldest and closest
friends. She went to Gorky on January 25, three days after Sakharov's
arrival. "His routine . . . had not yet been set," she recalled, ". . . and I
was able to stay with them for a month." Hesse was surprised by "a
stream of letters, vast numbers of them, ten and occasionally a hundred a day," that were reaching Sakharov. She began to sort them out
"because there were all kinds of letters; some greeting and supporting
him, some bewildered, some neutral ones in which people asked him to
explain his position." Within a week, Hesse was able to review and
tabulate all the letters that had arrived. She discovered that 70 percent

were messages of greeting; 17 percent neutral or expressing bewilderment; and only 13 percent abusive. Unfortunately, Hesse announced the results to Sakharov and Bonner. "From the very next day, we began to receive only abusive letters," the result of the KGB's "very attentive and well-organized monitoring and careful analysis of all conversations within the apartment."[171]

A more organized survey was soon attempted. Sometime in 1981, a demographer in Moscow organized an opinion survey about Sakharov. More than fifty interviewers were prepared to ask a short list of questions to a range of people. In all, more than 850 were approached. Their answers were then evaluated along a nine-point scale ranging from sharply negative ("an enemy, a spy, shooting him would not be good enough") to highly positive ("a hero, the conscience of the country"). Its results suggested that the Soviet people were far from unanimous in their approval of the regime's treatment of Sakharov. Many people responded with a straightforward "don't know" when asked their opinion (56 percent of the 245 blue-collar workers who participated, the highest percentage in this category); others, particularly engineers, scientific workers, and members of the liberal professions, expressed high levels of support (well over 50 percent). Even among Party members, one in four (out of 164 interviewed) expressed some degree of admiration for Sakharov.[172]

It was only in the late 1980s, when Sakharov was back in Moscow and a member of the Congress of People's Deputies, that the Soviet people had a chance to watch him on television. Now they could finally form opinions of their own based on more objective and unmediated information. One American friend noted that Sakharov's "persistent dedication to truth in the face of government denunciation, his freedom from bitterness or personal political ambition, his tireless efforts on behalf of individual victims of oppression, won him the unrivaled respect of the intelligentsia and later, after Soviet television made him known throughout the USSR, the general public as well."[173] In fact, Sakharov made such a vivid impression that a "poll" (it was actually a tabulation of readers' letters) published by *Argumenty i Fakty* in 1989 showed that Sakharov enjoyed a greater degree of respect among the public than Gorbachev. In a typical note, one of the respondents observed that "Sakharov is neither a gifted orator nor a sophisticated diplomat, but he consistently acts as a principled defendant of perestroika. He is a humanist, guided not by petty aims but by the highest moral goals."[174] Gorbachev was not about to accept such news patiently and soon summoned the editors of the three most prominent liberal journals—*Ogonyok, Argumenty i Fakty,* and *Moskovskie Novosti*—and made clear that such coverage was a personal affront. "I'll fire you, I'll destroy you," Gorbachev shouted at Vladislav Starkov, the editor of *Argumenty i Fakty.*[175] Starkov was not permitted to make a scheduled trip to the United States and Canada. He saw for himself that "Gorbachev was angry because we touched a personal nerve with him. The poll showed that he was not among the ten most popular people in the legislature. . . . Now we find that the father of glasnost is fighting with his own children."[176] But when Gorbachev tried to have Starkov replaced, the newspaper's staff all threatened to resign, and the Kremlin backed off.

It soon became possible to conduct public opinion polling of thousands of people based on genuine scientific methods. In November 1994, five years after Sakharov's death, a poll of 3,000 people was conducted by the Russian Center for Public Opinion and Market Research, under the direction of Yuri Levada. They were asked to evaluate nine major figures in Russian history—Nicholas II, Lenin, Stalin, Khrushchev, Brezhnev, Gorbachev, Yeltsin, Sakharov, and Solzhenitsyn—along a continuum from "significantly positive" to "significantly negative." Sakharov and then Solzhenitsyn scored the highest positive rankings, followed by Khrushchev, Nicholas II, and Lenin. The survey's results also reflected disappointment and bewilderment over the collapse of the Soviet Union and a precipitous decline in living standards. Brezhnev retained a significant level of respect; only Yeltsin, Gorbachev, and finally Stalin (in that declining order) had more negative responses than positive ones.

Another poll in the spring of 2003, written by the Washington-based Center for Strategic and International Studies in conjunction with the Russian Center for Public Opinion and Market Research, confirmed that Sakharov's standing remained high. In response to the question "If Sakharov were running for the Duma, would you vote for him?" 44 percent of respondents indicated they would either definitely or probably vote for him (19 percent expressed the likelihood they would not, leaving 37 percent unsure). This figure reflected consistent regard for him across all age groups above the age of thirty. A higher percentage of people under the age of thirty (who would have been teenagers or younger when Sakharov died)—54 percent—were not sure, and only 28 percent of those under 30 were likely to vote for him. Such polls could reassure Russian democrats that their most visible champion retained the respect of the Russian people whose memories of him were still vivid.[177]

In Russia today, Andrei Sakharov is commemorated in a host of inconsistent ways. Throughout the former Soviet Union, city squares and mountain peaks have been named for him. But his most substantial legacy remains within the handful of institutions, such as the Memorial Human Rights Society and the Andrei Sakharov Museum and Public Center, and the ranks of dauntless activists, young and old, who continue to challenge the Kremlin in an atmosphere of growing intolerance. It is no accident that Sakharov's close friend Sergei Kovalev has emerged as one of the most unsparing critics of Russian military action in Chechnya and one of the country's leading advocates of human rights. Kovalev is one of the few once-imprisoned dissidents from the Brezhnev era to have created a place for himself, however beleaguered, within Russia's fledgling democratic institutions, as chairman of the Human Rights Committee of the Russian Supreme Soviet, chairman of the Human Rights Commission, and human rights ombudsman.

Nonetheless, it is a bitter irony that a half century after Stalin's death, the dictator's influence on Russia outweighs the legacy of Sakharov and his fellow dissidents. In a poll conducted by the Russian Center for Public Opinion in 2003, 53 percent of respondents said that they looked on Stalin as a great historical figure, while in a separate poll, 36 percent said they believed that Stalin was more good than bad.[178] Such indications of public attitudes reflect the worrisome possibility that Stalin could join the pantheon of Russian national heroes, next to Peter the Great and Ivan the Terrible, whose ruthless exercise of power also created awe among the population, leaving many to forget the price in human suffering inflicted by their rule.[179]

Russia today does not resemble the liberal and prosperous country that people inside and outside its borders were hoping would emerge with the collapse of the Soviet Union. The betrayal of Russia's long-awaited political freedom has left a deep well of disappointment within the population. In a poll announced in the summer of 2003, 78 percent agreed with the statement that "democracy is a facade for a government controlled by rich and powerful cliques. Only 22 percent expressed a preference for democracy, whereas 53 percent positively disliked it."[180]

Still, much has changed for the better: Russians are generally free to worship as they please, to travel, to study in the West, to examine their country's history without the arbitrary limits of ideological censorship, to own land, and to establish small businesses. But such changes, however dramatic and necessary, cannot obscure the realities of everyday life. Two dismal wars in Chechnya, grinding and widespread poverty, ongoing ethnic tensions, an increasingly controlled and cowed press, official corruption and lawlessness, lack of free elections or democratic institutions in virtually all of the former Soviet Union—these conditions speak more of a country that has yet to dig out from under the rubble of Bolshevik and Stalinist dictatorship than of a country inspired by Sakharov's campaign for human rights.

Furthermore, Russia faces a mounting health and demographic crisis, whose dimensions would be unheard of in an advanced industrial democracy. Over the next half century, Russia's population could contract by one-third, from 145 million today to 101 million in the year 2050, a collapse brought on by low fertility rates and striking increases in HIV infections, heart disease, and tuberculosis. While women enjoy a current life expectancy of 72 years (seven years less than that of American women), Russian men face a dismal average of 58.2 years, almost sixteen years fewer than their American counterparts. Any society would face a formidable task in responding to such an overwhelming challenge. But Russia, with its fragile democratic institutions, can ill afford the social and economic chaos that is likely to result from a public health and demographic nightmare. As Murray Feshbach, the foremost Western scholar of Russian health care, has observed, "Epidemics invite chaos, and that's the last thing we want in a struggling democracy with huge arsenals of nuclear, chemical and biological weapons."[181]

The Communist Party was ousted from power in 1991. The collapse of the Soviet Union led to the removal of statues of Lenin and other Bolshevik leaders from public squares. But Stalin and Stalinism have not been repudiated altogether. Neither in the 1950s, after Stalin's death, nor since the breakup of the Soviet Union has there ever been a proper and thorough examination of the crimes of Stalin, of the KGB, or of the Communist Party itself, despite Khrushchev's initiatives at the Twentieth and Twenty-second Party Congresses. The country has never held trials for the perpetrators of the massive numbers of crimes committed between 1917 and 1991. In the fall of 2002, after a mass grave was discovered outside St. Petersburg, members of Memorial began to examine the site and sought assistance from the Federal Security

Bureau (FSB), the successor agency to the KGB. But the FSB refused to cooperate, "saying its archives held no information about burials there." (Memorial investigators believe the mass grave holds the remains of thousands of people.) Such reticence reflects the broader failure on the part of Russian society to confront its Soviet past. Irina A. Flige, who directs the St. Petersburg office of Memorial, bitterly observed that "the Communist regime was never properly held accountable, as happened in Germany after Nazism."[182]

Vladimir Putin, the current president of the Russian Federation, is a former director of the FSB. He rose within the ranks of the very organization that carried out unlimited, merciless repression under Stalin. Putin did not issue a word against Stalin and his legacy on March 5, 2003, the fiftieth anniversary of the dictator's death. It is this kind of calculated silence from Russia's political leadership that permits "the evil that Stalin exemplified [to be] treated as a legitimate part of the Russian national tradition," the journalist David Satter has noted.[183]

Elena Bonner had all this in mind when in April 2003 she argued against a proposal to erect a monument to Sakharov. "With one-third of its population living below the poverty line," she declared, "Russia waging a cruel and bloody war in which thousands of its soldiers and tens of thousands of peaceful citizens of Chechnya are dying—this Russia is violently contrasting with the idea of erecting a monument to Sakharov" in Moscow. Russia may well choose to look to Sakharov for inspiration someday—a monument to Sakharov would remind people of the ideal of justice—but "no monument can force society to re-evaluate its values," Bonner insisted.[184]

Sponsoring such a monument would be an easy step for Putin. In the fall of 2001 he did not hesitate to tell an American audience on National Public Radio that "at certain periods of time in the life of any nation, there will be people who turn on the light, if you will. They show a road for the nation to follow. Andrei Sakharov was one of those people: a visionary, someone who was able not only to see the future, but to articulate his thoughts, and to do so without fear."[185]

Such rhetoric is just another exercise in hypocrisy, the kind Russians have become accustomed to from their leaders. Tragically, the same week in April 2003 that a liberal federal legislator named Sergei Yushenkov initiated a proposal to build a monument to Sakharov, he was assassinated in the kind of shadowy attack that in 1998 claimed the life of Sakharov's friend and colleague Galina Starovoitova in St.

Petersburg. They are among 9 members of the country's parliament and 130 journalists who have been murdered with impunity. It would be a far greater tribute to Sakharov's memory and all he represented for the Kremlin to carry out a genuine investigation of these crimes, identify the perpetrators, bring them to justice, and thereby uphold the rule of law than for monuments to Sakharov to be erected in place of those that once commemorated a discredited revolution.

No one can predict where Russia is headed. Its contradictions and paradoxes remain too vivid to point to one particular kind of future or another. But if Russia is ever to deepen its commitment to democratic institutions, it will not look to tsars or commissars for inspiration; it will not look to the leaders who presided over the collapse of the Soviet Union or inherited the remnants of its political and economic arrangements. Russia will look to the life of Andrei Sakharov. In 1999 Boris Yeltsin, then president of Russia, nominated Sakharov as *Time*'s Person of the Century. Sakharov was "the real spiritual father of democratic change in Russia," Yeltsin observed. "I am intensely aware of how much we miss his wisdom, firmness and humanity today."[186] Sakharov's determined, nonviolent, and principled insistence on open, democratic, and responsible government provided an example for the Russian people to follow—toward a system of government that respects the lives and rights of each citizen while constructing the kind of social and political institutions that can be relied on to protect those rights. Only when this vision is realized can we say with confidence that the legacy of Andrei Sakharov has been assured.

## NOTES

1. *New York Times*, July 11, 1968, 1, and July 14, 1968, E10.
2. *Newsweek*, August 5, 1968, 41; *Time*, August 2, 1968, 26–27; *Christian Science Monitor*, July 23, 1968, 4.
3. Document 1, May 22, 1968
4. Document 3, June 13, 1968.
5. Ludmilla Alexeyeva, interview with author, Moscow, 2002.
6. Alexander Ginzburg's book on the trial appeared in English as *On Trial: The Soviet State versus "Abram Tertz" and "Nikolai Arzhak,"* trans. and ed. Max Hayward (New York, 1966).
7. Andrei Amalrik, *Will the Soviet Union Survive until 1984?* (New York, 1981), 15.
8. Andrei Amalrik, *Notes of a Revolutionary* (New York, 1982), 23. The text of Litvinov's conversation with the KGB can be found in Abraham Brumberg, ed., *In Quest of Justice: Protest and Dissent in the Soviet Union Today* (New York,

1970), 90–92. For information about the trials of Khaustov and Bukovsky, see Pavel Litvinov, ed., *The Demonstration in Pushkin Square* (Boston, 1969).

9. The full text of the "Letter to the Fourth Congress of the Union of Soviet Writers" can be found in Aleksandr I. Solzhenitsyn, *The Oak and the Calf* (New York, 1980), 458–62.

10. Boris Shragin, *The Challenge of the Spirit* (New York, 1978), 207.

11. Sakharov's foreword to Mark Hopkins, *Russia's Underground Press* (New York, 1983), vii.

12. Andrei Sakharov, "Letter to the Amnesty International Symposium on the Death Penalty," September 19, 1977, in his *Memoirs* (New York, 1990), 654.

13. Sakharov, *Memoirs*, 6.

14. See Elena Bonner, *Volniye Zametki k Rodoslovnoi Andreia Sakharova* [Random notes toward a genealogy of Andrei Sakharov] (Moscow, 1996).

15. Quoted in Vladislav Mokhov, "Grazhdanin Mira" [A citizen of the world], *Atom*, January 1998, 30. (This is a Russian-language journal published in Sarov.)

16. Sakharov, *Memoirs*, 114.

17. Ibid., 94.

18. Ibid., 97.

19. Ibid., 170.

20. Quoted in Vyacheslav Feodoritov, "On byl svetlym" [He was pure], *Atom*, January 1998, 6.

21. Sakharov, *Progress, Coexistence, and Intellectual Freedom* (New York, 1968), 25.

22. See Mikhail Heller and Aleksandr Nekrich, *Utopia in Power* (New York, 1986), 483.

23. Maximov's article appeared in *Krasny Flot* [Red Navy], June 14, 1952.

24. See the letter of eleven scientists to Beria in the Andrei Sakharov Archive (Harvard), folder S.II.2.6.1.51.

25. Sakharov, *Memoirs*, 164.

26. Quoted in Alec Nove, *Glasnost' in Action: Cultural Renaissance in Russia* (Boston, 1989), 30.

27. Sakharov, *Memoirs*, 164.

28. Ibid., 200.

29. Ibid., 207.

30. Ibid., 193–95.

31. *Atom*, January 1998, 9.

32. Sakharov, *Memoirs*, 203

33. Ibid., 215.

34. Ibid., 229, 263; Hedrick Smith, "The Intolerable Andrei Sakharov," *New York Times Magazine*, November 4, 1973, 56.

35. Sakharov, *Memoirs*, 234–35.

36. A copy of the transcript of the meeting of the Academy of Sciences of June 22–26, 1964, can be found in the Sakharov Archive (Harvard), folder S.II.2.9.01.1.

37. *Selskaia Zhizn'* [Rural life], August 29, 1964, ibid., folder S.III.1.01.0

38. The letter can be found ibid., folder S.III.1.2.28.4. Medvedev's book was

published as *The Rise and Fall of T. D. Lysenko,* trans. Michael Lerner (New York, 1969).

39. Sakharov, *Memoirs,* 224, 232.

40. Vladimir Bukovsky, interview with author, London, 1977.

41. Andrei Amalrik, *Will the Soviet Union Survive until 1984?* 15–17.

42. Ludmilla Alexeyeva, *Soviet Dissent: Contemporary Movements for National, Religious, and Human Rights,* trans. Carol Pearce and John Glad (Middletown, CT, 1987), 309.

43. Sakharov, *Memoirs,* 273.

44. Arkhiv Andreia Sakharova (Moscow), f. 1, op. 3, d. 6, ll. 1–2.

45. A somewhat abridged translation of the article can be found in Stephen F. Cohen, ed., *An End to Silence* (New York, 1982), 228–34. The text is drawn from Medvedev's journal "Politichesky Dnevnik."

46. Sakharov, *Memoirs,* 276. His letter to Suslov can be found in the Sakharov Archive (Harvard), folder S.II.2.4.26.

47. A copy of the appeal on censorship can be found in the Arkhiv Andreia Sakharova (Moscow), f. 1, op. 3, d. 1.

48. Sakharov, *Memoirs,* 275.

49. See Pavel Litvinov, comp., *The Trial of the Four: The Case of Galanskov, Ginzburg, Dobrovolksy, and Lashkova,* ed. Peter Reddaway (New York, 1972).

50. Kevin Klose, *Washington Post,* December 16, 1989, A24.

51. Alexander Solzhenitsyn et al., *From Under the Rubble,* trans. A. M. Brock et al. (Boston, 1975), 5. Sakharov and Solzhenitsyn met for the first time in August 1968. Solzhenitsyn described this and subsequent meetings in *Oak and the Calf,* 367–77.

52. *New York Times,* December 28, 1986, 14.

53. Alexeyeva, *Soviet Dissent,* 283.

54. *New York Times,* December 20, 1986, 8.

55. Document 77, March 7, 1974.

56. Transcription of Politburo meeting, as reported in Document 190, December 9, 1986.

57. Sakharov, *Memoirs,* 288.

58. Document 108, December 29, 1975.

59. A substantial section of the interview can be found in the appendix to Sakharov's *Memoirs,* 623–30.

60. Andrei Sakharov, "Interview with Western Correspondents," in *Sakharov Speaks* (New York, 1974), 204–5; the interview took place in Moscow on August 21, 1973.

61. See Oleg Kalugin, *Spymaster: My 32 Years in Intelligence and Espionage against the West* (London, 1994), 261–62.

62. Document 23, January 18, 1971.

63. Document 39, December 20, 1971.

64. Andrei Sakharov, *Moscow and Beyond* (New York, 1991), 32.

65. Document 144, August 26, 1980.

66. Vladimir Bukovskii, *Moskovskii Protsess* [Moscow trial] (Paris, 1996), 89. Yeltsin's government invited Bukovsky to be an expert witness at the 1992 trial of the Communist Party in the Constitutional Court of the Russian Federation. He

accepted on condition that he have access to documents that he wished to examine.

67. Anatoly Dobrynin, *In Confidence: Moscow's Ambassador to Six Cold War Presidents (1962–1986)* (New York, 1995), 512.

68. Amalrik, *Notes of a Revolutionary*, 26.

69. Pavel Litvinov, "O dvizhenii za prava cheloveka" [On the human rights movement], in *Samosoznanie* [Insights] (New York, 1976), 81.

70. *Newsweek*, November 22, 1982, 28.

71. Document 62, September 17, 1973.

72. Valery Chalidze, *To Defend These Rights* (New York, 1974), 49–50.

73. *Wall Street Journal*, July 23, 1975, 14; *New York Times*, August 1, 1975, 26 and 2. I am indebted to Daniel C. Thomas and his book *The Helsinki Effect: International Norms, Human Rights, and the Demise of Communism* (Princeton, 2001) for providing a good deal of information and source material for my discussion of the Helsinki Final Act. See also Joshua Rubenstein, *Soviet Dissidents* (Boston, 1985), for my initial evaluation of the effect of the Final Act on the fate of human rights in the Soviet Union.

74. Dobrynin, *In Confidence*, 346.

75. Thomas, *Helsinki Effect*, 93.

76. Dobrynin, *In Confidence*, 346.

77. Michael Ignatieff, "The Rights Stuff," *New York Review of Books,* June 13, 2002, 18.

78. *New York Times*, June 6, 1974, 16.

79. Dobrynin, *In Confidence*, 217.

80. Thomas, *Helsinki Effect*, 76.

81. Document 97, July 18, 1975

82. Sakharov, *Alarm and Hope*, 3–4.

83. Abram Tertz [Andrei Sinyavsky], *A Voice from the Chorus* (New York, 1978), 176.

84. "Meeting Zbigniew Romaszewsky," in Sakharov Archive (Harvard), folder S.IV.2.2.458. In addition, see a background report from Radio Free Europe dated January 29, 1980, titled "Reaction to Sakharov's Banishment"; the report describes contacts between Sakharov and dissidents in Eastern Europe.

85. Document 136, December 26, 1979.

86. Interview with Charles Bierbauer of ABC television, as quoted in *Chronicle of Human Rights in the USSR*, no. 37 (January–March 1980), 9.

87. *Chronicle of Current Events* (Amnesty International ed.), no. 44 (March 16, 1977), 185.

88. Peter Reddaway, "Soviet Policies on Dissent and Emigration: The Radical Change of Course since 1979," an unpublished colloquium paper delivered at the Kennan Institute for Advanced Russian Studies, August 28, 1984, 23.

89. *Chronicle of Current Events* (Amnesty International ed.), no. 63 (December 31, 1981), 58, 74.

90. *USSR News Brief: Human Rights*, 1982, no. 22 (November), 58.

91. *New York Times*, January 29, 1980, 1 and 8.

92. Elena Bonner, *Alone Together* (New York, 1986), 7.

93. Sakharov, *Memoirs*, 550.

94. *Smena*, no. 14 (July 1983), 26–27, quoted in Bonner, *Alone Together*, 41–42; *Newsweek* (Atlantic ed.), June 20, 1983, 52; Sakharov, *Memoirs*, 597; *New York Times*, December 9, 1983, 8.

95. Bonner, *Alone Together*, 108.

96. Sakharov, *Memoirs*, 520.

97. Sakharov, *Moscow and Beyond*, 32.

98. Bonner, *Alone Together*, 25–26.

99. Dobrynin, *In Confidence*, 552.

100. "Rabochaia zapis zasedaniia Politbiuro TSK KPSS po voprosu o reabilitatsii V. M. Molotova, G. M. Malenkova, L. M. Kaganovicha" [Working transcript of the session of the Politburo of the Central Committee of the Communist Party of the Soviet Union on the question of rehabilitating V. M. Molotov, G. M. Malenkov, L. M. Kaganovich], April 24, 1984. This transcript can be found in the collections of the Harvard Project on Cold War Studies, File 251, Document 13.

101. Orlov, *Dangerous Thoughts*, 260.

102. Mikhail Gorbachev and Zdenek Mlynár, *Conversations with Gorbachev: On Perestroika, the Prague Spring, and the Crossroads of Socialism* (New York, 2002), 84–85.

103. Rodric Braithwaite, *Across the Moscow River: The World Turned Upside Down* (New Haven, 2002), 116. Braithwaite was British ambassador to the Soviet Union during those years.

104. For the interview in *L'Humanité*, see Mikhail Gorbachev, *Selected Speeches and Articles* (Moscow, 1987), 329.

105. Sakharov, *Memoirs*, 607.

106. Mikhail Gorbachev, *Perestroika* (London, 1988), 108. Gorbachev, who attended law school, was quoting Article 6 of the French Declaration of the Rights of Man and Citizen, promulgated in 1789.

107. Unpublished essay by Alexander Daniel and Boris Belenkin, two veteran staff members of Memorial.

108. Document 108, December 29, 1975

109. See Irina Ratushinskaya, *Grey is the Color of Hope* (New York, 1988), for her account of life in the "small zone."

110. Orlov, *Dangerous Thoughts*, 296.

111. Jeri Laber, *The Courage of Strangers: Coming of Age with the Human Rights Movement* (New York, 2002), 258.

112. See the Web site www.ualberta.ca/~ulec/stus/timeline-01.html for biographical information about Vasyl Stus.

113. Alexander Daniel, interview with author, Moscow, 2002.

114. See *New York Times*, December 10, 1986, 3, and subsequent articles on December 11, 5, along with an editorial on December 13, 26. I contributed a tribute to Marchenko on the *Times* op-ed page on December 19.

115. Sakharov, *Memoirs*, 612.

116. Oleg Moroz, "Vozvrashchenie iz ssylki" [Return from exile], in *Andrei Dmitrievich: Vospaminaniia o Sakharove* [Andrei Dmitrievich: Reminiscences of Sakharov], ed. Tat'iana Ivanova (Moscow, 1990), 271.

117. *New York Times*, December 13, 1986, 26.

118. Anatoly S. Chernyaev, interview with author, Moscow, 2002.

119. Sakharov, *Memoirs,* 615–16.

120. I am grateful to Alexander Daniel for helping me understand the nuances of Gorbachev's call to Sakharov.

121. Sakharov, *Memoirs,* 611.

122. An initial decree was issued on February 2, 1987. See coverage in *New York Times,* February 8, 1, and February 11, 1.

123. Sakharov, *Moscow and Beyond,* 6.

124. Vladimir Bukovsky, "Gorbachev's Reforms: Where's the Beef?" *Wall Street Journal,* December 22, 1987, 18.

125. Sakharov, *Moscow and Beyond,* 6–7.

126. The open letter of Landa and Novodvorskaya was written in December 1986–January 1987; see "Materialy samizdata," Arkhiv samizdata 5891.

127. Sakharov, *Moscow and Beyond,* 12.

128. *New York Times,* April 1, 1987, 1; April 3, 1987, 1. Bill Keller reiterated these concerns seven months later, remarking that Sakharov was "partly estranged from the severest critics of the Soviet system, especially those who have emigrated to the West, because he continues to urge support for Mikhail S. Gorbachev, the Soviet leader, as the nation's best hope for change" (ibid., November 7, 1987, 1, 5).

129. See Nina Baytes, "Dissidents' Views of GLASNOST," Radio Free Europe/Radio Liberty, RL 238/87, June 24, 1987, for a well-informed summary of this controversy.

130. Thomas Remington, "A Socialist Pluralism of Opinions: Glasnost and Policy-Making under Gorbachev," *Russian Review* 48 (1989): 273.

131. Gorbachev and Mlynár, *Conversations with Gorbachev,* 68.

132. Sakharov, *Moscow and Beyond,* 9.

133. *New York Times,* December 25, 1986, 3.

134. Quoted in *Sipiscope,* published by the Scientists' Institute for Public Information, June–July 1987, 2–4, in Arkhiv Andreia Sakharova (Moscow), f. 1, op. 3, d. 109.

135. Stephen F. Cohen and Katrina vanden Heuvel, *Voices of Glasnost: Interviews with Gorbachev's Reformers* (New York, 1989), 298.

136. Anatoly S. Chernyaev, *My Six Years with Gorbachev* (University Park, MD, 2000), xvii, xv–xvi.

137. Cohen and vanden Heuvel, *Voices of Glasnost,* 115, 122.

138. *Wall Street Journal,* December 22, 1987, 18.

139. Andrei Sakharov, "A Letter from Exile," *New York Times Magazine,* June 8, 1980, 106.

140. See Strobe Talbott, *The Master of the Game: Paul Nitze and the Nuclear Peace* (New York, 1988), 358–61.

141. Sakharov, *Moscow and Beyond,* 56.

142. Sakharov, "Neizbezhnost' perestroika" [The inevitability of perestroika), in *Inogo ne dano* [No other way] (Moscow, 1998), 122–34. The article was dated March 25, 1988.

143. Sakharov, *Moscow and Beyond,* 46.

144. The text of Sakharov's remarks in Chelyabinsk is in Arkhiv Andreia Sakharova (Moscow), f. 1, op. 3, d. 110, l. 32.

145. Sakharov, *Memoirs*, 617.

146. Laber, *Courage of Strangers*, 294.

147. Cohen and vanden Heuvel, *Voices of Glasnost*, 179.

148. *New York Times*, December 27, 1986, 46; *Washington Post*, January 10, 1987, A24.

149. Sakharov discusses this interview in *Moscow and Beyond*, 7–8. There is also a long and fascinating account of how Moroz and Rost met with Sakharov and prepared their piece; see Moroz, "Vozrashchenie iz ssylki," in Ivanova, *Andrei Dmitrievich*, 271–366. Although the interview itself was never published, Rost published a profile of Sakharov in *Literaturnaya Gazeta* on November 16, 1988, which incorporated some of the earlier material.

150. *Moskovskie Novosti*, no. 45 (1987), 14.

151. Sakharov, *Moscow and Beyond*, 120.

152. *New York Times*, June 10, 1989, 4.

153. Elena Bonner, "On Gorbachev," *New York Review of Books*, May 17, 1990, 14.

154. Robert G. Kaiser, *Why Gorbachev Happened: His Triumphs and Failures* (New York, 1992), 284–86.

155. *New York Times*, February 16, 1989, 1.

156. Gorbachev and Mlynár, *Conversations with Gorbachev*, 65.

157. Sakharov, *Moscow and Beyond*, 10–11.

158. Bonner, "On Gorbachev," 17.

159. David Remnick, "The Struggle for Light," *New York Review of Books*, August 16, 1990, 6.

160. Amalrik, *Will the Soviet Union Survive until 1984?* 63.

161. Mikhail Sergeevich Gorbachev, *Memoirs* (New York, 1996), 293.

162. Sakharov, *Moscow and Beyond*, 130–131.

163. Ibid., xv–xvi.

164. David Remnick, "Mourning for 'Saint of Perestroika'" *Washington Post*, December 16, 1989, 1.

165. Ibid., 24.

166. David Shipler, "Soviet Dissident Movement Is at Low Ebb," *New York Times*, December 30, 1977, A6.

167. Document 49, February 18, 1973

168. A selection of these articles and letters can be found in the appendix to Sakharov's *Memoirs*, 631–40.

169. *Times* (London), December 20, 1986, 6.

170. This secret report to the Central Committee can be found in the Arkhiv Andreia Sakharova (Moscow), f. 3, op. 80, d. 639, ll. 68–75.

171. Natalya Hesse, "The Sakharovs in Gorky," *New York Review of Books*, April 12, 1984, 25–28.

172. Maksudov, "What Do You Think of Sakharov?" in Alexander Babyonyshev, ed., *On Sakharov* (New York, 1982), 111–18.

173. Sakharov, *Moscow and Beyond*, x.

174. *Argumenty i Fakty*, October 7–13, 1989.

175. Quoted in Joseph Gibbs, *Gorbachev's Glasnost: The Soviet Media in the First Phase of Perestroika* (College Station, TX, 1999), 125n33.

176. *Washington Post,* November 3, 1989, A2.

177. Sarah E. Mendelson and Theodore P. Gerber, "National Survey on How Russians View Human Rights, Democracy, and Military Reform, 2003," machine-readable data file, Center for Strategic and International Studies, Washington, DC.

178. *New York Times,* March 5, 2003, 3. The historian Richard Pipes reviewed a range of polling data and concluded that "the antidemocratic, antilibertarian actions of [Putin's] administration are not being inflicted on the Russian people but are actually supported by them" ("Flight from Freedom: What Russians Think and Want," *Foreign Affairs* 83 [May–June 2004]: 9).

179. David Satter, "Stalin's Legacy," *National Review Online,* March 14, 2003, 3.

180. Pipes, "Flight from Freedom," 11.

181. Murray Feshbach, "A Country on the Verge," *New York Times,* May 31, 2003, A25. Murray Feshbach is the younger brother of the late Herman Feshbach of MIT; he was a close friend of the Sakharov family and smuggled out material from the Soviet Union relating to Sakharov's dissident career in the 1970s.

182. *New York Times,* October 20, 2002, 6.

183. Satter, "Stalin's Legacy," 3.

184. "Sakharov's Widow Opposes Moscow's Plan to Build Monument," *New York Times,* April 17, 2003, A5.

185. National Public Radio, November 15, 2001.

186. *Time,* December 20, 1999, 29.

CHAPTER ONE

# Emergence of a Public Activist

I N MAY 1968 a secretary at the Installation, the secret community where Andrei Sakharov lived and worked with other nuclear scientists, handed security officials a manuscript copy of Andrei Sakharov's essay "Progress, Coexistence, and Intellectual Freedom." The KGB required her to pass along all material that the scientists shared with her. Sakharov was not naive; he fully expected her to alert the authorities, even as she typed the manuscript for him. But he had nothing to hide and was hoping that his essay would lead to a dialogue with Party officials. Andropov quickly summarized it for members of the Politburo, noting that it related both to general criticism of the Soviet regime and to recent defiant protests by a small group of activists. He also made sure to highlight Sakharov's support for the Prague Spring, a development that would only serve to reinforce suspicion of Sakharov himself.

## · DOCUMENT I ·

Andropov to Central Committee, May 22, 1968
The appearance of "Progress, Coexistence, and Intellectual Freedom"

A full member of the Academy of Sciences of the USSR, Andrei Dmitrievich Sakharov (born 1921; Russian; not a Party member; three times Hero of Socialist Labor; recipient of State and Lenin prizes; deputy director of research at All-Union Research Institute of Experimental Physics of the USSR Ministry of Medium Machine Building [Arzamas-16]), in recent years has repeatedly signed, at the request of antisocial individuals, politically immature documents, which were then sent to various government and state bodies.

On May 16, 1968, while at the Institute, Sakharov asked one of the typists to produce five copies of materials in his possession. Once information about the political nature of the document being duplicated was received, measures were taken that resulted in obtaining one copy of the document, starting with page 6.[1]

The attached document deals with issues pertaining to the political, economic, and social development of our society, mainly from an anti-Marxist position. It expounds the view that it is necessary to "reconsider the traditional approach in international affairs." It holds the Soviet Union accountable for the situation in the Middle East by permitting "the irresponsible encouragement of so-called 'Arab unity' (which in no way has a socialist character, . . . but is purely nationalistic and anti-Israel)." It calls for granting peoples the right "to decide their own fate by a free expression of their will" on the basis of the "[Universal] Declaration of Human Rights."

The author considers contemporary social development and discusses the danger of "the monstrously cruel dictatorial police regimes" of Stalin, Hitler, and Mao Zedong. He notes that "fascism in Germany lasted for twelve years, Stalinism in the USSR twice as long. While the two have much in common, there are also certain differences: Stalinism exhibited a more subtle kind of hypocrisy and demagoguery; it relied not on an openly cannibalistic program, like Hitler's, but on a progressive, scientific, and popular socialist ideology that was popular among the toiling classes and served as a convenient screen for deceiving the working class, and for weakening the vigilance of the intelligentsia and rivals in the power struggle. . . ."

In addressing the issue of the "threat to intellectual freedom," the author writes: "Today, intellectual freedom is the key to a progressive restructuring [perestroika] of the state system in the interests of mankind. This has been understood, in particular, in Czechoslovakia; we must sup-

1. Note that the KGB chairman does not know the title of the document. The fact that he reported such incomplete information indicates that he prepared the report in a great hurry; he was able to provide the first five pages five days later, on May 27, 1968. Perhaps the document he initially reported on on May 22 was actually obtained from samizdat and not from the typist at the Installation.

port their courageous initiative, which is so valuable for the future of socialism and all mankind."

. . . In the second part of the document, the author denies that capitalist society entails any contradiction between the means of production and the form of ownership, and claims that "both capitalism and socialism are capable of indefinite development by borrowing positive elements from each other (and, in fact, converging in a number of essential aspects)."

In conclusion, the author writes that "the capitalist world could not have failed to give birth to the socialist one, but the socialist world should not use armed force to destroy the ground from which it grew. Under present conditions this would be tantamount to mankind's suicide."

Andropov was now prepared to portray Sakharov in a more provocative manner. He emphasized that Sakharov was devoting less energy to weapons research and increasing amounts of time to antisocial activities. Furthermore, Andropov claimed that other dissidents, such as Pyotr Yakir, who was reputed to be one of the more adventurous figures among them, were now said to be asking Sakharov how to approach Yuli Khariton, the scientific director of Soviet nuclear weapons projects, to enlist him in their efforts. Leonid Brezhnev knew Sakharov personally and had been among the Soviet leaders to honor him earlier in the 1960s. So it was not surprising that Brezhnev, upon reading this report, appended a handwritten order that it be shared with Alexei Kosygin and Nikolai Podgorny, the other members of the triumvirate that was governing the country.

· DOCUMENT 3 ·

Andropov to Central Committee, June 13, 1968
Sakharov and the activity of other dissidents

According to information obtained by the Committee for State Security, certain hostile elements, in their demagogic attempts to prove the existence of "the Party's excessive interference in science and the arts," the necessity for "improving socialism," etc., are continuing their efforts to exploit the name of the well-known Soviet scientist Academician Sakharov by systematically asking him to endorse documents of politically harmful content. . . . In recent years, Sakharov has been paying less and less attention to creating nuclear weapons; for all practical purposes, he now avoids taking part in these tasks. According to the information available from of-

ficial sources and from our agents, Sakharov is characterized as an outstanding scientist, not only as a person possessing a wide range of knowledge in theoretical physics, but also as someone deeply interested in biology, medicine, literature, and politics. At the same time, during his work in
the collective of the All-Union Research Institute of Experimental Physics,
Sakharov was regarded as an apolitical person, who takes no part in public life and who is susceptible to outside influences. . . .

As the material obtained by agents shows, the people closest to Sakharov include some who are disseminating ideologically immature and
harmful works by Medvedev, Solzhenitsyn, and Ginzburg, which propagandize the idea of a "transfer of power from politicians to the technical
intelligentsia" and question the leading role of the Party in the task of
building communism. Material in the file of one individual, Zhivlyuk
(born 1936; Belorussian; member of CPSU; holds a candidate degree in
physics),[2] implicates him in having tried to use his contacts with scientists
(including Sakharov) to influence the decision of the authorities concerning the fate of Gabai and Khaustov, who were convicted under Article
190-3 of the Criminal Code of the RSFSR.

Zhivlyuk often meets and talks to Sakharov, who allegedly shares his
views on a number of issues concerning the politics and social development of the country. According to the same information, Sakharov, upset
by the lack of response to his repeated appeals to authorities, nevertheless
intends to seek a meeting with the CPSU's leadership and to raise the question of the inadmissibility of the recent unjustified repression of the creative intelligentsia, which reminds him of the "worst times of 1937."

The . . . material on . . .[3] Yakir shows that this subject and his associates not only are informed about the actual role of Academician Khariton
as the director of research for the whole task of developing Soviet nuclear
weapons, but also discuss with Sakharov the possibility of involving
Khariton in their activities, which are directed toward criticizing the policy of the CPSU and the Soviet government in the production and testing
of these weapons.

Currently Sakharov continues to work on a document of a political nature, which he has titled "Reflections on Progress, Coexistence, and Intellectual Freedom." In this document, together with a discussion of the
political, economic, and social development of our society, the author
advances a multistage scenario for the development of capitalist and so-

2. Equivalent to Ph.D.
3. Several words have been deleted from the declassified copy of this document;
they probably explained that material was obtained "by operational means."

cialist societies, which he believes will inevitably follow in the coming decades (by the year 2000).

Taking the above into account and in order to eliminate opportunities for anti-Soviet and antisocial elements to exploit Academician Sakharov's name for their hostile purposes, and in order to prevent him from committing politically harmful acts, we believe it would make sense for one of the secretaries of the Central Committee to receive Sakharov and conduct an appropriate conversation with him.

---

As human rights activists became familiar with Sakharov's essay and his full stature as a scientist, Andropov noted their desire to "exploit" Sakharov for their own political purposes. These activists were learning about Sakharov for the first time, just as the Western public was becoming aware that a principal designer of Soviet nuclear weapons had issued a manifesto criticizing the Kremlin. To reinforce the serious nature of their findings, KGB agents claimed to have evidence of a link between the dissidents and a foreign publisher with close ties to the émigré anti-Soviet organization NTS (Narodno-trudovoi soyuz, or the Popular Labor Alliance of Russian Solidarists).[4]

· DOCUMENT 4 ·

Andropov to Central Committee, July 18, 1968
Moscow dissidents linked to Andrei Sakharov

---

According to information obtained by the Committee for State Security, Litvinov, Grigorenko, and their confederates discussed (at their last regular gathering—the so-called Tuesdays at the Litvinov apartment) plans for continuation of their antisocial activities. In a conversation with our source, Litvinov said that they now seek new forms of activity, not excluding demonstrations and strikes. At the same time, they do not intend to abandon the dissemination of protest letters because they believe that, "despite persecution of their authors, the letters fulfill their role: they stir

---

4. NTS was an anti-Soviet émigré organization, founded in Belgrade in 1930 and later based in Frankfurt am Main, Germany; it published, through Possev-Ferlag, the journal *Grani* (Facets) as well as other periodicals and books. On the history of NTS, see B. Prianishnikov, *Novopokolentsy* [People of a new generation] (Silver Springs, MD, 1986). On the history of relatively recent infiltration, se Iu. Shchekochikhin, "Nash chelovek v NTS" [Our man in the NTS], an interview with the retired KGB colonel Ia. Karpovich, *Literaturnaya Gazeta*, December 15, 1990.

up public opinion." While demagogically asserting that his main goal is to "lay the foundation for the rule of law in our country," Litvinov simultaneously declares that he rejects "not only Bolshevism as a system, but Bolshevik methods as well." He considers his methods to be similar to those of the "Kadets."[5]

Grigorenko takes an especially active part in the discussions of new forms, tactics, and methods of antisocial activity. While giving high marks to the provocative actions of Litvinov and Bogoraz-Brukhman, Grigorenko said that now "another step is required. Life itself has come to our rescue. Sakharov is the next step. This is what we have to promote right now. But we already need to think about the third step. Every innovation, every new idea has its limits: there is a time to exploit it and a time to stop exploiting it; otherwise, it will turn into its own antithesis. Now, for the time being, we have to exploit Sakharov, and to exploit him to the hilt. But we have to think about the next stage, the third stage. And the third stage is the forthcoming conference of Communist parties. We have to have an opposition party of some sort; whatever form it may take, we have to have it here, in our country, in the land of the Soviets."

. . . On July 1, Litvinov, Bogoraz-Brukhman, and Marchenko were seen meeting with a French tourist, Jean Yves Clousier,[6] who represents a newspaper with close contacts to *Grani,* a publication of NTS. Clousier stated that his newspaper, in collaboration with other publishers, is preparing for publication two *White Books:* one on the trial of Ginzburg and Galanskov and another about "concentration camps."

During the meeting, Bogoraz-Brukhman gave Clousier documents (the content of which is unknown) that she had prepared and that had been approved by Litvinov and Marchenko.

Our agents have established that close contacts of Yakir (his wife, daughter, and son-in-law, Kim, as well as others) are very interested in events in Czechoslovakia, and that they intend to establish contact with citizens of Czechoslovakia to obtain information about events there. They prefer to establish contact with Czechs, not Slovaks. For the same reason, Yakir maintains contact with V. P. Lukin,[7] who works for the magazine *Problems of Peace and Socialism.* . . .

5. "Kadets" was the popular name for the Constitutional Democrats, a liberal political party, founded in 1905, that supported democratic reform under the tsar.
6. It has not been possible to establish the identity of this person.
7. Vladimir Lukin later became the Russian ambassador to the United States and chairman of the Russian Duma's Foreign Affairs Committee. He currently serves as human rights ombudsman for the Russian Federation.

Sakharov was now helping the Marxist historian Roy Medvedev compile additional material for his pathbreaking book on the purges, *Let History Judge*.[8] Sakharov's development of contacts with other dissident figures could only annoy the Politburo.

## · DOCUMENT 5 ·

Andropov to Central Committee, August 4, 1968
Sakharov and the dissident historian Roy Medvedev

---

Agents of the Committee for State Security have obtained a new version of R. A. Medvedev's manuscript, *Let History Judge* (a photocopy is appended). Medvedev has supplemented the manuscript with materials about physicists repressed in the past, with an analysis of their scientific potential, schools they represented in science, and evaluation of the ideas they did not bring to realization. Medvedev obtained this information from Academician Sakharov, with whom he has close relations.

Medvedev intends, in the near future, to complete *Let History Judge* and to begin an analysis and assessment of the contemporary situation (in connection with the deterioration in the domestic and foreign situation).

In assessing the measures of Communist parties in socialist countries with respect to events in Czechoslovakia, Medvedev declared: "The military occupation of Czechoslovakia would inevitably lead to a strong reaction in the USSR, but it seems that the pressure of Western Communist parties has restrained some of our own 'hawks' from such an insane action."

In June of this year, Medvedev obtained from Sakharov a revised copy of his article "Reflections on Progress, Coexistence, and Intellectual Freedom," which he permitted some of his acquaintances to read. He made copies of the text together with L. N. Petrovsky[9] (a member of the CPSU and researcher at the Central Museum of V. I. Lenin). In general, Medvedev endorses Sakharov's article, since, in his opinion, it calls for the democratization of intellectual life. At the same time, he also notes its

---

8. See the English translation in Roy Medvedev, *Let History Judge: The Origins and Consequences of Stalinism* (New York, 1971).

9. Leonid Petrovsky described what happened with Sakharov's manuscript in 1968 in *30 let Razmyshlenii . . . Andreia Sakharova: Materialy konferentsii* [30 years since Sakharov's "Reflections": Proceedings of a Conference] (Moscow, 1998), 214–16. Also see papers presented by Raymond Anderson, Gennadii Gorelik, Viktor Adamskii, and Alexander Gribanov in the same volume.

utopian character. Medvedev expresses concern about Sakharov's future; he believes it to be pointless for Sakharov to try "to put pressure on the government. . . ."

On August 25, a day before the following two reports were filed, eight activists held a demonstration in Red Square to protest the Warsaw Pact invasion of Czechoslovakia. They were Konstantin Babitsky, Larisa Bogoraz, Vladimir Dremlyuga, Vadim Delone, Pavel Litvinov, Viktor Fainberg, Natalya Gorbanevskaya, and Tatyana Baeva. At the same time, the KGB was growing increasingly concerned about Western fascination with dissent inside the Soviet Union, including the interest of the U.S. Congress.

## · DOCUMENT 6 ·

Tsvigun[10] to Central Committee, August 26, 1968
Growing Western interest in Soviet dissent

The U.S. Senate Judiciary Committee intends to publish, in the near future, a report on "Aspects of Intellectual Ferment and Dissent in the Soviet Union" prepared by Library of Congress specialists S. Yakobson and R. Allen.

The report is based on material from the trials of Brodsky, Sinyavsky-Daniel, Bukovsky, Galanskov-Ginzburg, and Chernovil; on letters sent to the West by Litvinov, Sakharov, Belinkov, L. Chukovskaya, Maltsev, Solzhenitsyn, and Voznesensky; and also on other documents that have reached the West and allegedly attest to the growth of an oppositionist mood in the USSR.

The authors of the report especially emphasize the connection of the "liberation movement" in the USSR with events in Czechoslovakia, with the renewal of nationalistic feelings in some Soviet republics, especially in Ukraine, and with the revival of religious beliefs. A large part of the report is devoted to the measures taken to suppress anti-Soviet manifestations among the intelligentsia.

In conjunction with the publication, one of the sponsors of the report (Senator Dodd) intends to appeal to world public opinion to protest "the suppression of intellectual freedom in the USSR."

10. Semyon Tsvigun was deputy chairman of the KGB.

Over the summer of 1968, Sakharov's essay provoked a good deal of
speculation and analysis in the United States and other countries about
its origins. But the Soviet government remained silent. The KGB now
presented the curious observation that the failure to repudiate it or in
some fashion to respond directly to Sakharov had induced many diplomats, including specialists in the U.S. State Department, to regard the
essay as signaling a shift in Soviet foreign policy. By pretending to ignore it, the regime created the unintended impression that it either
agreed with Sakharov or had somehow sponsored the publication of
his manifesto.

· DOCUMENT 7 ·

Tsvigun to Central Committee, August 26, 1968
How should the Kremlin respond to Sakharov's memorandum?

---

. . . Information has been obtained showing that government circles in
the USA regard the lack of official reaction in the Soviet Union to Sakharov's theoretical speculations as a sign that confusion has allegedly
permeated the ideological sphere in the USSR, and as a further sign that
Soviet policies and propaganda lack a clearly defined line. Peter Grose, a
*New York Times* correspondent who specializes in Soviet affairs, in a conversation with a Soviet official declared that State Department experts are
inclined to discern in Sakharov's essay the contours of a new orientation
that is gradually gaining ground in Soviet foreign policy. According to
these experts, the predominant opinion of our mid-level "Americanolo-
gists," who exert considerable influence on the formulation of our foreign
policy, is that rapprochement with the USA is the only reliable guarantee
of peace and an important factor for the containment of potential Chinese
expansion. Despite the Vietnam War (which, to a certain extent, has im-
peded the development of "pro-American" tendencies), and despite the
April plenary meeting of the CPSU Central Committee on ideological issues,[11] supporters of American-Soviet cooperation are allegedly continuing to bolster their position and to exert ever greater influence on Soviet
officials. The State Department experts find proof for their assessment in
the series of bilateral U.S.-Soviet agreements that have either already been

---

11. The plenum took a hard line on ideological issues; see the text in Robert H. Mc-
Neal, ed., *Resolutions and Decisions of the Communist Party of the Soviet Union,* 4
vols. (Toronto, 1974).

concluded or are now under discussion, as well as in the silence of Soviet ideological organs with regard to the issues raised in Sakharov's essay. Moreover, according to Grose, the State Department has information that, among high-ranking officials in Moscow, there has been widespread criticism of the decision of the April plenum of the Central Committee and of the related curtailment of Soviet-American cultural exchanges. It bears noting that interest in Sakharov's "theses" is not limited to U.S. government circles and propaganda agencies. In July of this year the Soviet embassy in Washington received several letters from ordinary Americans, who either expressed solidarity with Sakharov's views or sharply criticized them from a leftist point of view. In a conversation with a Soviet official . . . ,[12] a counselor at the Pakistani embassy, Kutub, stated that many members of the diplomatic corps, and especially diplomats from neutral countries, share the opinion that Sakharov's ideas confirm the widespread suspicion that a deal may be in the works between the USSR and the USA. In particular, Kutub was interested in knowing whether the transmission of Sakharov's essay to the West was a deliberate leak by the Soviet side to prepare public opinion for far-reaching initiatives in Soviet-American cooperation that are now being planned.

It also appears significant that [Ken] Weller, a representative of the *Daily World*,[13] the newspaper of the U.S. Communist Party, spoke positively of some of Sakharov's ideas, in the belief that they reflect current thinking in the Soviet Union. It is possible, however, that Weller regarded publication of the essay as an action sanctioned by Moscow.

· DOCUMENT 10 ·

Andropov to Central Committee, September 8, 1969
Sakharov and the scientific bureaucracy

On July 14 of this year, in a conversation with an officer of the Second Main Directorate[14] of the KGB (under the Council of Ministers of the USSR), Academician D. V. Skobeltsyn stated that on July 4 he had a lengthy conversation with Academician A. D. Sakharov about his starting to work at the Institute. During the conversation, Skobeltsyn asked what

12. The name was deleted from the declassified copy.
13. Successor to the *Daily Worker*.
14. The Second Main Directorate was the division of the KGB responsible for counterintelligence.

kind of research Sakharov intends to pursue in the Institute, what position he should be appointed to, and what was his general attitude. Skobeltsyn also asked Sakharov how he views publication of his hostile article in the foreign press. Sakharov responded that he would like the position of senior scientist and intends to study cosmic rays.

With respect to his article, "Progress, Coexistence, and Intellectual Freedom" (published in France by the magazine *Grani*), Sakharov stated that he had prepared this article together with a correspondent of *Literaturnaya Gazeta,* Ernst Henry.[15] According to Sakharov, he prepared another article in 1966 or 1967 (he does not remember the date) on antimissile defense, and then sent it to the government. He declared that this annoyed our military circles and that they began to harass him on the job. According to Sakharov, the second article was essentially a response written to defend him against attacks by the military. Sakharov believes that by publishing his article in a foreign journal, he has fulfilled some very great mission for humanity and for scientists around the world. Sakharov disagreed with Skobeltsyn's remark that his article subverts the prestige of our state and our government. He feels that he did the right thing, and he proudly stated that his article was published in millions of copies abroad.

In addressing political events in the world, Sakharov has views of his own. For example, he states that the cult of Mao Zedong is a kind of mindless disease and petty tyranny. But Sakharov believes that the cause of everything that is happening in China is that the Soviet Union and the USA could not join forces to help China solve its disastrous economic situation. Sakharov believes that we did seize Chinese territory. According to Sakharov, Mao's autocracy will eventually enable China to mobilize enough resources to build the hydrogen bomb, as well as the means to deliver and direct it against the USSR.

Skobeltsyn advised Sakharov to refrain from making any statements not connected to his scientific activities. Sakharov responded that he will consult Skobeltsyn before making any statement. Sakharov has been given the position of a senior scientist in the Theoretical Department of the Institute of Physics.

---

In the course of updating his colleagues on Sakharov's activities, Andropov noted that Sakharov had transferred a large sum of money from a bank account he had maintained at the Installation to three public charities. This was during his last visit to the Installation, when

15. For details on Ernst Henry, see Andrei Sakharov, *Memoirs* (New York, 1990), 268–70.

he collected his belongings and cleared out part of a cottage where he had lived since 1951. In subsequent years, Sakharov came to regret this act of largess. "I also did something I now believe was foolish," he later wrote. "This fit of generosity in which I transferred control over my money to the state now seems to me a mistake. A few months later I learned of a fund to assist the families of political prisoners, but could make only modest contributions."[16]

· **DOCUMENT II** ·

Andropov to Central Committee, September 15, 1969
Sakharov visits the Installation for the last time

———————

. . . From his first days at the Institute, Sakharov became actively involved in its work, and he presented several scientific reports to its theoretical seminar. To those around him he expresses satisfaction with his position at the Institute and with the way he is being treated.

From August 21 to 23, 1969, Sakharov traveled to Arzamas, visited the city's central savings bank, and left the following written declaration:

"I ask you to transfer, in equal shares, the whole sum deposited in my personal account #16267 (about 130,000 rubles or somewhat more) to the following public causes: (1) one-third for the construction and maintenance of medical and childcare facilities in our city; (2) one-third to the account of the 1969 Communist *subbotnik*,[17] to be used for the purposes stipulated by the decree of the Council of Ministers of the USSR (construction of an All-Union cancer center); and (3) one-third to the account of the Red Cross. In case it proves impossible to use the funds for any one of the stated purposes, the sum should be divided between the other two."

———————

Such hopes of Sakharov's renewed "loyalty" did not last long: six months later, Sakharov became heavily involved in an attempt to circulate and obtain public support for a letter on democratization addressed to Party leaders. Significantly, following the strategy of other dissidents, he approached high-ranking members of the Soviet elite. This new letter became known as Sakharov's second memorandum. It

16. Ibid., 299; he donated 139,000 rubles to official charities.
17. The "Communist *subbotnik*" [Saturday workday] was introduced in 1919, as a day when people "voluntarily" contributed uncompensated labor for public projects. In 1969 the regime established it as an "All-Union" event, encouraging mass participation and contributions.

addressed many of the same questions that he had raised in his first, but, significantly, Sakharov now signed it alongside two other independent-minded scholars: the physicist Valentin Turchin (who in 1973 would lead the first chapter of Amnesty International in Moscow) and Roy Medvedev, the dissident Marxist historian. This second memorandum was reprinted in the *New York Times* on April 3, 1970, just a few days after Andropov's note to the Central Committee. To the chagrin of Soviet officials, Sakharov was gaining a higher profile in the West while at the same time learning to work with other Moscow activists.

· DOCUMENT 12 ·

Andropov to Central Committee, March 30, 1970
The second memorandum
———————————

Enclosed is a copy of a letter on the "democratization" of socialist society in the USSR (written by Sakharov, Turchin, and Medvedev, and obtained by our agents), which is hereby transmitted for purposes of information.[18] The authors of the letter—A. D. Sakharov . . . , Turchin (holds a doctorate in physics; a member of the staff of the Institute for Applied Mathematics of the Academy of Sciences of the USSR), and R. A. Medvedev (holds a candidate degree in pedagogy; a staff member at the Research Institute for Vocational Education of the Academy of Pedagogical Sciences of the USSR)—are known for their politically harmful works: "Progress, Coexistence, and Intellectual Freedom," *The Inertia of Fear*,[19] and *Let History Judge*. According to agents' reports, while preparing the letter, the authors attempted to involve in its drafting Academicians P. L. Kapitsa, Ya. B. Zeldovich, L. A. Artsimovich, M. A. Leontovich, and I. L. Knuniants. For various reasons, they all declined to sign the letter. Sakharov intended to approach A. T. Tvardovsky, but (upon Medvedev's advice) did not do so. He did, however, meet with M. I. Romm and talked with him about the letter. V. A. Kaverin (a writer), P. I. Yakir (an instigator of antisocial manifestations), and several other people are allegedly aware of the letter's existence.

18. The letter, published in the *New York Times*, can be found in Andrei Sakharov, *Sakharov Speaks*, trans. and ed. Harrison E. Salisbury (New York, 1974), 116–34.
19. Written by Valentin Turchin, it appeared in English translation as *The Inertia of Fear and the Scientific Worldview* (New York, 1981).

The letter by Sakharov, Turchin, and Medvedev has allegedly been sent to Party and government authorities.

---

The KGB was acutely concerned about Sakharov, chiefly because of his willingness to associate with dissidents and the marked radicalization of his views. It therefore decided to gather systematic information by installing eavesdropping equipment in his apartment. The very fact that the KGB had to request permission to do so is extraordinarily telling: in the case of ordinary citizens, it would have proceeded on its own, but Sakharov's ranking in the nomenklatura was so high that the KGB had to request permission before invading his privacy. The file indicates that Brezhnev, Suslov, and others agreed to this proposal in May 1970.

·  DOCUMENT 13  ·

Andropov to Central Committee, April 20, 1970
The placing of eavesdropping equipment in Sakharov's apartment

---

. . . One cannot preclude the possibility that individuals hostile to the Soviet state (and also the Western press) will attempt to use the name of Academician Sakharov in the future, since he himself does not oppose such behavior and establishes contact with politically suspect individuals.

We believe that, in order to receive timely information on Sakharov's intentions and to discover the contacts inciting him to commit hostile acts, it is advisable to install secret listening devices in Sakharov's apartment.[20] Permission to do so is hereby requested.

---

20. This sentence was handwritten and underlined, evidently to keep the proposal secret from KGB typists (notwithstanding their security clearance).

# CHAPTER TWO

# Who's Afraid of an Organized Opposition?

B Y OCTOBER 1970 the KGB had finally defined its position toward Sakharov and his role among Moscow's human rights activists. It came to the conclusion that he could become a leader and that his philosophy could help provide a common approach for a growing and diverse culture of popular discontent. Andropov's reports began to dwell on the theme of an "organized or a de facto established opposition." The KGB always depicted an organized opposition as a product of foreign capitalist subversion and not as an authentic movement within the country.

At the same time, the first half of the 1970s marked a significant shift in Soviet foreign relations, as it sought to engage the West in a policy of détente. The Kremlin made a concerted effort to foster a positive public image as an acceptable, civilized partner. But it was difficult to develop a favorable image in the West while crushing a nonviolent opposition at home. As usual, creating the image was secondary to the requirements associated with sustaining absolute power.

Considering the broad variety of dissent in the USSR—nationalist, religious, cultural, and political—the KGB traditionally played one against the other. However, the defense of human rights provided a common language and facilitated a dialogue among various groups. Andrei Sakharov played a pivotal role in this process.

Sakharov and other scientists began to organize a "seminar" on human rights. This was the start of the Human Rights Committee, which Sakharov helped two young physicists, Valery Chalidze and Andrei Tverdokhlebov, establish.

· DOCUMENT 15 ·

Andropov to Central Committee, October 5, 1970
Sakharov and the Human Rights Committee

The Committee for State Security continues to receive information on the politically harmful activities of Academician A. D. Sakharov, which are incited by the enemy's special intelligence services and are actively used in the West for anti-Soviet and anticommunist propaganda. . . . In conversations with his confederates, Sakharov assesses policies of the Party and government from a negative standpoint, and he also shares the demagogic assertions of nationalistically minded individuals about the status of Jews in the USSR. Sakharov parades his views before foreigners as well. Thus, for example, on September 8, 1970, while meeting with a group of foreigners, Sakharov discussed "the democratization of Soviet society," "the compatibility of democratization with the Soviet structure of economic management," etc.

Currently Sakharov and Chalidze (a junior researcher at the All-Union Research Institute of Plastics) are discussing an idea planted by our adversary—the legalization of opposition activities in the USSR. They have in mind the creation of a so-called "Human Rights Seminar," by means of which they want to "help people defend their rights in a lawful manner." The organizers of this scheme attach special importance to "shielding the seminar from the controlling influence of the ruling party." They intend to create "around the seminar" a group of "correspondents," who will collect needed information "from without." The "Seminar," according to their plans, would have direct contacts with similar organizations abroad. Sakharov has agreed to head this "Seminar."

It should be noted that this is not the first time that antisocial elements have attempted to carry out the suggestions of Western ideological centers to create legal opposition groups and organizations in our country. All these attempts have been foiled by the Committee for State Security. The intention to organize a "Seminar" headed by Academician Sakharov creates a new, politically harmful situation. In view of the above, the Committee for State Security is taking measures to strengthen its control over Sakharov's behavior and to avert the harmful consequences of his activity. At the same time, it would seem to be expeditious to direct the Office of the USSR Procurator General to hold a prophylactic discussion with Sakharov and explain to him the illegality of his activities, which bring political and moral harm to the Soviet state.[1]

As Sakharov's efforts persisted, the prospects of a formally constituted organization recognized abroad loomed ever larger. Above all, it had become clear that the Human Rights Committee aimed to "assist Soviet citizens" and to intercede on their behalf. Readers of the Western press learned about these details two days before the Politburo received the following memorandum; on November 16, 1970, the *New York Times* and other Western newspapers reported on the establishment of the Human Rights Committee. For its part, the KGB also laid increasing emphasis on the role of foreign forces in exploiting the Sakharov case for anti-Soviet propaganda. Nonetheless, Sakharov remained mindful of his former work as a weapons researcher and kept his distance from the foreign press; he did not have his first interview with a Western reporter until October 1972.

· DOCUMENT 16 ·

Tsvigun to Central Committee, November 18, 1970
Sakharov is approaching other scientists to support
the Human Rights Committee

According to information received by the Committee for State Security, Academician A. D. Sakharov has intensified his politically harmful activity. He has begun to realize the idea of creating a so-called "Human Rights Committee,"[2] which, in his view, would assist Soviet citizens convicted of

1. Curiously, in November 1970 Andropov suggested through Yuli Khariton that Sakharov call him at KGB headquarters. Sakharov tried to call several times, but Andropov made himself unavailable. Perhaps Andropov at least momentarily entertained the idea of conducting a "prophylactic discussion" with him himself. See Andrei Sakharov, *Memoirs* (New York, 1990), 319.
2. The Human Rights Committee was established on November 4, 1970. The KGB

anti-Soviet activities in defending their rights. . . . Currently, Sakharov is attempting to enlist individual scientists to work in the "Committee." Although the "Committee" has not yet been officially registered, information about it has appeared in the bourgeois press and has been used by our adversary to ignite an anti-Soviet campaign in the West. Moreover, an attempt is being made to portray Sakharov as the leader of an opposition that purportedly exists in the USSR.

A number of correspondents from the USA, France, Britain, and other countries, who are accredited in Moscow, have been instructed by their agencies to meet with Sakharov and to interview him.

In addition, the Committee for State Security has information that Sakharov has begun work on a new article, in which he seeks to prove the necessity of "the democratization of Soviet society" and "socialist convergence." This pamphlet will be presented as a revised version of his earlier essay that was published abroad, "Progress, Coexistence, and Intellectual Freedom." He intends to finish work on this pamphlet by mid-1971. He is asking sympathizers to provide factual material for the pamphlet that he is preparing.[3]

. . . In order to undermine our adversary's attempts to use Sakharov's name and authority in carrying out acts of ideological subversion against our country, we believe that it would be useful to conduct a high-level substantive conversation with him and to consider the question of involving him in active scientific work.

---

Several weeks after the Human Rights Committee held its first press conference, on November 11, and disseminated its principles and charter, the KGB finally provided the pertinent texts to the Party leadership. In light of Sakharov's status, his name remains a handwritten insertion in the document; the names of Chalidze and Tverdokhlebov are routinely typed into the report.

---

has now correctly identified the group as a "committee," not a seminar, as in Document 15.

3. Reference here is apparently to the "memorandum" of 1971, which was intended as an aide-mémoire for a dialogue in which Sakharov and his colleagues on the Human Rights Committee still hoped to engage Party leaders. For the text of the "memorandum," see Andrei Sakharov, *Sakharov Speaks*, trans. and ed. Harrison E. Salisbury (New York, 1974), 135–58.

· DOCUMENT 17 ·

Andropov to Central Committee, December 4, 1970
The Human Rights Committee begins its work

The Committee for State Security of the Council of Ministers of the USSR reported, in 3163-Ts/ov dated November 18, 1970, that Academician Sakharov, Chalidze, and Tverdokhlebov had organized a so-called "Human Rights Committee."

They have now prepared the "Principles of the Human Rights Committee" and "Rules and Regulations of the 'Human Rights Committee,'" which they intend to circulate to various public organizations in the USSR and abroad in order to "establish working relations and exchange information and publications."[4] Both documents have been sent to the Association for Assistance to the United Nations in the USSR (copies are enclosed).

Among his followers, Sakharov propagandizes the idea of creating the "Committee," explaining that its exclusive goal should be to "study the problem of human rights in the USSR." At the same time, he considers it possible to protest, as a private person, the conviction of particular citizens on charges of anti-Soviet activity (Pimenov, Amalrik, and others).

In addition, information has been received that the Committee's organizers have enlisted Esenin-Volpin, a junior researcher at the All-Union Institute of Scientific and Technical Information, and Tsukerman, a scientist at the Institute of Chemical Reagents, as "Committee experts." The Committee for State Security is taking measures to determine the practical role of each member of the "Committee" and to contain their politically harmful actions.[5]

Sakharov's activities were becoming considerably more intense; even provincial religious dissenters managed to establish ties with him. His fame was quickly spreading through circles of the disaffected.

4. For the text of the "Principles and By-laws of the Human Rights Committee" (November 4, 1970), see International League for the Rights of Man, *Proceedings of the Moscow Human Rights Committee* (New York, 1972), 11–12, 16–18.

5. On November 23, 1970, *Pravda* carried a sharply worded editorial, "Neprimirimost' k burzhuaznoi ideologii" [Irreconcilability toward bourgeois ideology], warning the West—and liberals in the Soviet intelligentsia—that the Party would not permit external or internal threats to its ideological monopoly. This may well have been a direct response to recent dissident activity and appeals, including those by Sakharov; see *New York Times*, November 24, 1970, 3.

Sakharov himself later recalled that he received "stacks of letters and a constant stream of visitors seeking assistance."[6] The KGB now confirmed that claim. It devoted most of its attention to Sakharov's attempt to enlist the cooperation of Alexander Solzhenitsyn, and the row that ensued when a report of Solzhenitsyn's proposed collaboration (as a "correspondent" with the committee) was leaked to the Western press. (Solzhenitsyn was awarded the Nobel Prize for literature that fall; he was genuinely concerned that the actions of the Human Rights Committee could complicate his acceptance of the award.) The KGB also took pains to emphasize Sakharov's "vanity," especially his belief that his status and fame in the West made him immune to reprisals. Despite the allusion to putting "pressure" on Sakharov, the report ended with a curious vow to curb the activities of Chalidze, not Sakharov. And both Chalidze's and Solzhenitsyn's names, like Sakharov's, were written in by hand this time, so that even KGB typists would not be able to identify them.

## · DOCUMENT 18 ·

Andropov to Central Committee, December 16, 1970
Alexander Solzhenitsyn and the Human Rights Committee

---

According to information received by the Committee for State Security, Academician Sakharov and Chalidze . . . are taking measures to organize the practical activity of their so-called "Human Rights Committee."

Two representatives of the Orthodox Church from the city of Gorky gave Sakharov libelous documents (about the alleged persecution of believers by Soviet authorities), which he accepted for transmission to the West. Chalidze has begun to collect information "about the system of special distribution of goods in the USSR to members of the government," with the intention of "studying" this question from the standpoint of the "Human Rights Committee."

In an effort to expand the "Committee's" influence, Sakharov obtained the consent of the writer Solzhenitsyn to participate in its work as a so-called "correspondent." According to the "Committee's Rules and Regulations," "a person whose creative efforts contribute to the Committee's work" can be elected a "correspondent." Chalidze informed foreign cor-

6. Sakharov, *Memoirs*, 320.

respondents in Moscow about this. As a result, the Western press and radio published a report that Solzhenitsyn has joined the "Human Rights Committee."[7] Solzhenitsyn then expressed his intense indignation to Sakharov. The former believes that the publication of this fact in the Western press could interfere with his personal plans regarding his acceptance of the Nobel Prize. Chalidze and Sakharov have decided to publish a "denial" in the Western press which states that Solzhenitsyn had not joined the "Committee" but had only been elected as a "correspondent." On December 11, Chalidze contacted a BBC representative in Moscow and, at the latter's suggestion, Chalidze is preparing for publication a new written statement on Solzhenitsyn's participation in the "Committee."

In conversations with members of his entourage, Sakharov stresses his popularity abroad. He proudly asserts that his so-called "political activity" is currently more important than his work in science, if judged by the worldwide resonance that it has evoked. He declares that he "has become famous" thanks to publication of his essay in the anti-Soviet press in the West and in "samizdat" within the country, and that the Soviet government, in his opinion, is powerless to do anything with him.

On December 5, without notifying the Academy of Sciences of the USSR, Sakharov met in Moscow with an American physicist, Holman.[8] We have taken measures to inform the U.S. embassy in Moscow that Holman has violated the norms of behavior for a foreign scientist in our country. As a result, the embassy has decided to arrange his early departure from the USSR; he will leave the country on December 16. We shall use this incident to put necessary pressure on Sakharov. Simultaneously, the Committee for State Security is taking measures to curtail the antisocial activities of Chalidze.

---

In this revealing document, the KGB registered its alarm at the politicization of samizdat and drew attention to Sakharov's first memorandum, indicating that even amidst the profusion of samizdat literature it had achieved considerable renown. What is striking here is the KGB's recognition that the democratic movement had achieved a certain critical mass. A hitherto widespread, although discreet, culture of dissent, with considerable resonance among the intelligentsia, was

7. In fact, as Sakharov himself acknowledged, the status of "correspondent" was conferred on Solzhenitsyn without adequate explanation and was communicated to Western correspondents without Solzhenitsyn's consent, as reported in *New York Times,* December 11, 1970, 13. See Sakharov, *Memoirs,* 320.

8. Transliteration of the Russian spelling; no other information on this purported contact is available.

now leading to public demonstrations, the broad circulation of outspoken samizdat, and "a certain consolidation of like-minded people." Significantly, the dissidents themselves began to sense that they were on the verge of becoming an organized democratic movement, with supporters throughout the intelligentsia. This development worried many activists, who did not want to create an organized opposition with the inevitable hierarchy associated with a full-fledged organization. At the same time, the KGB emphasized that anti-Soviet circles, émigré organizations, and foreign intelligence services were now actively involved in fomenting such opposition. Aside from reporting efforts to tighten repression, it recommended that the Party redouble its efforts to thwart and rebut hostile propaganda.

· DOCUMENT 19 ·

Andropov to Central Committee, December 21, 1970
The spread of samizdat

An analysis of so-called "samizdat" literature that has been disseminated among the intelligentsia and students reveals that "samizdat" has undergone a qualitative change in recent years. If five years ago it was ideologically defective artistic works that mainly passed from hand to hand, documents of a programmatic political character are now acquiring even greater dissemination. Since 1965 more than 400 various studies and articles have appeared on economic, political, and philosophical questions; from various perspectives, they criticize the historical experience of socialist construction in the Soviet Union, assess the domestic and foreign policy of the CPSU, and advance various kinds of programs for oppositionist activity.

Many documents promote ideas and views that have been borrowed from the political platforms of Yugoslav leaders, the Czechoslovak supporters of Dubcek, and several Communist parties in the West.

An article titled "On Certain Social-Political Currents in Our Country" (written by R. Medvedev, well known for his antisocial activities) draws conclusions about the appearance in Soviet society of two parties with new intellectual currents and centers of ideological influence. It asserts that, within the CPSU, there are forces opposed to the current "conservatism" and in favor of a "decisive unmasking of all the crimes of the period of the cult of personality,[9] the purge of the state apparatus of bureau-

9. The "cult of personality" was the standard Soviet euphemism for the Stalin era.

crats, renegades, dogmatists, and careerists, and in favor of freedom of
speech, assembly, and discussions, for a replacement of censorship with
more flexible forms of Party control of the press, an expansion of workers'
self-rule, a change in the election system," etc.[10]

Among the scientific, technical, and part of the artistic intelligentsia
documents are being disseminated that preach various theories of "democratic socialism." According to the scenario of one such theory (that of
Academician Sakharov), the evolutionary path of the internal political
development of the USSR must inevitably lead to the creation of a country with a "truly democratic system." Mathematicians and economists
should therefore, in advance, work out a model so that it will be a synthesis of what is positive in the existing social and political systems.

A number of projects for the "democratization" of the USSR provide for
"limitation or elimination of the monopolistic power of the CPSU and creation of an opposition in the country that is loyal to socialism." The authors and disseminators believe that the current level of development of socialist democracy confers the right of oppositionist views to exist; they
demand that legal opportunities be given to express disagreement with official policies. They denounce as unconstitutional the criminal statutes that
punish anti-Soviet agitation and propaganda or the dissemination of deliberately false inventions that denigrate the Soviet state and social system.

On the basis of "samizdat" literature that is being prepared and disseminated, there is a certain consolidation among like-minded people, which
is vividly reflected in attempts to create something akin to an opposition.
Approximately in late 1968 and early 1969, people with an oppositionist
attitude formed a political center called the "democratic movement." In
their opinion, it has the three characteristics of opposition: "it has a leadership, activists, and relies on a significant number of sympathizers; without taking the precise form of an organization, it sets definite goals and
chooses a definite strategy; and it is striving for legality."

The main goals of the "movement," as formulated in issue 13 of *A
Chronicle of Current Events* (issued by the Moscow group of the "Democratic Movement" headed by Yakir),[11] includes the "democratization of
the country through the inculcation of democratic and scientific convictions in people, resistance to Stalinism, self-defense against repression,
and a struggle against extremists from any camp."[12]

10. See Roy Medvedev, ed., *XX vek* [Twentieth century] (London, 1976).
11. This is misleading and incorrect: the human rights movement was not headed by
Yakir or anyone else.
12. The quotation is accurate. It was taken from *Khronika Tekushchikh Sobitii*, no.

The centers for the dissemination of uncensored materials, as before, are Moscow, Leningrad, Kiev, Gorky, Novosibirsk, and Kharkov. In these and other cities, more than 300 people have been exposed; they call themselves "anti-Stalinists," "fighters for democratic rights," and "participants in the democratic movement." They engage in the publication of both individual documents and compilations (such as *A Chronicle of Current Events*, the *Ukrainian Herald*,[13] *Problems of Society*,[14] etc.) In 1970, a group of Zionist-minded elements in Moscow, Leningrad, and Riga began to publish a journal called *Exodus*.[15]

Western propaganda, along with foreign centers and organizations hostile to the Soviet Union, regard "samizdat" as an important factor in the political situation in the USSR. Illegally issued journals and collections are called the printed organs of the "democratic underground," "the free democratic press," etc. On the basis of a comparison of the issues of the "Chronicle of Current Events," one sees a "growing number of participants in the movement" and the presence of "constant and collective collaboration." The "Sovietologists" conclude that in the USSR there exists, and is developing, "a movement for human rights," which is acquiring "an ever more definite outline and political program."

The imperialist intelligence services (and associated anti-Soviet émigré organizations) not only count on the presence of oppositionist move-

---

13 (Amsterdam, 1979), 397. The same issue contained a review of "Pismo k rukovoditelyam Sovietskogo Soyuza" (Letter to the leaders of the USSR) by Sakharov, Turchin, and Medvedev dated March 19, 1970. This particular quotation, however, comes from another text that was also reviewed in the *Khronika*. It was attributed to an anonymous writer and titled "K voprosu, o tom chto delat" (Once Again: What Is to Be Done?). The reasoning in this essay reflected a Communist Party mentality and differed considerably from the traditional reasoning of the democratic movement in the USSR. The difference is clear in the next paragraph (prudently excluded from Andropov's report), which urged "loyalty to the Party and state leadership since its autocratic character corresponds to the reactionary mentality of the majority in the country, and the democratic movement should respect any popular will, even antidemocratic." Andropov may have been citing an article produced by his own specialists and promoted through samizdat.

13. "Ukrainskii visnyk" [Ukrainian herald] was an underground magazine modeled on *Khronika Tekushchikh Sobitii;* it first came out in 1970. See George Saunders, comp., *Samizdat: Voices of the Soviet Opposition* (New York, 1974), 421–26.

14. "Obshchestvennie problemy: Sbornik materialov" [Problems of society: A collection of materials] was edited by Valerii Chalidze; it appeared irregularly between 1969 and 1972.

15. "Iskhod: Sbornik dokumentov, posviashchennykh evreiskomu voprosu v SSSR" [Exodus. A collection of documents dedicated to the Jewish question in the USSR]. It began to circulate in samizdat in 1970; see "Khronika Tekushchikh Sobitii," no. 14 (Amsterdam, 1979), 451–52.

ments, but also endeavor to support them by resorting to the preparation and dissemination of false documents. Such documents include, for example, "The Program of the Democratic Movement of the Soviet Union," "Tactical Foundations,"[16] and "Time Will Not Wait."[17] Programmatic goals and recommendations for the organization of an underground struggle against the CPSU are also formulated.

The Committee for State Security is taking the requisite measures to terminate the efforts of individuals to use "samizdat" to disseminate slander against the Soviet state and social system. On the basis of existing legislation, they are under criminal prosecution; the people who came under their influence have been subjected to preventive measures.

At the same time, considering the ideological transformation of "samizdat" into a forum for expressing oppositionist sentiments and views and the attempt to use "samizdat" literature for purposes hostile to the Soviet Union, we recommend the following steps. It would be useful to instruct the ideological apparatus to prepare, on the basis of a study of the problem, the necessary ideological and political measures to neutralize and expose the antisocial elements in "samizdat." We also should take into account the factors that contribute to the appearance and dissemination of "samizdat materials."

---

As the Human Rights Committee continued to function, the KGB issued a summons to two of its members, Valery Chalidze and Andrei Tverdokhlebov. They were subjected to the customary intimidation routinely described by the KGB as "prophylactic measures." However, as KGB listening devices evidently confirmed, committee members were unimpressed, hoping that Sakharov's rank would shield the committee—and themselves—from reprisals. Moreover, Andropov warned, Western propaganda (including foreign broadcasts to the USSR) was exploiting the entire affair. Although still inclined to recognize Chalidze, not Sakharov, as the moving spirit behind the Human Rights Committee, the KGB nonetheless argued that Western propaganda now made it essential to conduct high-level talks with Sakharov to discourage his activism. In the margin of this document is a handwritten note to the effect that it was read by Mikhail Suslov.

---

16. Both documents were published by the underground organization known as the Democratic Movement in the Soviet Union, and later attributed to Sergei Soldatov (sentenced in 1975 to six years in a labor camp); see his memoir, *Zarnitsy vozrozhdeniia* [First signs of renewal] (London, 1984).

17. See "Khronika Tekushchikh Sobitii," no. 12 (Amsterdam, 1979), 372. This article was published under the pen names S. Zorin and N. Alekseev.

· DOCUMENT 20 ·

Andropov to Central Committee, December 30, 1970
Increased pressure on the Human Rights Committee

---

The Committee for State Security is taking measures to terminate the politically harmful activities of the so-called "Human Rights Committee." Chalidze . . . and Tverdokhlebov . . . have been summoned to the KGB. They were informed that, according to the joint decree of the All-Union Central Executive Committee and the Council of People's Commissars of the USSR of July 10, 1932 ("On the Procedure for Establishing Voluntary Associations and Their Unions"), the "Committee" they have created must be registered; otherwise, its operation is illegal. Chalidze and Tverdokhlebov were told that the creation of the "Human Rights Committee" has attracted the close attention of anti-Soviet organizations abroad and that it is being used for hostile propaganda. They have been warned that should the "Committee" engage in the dissemination of slander against the Soviet social system and the Soviet system of government, its organizers would face criminal charges.

Information has also been obtained that members of the "Committee" have discussed the fact that Chalidze and Tverdokhlebov were summoned to the KGB, but decided to continue their activities, for they believe that Sakharov's participation, with his name and authority, are sufficient guarantees for the existence of the "Human Rights Committee."

The appearance of the said "Committee" in the USSR has acquired, in the portrayal of Western radio and the press, an anti-Soviet slant; its importance is being deliberately exaggerated, primarily because of the participation of Academician A. D. Sakharov. All the radio broadcasts and newspaper articles put his name first, although the real organizer and ideologue of the "Committee" is Chalidze. . . .

Given this situation, the time has come to conduct a detailed conversation with Sakharov, the aim being to persuade him to cease his politically harmful activity. The task of conducting this conversation should be assigned to authoritative, high-ranking officials of the Party or government apparatus or (if this proves impossible for some reason) to responsible officials from the office of the General Procurator of the USSR and the Committee for State Security. . . .[18]

---

18. The final paragraph in the original document was underlined by the KGB to emphasize the point.

Two sensational cases drew the attention of Andrei Sakharov over the winter of 1970–71: of Angela Davis in the United States and of a group of Soviet Jews and other citizens who had attempted to hijack a plane in a desperate attempt to leave the country. Sakharov wanted to challenge both Washington and Moscow to observe human rights. The U.S. government took note of Sakharov's appeal, inviting him (along with other academicians who had earlier protested the prosecution of Davis) to attend the trial. The KGB report candidly admitted to intercepting mail, but then conceded that a telegram from the Nixon administration must be delivered to Sakharov; since the telegram was known to the world anyway, it would look foolish to confiscate it.

· DOCUMENT 22 ·

Andropov to Central Committee, January 13, 1971
The trial of Angela Davis in the United States and the trial of
Jewish would-be airplane hijackers in the Soviet Union

———————

I report that on December 28, 1970, Academician A. D. Sakharov sent a letter addressed to the Chairman of the Supreme Soviet of the USSR, Comrade N. V. Podgorny, and to the President of the USA, R. Nixon,[19] in which, while joining the Soviet scientists who had published a letter in defense of Angela Davis,[20] he expressed the hope that the American court would consider her case with absolute impartiality. At the same time, addressing himself to Comrade Podgorny, Sakharov claimed that those convicted in Leningrad of an attempt to hijack an airplane[21] had been moti-

19. Sakharov's letter to Nixon was delivered to the U.S. embassy in Moscow by Leonid Rigerman, who had a U.S. entry visa and could legally visit the U.S. compound.
20. *Pravda* published an appeal by Soviet academicians regarding the Davis case on December 26, 1970. One of the fourteen signatories was Sakharov's mentor, Igor Tamm; the letter was also signed by Pyotr Kapitsa. The previous August, a shootout had taken place at the Marin County Center in San Rafael, California, during an attempt by Jonathan Jackson to free his brother George. Angela Davis was accused of buying guns to help free George Jackson. Her trial began on February 27, 1972, before an all-white jury; she was acquitted on June 4. For Sakharov's letter to Nixon urging that American courts judge Angela Davis with "full impartiality and humanity," see *A. Sakharov v borbe za mir* [A. Sakharov in the struggle for peace], comp. Ia. Trushnovich (Frankfurt am Main, 1973), 193–94.
21. The Leningrad hijacking case involved a large group of people who had attempted to commandeer a small plane that carried no other passengers and escape abroad; the trial, held in December 1970, resulted in a draconian punishment, including two death sentences (for Eduard Kuznetsov and Mark Dymshits). Eventually, in the

vated by the authorities' "restriction on the legal rights of tens of thousands of Jews to leave the country," and he categorically rejected "the
charge of treason, as irrelevant to the act committed by the defendants."[22]

Because Sakharov had given a politically incorrect assessment of the decision of the Soviet court, we confiscated the copy of his letter to Nixon.
However, Sakharov gave another copy of the letter to Chalidze . . . who
sent it to the West through foreign correspondents in Moscow, and it has
been published there. On January 11, 1971, the International Telegraph
Office received an answering telegram (enclosed) from the U.S. Department of State in which the American side offers Sakharov assistance in
coming to the United States to "observe" the court hearing for Angela
Davis.[23] We have delayed delivery of the telegram for the time being.
Given the fact that the U.S. Department of State has sent Sakharov this
telegram, which may become known to the Western press, we deem it expedient to forward the telegram to the addressee. . . .

This extraordinary letter to General Secretary Leonid Brezhnev
(rather than the usual report addressed to the Central Committee)
probably represented a response to some direct request from Brezhnev's office. The report reflected the KGB's acute concern about the activities of the Human Rights Committee and of Sakharov in particular.
His rank lent prestige to the committee's work and credibility to claims

face of world criticism and domestic appeals (including one from Sakharov), the death
sentences were commuted. Another event contributed to this compromise by Soviet authorities. In a trial that December, a Spanish court condemned several Basque terrorists
to death, but that sentence was then commuted; a few days later, the Soviet court followed the example of its Spanish colleagues and commuted the sentences of Kuznetsov
and Dymshits. See *New York Times*, December 31, 1970; Sakharov, *Memoirs*, 321–25;
and Eduard Kuznetsov, *Prison Diaries* (Briarcliff Manor, NY, 1980).

22. Sakharov's appeal on behalf of Kuznetsov and Dymshits was dated December
27, 1970, and was addressed to Podgorny. It is listed in the bibliography in Sakharov's
*Memoirs*, 718. A copy is in the Andrei Sakharov Archive (Harvard), folder S.II.2.2.89.

23. The telegram was sent to Sakharov's office at the Lebedev Institute of Physics
(FIAN). According to the KGB translation, the American official, Martin U. Hillenbrand, wrote that he spoke on behalf of President Richard Nixon and offered the following statement: "Dr. Davis has been accused by the state of California of committing
a serious crime. I can assure you that her case, in accordance with the American judicial
system, will be considered impartially, like that of any other person who has been accused of committing a criminal offense. Her right to a fair trial, with the participation
of a jury and competent defense, will be fully observed. We also expect that, in accordance with the practice of our country, the case of Dr. Davis will be considered in an
open court and will be fully covered by representatives of the American and foreign
press." The American side then offered to arrange a visa so that Sakharov could attend
the trial, the same offer it had already made to the other academicians.

of an opposition movement within the Soviet intelligentsia. Indeed, as the appended report demonstrated, an appeal to the West loomed ever larger in Sakharov's strategy: the more famous he became in the West, the more likely Soviet authorities would listen to him.

Andropov proceeded to urge the Politburo to consider meeting one of Sakharov's demands in the fugitive hope it would curtail his activities: that Brezhnev himself agree to meet with Sakharov in order to show that the regime was at least taking his views seriously. This suggestion fell on deaf ears; any member of the Politburo who met with Sakharov would then have to assume responsibility for further decisions regarding this insubordinate and increasingly unmanageable academician. No one on the Politburo wanted to assume this kind of responsibility. Moreover, as Sakharov later demonstrated in August 1973, he was quite prepared to make public the substance of his conversation with a state official, as he would do after being summoned for a meeting with the deputy procurator general Mikhail Malyarov.

· DOCUMENT 23 ·

Andropov to Brezhnev, January 18, 1971
Sakharov, the Human Rights Committee, and the need to meet with him

————————

. . . First of all, it is necessary to emphasize that Academician Sakharov has recently abandoned scientific work and dedicated himself totally to "political" activity. He writes letters (which are sent to our authorities and also abroad) protesting the trials of individuals in the USSR who have committed grave crimes against the state. In the name of the "Human Rights Committee," he is conducting a voluminous correspondence with public organizations abroad. All this begins to create, in the view of world opinion, the impression that, in the midst of the Soviet scientific intelligentsia, there exists a legal organization that holds views contrary to the official policies of the Central Committee of the CPSU and of the Soviet government.

It must be recognized that, thanks to Western radio broadcasts and the bourgeois press, the creation of the so-called "Committee" has gained such wide publicity that it is viewed as some kind of "political force." Rumors about it are spreading in our country as well. The flow of letters addressed directly to Sakharov and to the "Committee" that approve the creation of such an "organization" in the USSR is increasing. The authors of the letters offer to establish contact, to collaborate, and to provide various kinds of assistance, including financial support. Most of the letters, written by Soviet citizens, contain complaints about the actions of local authorities, court sentences, etc.

Sakharov himself believes that this kind of activity gives him the reputation of an active, independent political figure and will force the leaders of the Soviet state to consider his views on issues of foreign and domestic policy. . . .

Sakharov talks with his closest associates about a meeting with you, and he is actively preparing for it. He is visibly worried about it, and it seems he is aware of the weakness of his political position.

Because of the above, I ask you, Leonid Ilyich, to consider the possibility of arranging a conversation with him at the Central Committee of the CPSU as soon as possible. I attach to this note a report on A. D. Sakharov based on the impressions of individuals close to him.

### [Appendix] Report

. . . [Sakharov] is described as an honest, compassionate, and conscientious person. He respects intelligent and knowledgeable people; he is principled and courageous in defending his principles; he lives in ideas and in theories; he can think about problems even in the least suitable places. He is absentminded and requires care, but he cannot abide having any sort of guards around him. . . .

He gives the impression of a typically eccentric scientist, who pays no attention to the minutiae of daily life. His dress is usually untidy, he wears old clothes, and his general appearance is one of neglect. He is interested in biology, literature, and politics; he has his own independent opinions on issues in these fields; they often differ from the official positions and he makes no effort to hide this.

Having made a great contribution to the creation of thermonuclear weapons, Sakharov felt his "guilt" before mankind, and, because of that, he has set himself the task of fighting for peace and preventing thermonuclear war. As a result, in 1968 he wrote an essay, "Progress, Coexistence, and Intellectual Freedom," in which he developed the familiar idea of Western philosophers, the so-called theory of convergence, which he advanced as the only alternative to world thermonuclear war. Currently Sakharov is rewriting this work and intends to offer it for publication to the publishing house Soviet Russia under the title "Reflections on Peaceful Collaboration, Progress, and Democracy."

. . . These "activities" of Sakharov have been condemned by many prominent Soviet scientists (Academicians Skobeltsyn, Khariton, Leontovich, Kapitsa, and others).[24] However, Sakharov stubbornly denies that his activities cause political harm to the state or serve as a source of anti-Soviet propaganda for the ideological centers of our adversary. . . .

A month after the above letter to Brezhnev, Andropov repeated his request that a high-ranking official meet with Sakharov, this time addressing the leadership collectively. Podgorny and Kosygin wrote on the document that they concurred with the proposal. Podgorny suggested that either Pyotr Demichev (secretary of the Central Committee in charge of ideological questions) or Dmitri Ustinov (secretary of the Central Committee responsible for the military-industrial complex) meet with Sakharov. Such a meeting never took place.

· DOCUMENT 24 ·

Andropov to Central Committee, February 12, 1971
Recommendation that a party leader meet with Sakharov

We report that Academician A. D. Sakharov has recently intensified his politically harmful activity, and some aspects of his behavior deserve, in our opinion, careful examination and the taking of urgent measures. . . .

The "Committee's" organizers (Chalidze and Sakharov) decided to form a subsidiary "Commission on the Problem of Political Prisoners." According to their plans, it is to collect and disseminate—through so-called samizdat in the USSR and also abroad—material about cases of alleged repression of individuals in the USSR for "political beliefs."

. . . Sakharov is striving to secure a meeting with leaders of the CPSU and the Soviet government, and he is preparing a so-called "Memorandum," which he intends to use for his meeting with the authorities. To judge from a conversation between Sakharov and Chalidze, one cannot exclude the possibility that this memorandum will be published in samizdat in the USSR (and possibly abroad). In the memorandum, Sakharov sets forth, in particular, the idea that our country will become "a barracks-

---

24. The KGB intentionally cited scientists who opposed Sakharov's human rights activities together with others who supported him, such as Leontovich and Kapitsa, to give the impression that all of Sakharov's colleagues condemned his activities.

like, bureaucratic, stratified, hypocritically dogmatic and demagogic, military-nationalist and aggressive society of pseudo-socialism. . . ."[25] . . .

---

Yuri Glazov was a little-known figure who had recently visited Sakharov.[26] The KGB was claiming, on the basis of what it could have learned only from listening devices, that Glazov engaged in a provocative conversation with Sakharov, trying to encourage him to support violence against the regime. Activists in the human rights movement consistently rejected the idea of using violence, so it is hard to believe that Glazov was trying to encourage Sakharov in that direction. Paradoxically, it is clear from Andropov's report that he had no complaint about Sakharov's response to Glazov's supposed questions. In its own way, the conversation must have been disheartening to the regime; Sakharov remained an outspoken dissident, but he was neither a traitor nor a fool, as Andropov would have preferred him to be. In the end, this document, like many others, tells us more about the KGB than it does about Sakharov.

· DOCUMENT 25 ·

Andropov to Central Committee, February 19, 1971
Two dissidents discuss the question of violence against the regime

---

. . . The circle of individuals around Academician Sakharov who are known for their hostile opinions is expanding. Lately, contact with him has been established by Yuri Yakovlevich Glazov (born 1929; Russian; not a Party member; holds a candidate degree in philology; previously served as a junior researcher at the Institute of the Peoples of Asia at the Academy of Sciences of the USSR; a Russian Orthodox believer). Glazov is attempting to establish rapport with Sakharov and to exert a certain influence on him.

---

25. This ellipsis is in the original document.

26. Yuri Glazov, a Moscow linguist and specialist in the Tamil language, became known in the human rights movement in 1968 during the campaign against the trial of Yuri Galanskov, Alexander Ginzburg, Vera Lashkova, and Alexei Dobrovolsky, as well as through his samizdat publications. In 1972 he emigrated to the United States, and the following year he testified before the Senate Foreign Relations Committee. See *Hearings before the Committee on Foreign Relations, United States Senate, June 12 and 23, 1973* (Washington, DC, 1973), 143–50. For his memoir about Sakharov, see Iurii Glazov, "Rannii Sakharov" [The early Sakharov], *Novy Mir*, 1996, no. 7, 165–71.

In 1968, Glazov, along with P. Yakir, L. Bogoraz, P. Litvinov, and others (twelve persons altogether), signed a letter to the Presidium of the Consultative Conference of Communist and Workers' Parties in Budapest.[27] From an anti-Soviet position, it described Soviet reality and the trial of Ginzburg, Galanskov, and others. The administration at his institute attempted, because of Glazov's behavior, to exert a positive influence on him, but he told the Academic Council of the institute that he is ready to "burn at the stake" for his convictions, and that he considers the trials of Sinyavsky, Daniel, Ginzburg, Galanskov, and others as repression of "dissenters" by Soviet authorities. The Academic Council of the institute decided to dismiss him for committing actions unbecoming a Soviet scientist. Currently Glazov is not employed anywhere and works as a freelance translator.

In a conversation with Sakharov soon after they met, Glazov told Sakharov of his admiration for the latter's "political" activity, praised its importance, and called Sakharov "the conscience of the contemporary thinking intelligentsia." With the goal of extolling Sakharov's role in the life of contemporary Soviet society, Glazov assured him that N. S. Khrushchev was removed from his posts because of Sakharov's memorandum to the Central Committee of the CPSU regarding Khrushchev's relations with scientists.[28]

At the same time that Glazov uses deliberate flattery, . . . he voices a firm belief that, because of Sakharov's fame and merits, an intensification of his "political" activity will not cause the appropriate organs to take repressive measures against him. . . . Glazov carefully draws an analogy between Soviet reality today and the situation in Russia in the 1870s. With this goal in mind, he recalls the terrorists of the People's Will and carefully probes Sakharov's attitude toward their methods.[29] Finding that Sakharov disapproves of terror as a method of political struggle, Glazov attempts to suggest that the time has come for this kind of action.

27. Published in "Khronika Tekushchikh Sobitii," no. 1 (April 30, 1968), 14–15 (Amsterdam, 1979). See also Peter Reddaway, ed., *Uncensored Russia: Protest and Dissent in the Soviet Union* (New York, 1972), 86–88; this volume contains an English translation of the first eleven issues of "Khronika Tekushchikh Sobitii."
28. This is a reference to Sakharov's campaign against Lysenkoism, which included a letter to Khrushchev on August 3, 1964, just two months before the latter's ouster. In his memoirs Sakharov repeated the rumor that "among the charges leveled at Khrushchev by Suslov, speaking for the Presidium, was the breakdown of communications with scientists evidenced by his having concealed Sakharov's letter from the Presidium for two weeks" (Sakharov, *Memoirs*, 237).
29. Narodnaya Volya (People's Will), established in 1879, resorted to political terrorism against the tsarist autocracy. Its victims included Alexander II, who was assassinated on March 1, 1881.

It is worth noting that Glazov has conducted discussions with other anti-Soviet individuals and expressed confidence that the shots fired by Ilin in the Kremlin will be repeated by today's youth. . . .[30]

In March 1971 the KGB arrested two Belgian tourists, J. M. Hemschoote and Hugo Sebreghts, for delivering anti-Soviet materials and representing an activist "Flemish Committee" with ties to the NTS. This incident attracted press attention both in Europe (*International Herald Tribune*, April 20, 1971) and in the USSR, where *Izvestia* published an article, "*Pod falshivoi lichnoi*" (Under a false mask), on the same day. The incident also increased concern about the international repercussions of the Human Rights Committee, which was now described as "created by Sakharov."

Both Hemschoote and Sebreghts were convicted and then immediately released and allowed to return to Belgium. At the time, human rights activists in Moscow believed that the whole operation had been engineered by the KGB in order to discredit the Human Rights Committee.

· DOCUMENT 27 ·

Andropov and Rudenko to Central Committee, April 7, 1971
The arrest of two Belgian tourists

. . . Sebreghts explained that he came to the Soviet Union in the guise of a tourist to carry out an assignment for the "Flemish Committee," which, as he knew, had ties to "NTS." He illegally brought to the USSR a bundle of literature and about thirty letters from different "institutions and people" with responses to the so-called "Sakharov Memorandum," which was published in the foreign press. In Moscow he gave it to Esenin-Volpin.

As Sebreghts testified, he had the task of discussing with Esenin-Volpin

30. Viktor Ilin (b. 1948) was a second lieutenant in the Soviet Army when he attempted to assassinate Leonid Brezhnev on January 22, 1969. Ilin was wearing a stolen militia uniform and fired sixteen times at a government car entering the Kremlin. He missed Brezhnev (whose car entered the Kremlin through another gate) but wounded several persons, one of whom later died in the hospital. Ilin was captured and sentenced to a special psychiatric hospital in Kazan; he was released in 1990. See Nikolai Zenkovich, *Vozhdi na mushke: Terakty i instsenirovky* [Leaders in the crosshairs: Terrorist acts and provocations] (Moscow, 1996), 200ff.

and Chalidze questions on measures to support the activity of the "Human Rights Committee," created by Sakharov.

A body search of Sebreghts resulted in the confiscation of a number of documents that he had received from Chalidze and others, including Yakir's declaration to the XXIV Congress of the CPSU and *A Chronicle of Current Events* (with slanderous content). These documents were intended for publication in the West.

The offenses committed by Hemschoote and Sebreghts come under the category of crimes covered by Article 70–1 of the Criminal Code of the RSFSR. However, taking into account information that Hemschoote and Sebreghts did not participate in a foreign anti-Soviet organization prior to their arrival in the Soviet Union, and considering the appeal of their relatives to the XXIV Congress of the CPSU and the request by the Belgian embassy in Moscow for an amelioration of their plight, we deem it possible to free them from criminal prosecution and expel them from the territory of the USSR.

After reviewing Sakharov's activities as a human rights campaigner, Andropov conceded that his efforts had helped to highlight problems as diverse as conditions in psychiatric hospitals, discrimination against national minorities, and the Jewish emigration movement. For the first time, the KGB learned of plans to nominate Sakharov for the Nobel Peace Prize. Andropov speculated that the rumor was simply a provocation by foreign intelligence agencies. Evidently still hopeful of turning Sakharov to "useful" scientific or public service, Andropov once again urged the leadership to meet with him.

· DOCUMENT 28 ·

Andropov to Central Committee, April 17, 1971
Sakharov's broadening activity

. . . As a result of enemy propaganda, the name of Sakharov is gaining even greater popularity inside the country as an "uncompromising fighter" against injustice. His apartment has become a place of pilgrimage for various kinds of "victims" of "arbitrary actions" by Soviet authorities. Some citizens come from remote regions of the country to Moscow specifically to meet with him.

Many people who have been denied permission to leave the country ask Sakharov to help them obtain exit visas. . . . He advises people to make "noise" each time an exit visa is denied, to publish relevant material in the USSR in samizdat, and to resort to the services of the bourgeois press and Western radio stations.

In his own actions, Sakharov vigorously uses the method he himself recommends by stirring up a deliberate hubbub about this or that issue. Thus he makes use of slanderous rumors that mentally ill patients undergoing compulsory treatment are given drugs that cause further mental degradation. Sakharov portrays these rumors as reliable information and lodges protests at official institutions. Simultaneously, through his connections, Sakharov gives copies of these slanderous, insulting attacks for publication in the West.

Lately, in an effort to extend the reach of his "political activity," Sakharov is thinking about joining the International Pugwash Movement of scientists.[31] To accomplish this, he submitted an application to join the movement to Academician M. D. Millionshchikov,[32] which has put the Soviet Pugwash Committee in a very difficult position.

The Committee for State Security has also learned that a representative of the so-called "Flemish Committee for Human Rights," Sebreghts (born in 1947, he was arrested for anti-Soviet activity and is being deported from the USSR), visited Chalidze and informed him that a group of foreign scientists allegedly plans to nominate Sakharov for the Nobel Peace Prize. Chalidze immediately reported this to Sakharov, who, in a conversation with Chalidze, expressed the opinion that "it would be ridiculous" for him to refuse the Nobel Prize. It cannot be excluded that the rumors of Sakharov's nomination for this prize have been inspired by the enemy's intelligence services for political purposes. . . .

The so-called "Human Rights Committee" that they created has established and maintains telephone contact with Tsukerman (formerly an employee at the Research Institute for Chemical Reagents, he emigrated for permanent residence in Israel). Chalidze and Sakharov plan to use their contact with Tsukerman to establish direct links between the "Human Rights Committee" in the USSR and analogous foreign organizations. Should that happen, given Sakharov's scandalous fame abroad, this might give rise to an unfavorable political situation.

31. Named after a village in Nova Scotia, the site of the first meeting in 1957, the Pugwash movement held international conferences to promote disarmament and peaceful applications of scientific discoveries. Today it is called the Pugwash Conference on Science and World Affairs; it was awarded the Nobel Peace Prize in 1995.

32. Mikhail Millionshchikov (1913–73), a vice president of the Soviet Academy of Sciences, had served as chairman of the Soviet National Committee of the Pugwash Movement since 1964.

Attempts made by the Committee for State Security (through scientists and specialists) to involve Sakharov in active scientific research, in socially useful work of nature conservation and against pollution of the environment, etc., have thus far failed to yield any results. In light of the above, a conversation with Sakharov at the Central Committee of the CPSU, which we proposed in our earlier reports, is now a matter of the utmost urgency.

---

Sakharov continued to focus on certain issues, especially the political abuse of psychiatry. And he and his fellow activists still hoped that the party leadership would agree to a meeting, although they did not believe that such a discussion would bring any tangible or positive result. This report was actually filed by Major General Grigory Grigorenko, the head of the Second Directorate of the KGB, dedicated to counterintelligence. He earned two pages in Oleg Kalugin's memoir, *The First Directorate: My 32 Years in Intelligence and Espionage against the West* (New York, 1994), 250–51.

· DOCUMENT 29 ·

Andropov to Suslov, May 13, 1971
An update on Sakharov and the Human Rights Committee

---

Lately members of the so-called "Human Rights Committee" (Sakharov, Chalidze, and Tverdokhlebov) have been discussing the following main questions:

1. In conversations among themselves, Sakharov, Chalidze, and Tverdokhlebov complain that the KGB has interfered with their work, because all the "Committee's archives" were confiscated during a search at Chalidze's residence (in connection with the case of an NTS agent, a Belgian citizen, Sebreghts, who has been deported from the USSR).[33] Chalidze declares that, at some later date, he intends to demand through court proceedings that the KGB return the material confiscated during the search. Chalidze is concerned that their "Committee" is actually not doing anything. No reports have been submitted to the "Committee" nor has the "Committee" produced any practical recommendations for the state organs on issues of law.

---

33. On the search at Chalidze's apartment, see Sakharov, *Memoirs*, 446–47. The KGB searched the apartment on March 29 and seized all material related to the Human Rights Committee.

2. Sakharov receives many letters, including some from the mentally ill. Hence Chalidze and Sakharov talk a lot about the need for the "Committee" to recruit, as an expert, a "reliable" psychiatrist. In their opinion, such an expert could clarify the "psychiatric problem," since they believe that in the USSR "dissenters" who are absolutely normal are being subjected to compulsory [psychiatric] treatment. With respect to this problem, "Committee" members intend to appeal to the International Congress of Psychiatrists, which, reportedly, will be held in Israel. However, here Chalidze expresses the reservation that they lack sufficient "arguments, and that they have almost no questions to which the authorities could not respond with demagogic but seemingly credible answers."

3. Chalidze is deeply concerned about popularizing the "Committee's" name inside the country and abroad. The most immediate task, as he sees it, is for the "Committee" to become a routine feature of Soviet life. Hence "Committee" members are pleased by the mere fact that the "Human Rights Committee" was mentioned at the union meeting of the All-Union Institute of Scientific and Technical Information, where the issue of Tverdokhlebov was discussed. A few days ago Chalidze received a letter from L. Rigerman. . . . In his letter Rigerman claims that authoritative international organizations are taking a great interest in the "Committee" of Sakharov, Chalidze, and Tverdokhlebov: they consider the "Committee" a solid organization for examining human rights in the Soviet Union and are anxious to cooperate in this area. Chalidze immediately informed Sakharov of Rigerman's letter as a piece of pleasant news: "I like the way things are going: first the 'Committee,' then straightaway the search. Everything is proceeding in a normal fashion; it looks like we are on a normal track."

4. All members of the "Committee" are expecting a conversation between Sakharov and one of the leaders from the Party or government. Chalidze insistently suggests to Sakharov the notion that he has to remind people one more time about the "Memorandum" that he sent to the Central Committee of the CPSU on March 5. "For example, a short note asking whether they are disposed to respond, and, if not, then I will know that I do not have to wait." All members of the "Committee" are of the opinion that the material Sakharov sent to the Central Committee of the CPSU should not be given wide publicity before the conversation takes place.

5. The main topic recently discussed by "Committee" members has been the behavior of Fainberg and Borisov, who are mentally ill and who are continuing their hunger strike in the Leningrad psychiatric hospital of the Ministry of Internal Affairs. Sakharov wrote about this matter to the

Minister of Internal Affairs, Comrade Shchelokov, offering to mediate between the hospital administration and the hunger strikers.[34] On this same matter, together with Academician Leontovich, he visited the Ministry of Health and called Comrade Rybkin (an officer of the Ministry of Internal Affairs) as well as Comrade Blinov (head of the Leningrad psychiatric hospital). In all these instances, he requested that the patients' wives and relatives be allowed to visit them, and offered his services to persuade Fainberg and Borisov to call off the hunger strike. All these officials gave Sakharov to understand, in no uncertain terms, that he was interfering in the business of others and asked him not to do so. In response, Sakharov threatened to cause "a big scandal."

6. On the eve of the May holidays, Sakharov attempted to contact Academician M. D. Millionshchikov regarding his application to join the Pugwash movement. However, he did not succeed in reaching him until May 3. Comrade Millionshchikov suggested that he and Sakharov discuss this subject further at a later time.

7. In April, Chalidze received a letter from the USA, from the " League for the Rights of Man,"[35] which invited the "Human Rights Committee" to become a collective member. The members of the "Committee" discussed this question and decided to join the "League."

---

Andropov again transmitted a report from a subordinate to update Suslov on Sakharov and the committee's activities. The KGB may have been ordered to provide a monthly report about him.

## · DOCUMENT 31 ·

Andropov to Suslov, May 31, 1971
Another update on the activities of the Human Rights Committee

---

. . . Many citizens, who consider Sakharov a "defender of the insulted and injured,"[36] continue to appeal to him for "help and advice."

Crimean Tatars visit Sakharov's apartment more frequently to complain to him about the refusal to give them residence permits and jobs in the Crimea. Sakharov promises to help them in their plight; he thinks that

---

34. See the full text in *Andei Sakharov v bor'be za mir*, 195–97.
35. The official name was International League for the Rights of Man, now International League for Human Rights.
36. The reference is to the title of Dostoevsky's novel *The Insulted and Injured* (1861).

"they do not want to give Crimean Tatars residence permits in the Crimea because they think that you will all be together there and will not forgive thirty years of humiliation."

There has been an increase in the number of collective letters addressed to Sakharov from Soviet citizens of Jewish nationality insisting on departing for Israel.

The essence of the advice that Sakharov gives to his visitors and correspondents is that, to resolve the issues that concern them, the key thing is to attract maximum public attention and to lay systematic "siege" to the relevant state institutions and officials.

In connection with the rising torrent of correspondence, members of the "Committee" discussed the question of choosing a "postmaster" for the specific task of analyzing and circulating mail.

Having abandoned any hope of recovering the materials that the KGB confiscated from Chalidze during the search, the "Committee" members are taking measures to create a new archive and intend to disperse it among several different locations, including the apartments of Sakharov and Tverdokhlebov. Sakharov has already collected what is in his opinion an amazing archive of "appalling cases."

. . . Sakharov, Chalidze, and Tverdokhlebov are intensifying efforts to collect material about the "unlawful" detention in psychiatric hospitals of Soviet citizens fighting for the "truth," about the use of physical coercion on them, and about the administration of "special medications that make them mentally ill." In this regard, acting through the League for the Rights of Man, the "Committee" intends to issue an "International Appeal" in an attempt to attract the attention of world public opinion to this issue.

Sakharov, Chalidze, and Tverdokhlebov discussed the admission of a new member to the Human Rights Committee, Igor Rostislavovich Shafarevich. Born in 1923, he is a corresponding member of the Academy of Sciences of the USSR and works at the Steklov Mathematical Institute of the Academy of Sciences of the USSR and at the Department of Mathematics of Moscow State University. (In the 1950s, Shafarevich received a prophylactic warning about his anti-Soviet tendencies.)

---

With the KGB increasing its pressure on members of the Human Rights Committee, Chalidze and Tverdokhlebov feared that they could be arrested, a move that would effectively close the committee. The political abuse of psychiatry was fast becoming a principal theme of the human rights movement; several of its leading figures, such as Pyotr Grigorenko and Natalya Gorbanevskaya, had recently been confined to psychiatric hospitals, and their supporters were eager to gain their release.[37] The Human Rights Committee was particularly involved in this effort.

It was unusual for a KGB memorandum to be addressed to another government official "personally," as was this report from Andropov to Suslov.

· DOCUMENT 34 ·

Andropov to Suslov "personally," August 23, 1971
On the political abuse of psychiatry

Sakharov and Chalidze have recently been discussing the question of expanding the so-called Human Rights Committee by enlisting new members, in particular Academician M. A. Leontovich. In this regard, Chalidze stated: "If Leontovich would join the Committee now, the question of the Committee's stability would be solved, even in the absence of Tverdokhlebov and myself." Later Sakharov told Chalidze that he had had a conversation with Leontovich, who declined to join the "Committee," but promised to help in its activities.

At a regular meeting in June, members of the "Committee" discussed a report by R. A. Medvedev . . . "On Politically Motivated Compulsory Psychiatric Hospitalizations" and the comments on this report by an "expert," A. S. Esenin-Volpin. As a result of the discussion, the "Committee" adopted an "Appeal" to the forthcoming World Congress of Psychiatrists, which will meet in Mexico this November.

Through this "Appeal" they intend to draw the attention of the Congress to certain specific questions related to the rights of persons certified as mentally ill. In the opinion of the "Committee," there are some legal and medical aspects to the problem of "politically motivated compulsory psychiatric hospitalizations" which require further study and democratization [sic].

As a result, the "Committee" intends to present the following proposals for discussion at the Congress:

1. The organization of a permanent commission of psychiatrists, repre-

37. There is an extensive scholarly and memoir literature about the struggle to expose the abuse of psychiatry. See especially Peter Reddaway and Sidney Bloch, *Psychiatric Terror: How Soviet Psychiatry Is Used to Suppress Dissent* (New York, 1977).

senting various countries, to study both the theoretical side of the problem and the actual situation.

2. The systematic publication in an international journal of the materials produced by this Commission.

3. The study of specific medical case histories, including examinations by international experts (if deemed necessary by the commission).

4. An appeal to the World Health Organization to support actions recommended by the commission.

Recently Sakharov and Chalidze have been trying to expand the "Committee's" activity by studying such problems as "psychiatry, political persecutions, and nationalism."

In June and July the Committee took steps to establish and extend contacts with various foreign human rights organizations. On June 29 the president of the "International League for the Rights of Man," J. Carey, informed the Committee by phone that the "League" had accepted the "Committee" as a member. The same day, Carey announced this at a press conference in New York and declared that the "Committee's" affiliation with the "International League for the Rights of Man" is an "important historical event." The "International League for the Rights of Man" was established in 1941, in the USA. It unites 31 national organizations in the United States, England, West Germany, Japan, Israel, and other countries; it has about 1,200 individual members. The "League's" budget is 8,000 dollars, which come from membership fees and private contributions. The "League's" mission is "to foster the implementation of the guarantees of political liberties not only in relations among states, but especially their observance within states." In reality, the activity of the "League" often assumes, under the influence of reactionary circles, a sharply anti-Soviet, anticommunist character. The "League" has consultative status with the U.N. (category B),[38] and maintains contacts with UNESCO and the International Labor Organization. Commenting on the "Committee's" joining the "League" at a regular gathering of the "Committee," Chalidze declared that "for the first time in half a century, a nongovernmental public association, which is not under the control of the Party or the government, has managed not only to survive for more than a half a year, but also to establish contacts abroad."

38. "Category B" refers to the accreditation of a group of nongovernmental organizations (NGOs) at the United Nations; another name for it is "special consultative status." "Category A" is applied to NGOs with mass constituencies, such as the International Confederation of Free Trade Unions.

In July, in a telephone conversation with René Cassin (president of the "International Institute for Human Rights" in Strasbourg, France; also a professor and winner of the Nobel Prize), Chalidze agreed to the "Committee's" joining the said "Institute" as a collective member. Simultaneously, he gave the "Institute" the publication rights to the collections of essays on "Problems of Society" that he had compiled. Chalidze designated Rigerman, who recently left the Soviet Union and now resides in New York, as the "Committee's" representative for publication of the "collections." We have also established that Chalidze is attempting to establish contacts with other foreign organizations ("Amnesty International," "International Front," and others). As can be seen, the "Committee's" members are establishing contacts with foreign organizations in an effort to raise its authority in world public opinion and strengthen its position inside the country. The increased frequency of contacts between Chalidze and foreign visitors to the Soviet Union attests to the fact that hostile propaganda centers are taking a noticeably greater interest in the "Committee."

On July 21, Chalidze was visited by a correspondent of the *Chicago Daily News*, G. Geyer, who came to the USSR as a tourist. Her purpose was to obtain an interview about the "Committee's" program and its practical activity. Responding to her questions, Chalidze took pains to underline the scholarly nature of the "Committee's" activity.

On August 9, Chalidze gave to Axelbank (a correspondent for the American press agency NANA),[39] material in defense of Kukui and Paladnik,[40] who were convicted of disseminating slanderous documents.

Bobkov
Head of the Directorate at the KGB of the USSR[41]

---

39. North American News Agency. Jay Axelbank was the Moscow bureau chief for *Newsweek*. His interview with Sakharov was the first to be published by a Western correspondent; see *Newsweek*, November 13, 1972.

40. The name of Raisa Palatnik was misspelled; she was arrested in December 1971 in Odessa, accused of disseminating samizdat, and sentenced to a labor camp for two years. Valery Kukui, an engineer from Sverdlovsk, tried to emigrate to Israel. He was arrested in March 1971 and sentenced to two years in a labor camp.

41. Filipp Bobkov was the head of the Fifth Directorate, established in 1967 to focus on all forms of ideological nonconformity. Dated August 18, 1971, this was the first report on Sakharov signed by Bobkov. From that moment on, Sakharov's file fell within his domain.

The KGB continued its close surveillance of Sakharov and the Human Rights Committee, making note of the following points: (1) increasing contacts between the committee and the International League for the Rights of Man in New York; (2) Chalidze's anxiety about Sakharov's meetings with foreigners, given his vulnerability to accusations of revealing state secrets; (3) Sakharov's reluctance to dismiss Soviet economic achievements altogether; and (4) a new intimate relationship between Sakharov and another human rights activist, Elena Bonner, who was increasingly to be depicted by the regime as a provocative and subversive influence on Sakharov's behavior.

## · DOCUMENT 36 ·

Andropov to Suslov, October 2, 1971
The impending marriage of Andrei Sakharov and Elena Bonner

Materials obtained by the Committee for State Security in August and September about the behavior of Academician A. D. Sakharov and other members of the so-called "Human Rights Committee" confirm that they (with the exception of I. R. Shafarevich) have regularly held meetings and discussed various questions concerning the current activity of the "Committee."

Recently interest in the "Human Rights Committee" has significantly increased on the part of the "League for the Defense of Human Rights" (USA). Its chairman, Carey, holds regular telephone conversations with Chalidze, informs him about the regular arrival of materials from the "Committee" to the "League" and the latter's relation to the "Committee," and shows interest in news pertaining to the activity of the "Committee's" members. At the request of Chalidze, the leadership of the "League" systematically sends him a significant quantity of material through the international mails, with information about the structure, tasks, and goals of the "League." Part of these materials reached Chalidze, who shared their contents with the members of the "Committee" and other people in his circle.

The "League" itself is undertaking an effort to establish personal contacts with the members of the "Committee." On September 25, an American clergyman Harrington arrived as a tourist in Moscow; a member of the "League," he intended to meet with members of the "Committee." It should be noted that Chalidze dissuaded Sakharov from meeting with Harrington, on the ground that the state security organs could cause the academician serious difficulties as "someone having access to state secrets." Sakharov concurred with Chalidze's arguments and decided to avoid meeting with Harrington.

Whereas Chalidze, in the question of meeting with the foreigner Harrington, took the correct position, he exerts a negative influence on the academician in those cases where, in Chalidze's opinion, Soviet administrative organs permit instances involving the "violation of human rights." For example, under Chalidze's influence, Sakharov continues to visit court sessions and to inform members of the "Committee" about the course of these trials. In particular, Sakharov attended the judicial proceedings of the Mikheev trial (who was accused of treason and anti-Soviet activities);[42] he also attended the session of the Supreme Court of the RSFSR that examined the appeal in the case of Kukui, who had been found guilty by the Sverdlovsk regional court of disseminating materials that discredit the Soviet state and social order.

There have also been many instances in which people known for their antisocial behavior (Z. M. Grigorenko, Delone, and Chalidze) appeal to Sakharov with requests to support their efforts to release Grigorenko and Gorbanevskaya from compulsory treatment [in psychiatric hospitals], to ameliorate the fate of the convicted believer Krasnov-Levitin, and to terminate the investigation of Bukovsky, who has been arrested for anti-Soviet activities. In the majority of cases, Sakharov promised his support, gave sundry advice, and promised to raise all these questions for consideration by the members of the "Committee."

It has also been established that Sakharov has received requests from [other] people (for the most part, mentally ill), including people from other cities. Some visitors, during their discussions with him, have advanced hostile comments. For example, one visitor attempted to persuade Sakharov that the Soviet Union is experiencing an economic crisis and that it is undemocratic. In reply Sakharov said: "We do have economic growth, but it is not sufficiently rapid. There exist a number of very great barriers to this growth. But there is growth. If there were no growth, then we could say that this is complete decay. But there is not decay, but

42. Dmitri Mikheev, a graduate student in the Department of Physics at Moscow State University, attempted to fly from Moscow to Austria using the ticket and passport of a Swiss student, François de Perrégaux, on October 2, 1970. Their trial took place on August 17–23, 1971. Mikheev was sentenced to eight years in a labor camp; Perrégaux was sentenced to three years.

growth. It proceeds in a rather contradictory fashion: in part, it is democratized, and in part there is significant economic improvement. All this is interrelated. . . . It is impossible to say that a communist democracy is incapable of advancing through economic formulas. . . ."

Recently there has been a change in Sakharov's personal life. He has become intimate with a teacher in Medical School No. 2, L. G. Bonner (born 1922; member of the CPSU; her parents were earlier subjected to repression, but later rehabilitated).[43] Bonner supports the negative manifestations and activity of Sakharov as a member of the "Committee" and makes multiple copies of the materials prepared by his fellow collaborators. Sakharov's intention to marry Bonner elicited a negative reaction on the part of his daughters, which has caused a tense situation in the family. . . .

---

For the KGB, there was nothing more provocative than cooperation among people representing various disaffected groups. Andropov was making note of efforts by Ukrainian nationalists to establish ties with human rights activists in Moscow.

## · DOCUMENT 38 ·

Andropov to Central Committee, December 15, 1971
Cooperation between Moscow activists and Ukrainian nationalists

---

. . . It has been established that nationalistic elements in Ukraine are maintaining close contact with so-called "democrats" in Moscow (Sakharov, Yakir, and others), and are taking practical steps to form a coalition with other anti-Soviet elements in Ukraine (Zionists, Tatar "autonomists," religious extremists, and others).

The organs of state security in their practical work are taking these facts into account, and they are taking measures to curb the hostile activity of the above individuals.

---

The following reports confirmed the attention that the Human Rights Committee continued to receive in the West. They also noted, more ominously, that Sakharov's views on the Soviet economy and the

---

43. The initial of Bonner's first name here is obviously incorrect, as her name is Elena; her nickname is Lusia. Sakharov and Bonner applied for a marriage certificate on December 2, 1971, and married on January 7, 1972.

legacy of Lenin's seizure of power were growing harsher. Sakharov was now prepared to publicize a broadening variety of human rights issues, including abolition of the death penalty, and, together with Bonner, to attend the trials of dissidents and help expose their arbitrary and unjust procedures.

· DOCUMENT 39 ·

Andropov to Central Committee, December 20, 1971
Sakharov's criticism of the regime grows harsher

Foreign propaganda centers continue to advertise vigorously the activity of the so-called "Human Rights Committee." In particular, Sakharov's appeal to the Supreme Soviet of the USSR, proposing that Soviet citizens be allowed to leave the country freely and that pertinent existing legislation be reviewed, has become widely known in the West. Attempts by the U.S. embassy in Moscow to disseminate Sakharov's appeal in Moscow, Leningrad, Kiev, and some other cities have been noted.

Thanks to propaganda tricks by the West, some citizens of the Soviet Union and other socialist countries are gaining a false impression of the role and capacity of the "Committee" and its members. For this reason, there has been a significant increase, for example, in the flow of domestic and international correspondence addressed to Sakharov, containing requests to appeal to the authorities about the opening of churches, granting official recognition of religious sectarian groups, meeting the demands of Crimean Tatar "autonomists," permitting specific individuals to leave the country, etc. Thus, in November, several letters mailed from Poland and Romania asked Sakharov to use his prestige and the "power" of the "Committee" to help the writers of the letters leave for permanent residence in capitalist countries.

Lately, under the negative influence of Chalidze, and as a result of his own irresponsible attitudes, Sakharov's political views have undergone a further degradation. In a conversation with his fifteen-year-old son, Sakharov declared: "The founder of the Soviet state committed colossal crimes, which then gave birth to a whole series of crimes." Further, he stated: "Before the Imperialist War [World War I], Russia was developing very quickly, and if peace had been preserved, today we would be richer than we are, because per capita food production—[even] without the mechanization of agriculture—would be greater than it is now." According to Sakharov, the contemporary state of the Soviet economy reminds him of "running in place: every year they tell a lot of lies and only create the illusion of progress."

On December 2, and notwithstanding his children's protests, Sakharov submitted an application to register his marriage with E. G. Bonner, an instructor at a medical school who has relatives in France and corresponds with them. Bonner is a member of the CPSU, but she not only fully shares and supports Sakharov's negative views, she also draws him into active antisocial activity.

On December 5 a group of antisocial elements led by Yakir attempted to organize a provocative crowd at the Pushkin statue in connection with the so-called "traditional day of the democratic movement." Sakharov and Bonner were among the participants at this gathering.

Of late Sakharov has completely abandoned his scientific activity at the Physics Institute of the Academy of Sciences of the USSR.

---

· DOCUMENT 40 ·

Pirozhkov[44] to Central Committee, December 28, 1971
Contacts between the Human Rights Committee and groups in Europe

---

Herewith is communicated information about the activity of the so-called "Committee for the Defense of Human Rights in the USSR." This information is based on correspondence of leaders of Zionist organizations in Western Europe.[45]

Formation of the committee was announced at a press conference in Brussels on June 4. Its leaders are Sakharov and Chalidze. The committee, operating illegally in the USSR, supports clandestine contacts with a number of Zionist and anti-Soviet organizations in West European countries.

Since last summer, the committee has been collaborating with the "International Institute of Human Rights" in Strasbourg. It was agreed that individual numbers of the institute's journal would be given materials to publish from the bulletin "Problems of Society" issued by the committee. The committee is also participating in preparatory work (under way in West European countries) to create an international organization of solidarity with the "oppressed" national minorities in the USSR. It proposed

---

44. Vladimir Pirozhkov served as deputy chairman of the KGB from 1971 until his retirement in 1989; see Vladimir Kriuchkov, *Lichnoe delo* [A personal case], 2 vols. (Moscow, 1996), 1:426.

45. The KGB collected the information by intercepting the correspondence.

that the goals of this organization are to consist in collecting information about the "national question" in the USSR, but also in preparing anti-Soviet actions in various countries. A publication called "Information Bulletin" is being planned for the dissemination of the materials that this organization collects. From this correspondence, it is evident that the "Committee for the Defense of Human Rights in the USSR"—for tactical reasons—asserts that its activity is not political and will not be used to harm the interests of the Soviet Union.

· DOCUMENT 42 ·

Andropov to Central Committee, May 26, 1972
Sakharov intervenes for political prisoners

In late March of this year, Sakharov and his wife Bonner traveled to Dushanbe, where he met with relatives and the lawyer of A. D. Nazarov, convicted by the Supreme Court of the Tadzhik SSR for disseminating slanderous fabrications defaming the Soviet state and social order.[46]

Sakharov is continuing to provide assistance in finding a lawyer to defend the interests of Kuznetsov, who is in prison for the attempted hijacking of a plane; he has also given financial assistance to Vail and Pimenov, who were convicted of antisocial activity. He is attempting to obtain the release of Borisov and Fainberg from compulsory [psychiatric] treatment.

Sakharov has prepared an appeal to the authorities suggesting amnesty for "political" prisoners and the abolition of the death penalty. This appeal was discussed in April with his sympathizers Chalidze, Tverdokhlebov, and Bonner, whose behavior can be characterized as provocative. The plan is to make the appeal public on the fiftieth anniversary of the creation of the Soviet Union and to solicit the largest possible number of signatures from well-known figures in science, literature, and art.

On May 11, Sakharov and Bonner attended a farewell dinner for Bonavia, a correspondent for the London *Times,* who has been expelled from the USSR for hostile activities.[47] Among those invited to the dinner were diplomats and correspondents from England, the United States, and other capitalist countries. Sakharov had a conversation with the British

46. Anatoly Nazarov was sentenced to three years in a labor camp for mailing a copy of Sakharov's essay "Progress, Coexistence, and Intellectual Freedom" to a friend.
47. This episode is described in David Bonavia, *Fat Sasha and the Urban Guerrilla: Protest and Conformism in the Soviet Union* (New York, 1973), 185.

ambassador. The instigators of antisocial actions and their active participants, Yakir, Rudakov, Shikhanovich, Stroeva, and others, were present at the dinner. . . .

---

· **DOCUMENT 43** ·

Andropov to Central Committee, May 26, 1972
Sakharov's appeals to the Supreme Soviet

---

Enclosed are the appeals to the Supreme Soviet of the USSR, produced by Academician Sakharov and obtained through operational means, proposing an amnesty for individuals convicted under Articles 70, 72, and 190 of the Criminal Code of the Russian Federation, and the abolition of the death penalty.

According to information received, Sakharov and his sympathizers have begun collecting signatures for these appeals, and they intend to publicize them on the 50th anniversary of the creation of the Soviet Union.

To the USSR Supreme Soviet: An Appeal for Amnesty[48]

On the anniversary of the formation of the USSR, we appeal to you to adopt decisions that correspond to the humanitarianism, democratic orientation, and fundamental interests of our society. Among such decisions, we urge you to adopt a law on amnesty. We believe that this law should provide, in particular, for the release of those who have been convicted for reasons that are directly or indirectly based on their convictions. In particular, those convicted under Article 190–3 and Articles 70 and 72 of the Criminal Code of the RSFSR and analogous articles in the codes of other Union republics, and all those convicted because of their religious convictions, and those convicted because of a desire to emigrate. In the same vein we urge you to reconsider the decisions made on similar grounds to confine persons in specialized or general psychiatric hospitals. The freedom of belief, discussion, and defense of one's own opinions constitute the inalienable right of everyone. At the same time, this freedom is the basis of a viable society. We also think that the law on amnesty (in accordance with juridical norms and humanitarian principles) should include the emancipation of all those whose incarceration exceeds what is now the estab-

---

48. English translations of both appeals are in Sakharov, *Sakharov Speaks*, 237–38.

lished maximum sentence (fifteen years) under judicial rulings that were adopted before the current law.

### To the USSR Supreme Soviet: On Abolition of the Death Penalty

Many people have long sought the abolition of the death penalty, believing that it contradicts moral sensibility and cannot be justified by any general social considerations. The death penalty has now been abolished in many countries.

On the anniversary of the formation of the Union of Soviet Socialist Republics, we call on the USSR Supreme Soviet to adopt a law abolishing the death penalty in our country. Such a decision would promote the extension of this humane act throughout the world.

During the early summer of 1972, several of Sakharov's appeals and statements were broadcast in Russian by Radio Liberty, the BBC, and the Voice of America. Andropov claimed that this material was based on letters that Sakharov had sent to Pyotr Yakir, which Yakir had then passed along to the West before his arrest on June 12, 1972. Elena Bonner does not believe that her husband sent letters to Yakir, so it is difficult to know why Andropov made such a claim. The arrest of Pyotr Yakir and Viktor Krasin was the beginning of a broad crackdown on the human rights movement. It is possible that Andropov sought to discredit Sakharov by linking him to Yakir, who was now under arrest and would soon be intimidated, along with Krasin, into testifying against scores of fellow activists.

## · DOCUMENT 44 ·

Andropov to Central Committee, June 26, 1972
Andrei Sakharov and the case of Pyotr Yakir

Western propaganda has recently and continually increased its use of all sorts of letters and "treatises" by Academician A. D. Sakharov for anti-Soviet purposes. . . . On June 23, the [foreign broadcast] stations of capitalist countries began a new series of broadcasts devoted to Sakharov's letters to Yakir, which, according to operational intelligence, Yakir sent to the West shortly before his arrest. Sakharov's letters contain crude attacks on Soviet reality and on the policies of the CPSU and the Soviet government. "Our society," writes Sakharov, "is infected with apathy, hypocrisy, obtuse egotism, and covert cruelty. The majority of the Party and government apparatus (as well as the more prosperous part of the intelligentsia) stubbornly cling to their open and covert privileges." Sakharov calls the Soviet system "bureaucratic and intolerant"; it is allegedly characterized by "the government's intervention in the lives of its citizens." . . .

Simultaneously, he attempts to cast himself in the role of the "reformer" in an area of social and economic relations. In particular, Sakharov advocates expanding the "private plots" of collective farmers, introducing "private trading enterprises" and "private medical practice," etc. In assessing Sakharov's recent letters, Western bourgeois propagandists stress that he goes "much further in them than in the previously published works." And our adversary is attempting to exploit this circumstance in its subversive activities. All this demonstrates that Sakharov's antisocial actions are objectively becoming more and more aligned with the subversive activity of our adversary's ideological centers. Under these circumstances, it is becoming necessary to react publicly to Sakharov's actions.

---

Sakharov and his colleagues continued to try to enlist the support of prominent figures in the Soviet intelligentsia. Several writers and the cellist Mstislav Rostropovich endorsed their appeals, but no other well-known scientists joined them.

· DOCUMENT 45 ·

Andropov to Central Committee, July 10, 1972
The dissidents approach other prominent figures

---

Through operational means, the Committee for State Security has established that Sakharov is intensifying his antisocial activity. Lately, this has been manifested, above all, in the collection of signatures for appeals to the authorities proposing an amnesty and the abolition of the death penalty. . . .

By July 1, the appeals had been signed by Sakharov, Chalidze, Tverdokhlebov, and Shafarevich (who listed themselves as members of the so-called Human Rights Committee); by members of the Writers' Union of the USSR (Chukovskaya, Maximov, and Vladimov); by Rostropovich, a cellist; and by R. A. Medvedev. They are all known as participants in various provocations.

Sakharov and his wife, E. G. Bonner, and also Shafarevich, asked Academicians Kapitsa, Knuniants, Novikov, Astaurov, and also Academician

Keldysh's sister, to sign the appeals, but they did not receive their support. The negative attitude of this group of prominent Soviet scientists toward yet another of Sakharov's provocative escapades has not affected his intention to continue collecting signatures. In the immediate future, Sakharov intends to secure the support of Academicians Maisky, Smirnov, and others.

The Committee for State Security is taking measures to contain Sakharov's activity and to limit his harmful influence on individuals by involving them in antisocial acts. We also deem it necessary to direct the Presidium of the Academy of Sciences of the USSR to take measures to exert the appropriate influence on Sakharov and to create a frame of mind among scientists that will not tolerate his actions.

---

In response to the attack on Israeli athletes at the Munich Olympics by Palestinian terrorists, Sakharov tried to join a group of Moscow Jews who intended to "conduct a silent protest in front of the Lebanese embassy." He was joined by his wife's son and daughter, Alexei Semyonov and Tatiana Yankelevich, and her husband, Efrem. They were all detained and kept in the drunk tank of a nearby police station for a few hours before being released. A month later, Tatiana Yankelevich was expelled from the Moscow University night school, where she was about to complete her work for a degree in journalism. Gradually Sakharov and Bonner saw her children "become hostages to [his] public activity"; Tatiana and Alexei, with their children, would be compelled to emigrate in 1977.[49]

· DOCUMENT 46 ·

Tsinev[50] to Central Committee, September 7, 1972
Moscow demonstration over the attack at the Munich Olympics

---

On September 6 a group of fifty citizens of Jewish nationality (including eleven women) attempted to stage a demonstration in front of the Lebanese embassy to protest the terrorist act carried out in Munich by an extremist Palestinian organization on September 5.

The Committee for State Security in cooperation with the Ministry of Foreign Affairs took measures to prevent this demonstration. These peo-

---

49. See Sakharov, *Memoirs*, 374–75.
50. Georgy Tsinev was a deputy chairman of the KGB.

ple were detained at the approaches to the embassy. Among those detained, as a check revealed, was Academician Sakharov. After an investigation and warnings about the inadmissibility of such actions, all those detained were released.

In February 1973, Alexander Chakovsky, the editor in chief of *Literaturnaya Gazeta,* published an article attacking Sakharov and his essay "Progress, Coexistence, and Intellectual Freedom" five years after it had appeared. Sakharov found the article to be "more condescending than critical," labeling him "a naive and conceited person."[51] Nonetheless, it was the first article in the Soviet press to be critical of Sakharov since his outspoken opposition to Lysenkoism in 1964 and marked a break in the conspiracy of silence that surrounded him. Andropov quickly objected and urged that Sakharov's name be banned from the official press, a suggestion that other officials soon endorsed by appending their signatures to the document.

· DOCUMENT 49 ·

Andropov to Central Committee, February 18, 1973
The first public denunciation of Andrei Sakharov

On February 14, 1973, *Literaturnaya Gazeta* published an article by A. Chakovsky, "What's Next?" On the whole, the content of the article does not raise any doubts and deserves a positive mark. But for the first time in the Soviet press, this article mentions Academician Sakharov as a person engaged in antisocial activity.

The Committee for State Security believes that reference to Sakharov in the official press can be used to expand the next anti-Soviet campaign in the Western press. It can encourage the antisocial activities of Sakharov himself and increase an unhealthy interest on the part of hostile elements inside the country.[52] We believe it would be expedient to ban mention of Sakharov's name in official publications of the Soviet press.

In November 1972, Valery Chalidze and his wife, with the regime's permission, flew to New York, where he had been invited to lecture on human rights. Three weeks after their arrival, he was stripped of his

51. See Sakharov, *Memoirs,* 382.
52. Chakovsky's article was reported in the *New York Times,* February 15, 1973, 3.

Soviet citizenship. Sakharov had understood that "this outcome was practically inevitable," and his inability to convince Chalidze of this danger caused some hard feelings between them. As Sakharov observed, "It was obvious that permission had been granted because the KGB was eager to get rid of a key figure in the human rights movement." Andropov documented the tensions within the Human Rights Committee and was happy to take credit for them. On the eve of Chalidze's departure, he had resigned as a member of the committee. Then in December, Andrei Tverdokhlebov also left the committee, in part because of Sakharov's attitude toward Chalidze's departure for the United States. Soon after, another veteran activist, Grigory Podyapolsky, a geophysicist, joined the committee, hoping to help Sakharov and Shafarevich carry on its work. But after a time they "began to feel that the committee had outlived its usefulness," issuing conventional appeals and calling them "committee documents."[53] By 1974, the Human Rights Committee was no longer active.

· DOCUMENT 50 ·

Andropov to Central Committee, March 1, 1973
Measures to compromise the work of the Human Rights Committee

As a result of measures taken by the organs of the Committee for State Security, the antisocial activities of the so-called "Human Rights Committee" decreased somewhat in 1972. This was assisted, in particular, by such measures as the compromising of the reputation of Chalidze and stripping him of Soviet citizenship, inciting disagreements and dissension among the members of the "Committee" and their sympathizers (which led to Tverdokhlebov's withdrawal from the Committee), suspensions of the tendentious journal "Problems of Society," and so forth. . . .

Andropov remained deeply concerned about Sakharov's connections to the West. But now a new challenge was emerging: Elena Bonner's mother and children received invitations from Israel, which made it possible for them to apply to leave the Soviet Union. Ruth Bonner was Jewish, so it was plausible for her and her grandchildren to claim relatives in Israel. But in the early 1970s, when the Jewish emigration movement was gaining permission for tens of thousands of Soviet Jews

53. See Sakharov, *Memoirs,* 380–81.

to emigrate, the regime required all would-be emigrants, whether or not they were Jewish, to apply for visas to Israel. Once they reached Vienna, Soviet emigrants could arrange to go to the United States. But the regime had its own reason for insisting on Israel as their ostensible destination: all the emigrating dissidents appeared to be Jews. And the Kremlin hoped to increase resentment among Ukrainians, Russians, and other nationalities against Jews and dissidents alike by making it appear that only Jews and dissidents could exercise the privilege of leaving the country.

·  DOCUMENT 51  ·

Andropov to Central Committee, March 13, 1973
Sakharov and increased contact with the West

. . . Lately foreigners have substantially increased the number of visits to the apartment of Sakharov and his wife, Bonner; these foreigners include correspondents accredited in Moscow and emissaries of such foreign "nongovernmental" organizations as "Amnesty International" and the "Herzen Foundation," who seek to obtain tendentious information from Sakharov. In many cases, Sakharov and his wife respond to these requests.

In addition, there has been an increase in the number of Sakharov's international telephone conversations with foreigners and letters to Sakharov from abroad which express support for his antisocial activities. In a telephone conversation in February, J. Carey (president of the "International League for the Rights of Man") invited Sakharov to become a member of the Advisory Council of the League. U Thant [former secretary general of the U.N.] has agreed to join this Council. The director of the organization "4,000 American Scientists,"[54] J. Stone, has sent Sakharov a letter offering to establish permanent contact between his organization and the "Human Rights Committee." In his letter Stone noted that his organization was founded in 1946 by nuclear scientists, that it enjoys the support of Nobel Prize laureates, and that its activities are identical to the goals of the "Human Rights Committee." Sakharov is inclined to accept these offers, but he has not yet given an official response.

Lately Bonner has been foisting on Sakharov the idea that repressive

54. The current name is the Federation of American Scientists.

measures may be employed against her relatives and is trying to convince him to leave the country. In January, Bonner's mother, son, daughter, and son-in-law received documents from Israel that give them grounds to apply to emigrate. This topic is constantly discussed in the Sakharov family. If Sakharov had earlier regarded the possibility of leaving the USSR as unrealistic, he is now, under the influence of his wife, wavering on this issue. . . .

----

Sakharov offered a novel idea for helping an imprisoned fellow scientist, the mathematician Yuri Shikhanovich. He offered to stand surety for him, hoping to gain his release from pretrial detention and draw attention to the case. Andropov also noted that Sakharov had met with the *New York Times* correspondent Hedrick Smith, a harbinger of more frequent contact with Western reporters.

## · DOCUMENT 52 ·

Andropov to Central Committee, March 28, 1973
The case of Yuri Shikhanovich

----

Academician Sakharov has petitioned the Committee for State Security to release Shikhanovich from pretrial detention, on Sakharov's personal surety.[55] Shikhanovich was arrested in September of 1972 on charges of violating Article 70 of the Criminal Code of the RSFSR.

Prior to his arrest, Y. A. Shikhanovich, who holds a candidate degree in pedagogical sciences and teaches at a vocational-technical school, was an instigator and an active participant in hostile acts. He took part in the illegal production, duplication, and dissemination of the anti-Soviet journal *A Chronicle of Current Events*. He signed a number of slanderous and provocative letters that were used for anti-Soviet propaganda in the West. During a search of Shikhanovich's apartment, more than three hundred anti-Soviet, slanderous, and politically harmful items were confiscated. These included Avtorkhanov's "Partocracy," Izgoev's "Socialism, Culture, and Bolshevism," and twenty-five issues of *A Chronicle of Current Events*.

On March 23, Sakharov was invited to the Regional Directorate of the KGB for Moscow and Moscow Oblast, which is responsible for prosecuting the criminal case against Shikhanovich. It was explained to him that,

----

55. The petition was signed by Andrei Sakharov and Elena Bonner. A copy can be found in the Andrei Sakharov Archive (Harvard), folder S.II.2.2.127.1.

according to Article 94 of the Code of Criminal Procedure of the RSFSR, a personal guarantee is acceptable only from trustworthy individuals. However, Sakharov does not enjoy the trust of the investigative organs, since his personal behavior does not correspond to the norms of our society. It was specifically emphasized that Sakharov, while privy to important government secrets, has established and maintains systematic contacts with foreigners (in contravention of instructions well known to him), and that he supplies them with tendentious material and information that is used abroad for anti-Soviet purposes. On these grounds, Sakharov's request was denied.

As established through operational means, in the early hours of March 24 Sakharov met with an American correspondent, Smith,[56] and his wife, and transmitted detailed information about the substance of his conversation with the organs of state security. During a discussion with Smith about Shikhanovich's situation, Sakharov's wife suggested: "Maybe there are some foreign scientists who would be willing to offer themselves as personal surety for their colleague, a mathematician." Smith quickly transmitted this information to the West, and Radio Liberty immediately broadcast it.

The Committee for State Security continues surveillance of Sakharov and his wife, Bonner, who lately has been playing an increasingly provocative role in the antisocial actions of her husband.

---

For the first time, Sakharov took concrete steps toward obtaining permission for Bonner's children to leave the country. Still, another four years would pass before they could travel to the United States.

## · DOCUMENT 53 ·

Andropov to Central Committee, April 12, 1973
Sakharov tries to help the children of Elena Bonner

---

On April 5, Academician Sakharov, together with his second wife, Bonner, visited the Visa Office of the Department of Internal Affairs attached to the Moscow City Executive Committee. They were accompanied by her

56. Hedrick Smith describes his first encounter with Sakharov in *The Russians* (New York, 1977), 588–96; he makes numerous references to Sakharov throughout the book. The *Washington Post* correspondent Robert Kaiser was also among the first American reporters to spend considerable time with Sakharov; see his description in *Russia: The People and the Power* (New York, 1976), 456–65.

children: a son, A. I. Semyonov (born 1956, a high school student), and a daughter, T. Yankelevich (born 1950; now a salesperson at the Moscow Book Store), together with her husband, E. V. Yankelevich (born 1950; an engineer at the Central Design Bureau of the Ministry of Communications). . . . [57] After formally introducing himself and identifying himself as their relative, Sakharov submitted the documents necessary for them to obtain permission to leave the country to work and study in the United States.

The invitation that Bonner's children received from the president of the Massachusetts Institute of Technology[58] indicates that they are invited for one year, but that the term of their stay in the U.S. could be extended. The Americans are offering salaries of $8,400 for [T. I.] Semyonova, $12,000 a year for Yankelevich, and [A. I.] Semyonov would also be fully provided for.[59]

In his conversation with officials of the Visa Office, Sakharov emphasized that the subject of his request is of "state importance." In his words, the president of the institute is an influential person, close to Kissinger, and he implied that refusal to allow [the children] to leave the country could "impact Soviet-American relations."

---

The summer and fall of 1973 marked a dramatic shift in the relationship between Sakharov and the regime. In May he granted a television interview to the Swedish correspondent Olle Stenholm. Coming after his interview with *Newsweek* and his meeting with Hedrick Smith of the *New York Times,* this interview made clear that Sakharov was now deciding to broaden his personal contacts with Westerners, a move that infuriated Soviet officials, who had long assumed that Sakharov would honor the commitment he made as a nuclear weapons researcher not to meet with foreigners or divulge state secrets.

Within days after the interview with Stenholm appeared, the Soviet press initiated an ugly and sustained campaign against Sakharov. If six months earlier Andropov had urged that Soviet officials refrain from attacking him publicly for fear that even negative publicity would draw undue attention to Sakharov and his ideas, now the regime aban-

57. The photocopy has a deleted section of about twenty-five characters in this first long sentence.
58. Jerome Wiesner.
59. The invitation was reported in the *New York Times,* May 3, 1973, 10.

doned all restraint. In quick succession articles and "letters" in the central press accused him of being a liar, of "distorting Soviet reality," and of opposing a reduction in international tensions. In one of the most disturbing attacks, forty of his fellow academicians stated that his actions were "thoroughly alien to Soviet scientists" and "discredit the good name of Soviet science." Even the renowned composer Dmitri Shostakovich was pulled into the act; his name appeared alongside those of eleven other figures in Soviet music in a harsh denunciation of Sakharov's "slanderous statements about socialist reality." Letters from workers and scientists in the national republics soon followed, lending themselves to a virtual chorus of condemnation.[60]

Other, more discrete actions accompanied these public attacks. As we shall see, Sakharov was called in that August for a "discussion" in the Office of the Procurator General (roughly the equivalent of the attorney general of the United States). There Mikhail Malyarov, the deputy procurator, spent an hour warning and berating Sakharov in a condescending and threatening tone. The fact that this document was prepared by both Andropov and Roman Rudenko, the procurator general, suggests that Soviet officials were seriously considering legal action against Sakharov. Within weeks, the authorities learned how little they had cowed Sakharov by reading his account of the conversation with Malyarov on the op-ed page of the *New York Times*. Andropov and Rudenko's report to the Central Committee bore little resemblance to Sakharov's more telling account. For them, Malyarov was helping to "educate" Sakharov and offering him the dialogue he had long sought with Party and government leaders. It is interesting to note that on September 4, in a note to Alexei Kosygin, Andropov sent Malyarov's own transcript of his talk with Sakharov, along with copies of Sakharov's interview with foreign journalists; this material has not been released.

Finally, that same summer other ominous events enveloped Sakharov and his extended family. Elena Bonner's son, Alexei, was refused admission to Moscow University and Tatiana's husband, Efrem Yankelevich, was dismissed from his job. Both the public and private nooses were tightening.

60. A sample of these articles and statements can be found in Sakharov, *Memoirs*, 631–40; the Stenholm interview can be found in the same volume, 623–30.

· DOCUMENT 55 ·

Andropov and Rudenko to Central Committee, August 2, 1973
A sustained public campaign against Sakharov

———————

. . . Lately . . . new motifs—openly hostile toward the Soviet Union—
have appeared in Sakharov's actions and statements. Thus, at the end of
last May, he gave an interview to a Swedish correspondent, Stenholm, in
which he directly stated that he is an enemy of the socialist system and
urged the West to take active steps against the policies of the Soviet Union.
As one such measure Sakharov recommended organizing more "groups"
and "committees" abroad to defend those hostile elements among Soviet
citizens that have been charged with criminal offenses.

Considering the above, and because such actions by Sakharov cannot
be left unpunished, it is necessary to summon him to the procurator general of the USSR and issue an appropriate warning regarding his illegal activity. . . .

———————

In an interview with a French correspondent, Sakharov emphasized
how important it was for the West to insist on democratization inside
the Soviet Union, even as it discussed limiting nuclear weapons and improving relations between East and West.

· DOCUMENT 56 ·

Andropov to Central Committee, August 14, 1973
Sakharov's call for democratization

———————

The Committee for State Security has established that one of the "leaders" of pro-Zionist elements in Moscow, K. Khenkin, a freelance translator, has established contact with Academician Sakharov. . . . With
Khenkin serving as an intermediary, on August 10 the correspondent
of the French press agency "Agence France-Presse" Dillon obtained a
lengthy taped interview with Sakharov. . . .[61] Having acknowledged in
the interview that the "process of rapprochement" is now taking place,

———————

61. The interview was published under the title "A Talk with Soviet Dissident Andrei Sakharov" by Edouard Dillon in the *New York Post*, August 23, 1973, IV, 4. Dillon was a guest at a meeting between Sakharov and the French writer Lucie Faure, wife
of the Speaker of the French Parliament. See Kirill Khenkin, *Okhotnik vverkh nogami*
[A hunter upside down] (Frankfurt am Main, 1979?), 286.

Sakharov also noted that this process contains "grave dangers." One is that "the authorities in our country . . . are already trying to use rapprochement not to democratize the regime, but to strengthen it and to make it harsher." In Sakharov's view, this is manifested in the repression of "freedom of thought in our country" and "in the growth of political repression." In this he cited "repression in Ukraine,"[62] the arrests of Shikhanovich and of other individuals, and he appealed to world public opinion "to do everything possible to save Shikhanovich from the threat of a terrible, virtually indefinite psychiatric confinement." In Sakharov's view, the West should use the emerging international situation to apply pressure on the Soviet Union. "Anything else will represent capitulation before our antidemocratic regime," declared Sakharov. "It will mean that the regime is forgiven for its sins; and it will have extremely grave, tragic consequences for the development of the entire international situation; it could lead to the dissemination of our disease throughout the world. The West should understand that if our country will not change in the direction of greater democratization, then any treaty with it will be extremely unreliable. The treaty will be effective only while political and economic necessities force us to seek rapprochement."

Sakharov appealed to the West to demand from the Soviet Union "an end to our isolation: . . . freedom to leave the country and freedom to return; the possibility of keeping Soviet citizenship and also of changing it freely. . . . In this connection, he depicted in a slanderous, perverted fashion actions of Soviet authorities taken with respect to individuals petitioning for permission to leave the country . . . ,[63] only a part of the wider issue of ending our isolation from the outside world, of introducing general intellectual freedom in our country. . . . There can be no rapprochement, no mutual trust if one side resembles a huge concentration camp."

Sakharov also claimed that 40 percent of the national income of the USSR is spent on the military and that the budget contains "camouflaged items," which are used for military purposes.

In the interview, Sakharov also spoke about members of the so-called "Human Rights Committee" and mentioned his desire to travel to the USA at the invitation of Princeton University. In conclusion, Dillon asked Sakharov to continue giving him information intended for dissemination in the West. If Sakharov's interview is published, it is deemed expedient to expel Dillon from the USSR.

---

62. In January 1972 KGB officials arrested at least nineteen Ukrainian dissidents.
63. The copy in the Sakharov Archive (Harvard) is not complete; it lacks one or more lines.

Sakharov's meeting with a prosecutor and a KGB officer was his first with representatives of the Kremlin in his role as a dissident. He did not come away deterred; at the close, he expressed his gratitude and hope that there would be further such talks, or, as he put it, "fruitful contacts with Soviet organs."

## · DOCUMENT 57 ·

Andropov and Rudenko to Central Committee, August 21, 1973
Sakharov is summoned to meet with a prosecutor

With the concurrence of the Central Committee of the CPSU (report 1837-A of August 2, 1973), on August 16 the first deputy procurator general of the USSR, Comrade M. P. Malyarov (together with an officer of the KGB of the Council of Ministers of the USSR), conducted a conversation with Academician Sakharov. During the conversation, Sakharov was informed that his actions (the preparation of slanderous and, lately, anti-Soviet material in the form of letters, statements, and interviews and their transmissions to bourgeois correspondents and other foreigners) are illegal and harm the interests of our state. His interview with the Swedish correspondent Stenholm, in which he calls our society "socially crippled, antidemocratic, lacking equality," etc., was especially open in its hostility.

He was further informed that during the time he had been engaged in top-secret work, he had accepted the appropriate obligation not to have contacts with foreigners and not to divulge information that he obtained by virtue of his work. However, it is obvious from reports in the foreign press that he is flagrantly violating this pledge. It was explained to Sakharov that his actions constitute a violation of the law. In this regard, Sakharov was informed that state organs cannot tolerate his antistate activity and categorically demand that it cease. In response Sakharov said that he does not consider his activity unlawful, since (in his view) the pledge, made in connection with his defense work, applies only to his past activities. On this point he was given reasoned explanations.

During the conversation, which lasted for a little more than an hour, an attempt was made to instill in Sakharov the idea that he has linked his activities to hostile forces in the West, that his slanderous material (letters, pictures) has been published by the most reactionary publishers (*Posev, Grani, Russkaya Mysl*, and the like), and that he has become the banner of antisocial elements. It was emphasized that the adversary uses him only because he speaks out against the existing order in our country, and that his activity finds no support among Soviet scientists.

The conversation has confirmed, once again, the view that Sakharov is an apolitical person who has a distorted perception and evaluation of the social and economic processes taking place in our country and in the world as a whole. His credo is "pure democracy," "universal freedom," and "convergence with bourgeois concepts in politics and ideology." For example, he states that he disagrees with V. I. Lenin's observation on the partisan nature of the press, and he therefore believes that "it makes no difference where my letters are published." In this regard, Sakharov said: "The important issue is what is published, not where it is published. I did not object to publication by *Posev* (the organ of the NTS). I believe publication is always useful. The fact that the program of the NTS has points that are completely unacceptable for me does not mean that the publisher *Posev* plays a purely negative role."

Later in the conversation, Sakharov attempted to expound on the right to propagandize "any opinion." In particular, he defended the slanderous activity of Amalrik, who is currently serving a sentence as a criminal offender, claiming that Amalrik's libelous essay "Will the Soviet Union Survive until 1984?" has the right to exist, since it reflects the author's conviction that "the Soviet system will not last long."

Sakharov attempts to portray ordinary bourgeois demagoguery as a manifestation of genuine democracy. "The Watergate affair," he declared, "where the president was in fact put on trial, is a sign of strength in the system. Nixon is an absolute scoundrel, his political career is over,[64] but the system shows here its positive side as well."

Sakharov may well put the main emphasis on weakening our struggle against our ideological enemies, including those who have embarked on a path of resistance to the Soviet system. Characteristic in this respect are his insistence on the need to abolish Articles 70 and 190-1 of the Criminal Code of the RSFSR, which establish criminal liability for anti-Soviet agitation and propaganda and for the dissemination of slanderous fabrications that defame the Soviet state and social system. On this basis, he believes that the sentences meted out to Galanskov, Ginzburg, Amalrik, and others under these articles are unjust. He advocates abolition of the death penalty. Following the logic of his thinking, and calling the so-called *Chronicle of*

---

64. The president was not, in fact, put on trial. Richard M. Nixon resigned on August 8, 1974, in the face of a pending bill of impeachment in the House of Representatives.

*Current Events* (produced by Yakir, Krasin, Kim, and others) the only "good publication" in our country, he regrets that it has ceased to exist.[65]

Sakharov received the requisite answers to these and other questions. At the conclusion of the conversation, Sakharov said: "I have listened to you attentively; I have not agreed with you completely, but I have taken note of everything said. For my part, I would like very much to restore some possibility for fruitful contacts with Soviet organs." It has become known that Sakharov informed foreign correspondents about this conversation.[66]

---

·  DOCUMENT 60  ·

Chebrikov to Central Committee, September 8, 1973
A meeting between Sakharov and Solzhenitsyn

---

On September 6, 1973, Solzhenitsyn invited Sakharov and his wife to his own wife's Moscow apartment. Sakharov accepted the invitation. During the visit he examined some documents that Solzhenitsyn had prepared. The latter approved Sakharov's antisocial activities but advised him, for the time being, to refrain from such activism, saying, "It is time to be silent." . . .

---

Solzhenitsyn had advised Sakharov to keep a low profile, knowing that the regime was on the offensive against him and the broader human rights movement. But two days later Sakharov invited more than a dozen correspondents to his apartment and reaffirmed his views on convergence and democratization.[67]

---

65. After no. 27 (October 15, 1972) "Khronika Tekushchikh Sobitii" did not reappear until May 1974. In no. 28 the editors explained the interruption: "Our reasons for discontinuing publication related to direct threats from the KGB to arrest people after each new issue. . . . But our silence might mean support, however indirect and passive, for the 'hostage tactics' used by the KGB. . . . For that reason the *Chronicle of Current Events* makes a second start." For the text of the statement by Tatyana Velikanova, Tatyana Khodorovich, and Sergei Kovalev, see *A Chronicle of Current Events*, no. 28 (Amnesty International ed., 1975), 8.

66. The last statement could refer to the fact that Sakharov made available to Western newsmen his record of the interview on August 18, but it could also refer to his meeting with Western correspondents in his apartment on August 21, when he once again described his encounter with Malyarov; see *New York Times*, August 22, 1973, 3. The *Times* published the full text of the interview August 29, 1973, 37. It can also be found in Sakharov, *Sakharov Speaks*, 180–92.

67. See Kaiser, *Russia*, 461, for an account of a press conference that fall in Sakharov's apartment.

· DOCUMENT 61 ·

Chebrikov to Central Committee, September 9, 1973
Sakharov holds a press conference

On September 8, at 3 P.M., fourteen correspondents representing various organs of the bourgeois press of Western countries visited A. D. Sakharov's apartment. Sakharov familiarized the correspondents with the contents of a "declaration" written by him. The text follows:

The campaign being conducted in the press about my last interview (as its main argument) accuses me of opposing détente, of being in favor of war. This is an unconscionable exploitation of the antiwar feeling of people who experienced the greatest suffering during the Second World War and who lost millions of sons and daughters. This is a deliberate distortion of my views. Beginning in 1958, I spoke out (in the press and behind closed doors) condemning nuclear testing in the atmosphere. I think that my statements made some contribution to the cause of concluding an agreement to stop nuclear testing in the atmosphere. In my basic published declarations (specifically, in the appeal for 'peaceful coexistence and intellectual freedom,' which was prepared in 1969 [sic]; in my memorandum that I issued in 1971 and its postscript in 1972), I wrote that the principal task before mankind is to eliminate the ultimate danger of nuclear war. Therefore I always welcomed, and welcome now, a reduction in international tensions and the efforts of governments to limit the arms race and to eradicate mutual mistrust. I have always believed, and believe now, that the sole way to resolve world problems is the path of mutual change, the path of convergence between the capitalist and socialist systems, accompanied by demilitarization, by an intensification of social protection for the lives of the working people, and the creation of a mixed economy. These unalterable views of mine were reflected in my recent interviews with foreign correspondents in Moscow. In these interviews I also emphasized the importance of mutual trust, one condition of which is a free press and the openness of society, as well as democratization, free dissemination of information and exchange of opinions, and respect for the basic rights of the individual, especially respect for the right of every person to choose the country where he wishes to live. I also drew attention to the danger of an illusory rapprochement, which is not accompanied by growth in trust and democratization. I think it is my right and duty to issue such a warning. How could such a warning be regarded as an attack against the easing of tensions? I spoke out in defense of the violated rights of my friends, those who are now in camps and psychiatric clinics: Shikhanovich, Bukovsky, Grigorenko, Plyushch, Amalrik, Borisov, Fainberg, Strokatova, and many others. I cannot consider this declaration to be slander against the Soviet system, as has been stated in the newspapers. I deem it necessary that the rights of people in our country be protected just as they are in those countries, which are now entering into new, friendlier relations with us. I also think that it is important that (as it is in these countries) our cities, villages, and our life be open for the eyes of outsiders as it is for our own eyes. This includes such institutions as places of incarceration, psychiatric hospitals, and the places where the so-called "conditionally freed" live and work. Let the chairman of the Red Cross take down the shutters from the windows of Soviet prisons, and let the chairman of the Red Cross stop the hand of the criminals who are giving injections of haloperidol to Leonid Plyushch in the hell of the prison psychiatric clinic at Dnepropetrovsk.[68]

The newspaper campaign, which has enveloped hundreds of people (many of whom are unquestionably honest and intelligent), has deeply saddened me, because this is yet another manifestation of the brutal acts in this country against our conscience, a coercion based on the unlimited material and ideological power of the state. I believe that it is not my declaration, but the newspaper campaign, which is so senseless and brutal towards its participants, that can damage the easing of international tensions.[69]

Sakharov told the correspondents that he would like to see his statement published in full in the Western press. Responding to the correspondents' questions, Sakharov alleged that there is not now, nor has there ever been, true democracy in our country, and that the exercise of all human rights remains a dream, a goal, but not a reality. According to him, current repression affects a very narrow circle of people who allow themselves freedom of opinion. Within this circle, the repressive actions are decisive and brutal, and affect almost everyone. This is achieved not just through court trials: more people are fired from their jobs and therefore lose their livelihood, since the state is the only employer in our country.

One of the correspondents asked Sakharov to comment on the possibil-

68. Haloperidol is a very strong tranquilizer and particularly dangerous if used to excess.
69. For the full text of this statement, see Sakharov, *Sakharov Speaks*, 208–10.

ity that he will be awarded the Nobel Prize. Sakharov replied: "I would be very touched, and it would seem to be a great honor for me. I think that, if this happens, it will be a great help for me and for those people and those causes that I support."[70]

---

Both Sakharov and Solzhenitsyn posed ideological dangers to the regime. Andropov proposed measures that sooner (for Solzhenitsyn) or later (for Sakharov) would neutralize their appeal and status in Soviet society. Solzhenitsyn would be forcibly sent to Western Europe five months after this memorandum was submitted, but the regime would still wait another six years before accepting Andropov's advice about what to do with Andrei Sakharov.

· DOCUMENT 62 ·

Andropov to Central Committee, September 17, 1973
Détente and the need to neutralize Sakharov and Solzhenitsyn[71]

---

Analysis of material in the possession of the Committee for State Security allows us to conclude that the enemies of détente have recently intensified their activities in their struggle against this Soviet foreign policy initiative in an attempt to turn, once again, the course of world events in the direction of the "cold war." In doing so, and in order to win public opinion over to their side, our adversaries are using lies to compromise the Soviet social system and sow seeds of mistrust among people who lack full and objective information on these issues.

Political figures, public organizations, mass media owned by large monopolies and controlled by the states—all are involved in this struggle. Special [intelligence] services are conducting subversive activities calculated to foment and provoke sensationalism over the so-called question of "civil rights in the USSR." As the activity of the special services and propaganda efforts of the enemy increase, it is becoming increasingly clear

70. At this moment the issue of the Nobel Prize acquired a special meaning for the KGB. The day before, on September 8, 1973, the *New York Times* published a statement by the mathematician Igor Shafarevich, the poet Alexander Galich, and the writer Vladimir Maximov proposing that the 1973 Nobel Peace Prize be awarded to Sakharov. Solzhenitsyn also nominated Sakharov; see Michael Scammell, *Solzhenitsyn: A Biography* (New York, 1984), 810.

71. At this point the Soviet leadership discussed Sakharov and Solzhenitsyn together as components of the same problem; see various materials on 1973 in Michael Scammell, ed., *The Solzhenitsyn Files* (Chicago, 1995), 241–43, 251, 256–58.

that the main thrust is to create, by using every form of political pressure, a situation that could cause a certain deformation in the structure of Soviet society. If that proves impossible, the hope is at least to cast doubt on any further normalization of relations between our country and the Western states.

The hysteria stirred up lately in the West around the names of Sakharov and Solzhenitsyn is directly subordinated to these goals and represents the product of a prearranged and coordinated program. Western propaganda centers are now soliciting Solzhenitsyn, who was known earlier in the West for his anti-Soviet attitudes, for direct collaboration—in the first place on ideological grounds, but also through large financial inducements. The former writer is now attempting to speak out as some kind of political figure and ideologue. In his latest writings, he does not hide his desire to convince mankind of "the illegitimate nature of socialism," its ideology and practice. Moreover, as has now become clear, Solzhenitsyn maintains conspiratorial contacts with people who were imprisoned earlier for political reasons. Solzhenitsyn's unpublished work, "The Gulag Archipelago," directly expresses the idea that these people have much in common, ideologically and otherwise, and hints at the possibility of their joining forces.[72]

In contrast to Solzhenitsyn, Sakharov is more restrained in his futile attempts to prove "the unacceptability of the Soviet system." Nevertheless, he is definitely degenerating into anti-Sovietism.

Although not uniting formally, they both act essentially in unison, playing up to Western reactionary circles and, in a number of instances, carrying out direct orders. Naturally, the imperialists, having found in Sakharov and Solzhenitsyn individuals who, through the force of circumstances, can still bark at Soviet power with impunity, go all out to maintain this possibility for them for as long as possible. In turn, Solzhenitsyn and Sakharov, emboldened by the Western reaction, are becoming more and more brazen. A very important factor pertinent to the situation is that both of them not only firmly believe that they can act with impunity, but are trying to convince their immediate entourage that this is so. In a conversation with a foreign correspondent, Solzhenitsyn has said bluntly: "You can be sure they will not touch one hair on my head."

72. The KGB was already well aware of this manuscript and had begun unraveling Solzhenitsyn's network of supporters in a vain attempt to disrupt its appearance in the West. But the Western public learned about *The Gulag Archipelago* only at the end of December 1973, when its publication in France was announced; see *New York Times,* December 29, 1973, 1.

The anti-Soviet activity of Sakharov and Solzhenitsyn, conducted with impunity, attracts the increasing attention of the Soviet people. In the absolute majority it arouses a feeling of outrage, but in certain circles of the intelligentsia and among young people, it sometimes inspires sentiments such as this: "Act boldly, openly, attract foreign correspondents, obtain support in the bourgeois press, and nobody will dare touch you." The development of such a tendency is fraught with negative consequences and compels one to consider more radical measures to terminate the hostile acts of Solzhenitsyn and Sakharov.

Today there is no real reason to believe that Solzhenitsyn and Sakharov will voluntarily renounce their hostile activities. Neither the conversations with Solzhenitsyn at the Central Committee of the CPSU and at the Writers' Union of the USSR nor the attempts to influence him with the help of representatives of society and through the press have had any effect. The conversations with Sakharov (at the Presidium of the Academy of Sciences of the USSR and with the heads of the institutes where he has worked) have also produced no results. The summons to Sakharov to come to the Office of the Procurator of the USSR (to warn him against further anti-Soviet steps) was used by him and by those around him for new hostile press conferences, where he directly appealed to the U.S. and other Western countries not to proceed with normalization of relations with the USSR without "extracting concessions from the Soviet leadership" for a "liberalization of the regime."

There is information that Sakharov and Solzhenitsyn intend to continue to meet with representatives of the reactionary Western press, to slander our country, and to recruit accomplices from the ranks of the Soviet people.

Under these conditions, it seems expedient to take a different approach to the question of Solzhenitsyn's and Sakharov's behavior.

1. Since there are documentary grounds to consider Solzhenitsyn's recent actions not as the mistaken aberrations of a writer, but as a premeditated activity, both legal and illegal, of a person deeply hostile toward the Soviet system, a criminal case should be initiated against him at the appropriate time, with the goal of putting him on trial.

2. Because this action is an extreme measure, it is possible to consider a less drastic solution: direct the USSR Ministry of Foreign Affairs to approach, through our ambassadors in Paris, Rome, London, and Stockholm, the governments of these countries with a suggestion that they offer Solzhenitsyn the right of asylum,[73] since, according to Soviet law, he

___

73. This list of cities omitted Bonn, West Germany. Andropov may well have been

would otherwise have to face trial. This plan could be put on a legal basis, either directly or through special channels. The governments concerned would be faced with a dilemma: either to offer Solzhenitsyn asylum or, should they decide otherwise, they would in effect have agreed with his being put on trial. It is possible that, faced with such a situation, official circles in Western countries would not (as is now the case) inflame passions so directly through propaganda organs about Solzhenitsyn and Sakharov.

3. It is extremely urgent that Academician Sakharov meet with one of the leaders of the Soviet government. There is little hope that Sakharov will change his behavior as a result of this meeting (he is ill, overwhelmed by his surroundings, and in a state of excitement). However, such a meeting would disarm critics who now reproach us because nobody from the leadership has talked with such a "respected" person (academician and three times a Hero of Socialist Labor) and tried to reason with him. Conversations along this line are taking place among good people abroad and even in our country. There is also a possibility that Sakharov, while making use of his impunity, is very much afraid that he will be "stripped of his Stars"[74] or that he will be expelled from the Academy [of Sciences]. Now, as a preventive measure, he repeatedly expresses such fears to Western journalists, who in turn stress in the press that the Soviet leadership will never take such a step and has no right to do so.

In light of this, in the course of the proposed conversation, perhaps it should be firmly stated to Sakharov that he can be deprived of his titles of Academician and of Hero of Socialist Labor if he does not cease his anti-Soviet statements (which also means losing the 800 rubles a month that he now receives for doing nothing).[75] As an alternative, Sakharov could be offered the possibility of going to work in Novosibirsk, Obninsk, or in some other city with a special regimen, in order to help him escape from his hostile surroundings and, above all, the Western press.[76]

Clearly, these actions would provoke an outcry in the West and possibly a new upsurge of anti-Sovietism as well as certain dissatisfaction in some fraternal parties and in progressive circles. There would also be talk among a certain (but small) segment of the Soviet population. But all this would not last long and would be of a transitory character.

---

already engaged in negotiations about Solzhenitsyn's exile, but at this stage, on September 18, 1973, chose not to share the information with the Politburo. Solzhenitsyn was sent to Frankfurt am Main in February 1974.

74. The medals of the Hero of Socialist Labor.

75. He was referring to money paid regularly to individuals of Sakharov's rank.

76. This line of reasoning was ultimately to lead to his exile to Gorky in 1980.

Left unresolved, the cases of Solzhenitsyn and Sakharov could linger on for a very long time, with all the negative consequences we have mentioned occurring in one way or another. The factor of impunity would undoubtedly work to our disadvantage.

4. To minimize the negative consequences of our actions with respect to Solzhenitsyn and Sakharov, perhaps pertinent information should be prepared for the leadership of socialist countries and a number of fraternal parties.

5. Since the anti-Soviet campaign attacks many aspects of our social and political structure and the Soviet way of life, our propaganda should pay special attention to this: we should publish theoretical material explaining the policies of our state and the many facets of our experience in building a communist society more actively. We should explain the essence of the democratic transformations in our country and simultaneously, both directly and implicitly, expose the views of Solzhenitsyn and Sakharov as the outlook of people for whom the victories of socialism are alien and hostile. It also seems necessary to make wider use of various international forums and conferences to conduct an active attack and unmask the reactionary Western circles that are obstructing the normalization of the international situation.

Material of this kind should be more vigorously promoted not only in the Soviet press but also abroad, by using the opportunities available to TASS, Novosti, and the State Committee on Television and Radio. Perhaps it would be worthwhile to develop a unified plan of action on this issue, even to the point of issuing specific directives to particular employees of public organizations and state institutions.

In their most recent documents, in seeking to hide their anti-Soviet views and to attract the sympathy of various categories of the population, Sakharov and especially Solzhenitsyn have been attempting to speculate demagogically on such issues as the question of "the role of the Russian people in the Soviet state," "the plight of women under socialism," the legitimacy of the "military draft" in our country, and the protection of historic monuments (including the allegedly flawed reconstruction of Moscow). Hence it might be expedient for the mass media to draw proper attention to these issues.

6. The Committee for State Security should use its facilities to acquire and transmit (for purposes of propaganda and counterpropaganda) more documentary material that unmasks the following: links between reactionary forces obstructing détente and our adversary's special services; the instigation of various kinds of anti-Soviet campaigns by the intelligence services of the imperialist countries; and the connections of the renegades

of our society (such as Solzhenitsyn, Sakharov, and others) to intelligence services and anti-Soviet centers abroad. We ask that this be considered.

---

The right to emigrate was of particular importance to Sakharov. As he wrote to the U.S. Congress in September 1973, "If every nation is entitled to choose the political system under which it wishes to live, this is true all the more of every individual person. A country whose citizens are deprived of this minimal right is not free even if there were not a single citizen who would want to exercise that right."[77] By 1973, as a result of an international campaign to allow Soviet Jews to emigrate, the U.S. Congress was growing increasingly involved in the issue, and there was considerable support for an amendment to a trade bill (the Jackson-Vanik amendment) that made extension to the USSR of the lowest regular tariff rates—most favored nation status—dependent on the Soviets' willingness to permit freer emigration. In 1972 and 1973 60,000 Jews left the country, most of them for Israel. But the regime still prohibited many others from leaving, dismissing them from their jobs and even arresting some refuseniks in order to instill fear and anxiety in anyone who thought of applying for an exit visa. Sakharov supported the Jackson-Vanik amendment, lending his prestige to the one human rights issue that Congress could affect most directly. As the KGB learned, Solzhenitsyn did not agree with Sakharov's approach; for Solzhenitsyn, the right to emigrate should not be elevated above broader questions of freedom within the country. He believed that people should stay and continue to press the regime for greater freedom. Sakharov understood that for many people staying would result in great hardship.

## · DOCUMENT 63 ·

Tsvigun to Central Committee, September 18, 1973
Sakharov on the right to emigrate and the Jackson-Vanik amendment

---

The Committee for State Security reports that on September 17, 1973, Solzhenitsyn's wife invited Academician Sakharov and his wife to her apartment and had a two-hour conversation with them.

During the conversation, Sakharov was handed a letter from Solzheni-

---

77. "A Letter to the Congress of the United States," in Sakharov, *Sakharov Speaks*, 212.

tsyn commenting on Sakharov's provocative "Open Letter to the U.S. Congress," in which he raised the question of the right of all citizens desiring to change their country of residence to leave the Soviet Union freely.

Expressing Solzhenitsyn's view, his wife persistently argued the necessity for an additional appeal by Sakharov to world public opinion on a wider range of issues pertaining to the alleged lack of liberties in the Soviet Union. In her opinion, the issues raised in Sakharov's letter "nevertheless sound like a minor detail compared with the broad scope of today's issues. On one hand, these unquestionably are very important questions; on the other hand, they are derivative [from more basic issues]. If there were internal freedom, even a little, then the emigration issue would undoubtedly be resolved as a consequence. The freedom you seek is true (whereby each could go wherever he wants), but it should be the result of some kind of rights at home." Arguing in support of this view, she declared: " Last June, they issued an edict that denies seasonal workers the possibility of travel. This is real serfdom, which is becoming stronger and stronger."

Responding to Sakharov's objection that the Americans are afraid "to widen the issue beyond the Jewish problem," Solzhenitsyna stressed that, in any event, such a [broader] appeal by Sakharov will have a great propaganda effect: "The many thousands who have started putting two and two together, who are now paying attention and reading, will simply not do it at another time. And upon reading it, they will come to the conclusion that there really is no freedom here. That is simply much more terrible than the lack of freedom to emigrate. . . . This issue is petty compared to what Sakharov could say from the pedestal upon which he is now standing. There are also now forces in the Congress that pose the question more broadly, and reflect the new understanding that you and Sanya [Solzhenitsyn] have hammered into their brains."

Solzhenitsyna expressed the opinion that a possible increase in emigration from the USSR would be "a temporary tactical maneuver," just like, for example, the current "cessation of jamming."[78]

During the conversation, Sakharov, while generally sharing Solzhenitsyn's position, nonetheless indicated that such an approach is not expedient now. For all practical purposes, Sakharov retained his earlier point of view.

---

78. On September 11, 1973, the Soviet Union stopped jamming the broadcasts of the Voice of America. At the same time, the Voice of America began to present more music and less news. The dissidents came to believe that the Nixon administration changed the content of its programs as a gesture to the Kremlin; see *New York Times,* December 25, 1975, 42.

As part of its broad assault on the human rights movement, the regime was now considering more forceful and concrete measures for dealing with Sakharov and Solzhenitsyn, the two most heralded independent figures in the country.[79]

· DOCUMENT 64 ·

Chebrikov and Rudenko to Kosygin, September 28, 1973
Proposals on how to deal with Sakharov and Solzhenitsyn

———————

To: Comrade A. N. Kosygin

In accordance with your directive, we hereby present the draft report for the Central Committee of the CPSU (revised to take into account the exchange of opinion at the Commission meeting) and other materials on the matter of Sakharov and Solzhenitsyn.[80]

R. Rudenko
V. Chebrikov

[Memorandum] to the Central Committee—September 1973

In accordance with the instructions of the Politburo of September 17, we have examined the question of the anti-Soviet activity of Sakharov and Solzhenitsyn, which they have conducted for some years, but recently—under the conditions of détente—with particular fervor.

Sakharov and Solzhenitsyn have conclusively revealed themselves to be enemies of the socialist system. They have issued a whole series of statements against policies of the Communist Party and the Soviet state. In

79. Officials in the West were also paying close attention to the fates of Solzhenitsyn and Sakharov. On September 17 the U.S. Senate approved an amendment sponsored by Walter Mondale expressing the "sense of the Senate" in support of Sakharov, Solzhenitsyn, and others. The amendment called on President Nixon to impress upon the Soviet government the "grave concern" of the American people about conditions in the USSR; see *New York Times*, September 18, 1973, 11. A month later, on October 16, Premier Alexei Kosygin met with Danish Premier Anker Jorgensen and had to answer criticism on the Soviet handling of the Sakharov case; see *New York Times*, October 17, 1973, 18.

80. The supplementary materials consisted of extracts from several documents issued by Sakharov: "Progress, Coexistence, and Intellectual Freedom," June 1968; "Memorandum," March 1971; "Postscript to the Memorandum," July 1972; "Interview with Stenholm," May 1973; "Interview with Dillon," August 1973; and "Open Letter to the Congress of the United States," September 1973.

essence, they have united with reactionary circles of imperialist countries, and are acting in concert with their special services against the policies of the CPSU and the Soviet government, which are directed toward a relaxation of international tensions and peaceful coexistence among states.

During the period of August and September alone, Sakharov has conducted three press conferences in his apartment for foreign correspondents, given several interviews, and transmitted a number of statements to the foreign press, including an "Open letter to the U.S. Congress." In his statements and meetings with foreign correspondents, Sakharov persistently appeals to the West not to accept rapprochement with the USSR without "extracting from the Soviet leadership concessions" of an ideological and political nature. Sakharov portrays the Soviet way of life in a slanderous manner and attacks the state, political, and social systems of our country. (A report about materials on the hostile activity of Sakharov is appended.)

Exploiting his status and achievements, and relying on the assistance of his entourage and Western reactionary circles, Sakharov has come to believe that he can conduct his anti-Soviet activity with impunity.

There is evidence that Sakharov intends to continue to meet with representatives of the bourgeois press, slander our country, and induce Soviet citizens who share his views to participate in his hostile activities.

Having weighed all these factors and taking into account the international situation, we submit for consideration the following measures to terminate the hostile activity of Sakharov:

1. Direct the deputy chairman of the Council of Ministers of the USSR, Comrade V. A. Kirillin; the president of the Academy of Sciences of the USSR, Comrade M. V. Keldysh; and the director of the Lebedev Physics Institute, N. G. Basov, to invite Sakharov to the Academy of Sciences of the USSR and conduct an appropriate conversation with him. Sakharov should be told that the Soviet public is outraged by his behavior and that he should stop his antisocial activity and cease making anti-Soviet statements. Sakharov should be told that his circle contains people who are connected with the special services of Western countries and are paid for performing certain tasks (including the task of instigating statements by Sakharov himself). The situation is exacerbated by the fact that Sakharov, having started down the path of criminal actions, has stopped doing any science, and that the Physics Institute is paying him his salary for no reason. Depending on Sakharov's reaction, it could be intimated to him at the end of the conversation that one solution to the current situation would be for him to leave Moscow for one of the cities in the country with a special [security] regimen and engage in scientific work there.

2. Should the conversation with Comrades Kirillin, Keldysh, and Basov fail to produce positive results, direct Comrade R. A. Rudenko to summon Sakharov to the Office of the Procurator General of the USSR and, on the basis of documentary material about his hostile activity, explain to Sakharov once again that his actions are violating the laws of our country and that criminal charges should be initiated against him. However, we believe that Sakharov is able to reflect on his actions once again and to renounce making hostile statements. In this case, he could do useful work in our society. In the course of the conversation, obtain the appropriate signed agreement from Sakharov.

3. The next step could be to dismiss Sakharov from his position at the Lebedev Physics Institute (FIAN), where he is still listed as a senior research scientist.

4. If Sakharov still continues to engage in hostile activities, direct Comrade R. A. Rudenko to summon Sakharov a second time to the Office of the Procurator General of the USSR and inform him that he is being charged under Article 190–1 of the Criminal Code of the RSFSR. This article states: "Systematic oral dissemination of fabrications, known to be false, that defame the Soviet state and social order, or the fabrication and dissemination of works with such content in written, printed, or other forms, is punishable by deprivation of freedom for up to three years, or by corrective labor for up to one year, or by a fine of 100 rubles."

The Office of the Procurator General of the USSR should be instructed to conduct the investigation of the criminal case against Sakharov in an accelerated fashion, such that the case can, within a short period of time, be heard in the Supreme Court of the RSFSR. As punishment, Sakharov could be exiled to one of the cities under a special [security] regimen, where he would be given a comfortable apartment and work. His period of exile must preclude any contact with foreigners and the people in his current circle.

In pronouncing the sentence, the Supreme Court of the RSFSR should petition the Presidium of the Supreme Soviet of the USSR to revoke Sakharov's title of triple Hero of Socialist Labor and his government awards, and the Council of Ministers of the USSR should revoke his Lenin and State prizes.

5. The Commission also deems it necessary to rescind Sakharov's title of "academician" in the Academy of Sciences of the USSR, but to do this later (after the government's measures against Sakharov have been taken).

At the same time, direct the Department of Science in the Central Committee to take, jointly with the Presidium of the Academy of Sciences of the USSR, further steps to unmask Sakharov's criminal behavior before the scientific community.[81]

It should be kept in mind that implementation of the proposed measures against Sakharov and Solzhenitsyn may cause certain political problems. This action will lead to vigorous anti-Soviet outcries in the West; it may encounter less than full understanding in some fraternal parties and require additional explanations inside the country.

In the final analysis, however, measures against these individuals will be understood correctly and will not influence the implementation of major political initiatives of the Soviet state. As for the long-range impact on foreign affairs, the firmness displayed on these issues should have the positive effect of demonstrating yet again that any hopes of winning ideological concessions from the Soviet Union are groundless.

At the same time, in order to create more favorable conditions for implementing the proposed measures and ensuring that the public has a correct understanding of our measures, it is necessary to do the following:

1. Have departments of the Central Committee of the CPSU prepare information about Sakharov and Solzhenitsyn for the leaders of socialist countries, for certain fraternal parties, and for some international organizations, together with an explanation of our measures and of our position on this issue. They should also ensure that appropriate instructions are given to groups and delegations going abroad.

2. Direct the Ministry of Foreign Affairs of the USSR and the Committee for State Security of the Council of Ministers of the USSR to prepare and submit to the Central Committee of the CPSU proposals on instructions to the heads of Soviet establishments abroad in connection with the hostile activity of Sakharov and Solzhenitsyn. The purpose is to arm Soviet representatives abroad with the materials needed for active work to unmask any anti-Soviet commotion.

3. It would be expedient to intensify propaganda in our press to explain the policies of the CPSU and the Soviet government, the experience of building a communist society, and the essence of democratic transformations within the USSR. The media must also be more decisive in unmasking the slander of our system and Marxist ideology. In particular, we deem it necessary to publish, in the near future, detailed articles in the journal *Kommunist* and the newspaper *Pravda* that unmask the political machinations of Sakharov and Solzhenitsyn.

81. The photocopy in the Andrei Sakharov Archive (Harvard) has a deleted section equivalent to nine or ten lines.

Commission TASS, Novosti, and the State Committee on Television and Radio to prepare material that shows the political face of Sakharov and Solzhenitsyn and the character of their criminal activity and that explains our own position on these questions.

4. Have the Committee for State Security of the Council of Ministers of the USSR transmit to the appropriate organs on a regular basis, for use in propaganda and counterpropaganda activities, documentary material exposing the instigation by the special services of imperialist countries of anti-Soviet campaigns of various kinds and the links between these services and renegades like Solzhenitsyn and Sakharov. At the same time, intensify the work on the people around Sakharov so as to make for a healthier environment and prevent people with hostile views from uniting around him. Act more vigorously to keep foreign correspondents away from Sakharov and carry out a number of other operational measures.

### Resolution of the Central Committee
### "On the Question of Sakharov and Solzhenitsyn"

[It is resolved] to agree with the recommendations regarding this question as presented in the report by Comrades Kosygin, Suslov, Shelepin, Kuznetsov, Keldysh, Chebrikov, and Rudenko.

---

As the KGB continued its tight surveillance of Sakharov, it learned of his steadfast support for freer emigration, including the emigration of the country's ethnic minority of German origin. According to the KGB's report, he was also making harsher statements about Soviet history. If earlier he had regarded the Bolshevik revolution as inevitable, he was now prepared to denounce it altogether and even look upon the recent overthrow of Salvador Allende in Chile by a military junta as the kind of action that could have saved Russia in 1917.

### · DOCUMENT 65 ·

Andropov to Central Committee, October 19, 1973
Sakharov is growing harsher in his criticism

---

The Committee for State Security reports that A. D. Sakharov and A. I. Solzhenitsyn, despite preventive measures already taken, continue to discredit the foreign policy of the Soviet state through their provocative conduct. They are strengthening their contacts with foreigners and becoming more active in transmitting slanderous statements.

Recently Sakharov has been acting as an ardent defender of Israel's aggressive policies. He has publicly accused the Soviet Union and other socialist countries of "one-sided support of the Arab states" and demands that his appeals in support of Israel receive extensive publicity.

Bourgeois propaganda organs are commenting extensively on Sakharov's pro-Israel statements. They are trying to incite American Zionists to voice solidarity with him; they are making it clear to Sakharov that, for their part, they are ready to promote his "mission" in the Soviet Union. As Sakharov's associate Glazov (who recently emigrated to the U.S.) told him over the telephone: "The Jews of America are in fact the only large segment of the population here who understand the situation in the Soviet Union and are ready to respond to it. These people are actually interested not only in the Jewish problem, as is often the case, but also in broader issues. As you know, they have a very special attitude toward you in particular."

In a conversation with [Richard von] Weizsäcker (deputy chairman of the CDU/CSU in the West German Bundestag) last September, Sakharov asked for help in resolving the problem of emigration for Soviet citizens of German nationality to the Federal Republic of Germany. In answer to questions by a Weizsäcker aide about the significance of the Great October Socialist Revolution for our country, Sakharov declared: "I think that history might have developed more favorably without the October Revolution."

In this conversation Sakharov expressed approval of the American Congress's resolution on Jewish emigration from the Soviet Union: "This is a very good resolution. It does not deal with just Israel, but with all questions of leaving the country. It should also concern Germans." He expressed the hope that the Bundestag will adopt a similar resolution.

Sakharov persists in making slanderous statements about the use of psychiatric hospitals in our country to punish "dissidents." He systematically supplies the West with information to prove his view. The English psychiatrist Louer[82] informed Sakharov about a forthcoming conference of English psychiatrists. In one of their telephone conversations, he read out the main propositions and suggested that Sakharov comment on them in his next appeal to the world community devoted to this subject.

Heeding Louer's request, Sakharov and other members of the so-called

---

82. Dr. Gerard Low-Beer. The issue of psychiatric abuse of political prisoners became increasingly acute as Andropov and his colleagues came to rely on this measure; see details in Vladimir Bukovskii, *Moskovskii protsess* (Moscow, 1996), 144–61.

"Human Rights Committee" (Shafarevich and Podyapolsky) composed and passed on to the West a statement on the alleged misuse of psychiatric hospitals in our country for political purposes.

Characteristically, Sakharov now makes more frequent anti-Soviet attacks in his meetings with Soviet citizens. For example, in his conversation with Nekrasov (a Kiev writer), Sakharov made the following remark about an appeal to the Chilean military junta that he signed: "In this letter I did not defend the junta. I am defending it at this table. The junta is a Kornilov revolt, just one that succeeded. If Kornilov had succeeded, he would have shot 500 Bolsheviks. Or 10,000. And he would have saved 40 million persons destroyed by the Bolsheviks. But Kornilov's revolt failed, unfortunately."

Since Sakharov and Solzhenitsyn are not only continuing their provocative activity but also even more actively offering their services to reactionary imperialist and especially Zionist circles, we think it expedient to examine the recommendations made by Comrade Kosygin's Commission, taking into account the considerations contained in the Memorandum of the Committee for State Security no. 2239-A dated September 17.

Portrait of Andrei Sakharov by Yousuf Karsh, 1989 (© Yousuf Karsh, published by permission of The Estate of Yousuf Karsh)

Portrait of Andrei Sakharov and Elena Bonner by Yousuf Karsh, 1989
(© Yousuf Karsh, published by permission of The Estate of Yousuf Karsh)

Bonner and Sakharov in Moscow, 1973 (© Stern Magazine, published by permission of Syndication Picture Press, Hamburg)

Bonner, Sakharov, Pavel Litvinov, and Dina Kaminskaya in Moscow on the eve of Litvinov's departure from the Soviet Union, March 1974 (The Andrei Sakharov Archive)

Mikhail Litvinov, Bonner, Viktor Nekrasov, and Lev Kopelev bid bon voyage to Pavel Litvinov, March 1974 (The Andrei Sakharov Archive)

Bonner leaves Moscow for Italy, August 1975 (The Andrei Sakharov Archive)

Sakharov at an improvised press conference in the Moscow apartment of Yuri Tuvim after the announcement of the 1975 Nobel Peace Prize, October 9, 1975 (The Andrei Sakharov Archive)

A gathering of human rights activists in Moscow. Seated, left to right: Naum Meiman, Sofia Kalistratova, Pyotr Grigorenko, Zinaida Grigorenko, Natalya Velikanova, Father Sergei Zheludkov, and Sakharov. On the floor: Genrikh Altunyan and Alexander Podrabinek. The man standing at the left is unidentified. (The Andrei Sakharov Archive)

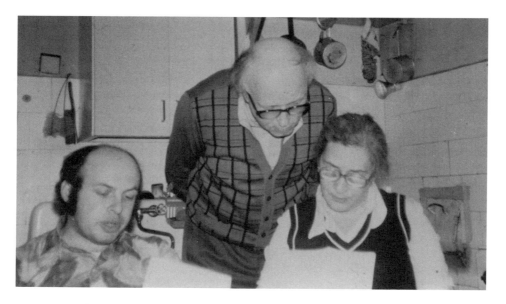

Anatoly Shcharansky (today Natan Sharansky) with Bonner and Sakharov as they work on a report for the Moscow Helsinki Watch Group, October 1976 (The Andrei Sakharov Archive)

A refusenik scientific seminar, Moscow, 1976. Seated in front: Elias Essas, Sakharov, Yakov Alpert, Veniamin Fain (Courtesy Frayerman)

Bonner, Sakharov, Lev Kopelev, and Raisa Orlova in Sukhumi, Georgia, 1978 (The Andrei Sakharov Archive)

Sakharov during the trial of Anatoly
Shcharansky in Moscow, June 1978
(© Vladimir Sichov, published by
permission of Sipa Press)

Andrei Sakharov and Elena
Bonner, *The New York Review
of Books,* April 12, 1984
(© David Levine)

THE OTHER AGGRESSION

© 1980 by Herblock in
*The Washington Post*

Sakharov and Bonner in Gorky, January 1980 (The Andrei Sakharov Archive)

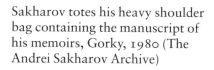

Sakharov totes his heavy shoulder bag containing the manuscript of his memoirs, Gorky, 1980 (The Andrei Sakharov Archive)

Sakharov and Liza Alexeyeva, Gorky, 1980 (The Andrei Sakharov Archive)

Sakharov and Bonner in Gorky after his long hunger strike in 1984 (The Andrei Sakharov Archive)

Sakharov and Edward Teller at the Ethics and Public Policy Center dinner,
Washington, DC, November 16, 1988 (© The Ethics and Public Policy
Center, by permission of The Ethics and Public Policy Center)

Bonner by the bier of Sakharov, Moscow, December 17, 1989
(© L. Sherstennikov)

Muscovites crowd the streets for a glimpse of Sakharov's funeral procession, December 18, 1989 (© The Yomiuri Shimbun, published by permission of The Yomiuri Shimbun)

Tatiana Yankelevich, Boris Yeltsin, and Lech Walesa with Bonner after Sakharov's funeral (The Andrei Sakharov Archive)

Andrei Sakharov in front of his apartment building on Chkalov Street,
Moscow, June 1987 (© Richard Sobol)

# CHAPTER THREE

# Counterattack

## Disorganizing the Opposition

THE SUMMER AND FALL OF 1973 marked the first sustained crisis of the human rights movement. After the arrest of Pyotr Yakir and Viktor Krasin in 1972, the regime was able to compel both men to cooperate, and more than two hundred other people were then interrogated. Publication of *A Chronicle of Current Events* was suspended in the fall of 1972 and did not resume until May 1974. Yakir even tried to persuade Sakharov to stop his dissident activities, urging him not to allow his name to be used, as Yakir now claimed his had been used, "for purposes of propaganda against our homeland."[1] Viktor Krasin also tried to dissuade his former colleagues, addressing a letter to his "friends who are free" to warn them that the state had the right to defend itself. The *Chronicle* summarized his message: "The defeat of the 'Democratic Movement' should be acknowledged. The cessation of all opposition activity is not sufficient to save people from repressions. The authorities require guarantees, and these guarantees can be assured only by all-round cooperation with the investigation. Krasin calls upon people to overcome the psychological barrier and testify freely, not only about their own activities but also about those of others."[2]

1. Yakir's letter to Sakharov, dated April 3, 1973, was published in *Chronicle of Human Rights in the USSR*, no. 2 (New York, April–May 1973), 11–12.
2. *Chronicle of Current Events*, no. 28 (December 31, 1972), 67 (Amnesty International ed., 1975).

Yakir and Krasin went on trial on August 27, 1973, for "anti-Soviet agitation and propaganda." One witness, the notorious psychiatrist Andrei Snezhnevsky, gave testimony that unintentionally confirmed the effectiveness of the dissidents' approach. Snezhnevsky informed the court that at international conferences he had been embarrassed by reports in the *Chronicle* that healthy people were confined in Soviet mental hospitals because of their political ideas or dissident activity. Such claims, he assured the court, were unfounded. A week after their trial and conviction, Yakir and Krasin appeared at a news conference with foreign journalists and claimed, as they had done in court, that material in the *Chronicle* was "libelous." Part of the news conference was broadcast over Soviet television. One of the viewers was General Pyotr Grigorenko; he was watching from a mental hospital in Chernyakhovsk.

In the short term, the KGB achieved a tactical victory. The network of active dissidents was severely disrupted. Many were intimidated into silence, into leaving the country, even into betraying themselves and their friends.

One activist was overcome altogether. Ilya Gabai, a respected teacher and poet, was released from a labor camp in May 1972 after serving three years for defending the Crimean Tatars. After Yakir's arrest, Gabai was among those summoned for repeated interrogations. He refused to cooperate, but Yakir's betrayal demoralized him; they had been close friends for many years. On October 20, 1973, Gabai committed suicide by jumping from the balcony of his apartment.

But if the KGB could feel proud of its crackdown, the Party leadership had reason to be dissatisfied. As many of the following documents show, contacts between human rights activists and the Western public proliferated. Moreover, the KGB had a fundamentally flawed understanding of what Sakharov and his fellow activists were up to. Andropov and the KGB represented the human rights movement to the Politburo as a kind of political opposition, a political movement that was too dangerous to recognize. But the human rights movement was not primarily a political phenomenon. It was a loosely organized movement of activists who were taking a stand, each in his or her own way, against lies and oppression. They might have to "lie low for a time," as Solzhenitsyn advised Sakharov to do that fall, but sooner or later, as long as the regime persisted in carrying out repression, dissidents such as Sakharov would continue to stand up to the regime.

At the same time, foreign developments intruded on the lives of Sakharov and his dissident colleagues. In October 1973 the Yom Kippur War in the Middle East brought a sense of crisis throughout the world. Sakharov "made a statement calling for a peaceful settlement." About a week later, "two men who looked like Arabs" rang his doorbell. Sakharov let them in and they immediately announced that they were from "the Black September group" and accused him of publishing "a statement damaging to the Arab cause." When Sakharov and Bonner made clear they would not "write or sign anything under duress," their visitors reminded them of their children and grandchildren, an outright threat that Sakharov could not ignore.[3] Attempts to intimidate them were later repeated.

After Stalin's death in 1953, the regime gradually opened the country to more foreign visitors. In 1957, at the World Youth Festival in Moscow, the presence of thousands of relaxed, carefree young people from the West made a profound impression on Soviet students, who were not accustomed to this cultural style. The regime miscalculated; it did not anticipate how attractive Western clothing, art, and music would be to Soviet youth.

Now in 1973, with the convening of the World Congress of Peace-Loving Forces for the first and only time in the Soviet Union (the organization had always been a mostly pro-Soviet affair, no matter where its meetings were held), the regime had to contend with Western activists who were eager to come to Moscow and show their solidarity with the dissidents. It was around the time of this conference that Sakharov was threatened by people claiming to represent Black September; perhaps they embodied Andropov's stated intention to "detect and deter subversive actions." But his reports to the Politburo made no reference to this harassment. The KGB's operational reports were probably more candid.

## · DOCUMENT 66 ·

Andropov to Central Committee, October 21, 1973
The World Congress of Peace-Loving Forces comes to Moscow

At the initiative of the World Council for Peace and other international organizations, the World Congress of Peace-Loving Forces will begin its work in Moscow on October 25.

3. Andrei Sakharov, *Memoirs* (New York, 1990), 392.

Since this forum will have an extremely broad range of representation and will include both supporters of détente and reactionaries who oppose peaceful coexistence, the Congress has attracted the close attention of intelligence agencies, the enemy's ideological centers, and foreign organizations. They are making an effort to include their agents and emissaries in international and state delegations, with the intention of using the platform of the Congress . . . to issue demagogic statements and make hostile attacks on the Soviet state. . . .

For example, representatives of the American "Committee for Responsible Nuclear Policy" intend to speak in defense of Sakharov and Solzhenitsyn at the Congress. American delegates of the "War Resisters League" want to use the Congress platform to demand the "release of political prisoners" who allegedly number 15,000 in the USSR. Such organizations as "Amnesty for Dissenters," "Student Struggle for Soviet Jewry," "National Conference on Soviet Jewry," and others are involved in drawing up a list of prisoners. The organization "Amnesty International," known for its hostile activities, as well as the "International Association of Antiwar Activists," the "International Conference for Disarmament and Peace," and the "League for the Rights of Man" are attempting to put the question of "persecution of dissenters" on the agenda of the Congress. A parliamentary group of the Socialist Party of the cantonal parliament in Geneva intends to make an attempt to have the Congress discuss "freedom of the press and literature in the USSR."

. . . Delegations are preparing various "addresses," "petitions," and "demands" that they intend to circulate in Moscow among Congress participants and Soviet citizens.

Information has been obtained that staff members of the enemy's intelligence agencies and subversive ideological centers will come to Moscow during the time of the Congress's work.

Information has also been received that on the eve of the Congress's opening, extremist elements (from the ranks of ethnic Germans and Jews desiring to emigrate, as well as Crimean Tatar autonomists) are intensifying their activity. In particular, they are preparing various slanderous documents for transmission to foreign guests and are planning antisocial actions during the Congress.

The Committee for State Security realizes that the irresponsible demagogic statements and provocations of foreign delegates to the Congress may evoke increased activity on the part of antisocial and hostile elements among Soviet citizens. Consequently, it intends to take steps to contain the harmful influence of foreigners. At the same time, Soviet citizens known for their antisocial and hostile orientation are being kept under close surveillance in order to prevent possible undesirable excesses on their part. . . .

One of the delegates to the World Congress of Peace-Loving Forces was a Russian-speaking Danish pastor named Jörgen Laursen Vig, who visited with Sakharov. Sakharov struck a highly pessimistic tone with his visitor, denouncing the USSR as the principal threat to world peace and expressing deep anxiety over the "psychology of the masses." This was a familiar refrain in Russian intellectual and political history, where revolutionaries and reformers had run aground seeking support from the peasants. If the quoted material is accurate, it helps to explain why Sakharov placed so much emphasis on pressure from abroad to reform the Soviet system.

· DOCUMENT 67 ·

Andropov to Central Committee, November 11, 1973
Sakharov meets with a foreign delegate to the World Congress
of Peace-Loving Forces

. . . Realizing that he cannot find support for his anticommunist conceptions in the Soviet Union, Sakharov is attempting to advertise them through the bourgeois propaganda machine and is consequently expanding his contacts with foreigners. He systematically provides them with provocative declarations, appeals, and protests; he also gives them interviews in the same vein.

Sakharov expressed his hostile views in the most concentrated form during discussions with some participants in the World Congress of Peace-Loving Forces when it met in Moscow. Thus, during a meeting with the theologian Vig (a member of the Danish delegation),[4] Sakharov asserted: "Our state, it seems to me, is the most important source of tensions in the world. The Soviet system is not among the progressive forces." In his opinion, the only reason why a new world war has thus far not broken out is that the Soviet Union is not sufficiently powerful to fight the great powers.

Sakharov declared that "if the Soviet Union were ten times more powerful, it would start a third world war. If we were strong, we would strive for world domination."

4. Vig wrote a report on his conversations with Sakharov. His account differs markedly from Andropov's; see Andrei Sakharov Archive (Harvard), folder S.I.1.34.01.

In reply to Vig's question about what needs to be done to make the struggle for peace more effective, Sakharov responded: "Liquidate, diminish the main threat to peace around the world—i.e., the Soviet system."[5]

Attempting to persuade his interlocutor about the need to make world public opinion cognizant of the "truth" about our country, Sakharov said: "It seems to me that one should tell about everything that happened here in the past, and tell what our country really represents. One need not fear that this is anti-Soviet propaganda. Above all, one needs to know the truth. And everyone should understand the internal processes that are transpiring in our country, their course, and their connection with economic and political structures. These interrelationships are very important; one needs to analyze all this. For example, one should do this as [Milovan] Djilas did earlier in his book *The New Class*. . . . Our horrific history has done something terrible to the psychology of the masses. The psychology of our masses is such that it is difficult to imagine anything good for this country in the immediate future. The terrible time of the 1930s has changed the psychology of people. It seems to me that our state, given this psychology and these conditions, has the worst conditions of life, [worse] than all other countries. . . . When we read anything about German life during the fascist period, we also recognize much that is in common. That is true too of mass psychology. We often say that we have psychological fascism."

Sakharov drew Vig's attention to alleged facts about the persecution of believers: "I do not regard myself as a believer, but I have a positive attitude toward religion. . . . You know, for example, what has been done to religion in Russia from the first years of the revolution to the present day. How many people have suffered for this? Now too it is very bad. Perhaps there were years when it was simply horrible. And now, apparently, half of the men and women in the camps and [psychiatric] hospitals are believers. . . . Our camps apparently have the largest number of prisoners, more than in other European countries."

In response to Vig's question about what the West should demand, Sakharov said: "Two things: political amnesty and the freedom to emigrate. . . . This is now a servile land. But if it becomes possible to leave, it will have to become free."

With respect to the causes of the emergence of the current crisis in the

5. Pastor Vig (b. 1918) spoke Russian; his conversation with Sakharov took place without interpreters. KGB reports never make clear in what language a conversation took place, who was translating, or whether it was using a transcript of the tapes in the original language or a translation recorded at the time.

Middle East, Sakharov defended the position of Israel and accused the Soviet Union of giving one-sided support to the Arab states and of direct collaboration in instigating a military conflict. . . .

The first volume of Solzhenitsyn's monumental account of Stalin's labor camp system, *The Gulag Archipelago,* was published in Paris at the end of December. The regime responded with an orchestrated public campaign of threats and denunciations. Sakharov was among the people, in the West and inside the Soviet Union, who spoke up in Solzhenitsyn's defense. In two interviews and in written statements he applauded Solzhenitsyn for challenging the regime with the truth. For Sakharov, *The Gulag Archipelago* was "a stone that will finally shatter the wall dividing mankind. It is a wall of mistrust and lack of understanding created by lies, wickedness, cowardice, and stupidity."[6]

For several months the regime had linked Sakharov and Solzhenitsyn together. So it was not surprising that when otherwise ordinary citizens began distributing appeals, they called on people to defend both men, although at the moment it was Solzhenitsyn's head that was on the block. A few weeks after this report was filed, the KGB identified the miscreants as a Leningrad couple named Verdi. When Tsvigun reported on the investigation on February 25, he made a point of revealing that their parents had been arrested under Stalin.

## · DOCUMENT 73 ·

Andropov to Central Committee, January 29, 1974
Leaflets in support of Alexander Solzhenitsyn and Andrei Sakharov

On January 26, 1974, in the subway stations and public parks in Leningrad, unidentified persons distributed politically harmful leaflets calling for people to speak out in defense of Solzhenitsyn and Sakharov. The proclamations were drawn by hand and bore the signature "Yemelia." They had been duplicated on a photocopying machine. Two hundred thirty-five copies were confiscated at the distribution points. The Committee for State Security has taken active measures to find the people who wrote and distributed the leaflets.

6. Quoted in Michael Scammell, *Solzhenitsyn: A Biography* (New York, 1984), 832.

With Solzhenitsyn in the West, Andropov saw an immediate need to reevaluate the regime's treatment of Sakharov, so he proposed to suspend public statements against him for up to half a year. He also wanted to clarify if Sakharov could realistically be said to know state secrets; almost six years had passed since he had last worked on weapons development. At this point, it is hard to know if Andropov was considering arresting Sakharov, expelling him, or taking even more drastic measures.

·  DOCUMENT 77  ·

Andropov to Central Committee, March 7, 1974
Proposals on how to handle Sakharov

The intelligence services and propaganda agencies of the United States have begun to conduct yet another premeditated anti-Soviet action, announcing the publication of a book of articles titled "Sakharov in the Fight for Peace."[7] The book contains libelous and biased "letters," "appeals," and "declarations" by Sakharov between 1970 and 1973, as well as the essay "Progress, Coexistence, and Intellectual Freedom" (which the West has repeatedly and actively used for ideological sabotage against the USSR and other socialist countries). At the request of the publishers, in December 1973 Sakharov wrote and illegally sent abroad a preface for this book (a copy is enclosed), which contains libelous fabrications about Soviet life and flagrant attacks on the domestic and foreign policy of the Soviet state. . . .

Based on our study of the West's reaction to the measures taken against Solzhenitsyn and the enemy's possible actions with respect to Sakharov, we think it advisable to make no public statements against Sakharov for the next five or six months. This may create the impression that Sakharov is deprived of the opportunity to coordinate his hostile activities with Solzhenitsyn, and that he no longer represents a particular threat to Soviet society.

Because Sakharov is in constant contact with foreigners and because some of them express interest in his past scientific activity, we deem it useful to create a special commission to determine whether the information

---

7. The report is referring to Andrei Sakharov, *Sakharov Speaks,* trans. and ed. Harrison E. Salisbury (New York, 1974).

he obtained during his work in the Ministry of Medium Machine Building still constitutes a state secret.

Sakharov grew increasingly concerned about the mistreatment of political prisoners in Soviet labor camps and prisons. By declaring a hunger strike, he hoped to draw attention to their plight. The KGB assured the Party it would intervene if the hunger strike threatened Sakharov's health. Four months later, on October 30, Sakharov would give a press conference to mark Political Prisoners Day.[8]

· DOCUMENT 80 ·

Andropov to Central Committee, July 1, 1974
Sakharov declares a hunger strike in support of Vladimir Bukovsky
and other political prisoners

Recently Academician Sakharov drafted and sent to the West about ten letters and statements that describe the internal situation in our country in libelous terms and call upon the world community to speak out openly against continuing violations of civil rights allegedly occurring in the Soviet Union. Sakharov indulges in similar unfounded speculation in conversations with foreign correspondents whom he quite frequently invites to his apartment.

On June 28, Sakharov organized another "meeting" with foreign correspondents at his apartment and handed them a statement in which he announced a hunger strike "as a sign of protest against illegal and cruel repression of political prisoners" and in particular Bukovsky (convicted of anti-Soviet activities). In answer to a question as to how long he intended to fast, Sakharov replied that this would depend on "the reaction of the Soviet authorities" to his statement. On June 29 it was established that Sakharov's "hunger strike" is primarily symbolic in character, since he is taking glucose and drinking juices and mineral water.

The Committee for State Security is taking measures to contain the effects of Sakharov's antisocial behavior. In case the hunger strike becomes dangerous to Sakharov's health (this, according to doctors, may occur in ten to twelve days), he will be hospitalized and force-fed.

8. This was the beginning of the tradition of marking October 30 as Political Prisoners Day in the USSR. Prisoners in Mordovia and Perm reportedly initiated this idea with the intention of holding hunger strikes on that date; see *Chronicle of Current Events*, no. 33 (Amnesty International ed., 1976), 108–9.

### · DOCUMENT 83 ·

Andropov to Central Committee, October 10, 1974
Elena Bonner invited to Italy for medical treatment

---

The Committee for State Security reports that in September invitations to come to Italy for medical treatment were sent to Academician Sakharov's wife, Bonner. Bonner has long suffered from cataracts. She was treated for this condition in a hospital, but without positive results.[9] She told an acquaintance[10] living in Italy about this, and that led to the invitation. . . .

---

### · DOCUMENT 85 ·

Andropov to Central Committee, November 19, 1974
Sakharov's contacts with the U.S. embassy

---

Sakharov is known to have submitted, in 1973, the documents of the children of his second wife, Bonner, to the Visas and Registrations Department of the Main Administration of Internal Affairs of the Moscow City Executive Committee, with a request to authorize their trip to the USA (reported to the Central Committee of the CPSU on April 12, 1973).

On October 22, Sakharov sent a letter to the U.S. ambassador in the Soviet Union, asking him to appeal to Kissinger regarding the trip for Bonner's children to the USA.

On November 13 an employee of the U.S. embassy visited Sakharov in his apartment and handed him an invitation to visit the ambassador. Later that same day Sakharov called the embassy and said that he was ready to meet the ambassador on November 14 or 15. Sakharov was told that the consul would receive him on November 21.

In the opinion of the Committee for State Security, the Ministry of Foreign Affairs must apprise the U.S. ambassador to the Soviet Union that contacts between the American embassy and Sakharov will be viewed negatively by the Soviet side and will be regarded as a step contradictory to the

---

9. Notwithstanding the official Soviet line that Bonner had access to world-class medical treatment, Andropov here concedes that her treatment in the USSR did not bring "positive results."

10. Nina Harkevich, a physician and professor at the Accademia dell' Arte in Florence; the declassified copy deleted her name.

interests of the further development of Soviet-American ties and contacts. Sakharov has become notorious for his disloyal attitude toward state organs and for his regular participation in antisocial actions, which are intended to denigrate Soviet reality and to damage relations between the Soviet Union and other countries, including the United States of America. . . .

As concern about Sakharov's behavior continued, Andropov sought to demonstrate growing evidence of official American involvement in attempts to organize a foreign trip for members of his family. With the backing of the Ministry of Foreign Affairs, Andropov proposed to lodge a stern protest with the U.S. embassy about "inappropriate contacts" with Sakharov.

· DOCUMENT 87 ·

Andropov to Central Committee, January 11, 1975
Continuing concern over Sakharov's contacts with American officials

In accordance with an authorization (based on the memorandum sent to the Central Committee on November 19, 1974), the Ministry of Foreign Affairs of the USSR issued a verbal note to the American chargé d'affaires in the USSR about the undesirability of embassy personnel maintaining contacts with Sakharov. Notwithstanding this, that same day Sakharov and Bonner's daughter and son-in-law were received at the American embassy, where they remained for thirty minutes.

From the materials obtained by the Committee for State Security, it is apparent that Sakharov is satisfied with the meeting and especially with the letter the Americans gave him for Bonner's daughter and son-in-law. The letter contains the following text:

"Secretary of State Kissinger asks me to inform you that the State Department was recently in contact with Dr. Jerome Wiesner, president of the Massachusetts Institute of Technology, and that Dr. Wiesner fully understands your situation. Dr. Wiesner has again expressed the hope that you will nevertheless be able to come to the Massachusetts Institute of Technology. The embassy has already received instructions to discuss with competent Soviet authorities your desire to go to the Institute. Please inform the embassy of any change in the status of your application.
Sincerely yours,
Leonard Williams, U.S. Consul

The text of the letter, in our opinion, shows that the Americans are interested in maintaining contacts with Sakharov. This position of the embassy suits Sakharov. Despite the fact that the Office of Visas and Registrations of the Main Administration of Internal Affairs of the Moscow City Executive Committee has refused to authorize Bonner's daughter and son-in-law to go to the USA to study, Sakharov continues his attempts to secure a favorable decision on this question. For this purpose, on December 23, 1974, Sakharov (together with Bonner's daughter and son-in-law) again visited the American embassy, where the consul, Williams, received him. Sakharov informed Williams that Bonner's daughter and son-in-law had been denied permission to go to the USA. He received assurance that the Americans share his concern in this matter and are continuing to assist in their efforts to arrange their trip to the USA.

The Committee for State Security proposes that the Ministry of Foreign Affairs of the USSR once more invite a representative from the U.S. embassy and draw his attention to the inappropriateness of contacts between the embassy and Sakharov. It should be emphasized that the Soviet side shall regard the continuation of such contacts as inciting Sakharov to commit hostile acts against the Soviet Union.

The draft of this oral statement to the U.S. embassy is attached. It has been approved by the Ministry of Foreign Affairs of the USSR (comrade V. V. Kuznetsov). We hereby request approval.

Appendix: Draft of the Oral Statement to the U.S. Embassy in Moscow

The contacts between the U.S. embassy and A. D. Sakharov were discussed in a recent conversation with representatives of the embassy. In the words of the representatives of the embassy, the subject of these contacts is the appeal by "Sakharov's [sic] children—Tatiana Semyonova and her husband Yankelevich—for assistance in arranging their travel to the USA for study. It has become known that at the end of December 1974 Sakharov once again visited the U.S. embassy.

In this regard, the attention of the embassy is drawn to the fact that, insofar as Semyonova and Yankelevich are adults and are capable of deciding their fate on their own, the embassy has not the slightest grounds for entering into contact with Sakharov on this question. This is all the more true if one takes into account the fact that Sakharov has absolutely no blood relationship to Semyonova and Yankelevich.

The Soviet side will regard the continuation of inappropriate contacts with Sakharov on this question as inciting Sakharov to commit hostile acts against the Soviet Union. The Ministry hopes that the American side will give due attention to this notice.

---

· DOCUMENT 88 ·

Andropov to Central Committee, February 27, 1975
Invitations to Elena Bonner for medical treatment in Europe

---

E. G. Bonner, the wife of Academician Sakharov, continues to receive various kinds of invitations from foreign citizens to go abroad for medical consultations and treatment. For example, in January 1975, Nisel, an employee of an eye clinic in Bern (Switzerland), wrote to Bonner: "Dear Mrs. Sakharov: Mr. Foss has asked me to invite you for a consultation in connection with your eye disease and, if necessary, to admit you to our clinic for an operation. Please come for an examination on February 14, 1975."

At the beginning of February, the Swiss ambassador in the USSR, R. Fessler, sent Bonner a letter in which he wrote the following: "According to the Evangelical-Reform State Church of the Canton of Zurich, you have been invited for medical treatment in Switzerland. The Embassy therefore has the right to issue you an entry visa. Please send us your passport and complete the enclosed application."

The heightened activity surrounding Bonner's trip abroad shows that certain circles in the West are hoping thereby to rekindle interest in the "onerous" situation of Bonner and Sakharov and to exploit this circumstance in the next wave of propaganda. At the same time, an attempt is also apparently being made to sound out the attitude of competent Soviet organs toward Sakharov and our reaction to his public statements.

Taking into account the fact that Bonner has applied for an exit visa to Italy in November 1974 and that her trip abroad is undesirable, the Committee for State Security deems it appropriate to inform Bonner (through the Office of Visas and Registrations) that her request for an exist visa is denied. The Office of Visas and Registrations will also explain that she can invite a foreign specialist to come to the USSR for a consultation. . . .

---

## · DOCUMENT 89 ·

Andropov to Central Committee, March 29, 1975
Sakharov insists on his wife's right to seek medical treatment in the West

---

The Committee for State Security of the USSR Council of Ministers reported to the Central Committee of the CPSU (no. 463-A on February 27, 1975) regarding the request of Sakharov's wife Bonner to go to Italy for medical treatment.

In accordance with the authorization granted on March 24, 1975, Bonner . . . was informed that her request for an exit visa for travel abroad has been denied. . . . Bonner and Sakharov declared that the issue was not so much treatment as Bonner's departure on the basis of a private invitation to Italy. They categorically demand [that the visa be issued].

The same day Sakharov, at Bonner's initiative, sent a provocative letter to the president of the USSR Academy of Sciences, Comrade Keldysh (a copy of the letter is attached).

. . . In our opinion, the escapade surrounding Bonner's trip to Italy is another provocation of certain circles in the West, which are seeking to use Sakharov's antisocial activity for their own ends.

To: President of the USSR Academy of Sciences,
Academician M. V. Keldysh

Dear Mstislav Vsevolodovich:

A year and a half ago, in response to a declaration by the president of the National Academy of the U.S., Dr. Handler, you assured the world community that "not a hair will fall off the head of Academician Sakharov." In the course of the same year and a half, my family has been subjected to every kind of harassment. But this is not what forces me to remind you of your words. My wife, Elena Bonner, was at the front for four years of war. She is an invalid (grade 2) of the Great Patriotic War. For thirty years she has been suffering from a difficult and complicated eye disease as a result of a concussion. One year ago the disease entered a more acute phase and she is now in danger of complete blindness. In spite of her doctors' high qualifications and treatment, because of a number of circumstances (associated with me and my activity) we do not have any hope of effective help in the USSR. Last August the Italian Union of Ophthalmologists sent a letter to my wife inviting her to come to Italy for treatment at an eye clinic with all the resources of world medicine. The invitation from the doctors was supported by a personal invitation from our old friend Nina Harkevich, who lives in Italy. The letters with invitations wandered about for some two months and were delivered only after a stir was raised in the Italian press.

On October 27, 1974, my wife filed an application for permission to travel abroad. Five months passed. Yesterday, March 24, 1975, the deputy director of the Moscow Office of Visas and Registrations, V. T. Zolotukhin, informed us that my wife had been denied permission. I consider this unfounded denial to be an instance of persecution directed at me for my public activity. Knowing your influence in the Central Committee of the CPSU and in other ruling circles and knowing that you are in charge of scientific and international contacts, I request your assistance in reaching a positive solution to this problem. For the last several months, my wife's vision has been rapidly and irreversibly deteriorating. I ask you to intercede as soon as possible and inform me of the results. If, in the next few days, my wife does not receive permission for the trip, I will be forced to take measures that, under other circumstances, I would prefer to refrain from taking. I will appeal to the world scientific community, and in particular to the president of the U.S. National Academy of Sciences, Dr. Handler, with an open letter, which will urge scientists to act decisively against the persecution of their colleague and to use all means of pressure at their disposal, including a scientific boycott. I will appeal to the veterans of the Second World War around the world and ask for their support. I hope that in the year of the thirtieth anniversary of the war's conclusion and in the International Year of Women, this defense will be effective. I will raise the question of my traveling together with my wife, believing that thereby the trip will receive the strongest international support. I will also find other means to attract international attention to the problem that is now most important to me personally. I will also be forced to publish this letter of mine addressed to you.

Respectfully yours,

A. D. Sakharov
March 25, 1975

·  **DOCUMENT 92**  ·

Andropov to Central Committee, April 30, 1975
On the right to leave one's country

On April 17 of this year, at the request of the organizers of the forth-coming meeting of the so-called "National Conference in Defense of So-

viet Jewry" (to be held on May 5, 1975, in Washington, D.C.), Sakharov
prepared the following statement:

I am grateful for the opportunity to speak at this meeting. The problem of Jewish emigration from the USSR to Israel, which is of special
concern for all present here, is extremely important for many reasons.
It is important for people who leave the country, often constituting the
central event in their life. For the Jewish nation in a broad sense, Jewish emigration to Israel is one of the most significant phenomena in the
many millennia of the tragic history of the Jews. Each case of unfounded denial of permission to emigrate, persecution, repression,
provocation, and conviction means a great human misfortune. It is
very important for the world community to pay attention to each
such instance—such as the "Leningrad airplane case" of Kuznetsov,
Dymshits, Murzhenko, Fyodorov, Altman, Mendelevich, the Zalmanson brothers, Penson; the provocative trials of Khantsis, Feldman,
Shtern, Nashpits, Tsitlyonok; and the fate of the "refuseniks" Davidovich, Slepak, and others.

I would now like to discuss some other questions of general significance. Soviet authorities do not overtly challenge the right of free
choice for one's country of residence, which is proclaimed in Article 13
of the Universal Declaration of Human Rights. But in fact this right is
subject to very serious unwarranted restrictions, which are encountered by all those seeking to emigrate (regardless of nationality). These
restrictions are a manifestation of the closed and unlawful character of
Soviet society; they represent, therefore, a direct threat to international
trust and peaceful relations between states. It is very important that
Jews in the USA, as well as government leaders, people prominent in
culture and business, all those who have influence in society, be aware
that support for Jewish emigration alone would signify an inadmissi-
bly narrow view of a much larger problem. I want to mention, in particular, the emigration of ethnic Germans from the USSR. To a greater
extent than any other people, Germans have encountered the cruelties
of deportation, persecution, discrimination, eradication of their national culture, and everyday national oppression. About thirty Germans active in the cause of repatriation are now confined in the strict-
regime camps of Kazakhstan and other republics. Their families do not
receive any relief from abroad. Absolutely no foreign assistance is
granted to thousands of Germans who, for years and decades, have
been denied permission to emigrate to the Federal Republic of Germany, and often they are deprived of basic necessities of life. Until
now, Germans of the Federal Republic of Germany, the United States,
and other countries with large German communities have shown little

activism at either the personal or political level. There is a lot they could learn from Jewish communities, with their splendid traditions of mutual support. A great many Germans, Ukrainians, Lithuanians, Latvians, Estonians, Russians, and people of other nationalities encounter similar difficulties. Another important category includes people persecuted by authorities mostly for political and religious reasons (for example, Pentecostals and Baptists), who want or are forced to emigrate.

In the majority of such cases, the authorities suggest that one apply for emigration to Israel. This is part of the authorities' tactics, which derive from considerations of propaganda as well as foreign and domestic policy (anti-Zionism and anti-Semitism).

Marchenko's case, which became famous because of his principled position (not to yield anything to the KGB, even when leaving), is a typical example. Marchenko, who wrote a book on Soviet camps, received an invitation from the USA. But the authorities suggested that he apply for emigration to Israel. He refused and was sentenced to four years of exile. This tactic of the Soviet authorities (to grant permission to emigrate only to Israel) partly explains why a high percentage of emigrants who formally left for Israel in fact go to other countries. This apparent diversion of emigrants should not worry Jewish organizations; it occurs because these people never intended to go to Israel.

The last and very important issue concerns discussions surrounding the trade law. The president of the United States, reflecting a viewpoint prevalent among certain politicians and businessmen, has said that the amendment to the trade law has proved to be counterproductive in securing freedom of emigration (in contrast, allegedly, to the methods of quiet diplomacy) and dealt harm to the economic interests of the USA. I think that such a pragmatic and shortsighted attitude is equivalent to capitulation in the face of Soviet blackmail and is completely objectionable in this question of principle. An analysis of the whole course of events shows that the true cause of the current difficult situation was a lack of unity of understanding and of sufficient altruism in the West. It is intolerable that not only did Congress's initiative fail to elicit support from other Western countries, from their parliaments or public leaders, but that, on the contrary, after the USSR refused to sign the trade agreement, they vied with one another in offering credits. It is sad that in the USA the principles behind the amendment were not fully explained and became a subject of political conflict. . . .

To create the needed unity of the West, international Jewish organizations—which are influential in many countries—can play a major role. I urge the participants of this conference to develop a program of action designed to forge such unity.

Sakharov had this statement delivered to the West through his Moscow connections with Zionist extremists. . . .

Pressure kept increasing on the regime to permit Elena Bonner to seek medical treatment in Italy. Andropov reported that six Nobel laureates were appealing on her behalf. Andropov's note was personally signed on the first page by every Politburo member, an indication of how sensitive the issue was becoming.

## · DOCUMENT 94 ·

Andropov to Central Committee, June 22, 1975
Nobel laureates appeal on behalf of Elena Bonner

In May 1975, a group of six West European Nobel laureates, including the director of the so-called "International Institute for Human Rights," René Cassin (France), and the West German writer Heinrich Böll, forwarded an appeal to the leaders of the CPSU and of the Soviet government, with a request to allow Sakharov's wife, Bonner, to travel abroad to receive medical treatment.

In this connection it seems appropriate to prepare and send an official response to the signatories from the USSR Ministry of Health. It should state that, according to well-established practice in the USSR, Soviet citizens (regardless of their social and official rank) are allowed to travel abroad for medical treatment only when our country's medical science cannot guarantee the patient's cure and when foreign medicine in a particular branch of medical practice is clearly superior. . . .

Under these circumstances Bonner's refusal to accept medical care in the USSR and her insistent demand to obtain it abroad seem to be motivated by reasons unrelated to the treatment of her disease. . . .

Telegram (translated from the French)
From France
May 15, 1975
To: Chairman of the Council of Ministers Alexei Kosygin
Moscow

The undersigned Nobel laureates make an urgent appeal to Soviet authorities and to [General] Secretary Brezhnev to permit Mrs. Elena Sakharov to travel to Italy. Mrs. Sakharov has been denied a passport many times even though she needs major lifesaving surgery. The undersigned, motivated solely by humanitarian considerations, ask that Mrs. Sakharov be allowed to travel immediately to Italy for radical treatment and that she be guaranteed the possibility of returning to the USSR.

Sir Derek Barton (Great Britain), Heinrich Böll (Federal Republic of Germany), Alfred Kastler (France), Max Perutz (Great Britain), F. Sanger (Great Britain)[11]

---

Faced with more demands by Sakharov for Bonner's right to seek medical treatment, Andropov reaffirmed his opposition to granting permission. With the support of the foreign minister, he warned that foreign "intelligence services" would exploit the trip by insisting on Sakharov's right to travel as well. As a note in the margin indicated, during the Politburo meeting "the question was resolved"—in the negative.

## · DOCUMENT 96 ·

Andropov to Central Committee, July 9, 1975
Sakharov continues to insist on his wife's right to seek medical treatment in Italy

---

In the last two years Sakharov, under the influence of his wife, Bonner, has appealed to the world community repeatedly with a provocative demand to help her to go abroad. They have attempted to use her eye disease as a pretext.

Bonner does, in fact, suffer from a cataract in the left eye and glaucoma in the right eye. For this purpose, in 1975 she consulted one of the most prominent Soviet specialists, Professor M. M. Krasnov, who advised surgery.[12] However, Bonner refused to undergo an operation and received treatment at the Moscow Ophthalmologic Clinic, but was discharged at her own insistent demand. . . .

Notwithstanding these explanations, Sakharov and Bonner continue to

---

11. There were six signatures in the original French text, including René Cassin's. For some reason, the Russian translation omitted his name.

12. But Professor Krasnov refused to admit Bonner to his hospital. At the other eye clinic where Bonner was sent, one of the doctors confessed, "We do not know what they are planning to do with you, but you ought to get yourself out of here as fast as you can"; see Sakharov, *Memoirs*, 411. Bonner had to seek an operation abroad.

exploit this circumstance for provocative purposes, attempting thereby to arouse interest and corresponding public support in the West. On July 7, 1975, Sakharov prepared a new appeal on this matter (a copy is enclosed).

The Committee for State Security deems Bonner's travel outside the USSR undesirable, since it will be used by the intelligence services of capitalist countries for anti-Soviet purposes, and also for organizing a campaign to support Sakharov's travel abroad. The Ministry of Foreign Affairs (Comrade A. A. Gromyko) supports this proposal. We request your approval.

Text of Sakharov's Letter to L. I. Brezhnev
To: Comrade Leonid Ilyich Brezhnev
General Secretary of the Central Committee of the CPSU

Dear Leonid Ilyich Brezhnev:

I request permission for my wife Elena Georgievna Bonner to travel for treatment abroad on the basis of a private invitation. It has become known to me that Mr. Willy Brandt spoke with you about this. . . .

[My wife's] eye disease has begun to progress rapidly and each month brings irreversible changes and threatens her with total blindness. On the basis of detailed consultations, we know that in a number of foreign countries the possibilities for operating in this specific case are significantly greater than those in this country.

Since September 1974, the Office of Visas and Registrations has been reviewing the private invitation from our old friend Dr. Nina Harkevich. During this time, my wife has received a whole series of new invitations: from our relative Mme Tanya Maton in France and from friends and people whom we do not know in other countries. . . . We are most interested in a trip to the USA, since the level of ophthalmology there is highest, but my wife has no relatives there. In view of the exceptional urgency of this case, I ask you to have this request reviewed by a responsible official in the Office of Visas and Registrations of the Ministry of Internal Affairs who has the authority to make a decision.

With respect,

A. D. Sakharov, Academician, three times Hero of Socialist Labor[13]

---

Sakharov's constant appeals to gain permission for his wife to see doctors in Italy finally came to a positive conclusion in the summer of

---

13. Andropov missed the absurdity of sending the letter to Brezhnev two days after it had already been delivered.

1975. As Andropov made clear to his colleagues, Sakharov was threatening to involve Western leaders who were about to gather in Finland that August to conclude the Helsinki Final Act. Andropov was wary of Sakharov's intentions; hence his indication that he had discussed the problem with Foreign Minister Gromyko.

Bonner was informed by telegram that her request was granted and that she could come immediately to OVIR (the Office of Visas and Registrations) to pick up her papers; she then made plans to leave by train on August 9. But her trip was disrupted by a frightening incident. Tatiana's two-year-old son suddenly became ill and went into convulsions. An emergency team quickly arrived and was able to help Matvei, although he required an overnight stay in the hospital before the doctors assured his anxious parents that he would be fine. Still, the family believed he had been given some kind of convulsant, "less with the aim of harming the child than of delaying [Bonner's] departure."

Elena Bonner rescheduled her trip for a week later. Even then, the KGB was not finished with its tricks. On the day before she was to leave, an envelope postmarked in Norway arrived with "horrifying photographs, all involving injuries to eyes." As Sakharov described them, "they looked like ads for horror movies: . . . eyes gouged out with a dagger, a skull with a knife driven through one eye socket." Bonner left for Italy on August 16 and a surgeon in Siena operated on September 4, successfully halting the glaucoma. But two days later Sakharov was treated to one more ugly prank. He "received false information . . . that the operation had been a failure."[14] None of these details made it into Andropov's reports to the Central Committee, and as has been noted before, the "operational files," which might cast light on these incidents, are said to have been destroyed.

## · DOCUMENT 98 ·

Andropov to Central Committee, July 18, 1975
Bonner receives permission to travel abroad

Since 1973, Academician Sakharov has been constantly raising the question of his wife E. G. Bonner's departure abroad for medical treatment through a private invitation.

The petitions by Sakharov have been considered at different levels, and

14. Sakharov, *Memoirs*, 427–28.

it was decided to deny Sakharov's request because once Bonner was abroad she might subsequently attempt, on the pretext of family reunification, to obtain permission for Academician Sakharov to go abroad. . . .

On July 18 Bonner applied once again for an exit visa to go to Italy. When that application was also rejected, Sakharov (as our sources have reported) prepared a letter to the Central Committee of the CPSU, the Supreme Soviet of the USSR, the Council of Ministers, and the Presidium of the USSR Academy of Sciences. He alleges that his wife cannot get treatment in the USSR because of interference by the organs of State Security. Therefore, he, Sakharov, again insists that his wife E. G. Bonner be given permission to go abroad for treatment.

In this same letter, Academician Sakharov states that if his request is once again ignored, on the day that the heads of state meet in Helsinki he will announce his renunciation of his three Hero of Socialist Labor awards, laureate of the Lenin and State prizes, and all other state awards.

In conversation with his wife, Sakharov declared that he is disposed to think about self-immolation.[15]

The Committee for State Security believes that Sakharov's entire behavior is overtly provocative, being calculated to resolve this question with the aid of world public opinion or to harm the prestige of the Soviet state on the eve of the European conference. One can assume that after such a statement, appeals in support of Sakharov's position to the leadership of the Soviet state will ensue. Moreover, one cannot rule out appeals from some Communist parties, especially the Italian.

Given the above, we deem it expedient—even before receiving the letter from Academician Sakharov—to summon Bonner to the Office of Visas and Registrations and to inform her that she is given permission to go to Italy in accordance with the established procedure. At the same time, she is to be officially informed that she must not expect that her husband, Academician Sakharov, as the bearer of important state and military secrets, will receive permission to join her abroad. Agreement on this has been given by the Ministry of Foreign Affairs (Comrade A. A. Gromyko).

This measure, in our opinion, would make it impossible for Sakharov to indulge publicly in political speculation on the eve of the European conference. . . .

---

15. According to Elena Bonner (interview with author, Brookline, MA, 2003), this was an absolute lie; Sakharov was never concerned with issues of prestige and never talked about self-immolation.

## · DOCUMENT 100 ·

Chebrikov to Central Committee, September 27, 1975
The appearance of Sakharov's *O strane i mire* [My country and the world]

---

The Committee for State Security reported (in no. 1597-A of June 22, 1975) that Academician Sakharov was writing a libelous attack titled "My Country and the World." According to information received, in late June or early July Sakharov sent this libel for publication abroad, using his contacts among foreigners.

In July this essay was published in the USA as a separate Russian-language book.[16] At the present time, arrangements are under way in Italy and the United States to publish it in several Western European languages. Separate chapters and excerpts have appeared in the American magazine *Time*[17] and in the Milan *Giornale Nuovo*, and they have been extensively discussed on short-wave broadcasts of "Voice of America," "Die Deutsche Welle," "Radio d'Italia," and others.

To stir up publicity for this libelous tract, the bourgeois press and radio present it as Sakharov's "political testament," summarizing his activity as "the leader of dissenters and a fighter for civil rights in the Soviet Union."

Sakharov's libelous attack consists of seven sections: Introduction; Soviet Society; The Freedom to Choose One's Country of Residence; Disarmament; Indochina and the Middle East; The Liberal Intelligentsia of the West: Its Illusions and Responsibilities; Conclusion.

This libelous work contains a malicious calumny directed against the Soviet Union and socialism, claiming, in particular, that there is "no democracy," that the Soviet people live in "poverty," that national minorities are "oppressed," that there is "persecution" for political and religious reasons. It demands freedom of information and the free movement of people. Touching upon problems of international relations, Sakharov raises questions about disarmament, points out mistakes by Western countries in their political and economic relations with the USSR, warns the West against the danger that the Soviet Union poses for the capitalist world, and urges the West to unite to exert pressure on the USSR and socialist countries.

Sakharov's new work shows a further evolution toward open anti-Sovi-

---

16. Andrei Sakharov, *O strane i mire. Sbornik proizvedenii,* published in English as *My Country and the World,* trans. Guy V. Daniels (New York, 1975).
17. See *Time,* August 4, 1975.

etism and direct complicity with the forces of international reaction. Even now the foreign press and radio are powerless to conceal this.

For example, the radio station "Die Deutsche Welle," in its broadcast of August 25, reported that the work "is an indictment of Soviet society and represents a summary of Sakharov's political ideas in his role as leader of the domestic Soviet opposition. . . ."

On October 9, 1975, the world learned that Andrei Sakharov would be awarded the Nobel Peace Prize. For the regime, the announcement echoed earlier awards to Boris Pasternak and Alexander Solzhenitsyn, each of whom had received the literature prize for works that defied Soviet literary norms. Within days the regime launched a massive propaganda campaign, seeking to discredit Sakharov at home and in the West. Seventy-two full and corresponding members of the Academy of Sciences signed a letter denouncing him in *Izvestia*. *Trud* claimed that Elena Bonner had chosen this "propitious moment" to visit Europe "as the wave of her husband's fame was cresting in the West." "It was, of course, the KGB who had actually chosen the moment—and they could kick themselves for it," as Sakharov rightly observes in his memoirs.[18] Reading these harsh memorandums, it is curious to keep in mind that at the same time, the *Great Soviet Encyclopedia* was about to issue volume 23, which would contain a brief respectful entry on Sakharov, accompanied by his photograph. There was no mention, of course, of his human rights activity and only the misleading information that "in recent years, he has left scientific work."[19] Perhaps the encyclopedia was obliged to carry this entry because Sakharov retained the rank of academician. Nonetheless, it seems the regime was still not sure how to deal with him.

·  DOCUMENT 101  ·

Andropov to Central Committee, October 10, 1975
Sakharov receives the Nobel Prize for peace

On Measures to Compromise the Decision of the Nobel Committee to
Award the Peace Prize to A. D. Sakharov (excerpts)

On October 9, the Nobel Committee adopted a resolution to award Sakharov the Peace Prize, obviously for provocative purposes, in order to

18. Sakharov, *Memoirs*, 430.
19. *Bolshaia Sovietskaia Entsiklopediia [Great Soviet encyclopedia]*, vol. 23 (Moscow, 1976), 13.

support his anti-Soviet activities and on that basis to consolidate hostile-minded elements within this country. . . .

We consider expedient the following measures:

1. Direct the Central Committee's Department of Science and Education Institutions and Department of Propaganda, in cooperation with the Presidium of the USSR Academy of Sciences, to prepare, on behalf of the Presidium of the Academy of Sciences and prominent Soviet scientists, an open letter to be published in *Izvestia* condemning the action of the Nobel Committee in awarding the Peace Prize to a person who has embarked on the path of anticonstitutional, antisocial activity, which, to our great sorrow, unwittingly compromises the above-mentioned august body.

2. The editorial board of the newspaper *Trud* should publish a satire portraying the award of the Nobel Peace Prize to Sakharov for the sum of $122,000 as a reward from Western reactionary circles for his continual slandering of the Soviet social and state order.

3. Transmit to the West via the news service APN materials that support the idea that awarding the Peace Prize to a person who has spoken against détente . . . goes against the policy of the Soviet government and worldwide progressive forces, which is structured toward achieving international détente and disarmament.

4. Using the channels of the KGB, promote articles in the West showing the absurdity of the decision to award the Peace Prize to the inventor of a weapon of mass destruction.

5. When pressured to allow Sakharov to go abroad to receive the Nobel laureate medal and cash award, it appears necessary to refuse him permission on the grounds that he is in possession of state and military secrets. In case other options arise, the matter should be resolved according to the demands of the specific situation.

---

· DOCUMENT 102 ·

Andropov to Central Committee, October 28, 1975
Response to the Nobel award

---

The Committee for State Security of the USSR Council of Ministers has received intelligence information showing that congratulations were sent to Sakharov on the occasion of the award of the Nobel Peace Prize by "Amnesty International," the "Association of Soviet Jews Living in Israel," the "Ecumenical Peace Council," the "Organizing Committee for Sakharov Hearings," the émigrés Z. Shakhovskaya, Galich, Maximov, and several others. More than one hundred Soviet citizens, most of them hostile to the state and social system of our country, also sent congratulations to Sakharov (Turchin, Zheludkov, Khalif, Nekrich, Gastev, Barabanov, Azbel, Grigorenko, Orlov, Shikhanovich, Albrekht, Kopelev, Voinovich, Shafarevich, and others).

In connection with the Peace Prize announcement, Sakharov received journalists accredited in Moscow from the United States, England, the Federal Republic of Germany, Italy, Canada, Sweden, Norway, and several other countries.

At the press conference for foreign journalists organized on October 10, Sakharov read a prepared statement in which he noted, among other things, that he "considers the Nobel prize to be recognition not only for his own achievements, but for those of his confederates, of all those in this country who have fought for freedom of opinion, for human rights, for openness, and, above all, for those who have paid a high price for this— the loss of their liberty."

In response to a journalist's question about what the laureate felt, Sakharov answered: "Awards have been bestowed on me on many occasions, but this one is certainly much more significant. Naturally, I am happy and proud."

In subsequent meetings with foreign journalists, Sakharov continually expressed the idea that "the Helsinki conference presents opportunities to put pressure on the Soviet Union." For instance, in his conversation with an English journalist, he urged: "It is now very important to increase the pressure of world public opinion to defend human rights in the Soviet Union, such as the right to choose one's country of residence. Now, after the Helsinki conference and after the award of the Peace Prize to me, I hope better conditions have been created for such activity."[20]

Sakharov explained that "the task of the West is to use the tools at its disposal to ensure that the Soviet Union fulfills its obligations." He declared that "I want people in the West to work more actively and to understand the dangerous nature of our system better. This is very important."

In his discussions with journalists Sakharov devoted much attention to the "problem" of so-called political prisoners. "These days," he declared,

20. "Basket 3" of the Final Act of the Conference on Security and Cooperation in Europe, signed in Helsinki on August 1, 1975, contained provisions on human rights, freedom of movement, and other humanitarian issues. Basket 1 secured existing borders; Basket 3 made all thirty-five signatory countries, including the Soviet Union and the Eastern bloc countries, accountable on the critical issue of human rights.

"when I am being paid such an honor, when I have been given a rostrum to address the whole world, I want to say that I am constantly thinking about my friends, about those who are now in prisons, and those who are awaiting trial." All his verbiage on this subject essentially urged Western countries to put pressure on the Soviet Union to declare a general political amnesty in this country.

During Sakharov's meetings with foreign journalists, various scenarios for a possible trip to Oslo to attend the Nobel award ceremonies were discussed.

The Norwegian ambassador in Moscow, Petter Graver, sent a congratulatory letter through his staff and assured Sakharov that "the Embassy will render any assistance necessary in organizing his trip to Oslo to receive the prize."

The BBC correspondent [Philip] Short remarked that "the conduct of the Norwegian ambassador contrasts sharply with the behavior of Gunnar Jarring [Sweden's ambassador to the USSR], who tried to avoid any action that would evoke the disapproval of the Soviet authorities when Solzhenitsyn was awarded the Nobel Prize."

Foreign journalists and others who congratulated Sakharov attempt to depict him as an "uncompromising and courageous fighter for human rights in the USSR" who has contributed "greatly" to bringing countries and peoples together. American journalists believe that "he has such stature in the dissident and freedom of emigration movements that he is venerated as a god."

In response to the adulation of foreigners and his few "admirers" among Soviet citizens, Sakharov has repeatedly asserted that "this prize and the international recognition expressed by it impose additional responsibility" on him and that he will try to measure up to his "new expanded obligations."

At the same time, because of the declaration by seventy-two Soviet academicians published in *Izvestia*, who condemn his antisocial and antistate position, as well as the provocative activity of the Nobel committee in conferring the Peace Prize, Sakharov displays nervousness and shows noticeable anxiety. Sakharov is especially concerned that the statement was signed by a great number of well-known scientists who are members of the Academy of Sciences. Though in his interviews with foreign journalists Sakharov maintained that Soviet scientists had signed the document "under pressure from the authorities," he conceded that he was "surprised and upset by the campaign the authorities were waging against him," that "it is making the situation more complicated."

Privately, Sakharov has expressed[21] concern about his possible expulsion from the Soviet Academy of Sciences. In conversations with foreign journalists, he declared that "such a decision could not be ruled out." Nevertheless, Sakharov, referring to an analogous situation in 1973, expressed doubt that measures involving the Academy of Sciences would really be taken against him—the initiators of his possible expulsion would not be able to gather the required number of votes (two-thirds).

Despite this, in his talks with foreign journalists, with his allies and in a telephone conversation with his wife Bonner, now in Italy, Sakharov continues to maintain that he "is facing a struggle" but that his "cause will prevail." . . .

[Enclosed document]

We hereby report that seventy-two members of the Academy have signed the statement of Soviet scientists protesting against the award of the Nobel Peace Prize to A. D. Sakharov. The document was not signed by:

Academician Ya. B. Zeldovich, who claimed that the letter had to be written in a different spirit and that he was thinking of preparing an individual letter;

Academician Yu. B. Khariton, who did not believe that such a letter had to be dispatched because members of the Academy of Sciences, including himself, had already protested against actions of Academician Sakharov;

Academician P. L. Kapitsa,[22] who believed that it was necessary to invite Sakharov for a discussion at a meeting of the Presidium of the Academy of Sciences and only then to decide upon the appropriate reaction to his conduct;

Academician L. B. Kantorovich, who claimed that he, being himself a recent Nobel laureate, considered it inopportune to sign a collective letter and was thinking about making an individual protest;

---

21. Several words have been omitted here, probably identification of the person who reported the conversation to the KGB.

22. The name of the great Russian physicist Pyotr Kapitsa appeared in a similar context during the Politburo meeting on Sakharov and Solzhenitsyn, when Andropov said: "Not long ago Comrade Keldysh called me and asked why we didn't take any measures regarding Sakharov. He says that if we remain inactive on Sakharov, then how will such academicians as Kapitsa, Engelgard, and others behave in the future?" See Michael Scammell, ed., *The Solzhenitsyn Files* (Chicago, 1995), 284. It is difficult to believe that Keldysh asked Andropov such a question; perhaps the KGB chief wanted to introduce Kapitsa's name for reasons of his own.

Academician V. L. Ginzburg, who did not sign the letter citing personal reasons.[23]

The USSR Academy of Sciences asks for permission to publish the statement on October 25 of this year. . . .

Acting President of the USSR Academy of Sciences Academician V. A. Kotelnikov

Acting Academic Secretary, Presidium of the USSR Academy of Sciences, Corresponding Member of the USSR Academy of Sciences G. K. Skriyabin

[The material was then submitted to the Politburo for its review.]

. . . We think it expedient to publish the Soviet scientists' statement in the newspaper *Izvestia* on October 25 of this year.

On the statement made by Soviet scientists in connection with the award to Academician Sakharov of the Nobel Peace Prize.

The issue was submitted by Comrades Kotelnikov, Skriyabin, Trapeznikov.

Voted by:

Brezhnev—coordinated with Comrade Chernenko
Andropov—corrections
Grechko—yes
Grishin—no corrections
Gromyko—agree
Kirilenko—reported to K. Chernenko
Kosygin—no corrections
Kulakov—on vacation
Kunaev—on vacation
Mazurov—on vacation
Pelshe—[illegible]
Podgorny—yes
Polyansky—no corrections
Suslov—sick
Shcherbitsky—[illegible]
The original copy
P1867
October 25, 1975

23. So far as is known, all five academicians survived the affair unscathed, despite their refusal to cooperate.

The scientists' letter was sent to TASS and to the newspaper *Izvestia,*
October 25, 1975.

---

On October 15 the Politburo forbade Sakharov to go to Oslo to receive the Nobel Peace Prize. This measure reinforced support for Sakharov in the West and led to protests on his behalf. Inasmuch as Andropov could make only vague allusions to "measures to contain the
anti-Soviet commotion" over the visa denial, it is obvious that he was
referring to a damage-control operation.

· DOCUMENT 103 ·

Andropov to Central Committee, November 12, 1975
Sakharov is not permitted to travel to Oslo for the Nobel ceremony

---

In connection with the award of the Nobel Peace Prize, Sakharov applied to the Office of Visas and Registrations . . . on October 20 for permission to go to Norway from December 3 to 17 in order to participate in
the award ceremonies for the prize.

In accordance with the decision of the Politburo of the CPSU Central
Committee on October 15 (no. P-192/41),[24] Sakharov was invited to the
Office of Visas and Registrations, where he was told the following:

"Your application for permission to travel to Norway has been examined. Because you are a person possessing especially important state secrets, you are denied permission to travel abroad for reasons of state security." Having heard the refusal, Sakharov declared that he believes the
decision resulted from the fact that the government considers him politically suspect and that he finds this insulting. While still in the building of
the Office of Visas and Registrations, Sakharov informed the Reuters correspondent [Patrick] Worsnip of the refusal to grant him permission for a
trip abroad.

In a phone conversation with a correspondent of Agence France-Presse,
Sakharov emphasized: "This decision is an insult not only for me, but also
for the Nobel Committee. This is a challenge to world public opinion. The
decision can be revised if there is support on the part of the world community."

In his conversation with a UPI correspondent, Sakharov declared that

---

24. This document has not been released by Russian authorities. The Politburo required five days to follow Andropov's recommendations, which were dated October
10, 1975.

he was appealing to the world community to have the decision reversed. The Committee for State Security is taking measures to contain the anti-Soviet commotion provoked by the refusal to authorize Sakharov's travel abroad. . . .

---

After the announcement of the award of the Nobel Peace Prize to Sakharov, Elena Bonner gave a press conference in Italy on November 7. She was outspoken in her denunciation of Soviet policies. Her presence in the West on top of the award to Sakharov infuriated the regime. Andropov reported on Bonner's remarks in Italy in a particularly provocative manner. Three days later, in a second report, Andropov, joined by Roman Rudenko and Dmitri Ustinov—the heads of the Procuracy and the Ministry of Defense, respectively—directly proposed to subject Sakharov and Bonner to administrative exile by sending them to the closed city of Sverdlovsk-44, a town specifically built for nuclear weapons production; it was located close to the old Russian city of Verkh-Neivinsk. Inasmuch as no mention was made of the Academy of Sciences (which had one of its thirteen branches in Sverdlovsk-44), and given the reference to the Ministry of Medium Machine Building, which was actually responsible for every aspect of atomic research and armaments, Soviet authorities evidently planned to compel Sakharov to work in his field of research. Nevertheless, although this was not the first time Soviet officials had considered exiling Sakharov, the decision was again shelved. As the following undated statement reveals, Brezhnev himself was involved in reaching the Kremlin's decision: "The question of the administrative expulsion of Sakharov from Moscow was discussed twice at the Politburo of the Central Committee of the CPSU, under the agenda of November 1975 and January 1976 meetings. It was judged expedient to postpone temporarily the study of this question. Comrades L. I. Brezhnev and Yu. V. Andropov thoroughly informed members of the Politburo of the Central Committee of the CPSU about this problem."[25]

Sakharov, like Pasternak and Solzhenitsyn before him, was not permitted to go to accept the award in person. Elena Bonner extended her stay in Europe and read Sakharov's acceptance speech in Oslo on December 10. On that day he was in Vilnius, the capital of Lithuania, to show solidarity with his friend Sergei Kovalev, who was on trial for

---

25. From an attachment to Document 105, November 16, 1975. The attachment was inserted much later. It is not included in this volume but can be found at www.yale.edu/annals/sakharov/

"anti-Soviet agitation and propaganda." Along with others, Sakharov was not permitted to enter the courtroom.

## · DOCUMENT 104 ·

### Andropov to Central Committee, November 13, 1975
### Press conference by Elena Bonner in Italy

On November 7 of this year the editors of the newspaper *Tempo* arranged a press conference with Sakharov's wife Bonner, who is temporarily in Italy on a private invitation. . . .

One cannot help noticing Bonner's intemperate tone and the overtly anti-Soviet character of her statements throughout the conference. . . . While answering questions, Bonner asserted that "for the last 56 years the people of the Soviet Union have had a difficult history. The period of extermination of people and ideas under Stalin has left a deep imprint of inertia and fear. This inertia prevents people from thinking independently, and therefore they do not think at all."

In answer to the question whether there is freedom of religion in the USSR, she replied: "No, there is not. The insignificant number of churches is under the control of the state. Many forms of religion are persecuted. In particular, the Catholic faith is persecuted. The camps are overflowing with believers.

"Our camps," continued Bonner, "are full of members of the intelligentsia and representatives of the working class. Many people are starting to think and to doubt Marxist principles."

In answer to the question of one journalist, whether it was true that the Communists themselves killed Marxism in Czechoslovakia and Poland, Bonner replied: "Communism was killed by the Soviet tanks that entered Prague. I think Soviet tanks are always ready to kill the illusion of Marxism in other countries as well."

One correspondent asked Bonner the following question: "We in Italy miss order and therefore sympathize with communism, which guarantees order. Do Russians like order?" Bonner answered: "I think not. But I would like to remind you of the time when Italy had order too—that was in the time of Mussolini."

In answer to the question whether there was disagreement in the leadership of the CPSU about Soviet dissidents, Bonner said: "We do not know what goes on in our ruling circles. Whatever appears in the press is only something that has been examined and prepared beforehand; there is never a [true] discussion on the pages of the press. In my opinion, the only thing that goes on in our higher circles is the struggle for power." . . .

·  DOCUMENT 105  ·

Andropov, Ustinov, and Rudenko to Central Committee, November 16, 1975
The broad challenge posed by Sakharov and a proposal
to expel him and his wife from Moscow

The Committee for State Security of the USSR Council of Ministers and the USSR Procurator's Office have reported to the Central Committee of the CPSU about Sakharov's anti-Soviet activities. . . . Recently, having embarked on the path of an open struggle against Soviet power, he is divulging state secrets to the enemy that pertain to the most vital defense issues of the country.

On November 29, 1974, in his talk with the American journalist H. Smith, Sakharov commented on the Vladivostok agreement to limit offensive strategic arms and stated that "we can convert half of our missiles into MIRV warheads [*kassetnye boegolovki*]," that "our missiles are larger than American missiles in terms of both size and throw weight," and that "the Soviet Union will modernize its missiles while keeping their numbers constant." While developing Smith's idea about the uselessness of air defense systems, Sakharov said that "we decreased them by half without compromising the defense of the Moscow area."

In December 1974 Sakharov attempted to convince the American journalist Axelbank that "the content of the agreement does not appear to be very satisfactory. Its deficiency consists in the fact that they agreed upon the number of missiles, but did not stipulate such characteristics as type, capacity, explosive power, and total takeoff weight. That is why the agreement appears not to create parity but rather to give the Soviet side a unilateral advantage. In a situation where the takeoff weight of the Soviet missiles is about three times greater than that of the Americans, without any agreement about the throw weight of missiles, an agreement establishing parity in the number of missiles is tantamount to giving an advantage to the Soviet Union."

In January 1975, during the customs inspection of the luggage belonging to the Canadian journalist D. Levy, a tape recording of his discussion with Sakharov was confiscated. In this conversation Sakharov asserted, in particular, that "nuclear weapons are manufactured by the Ministry of Medium Machine Building and missiles are built by the Ministry of General Machine Building. . . . Soviet launch sites are grandiose underground structures; a large number of military building detachments are used in their construction. . . . We already have the first MIRV warheads, which were first tested in the fall of 1973. Obviously, the industry [to produce them] has already begun operations. Their number is still small (approximately 1,200). We produce them on the basis of existing missiles by replacing the powerful warheads of existing or newly built missiles with separately targetable warheads. . . . The agreement was concluded in accordance with our technical policy—i.e., not to manufacture a great many missiles, but to make them more powerful. . . . The Soviet Union has 2,400 warheads, of which 1,200 can separate into eight warheads. This is an extraordinary number."

In the opinion of experts, the above information is highly confidential and constitutes a state secret. (The conclusion of a commission in the Ministry of Medium Machine Building is enclosed).[26]

As someone who opposes Soviet foreign policy and who seeks to compromise this country's position at the Conference on Security and Cooperation in Europe, Sakharov initiated the so-called "International Hearings on Human Rights Violations in the USSR." Offering a new libelous attack called *My Country and the World* (written by Sakharov and now widely disseminated in the West) as testimony against the Soviet system, the organizers of the "Hearings" exploited [Sakharov's work] to confirm "the fact of persecution" of national minorities in the USSR, the "trampling" of political and religious freedoms, and the "repression" of citizens for their political convictions. . . .

The Procurator's Office and state security organs, in an effort to bring Sakharov to his senses and avert his final political downfall, have taken every possible measure—through Party, Soviet, and public organizations. He has received repeated admonitions from many of his colleagues at the Academy of Sciences as well as responsible officials in the Party and state apparatus. Comrade V. A. Kirillin, deputy chairman of the USSR Council of Ministers of the USSR, spoke with him on behalf of the government.[27]

---

26. This document has not been declassified and released.

27. Vladimir A. Kirillin was appointed to the Central Committee in 1966, was deputy chairman of the USSR Council of Ministers (1965–80), and served as chairman of the State Council on Science and Technology. He was a physicist, academician, and at one time vice president of the Academy of Sciences (1963–65). The only known conversation between Sakharov and Kirillin took place in the late spring of 1967; see Sakharov, *Memoirs,* 275.

Sakharov's actions have been condemned by a broad spectrum of public opinion in the Soviet press. In 1973 he received an official warning from M. P. Malyarov, deputy procurator general of the USSR, and from the KGB. Sakharov's wife, E. G. Bonner, also received a warning about her antisocial activities at the KGB of the USSR Council of Ministers. . . .

A new démarche aimed at intensifying Sakharov's antisocial activity was the provocative award of the Nobel Peace Prize. The Western press does not even conceal the fact that he was awarded the prize for his anti-Sovietism. Thus the Swedish paper *Dagens Niheter* announced that "the Nobel Committee, through its selection of laureates, in recent years has displayed such poor judgment about candidates that it has seriously compromised the Peace Prize." The English newspaper [*Manchester*] *Guardian* stated that if "peace means nothing but political détente, then the Norwegian committee has chosen the wrong person for the Peace Prize." Moreover, the award of the Nobel Peace Prize to Sakharov is an attempt by the enemy to present Sakharov as a symbol of the struggle against socialism. It aims not just at stimulating but at legalizing his anticonstitutional activity.

Although Sakharov is not the leader of any organization, in fact he is the center of a group of people who, flouting the laws of our country, have systematically given him every kind of assistance in conducting his anti-Soviet activity. A number of people from this group have been prosecuted and punished. . . .

The actions committed by Sakharov and Bonner are punishable. Under Soviet laws criminal proceedings may be started against them. One has to consider, though, that the punishment of Sakharov through court proceedings may evoke a serious negative reaction.

Hence it appears appropriate to take administrative measures against Sakharov and his wife Bonner so that they cannot engage in hostile activities. It is proposed to expel Sakharov and Bonner, by means of an administrative decree of the Presidium of the USSR Supreme Soviet, to the town of Sverdlovsk-44.[28] It is closed to foreigners for security reasons but affords the opportunity to provide [Sakharov and Bonner] with work and suitable housing.

At the time of their resettlement, inform Sakharov and Bonner that they are forbidden to leave the place of their residence without special permission and that they must observe the established regimen. Authorize the organs of state security to enforce the appropriate regimen, even through the use of force, if necessary.

28. The name of Sverdlovsk-44 was inserted by hand in the typescript.

One must assume that the administrative resettlement of Sakharov and his wife will evoke an anti-Soviet campaign in the West. However, this will entail smaller political costs than permitting Sakharov to act with impunity in the future or putting him on trial for criminal activities. It is expedient to publish a press release about the decision to relocate Sakharov and Bonner and to explain the necessity of this measure. . . .

At the same time, we deem it possible to direct the Department of Propaganda of the CPSU Central Committee (with the assistance of the appropriate ministries and agencies) to prepare and conduct the requisite propaganda. This includes publication of materials in the press and broadcast of reports on radio and television. The International Department and the Department of the Central Committee, together with the USSR Ministry of Foreign Affairs, should prepare appropriate instructions for ambassadors of the USSR and information for the leaders of socialist countries and fraternal Communist parties. . . .

Attachment 1
Resolution of the CPSU Central Committee (draft)

1. Approve the draft of the decree of the Presidium of the USSR Supreme Soviet and adopt the text of the press release concerning this issue (attached).

2. Direct the Department of Propaganda of the CPSU Central Committee, with the assistance of the appropriate ministries and agencies, to prepare and conduct propaganda measures pertaining to the resettlement of A. D. Sakharov and E. G. Bonner.

3. Direct the International Department and the Department of the CPSU Central Committee, together with the USSR Ministry of Foreign Affairs, to present proposals to the CPSU Central Committee on instructions for Soviet ambassadors and for the leadership of fraternal parties about the measures taken with respect to A. D. Sakharov.

Secretary of the Central Committee

Attachment 2

[Draft of press statement]
Office of the Procurator General of the USSR

For the past several years, Academician A. D. Sakharov has been openly pursuing anti-Soviet activities. Unable to elicit support inside the Soviet

Union, he advances his antisocialist ideas in the West, where the adversaries of international détente and open enemies of peace among peoples are actively using his name and socially harmful actions for anti-Soviet purposes.

It has already been reported in the Soviet press that Sakharov systematically makes anti-Soviet statements, slanders Soviet reality, and disseminates flagrantly false fabrications that discredit the Soviet state and social order. Sakharov's accomplice and, in many cases, the instigator in these actions is his wife, E. G. Bonner.

Party, Soviet, and social organizations have done a great deal to help Sakharov understand his errors and avert his final political downfall. The USSR Academy of Sciences and Sakharov's colleagues have attempted to explain to him the pernicious nature of his activities and endeavored to bring him back to scientific and social activities worthy of a Soviet scientist. This was also the aim of discussions with Sakharov at the State Committee for Science and Technology (USSR Council of Ministers). And, finally, a warning has been given to him at the Office of the Procurator General of the USSR. Unfortunately, Sakharov ignored all these warnings and the concern extended to him.

Recently there have been instances when Sakharov blatantly divulged important military secrets to which he had had access during his previous work.

Given the need to protect the defense interests of this country and to prevent any further disclosure of state secrets, and, at the same time, given the inexpedience of pursuing criminal prosecution of Sakharov because of his previous accomplishments in science, the Presidium of the Supreme Soviet of the USSR has approved the administrative resettlement of A. D. Sakharov and his wife E. G. Bonner from the city of Moscow.

Normal conditions for work and life have been created at Academician Sakharov's new place of residence.

Attachment 3

Confidential

Decree of the Presidium of the Supreme Soviet of the USSR on the Administrative Resettlement of A. D. Sakharov and E. G. Bonner from Moscow

Given the need to terminate the association of A. D. Sakharov and his wife E. G. Bonner with citizens of capitalist countries (since these contacts result in the disclosure of secret information that can cause serious harm to the country's defenses), and, at the same time, considering it inexpedient to subject Sakharov to criminal prosecution out of respect for his earlier accomplishments, the Presidium of the Supreme Council of the USSR decrees:

1. Direct the Office of the Procurator of the USSR and the Committee for State Security of the Council of Ministers of the USSR to resettle, by administrative decree, Andrei Dmitrievich Sakharov and his wife Elena Georgievna Bonner from the city of Moscow to the city of Sverdlovsk-44.

2. The Executive Committee of the Sverdlovsk Regional Council of Workers' Deputies and the Ministry of Medium Machine Building of the USSR are to take measures to provide Sakharov and Bonner with work and housing.

3. The Committee for State Security of the USSR Council of Ministers and the USSR Ministry of Internal Affairs must take measures to prevent Sakharov and Bonner from having contact with foreigners and antisocial elements, and to provide surveillance over Sakharov and Bonner so as to guarantee their compliance with the established regimen at their new residence.

Chairman of the Presidium of the USSR Supreme Soviet
Secretary of the Presidium of the USSR Supreme Soviet

· DOCUMENT 106 ·

Andropov to Central Committee, November 30, 1975
Sakharov's speech for the Nobel ceremony

The Committee for State Security of the USSR Council of Ministers has received information[29] that, because his application to travel to Norway was denied, Sakharov has authorized his wife Bonner, now on a private visit to Italy, to represent him at the Nobel Peace Prize ceremony in Oslo on December 10, 1975.

In this connection, Sakharov has prepared a so-called "Open Letter to the Nobel Committee" and a speech, which, according to the established tradition, is delivered by the laureate after receiving the prize (copies are

29. About twenty letters were deleted here, probably "through operational means."

attached).[30] On November 24 he dictated the text of these documents to his wife[31] and, in his apartment on November 26, he gave them to the correspondents of several foreign newspapers. . . .

· DOCUMENT 107 ·

Andropov to Central Committee, December 8, 1975
Demonstration in Moscow's Pushkin Square

On December 5, a group of antisocial elements gathered at Pushkin Square with the provocative purpose of making a "silent protest" against the "violation" of civil rights guaranteed by the Constitution of the USSR.

At the square near the Pushkin monument, the following people were present: Sakharov, Semyonova (Bonner's daughter), Yankelevich (Semyonova's husband), Salova, Shatunovskaya, Ioffe, Lunts, Genkin, Podyapolsky, Kristi, Irina Yakir, Grigorenko, Tatyana Litvinova, and others, about thirty people in all. At 6 P.M. some of them removed their hats.

At the same time, the following foreign journalists were present in the square: Wren, Shipler, Krimsky, James, and Pont (USA); Brane, Muller (England); Levy (Canada); Mayer, Engelbrecht, Pleitgen (Federal Republic of Germany); Fredrickson (Norway); Hostad (Sweden); Wan Wei, Shen Yimen (China); and Yamaguchi (Japan). Some journalists took pictures of the participants in the meeting.

After five minutes, the participants left the square. There were no incidents during the demonstration. . . .

Ever since the trial of Sinyavsky and Daniel in February 1966, several leading figures in West European Communist parties had been prepared to denounce political repression in the USSR. These voices grew louder as the concept of Eurocommunism began to emerge, with its implicit emphasis on the independence of Communist parties in France, Spain, and Italy, where they had to compete for votes in democratic elections. (After the death of Franco in 1975, the Spanish Com-

30. The *New York Times* published the speech December 13, 1975, 6; it was later reprinted in Sakharov's *Alarm and Hope,* trans. Efrem Yankelevich and Alfred Friendly Jr. (New York, 1978), 3–18. It is not clear what "open letter" Andropov was referring to.

31. Several words in this line were expunged from the copy provided to the Sakharov Archive; they probably explained that Sakharov's telephone conversation with Bonner had been taped.

munist party was permitted to organize legally. Communist parties in Albania, China, and Yugoslavia were already independent of Soviet control, but they were not pressing for greater democracy or protesting against political trials in Moscow.) Aside from the degree to which these parties were ever truly independent of Moscow, appeals to them by Soviet human rights activists—which at times were favorably received—compromised Soviet propaganda and provoked hard feelings among Soviet leaders.

In December 1975, the French Communist Party raised questions about a film "said to be shot clandestinely in a Soviet prison camp and said to show 'intolerable conditions,'" the Associated Press reported. "If 'such injustifiable [sic] facts' about the camp were confirmed, they 'could only damage socialism' and the good name of the Soviet Union, the party added."[32] Three years later, in July 1978, after the conviction of Anatoly Shcharansky on charges of treason, Enrico Berlinguer, head of the Italian Communist Party, declared that "convictions for crimes of opinion cannot be tolerated." The French Communist Party asked for the release of Shcharansky and Alexander Ginzburg, who was convicted at the same time. In Paris, Communist Party members marched alongside Jewish and Zionist organizations, and some people in the crowd were heard to chant, "KGB equals Gestapo" and "Socialism, yes—Gulag, no."[33]

Andropov was already angry in 1975. The KGB regularly passed huge sums of money to Western Communist parties, so Andropov and his Party colleagues looked on even modest gestures of independence as presumptuous ingratitude.

Still, there is a curious dimension to the following document. In response to calls from Western European Communist parties for greater freedom in the Soviet Union, Andropov reminded his colleagues of how many hundreds, even thousands of people had been arrested on political charges since 1953, the year of Stalin's death. Then he went on to emphasize, as if he sensed a lack of resolve within the Politburo, that "a renunciation of active measures to terminate the politically harmful activities of 'dissidents' . . . could be fraught with the most serious negative consequences." The Party, in other words, continued to rely on force and the threat of violence to maintain power. It could not foresee the consequences if that threat were ever removed.

32. *New York Times*, December 14, 1975, 14.
33. *Time*, July 24, 1978, 24.

## · DOCUMENT 108 ·

Andropov to Central Committee, December 29, 1975
Appeals to Western Communist parties and the need
for continuing internal repression

Recently bourgeois propaganda is actively exploiting, for purposes of subversive activities against the Soviet Union and other socialist countries, certain declarations by the leaders of the Communist parties of France and Italy about issues pertaining to Soviet democracy, the rights and liberties of citizens, and the interdiction of activities by antisocial elements. The materials transmitted by Western radio stations are becoming known to a broad circle of Soviet citizens, who express perplexity over the position taken by the leadership of the French and Italian Communist parties.

At the same time, the "special" views of the leaders of these parties serve to encourage hostile elements like Sakharov, Medvedev, and several others. They see such views as a manifestation of "solidarity" with their own position on the question of "human rights," "the persecution of dissenters," etc. According to agents' reports, Sakharov recently said: "The position of the Italian Communists corresponds to our views and opinions." Highly revealing in this regard is the fact that the wife of the well-known anti-Soviet activist, Plyushch, sent an appeal to G. Marchais,[34] in which she emphasized that "Plyushch shares many of the views of Marchais." Solzhenitsyn used similar references to justify his own antistate activities.[35]

The problem created by the statements of certain leaders in the French and Italian Communist parties, apart from the ideological and theoretical dimension, also have a practical side linked to the security of the Soviet state.

In this case, [our] friends[36] have long since been retreating in the face of the enemy's propaganda pressure. *L'Humanité* has advanced a thesis about giving, under the conditions of socialism, freedom of action to those who "assert their disagreement with the system established by the majority." Objectively, this thesis assists the enemies of socialism in their at-

---

34. Georges Marchais was the general secretary of the French Communist Party.

35. It was a routine tactic in the dissident movement to quote West European Communist leaders as a way to counter Soviet propaganda. It is not clear if Solzhenitsyn did so too, since his determined anticommunism would have gotten in the way of any sympathy he might have felt for West European Communist officials.

36. "Our friends" was a euphemism for foreign Communist parties.

tempts to create, in the Soviet Union and other socialist countries, a legal
opposition and to undermine the leading role of the Communist and
Workers' parties.

The intelligence services and ideological centers of imperialism seek to
discredit Soviet laws and to depict them as archaic, dogmatic, and contrary to the spirit of international documents (in particular, the [U.N.]
"Declaration of Human Rights"). Unfortunately, these have something in
common with certain statements about democratic freedoms under socialism that have appeared in the Communist press of Italy and France.
These ignore the real conditions of the class struggle in the contemporary
era and underestimate the subversive activity of world imperialism and its
agents.

Comrades who made such declarations, even after the events in Hungary and Czechoslovakia, do not wish to see that under conditions of developed socialism—notwithstanding the monolithic political unity of society—anti-Soviet tendencies nonetheless persist, in one or another form,
to a greater or lesser degree.

The available data attest to the attempt by the intelligence services and
ideological centers of the enemy to unite the actions of hostile elements,
whatever their proclivity. Work is being especially actively conducted to
create an anti-Soviet illegal press organ, which is intended to play the role
of an organizational center.

In their subversive activities against the Soviet Union, enemies count on
those elements that, because of their past ties to the exploiting classes, and
because of their politically harmful and criminal activity, can become involved in the anti-Soviet struggle. In our country, this means former collaborators and members of retaliatory detachments of the German fascist
occupiers, the Vlasovites,[37] members of the armed bandit underground
(in Ukraine, the Baltics, Byelorussia, certain areas of Central Asia, and the
northern Caucasus), nationalistic and other elements hostile to the Soviet
system. The number of such people runs to hundreds of thousands. Many
of them have atoned for their guilt and perform honest labor. But in this
category there are also those who do not pass up an opportunity to inflict
harm on Soviet society and, under certain circumstances, will embark on
an open struggle, or even armed assault.

The organs of state security are taking measures to study the situation in

37. Military units recruited by the Germans among Russian prisoners of war during
World War II. Lieutenant General Andrei Vlasov, who was captured in 1942, accepted
the command of these forces. To the KGB, then, anyone who resisted Soviet rule during
and after World War II was a Vlasovite. Solzhenitsyn was a "literary Vlasovite."

this environment and to exert control over the activity of people who harbor anti-Soviet ideas. Guided by the requirements of Soviet laws, the KGB will act decisively to interdict especially dangerous state criminals.

As for measures to persecute the so-called "dissidents" (by which the West usually means those who violate Article 70 [anti-Soviet agitation and propaganda] and 190-1 [dissemination of flagrantly false libel that discredits the Soviet system] of the Criminal Code of the RSFSR, the statistical data appear as follows. For the period from 1967 (Article 190-1 was introduced only in September 1966) through 1975, the courts convicted 1,583 individuals for violating the above two articles. For the previous decade (1958–66), the number of those convicted of anti-Soviet agitation and propaganda amounted to 3,448 individuals.[38] Incidentally, 1958 belongs to the time that is often called the "period of liberalization"; it was also the year to which N. S. Khrushchev referred on January 17, 1959, when he declared the absence of "criminal prosecution for political crimes." In 1958, the number of people convicted under article 70 was 1,416 individuals (i.e., almost as many as during the previous ten years).

On December 20, 1975, there were 860 people in corrective labor institutions for committing especially dangerous state crimes. This includes 261 individuals who were convicted of anti-Soviet agitation and propaganda and who are held in two corrective labor colonies.

This decrease in the number of state crimes is the result of a further strengthening of the moral and political unity of Soviet society, the loyalty of Soviet people to the socialist cause, and the decisive interdiction of anti-Soviet activities by hostile elements.

In accordance with directives of the Twenty-fourth Party Congress[39] and the Central Committee, the organs of state security emphasize preventive-prophylactic work to avert state crimes. During the period 1971–74, prophylactic measures were taken against 63,108 individuals. During this period, prophylactic measures alone sufficed to terminate the activity of

---

38. When Vladimir Bukovsky saw these figures, he observed, "These [prisoners] were only the ones the regime had to openly acknowledge as its political opponents. They did not include prisoners who were confined in psychiatric wards, exiled abroad, convicted of trying to cross the border illegally or high treason, or convicted as 'religious people' or in fabricated criminal cases. We don't know anything about them": Bukovskii, *Moskovskii protsess* (Moscow, 1996), 91.

39. The Twenty-fourth Congress of the CPSU, March 30–April 9, 1971, was the most recent. In citing the decisions of the Congress, which formally carried the highest authority, Andropov was reminding his colleagues in the Politburo that the KGB acted only as an instrument of the Party leadership and that they shared responsibility for the suppression of dissent.

1,839 anti-Soviet groups that were still in the gestation stage. Prophylactic measures continue to dominate the activity of security organs.

In addition to prophylactic measures, use was (and is being) made of other operational measures besides criminal prosecution. It proved possible to disrupt, at the formative stage, a number of dangerous nationalistic, revisionist, and other anti-Soviet groups. Compromising the authoritative figures who incited antisocial tendencies made it possible to avert undesirable consequences in a number of regions of the country. Such measures as depriving people of Soviet citizenship and deportation abroad (Solzhenitsyn, Chalidze, Maximov, Krasin, Litvinov, Esenin-Volpin, and others) proved their worth. An improvement in the operational situation also ensued from granting permission to many extremists to leave the Soviet Union for Israel.

Nevertheless, it is impossible at this time to renounce the criminal prosecution of people who oppose the Soviet system, for this would entail an increase in especially dangerous state crimes and antisocial manifestations. Experience shows that the activities of "dissidents," which initially was limited to anti-Soviet propaganda, in a number of cases subsequently assumed such dangerous forms as terrorist activities, an organized underground for purposes of overthrowing Soviet authority, establishment of ties to foreign intelligence services that engage in espionage, etc.

From the foregoing, it follows that a renunciation of active measures to terminate the politically harmful activities of "dissidents" and other hostile elements (as the French and Italian comrades want) could be fraught with the most serious negative consequences. It is impossible to make concessions of principle on this question, since these would inevitably lead to further unacceptable demands on us.

The foregoing confirms the correctness of our Party line to wage a decisive battle "to protect Soviet society from the activities of harmful elements." Accordingly, the organs of state security will continue to take resolute measures to terminate any anti-Soviet activities on the territory of our country. It is expedient to conduct a well-proved policy of combining prophylactic and other operational-chekist[40] measures with criminal prosecution in those cases where it is essential.

The KGB will strictly see to it that the so-called "dissidents" cannot cre-

---

40. The word "chekist" is derived from the original name for the secret police, Cheka, an acronym for All-Russian Extraordinary Commission. It was under Lenin that terror against enemies, real and perceived, was initiated. The name was proudly accepted within the Soviet security community and used each time they wanted to emphasize the continuity of the secret police tradition.

ate an organized anti-Soviet underground and carry out anti-Soviet activities. This pertains as well to activities from a "legal position" (Sakharov's "Human Rights Committee," the "Amnesty International Group," the holding of meetings with definite political goals, etc.).

It would be desirable, at an appropriate time, to hold appropriate discussions with French and Italian comrades at a high level. One could explain to them that the struggle with so-called "dissidents" is not an abstract question of democratization for us, but vitally important for ensuring the security of the Soviet state. Our measures to interdict the activities of "dissidents" and other anti-Soviet elements in no way bears a "massive" character, but concerns only specific individuals, who have not abandoned their activities after the appropriate official admonitions and warnings. These measures are based on socialist legality and are in complete compliance with Leninist principles for the development of a socialist democracy. In conducting more vigorous actions, as far as possible we take into account the interests of our friends who are working under the conditions of bourgeois-democratic states.

Consequently, the statements of the French and Italian comrades on questions of democratic freedoms under socialism evoke perplexity among the Soviet people. It seems more efficacious for our propaganda to demonstrate more fully the advantages of the Soviet social and state order, the true popular character of Soviet democracy, and the deep interest of the workers in our country in the unconditional observance of laws, which confer on Soviet citizens the broadest social and political rights. One should also give special attention to the fact that the Soviet constitution provides for the exercise of those rights and liberties, including freedom of speech and assembly, but only "in accordance with the interests of the workers and for purposes of strengthening the socialist order." It is precisely on this class basis and in full compliance with the laws that the antisocialist activities of the "dissidents" are curbed. They are convicted not for their "nonconformity" but for active criminal deeds and subversive activities against the socialist order. It should be emphasized that the antisocialist activities of hostile elements are linked to the influence of bourgeois propaganda, with the organized subversive activities of imperialist intelligence services and anti-Soviet centers. Yakir, Dzyuba, Krasin, and others have publicly admitted such connections.

One must show that real socialism is the embodiment of Leninist ideas about the functions and role of the state in the period of communist construction. One must also make clear the purpose of measures aimed at defending the accomplishments of socialism. It is essential to emphasize the

special responsibility of fraternal parties holding power for the fate of society and the state.

On the eve of the Twenty-fifth Party Congress, which was held from
February 24 to March 5, 1976, KGB agents obtained a copy of
Sakharov's appeal for a general amnesty for prisoners of conscience in
Eastern Europe and the Soviet Union. The appeal was directed not
only to the party leadership but also to "foreign [Communist] delega-
tions" and Western socialist parties that were also participating.

· DOCUMENT III ·

Andropov to Central Committee, February 21, 1976
Sakharov appeals on behalf of prisoners of conscience

The Committee for State Security has obtained information that Academician Sakharov has prepared an "appeal" to delegates and guests of
the Congress, leaders of the CPSU, and foreign delegations. It has the following content:

We ask for your assistance in resolving a question of great moral and political significance. Thousands of people are confined in the camps of Perm
and Mordovia, in the horrific prison in Vladimir, in tens of other camps,
and in prison psychiatric hospitals; they are suffering for their convictions
or for nonviolent actions that would never be considered a crime in any
democratic country. There are people among them who, heeding the call of
their conscience, spoke in defense of the victims of repression and in defense of glasnost. There are religious believers and people who wish to emigrate, including Germans, Jews, Russians, Ukrainians, Armenians, Lithuanians, and others. Nowadays all this cannot be refuted by propagandistic
lies. The question of political amnesty is just as acute as in many other
countries, including the socialist countries of Eastern Europe. Today we
fear for the life of Mustafa Dzhemilev in an Omsk prison and Mihajlo Mi-
hajlov in a Yugoslav prison. We are calling for a general political amnesty
and legislation to ameliorate conditions in places of confinement for all
categories of prisoners. Only after this disgrace, this unbearable stress
weighing on people's conscience, is eliminated can one start thinking about
improving the moral, political, and even economic situation in the country.
A political amnesty in the USSR and in other countries of Eastern Europe
would be a genuinely historic act of great significance for the whole of
mankind. It will make a general political amnesty everywhere in the world

possible and will thus contribute to a better understanding between peoples, to a true détente, to a more humane world, to peace. We hope that this will be widely appreciated both in our country and abroad.

This letter is supposed to be signed by Sakharov and by his remaining sympathizers Orlov, Turchin, and Amalrik. . . .[41]

---

The following two documents related to two political trials: those of Andrei Tverdokhlebov in Moscow and Mustafa Dzhemilev in Omsk, more than a thousand miles east of the Soviet capital. Both trials were scheduled to open on April 6, but then each was postponed in order to confuse their supporters. "This was no coincidence," Sakharov remembered. "The KGB wanted to make sure that no one could attend both trials." Sakharov decided it was more important for him to go to Omsk. In Moscow, at least, foreign correspondents could be in touch with Tverdokhlebov's supporters and join them outside the courtroom, whereas "there was reason to fear that little information about [the trial in Omsk] would be reported with any speed." (According to Sakharov, the KGB cut off the city's long-distance telephone service during Dzhemilev's trial.)[42] In Omsk Sakharov and Bonner experienced a crude confrontation with police outside the courtroom.

Dzhemilev and Tverdokhlebov were both convicted; Dzhemilev was sent to a labor camp for two and a half years, while Tverdokhlebov got off with a lenient sentence of five years of internal exile. Later that year, Sakharov and Bonner undertook a difficult trip to visit Tverdokhlebov at his place of exile in Nyurbachan, a small, remote settlement in Yakutia; to reach him they had to walk about twelve miles on a deserted forest road. Sakharov tore a ligament in his leg during the trip and required a cast to ensure its recovery.

### · DOCUMENT 112 ·

Andropov to Central Committee, April 15, 1976
The trials of Andrei Tverdokhlebov and Mustafa Dzhemilev

---

The Committee for State Security of the USSR Council of Ministers reports that on April 14 Sakharov and his wife Bonner committed acts of

---

41. This appeal was published in *Chronicle of Current Events*, no. 39, 214 (Amnesty International ed., 1978). It was signed by these four activists and by General Pyotr Grigorenko and dated February 23, 1976, two days after Andropov's report.
42. Sakharov, *Memoirs*, 449, 451.

hooliganism at the courthouse in the city of Omsk. They went there for the beginning of the trial of Dzhemilev, who has been indicted for disseminating flagrantly fallacious fabrications discrediting the state and public order of the Soviet Union.

Sakharov and Bonner tried to enter the courtroom, but all the seats had already been taken. In response to warnings by on-duty police officers that there were no vacant seats in the room, Sakharov caused an uproar: he slapped the two policemen in the face, shouting, "Take that, you puppies, from Sakharov." Bonner also struck the face of the commandant of the courthouse who was trying to restore order.

Sakharov and Bonner were detained and brought to the police station. In his written statement Sakharov admitted that he had in fact struck the policemen, but claimed that he did so only after the police tried to twist his arms. He categorically refused an offer to undergo a medical examination in order to support his statement. Bonner claimed in her statement that her actions had been premeditated and that she knew what she was doing. After all the necessary papers were completed, Sakharov and Bonner were released.

·  DOCUMENT 113  ·

Andropov to Central Committee, April 16, 1976
More on the trials of Tverdokhlebov and Dzhemilev

On April 14–15, 1976, trials were conducted of A. N. Tverdokhlebov in Moscow and M. Dzhemilev in Omsk. They were indicted for disseminating deliberately false fabrications that discredit the Soviet state and social system.

Tverdokhlebov, proved guilty by an abundance of evidence and by the testimony of sixteen witnesses, admitted that between 1970 and 1975 he produced and disseminated various libelous documents. In his final statement, he attempted to justify his criminal actions by demagogic references to the provisions of the Final Act of the Helsinki Conference, the Declaration of Human Rights, and so forth. As a result, the court decided to deprive him of the right to make a final statement. Tverdokhlebov was sentenced to five years of exile.

The court proceedings also found Dzhemilev guilty. In his final plea, Dzhemilev claimed that he adhered to his ideological views and intends to continue his hostile activities. The court sentenced Dzhemilev to two and a half years of imprisonment.

The citizens attending the trials approved the verdicts.

Antisocial elements attempted to influence the court proceedings. Thirty-five to forty people assembled near the Moscow Municipal Court tried to disturb public order by shouting in support of Tverdokhlebov.

Sakharov and his wife Bonner arrived in Omsk and committed hooligan actions directed against the police and representatives of the public. . . .

The acts of Bonner and Sakharov have been documented. They may be regarded as a criminal offense according to Article 191–1, Part II of the Criminal Code of the RSFSR (forcefully resisting a policeman or a member of the voluntary militia[43] while he is performing his duty of maintaining public order).

For the time being, it has been decided only to issue an official warning to Bonner and Sakharov and not to indict them for a criminal offense. We plan to use the fact of Sakharov and Bonner's criminal activities in the steps we are taking to expose their antisocial activity. . . .

---

· DOCUMENT 115 ·

Andropov to Central Committee, August 26, 1976
Sakharov and Bonner visit Andrei Tverdokhlebov in his place of exile

---

In April 1976 the Moscow Municipal Court sentenced A. N. Tverdokhlebov (one of Academician Sakharov's closest associates) to five years in exile for consciously disseminating false fabrications that discredit the Soviet state and social system. The village of Nyurbachan of the Yakutsk ASSR was designated as Tverdokhlebov's place of exile.

As is known, Sakharov and his wife did not attend Tverdokhlebov's trial because they were in another city. However, desiring to provide moral support to Tverdokhlebov and to smooth over the negative reaction of their friends,[44] on August 13, 1976, Sakharov and Bonner left Moscow by plane for Nyurba, a district capital in Yakutia. Their repeated attempts to find transport to take them the twelve miles from Nyurba to Nyurbachan were unsuccessful.[45] As a result, that night the Sakharovs started out on foot. To use their own words, they experienced many fears that night, and

---

43. Civilians recruited as an auxiliary security force.

44. Andropov was insinuating that Sakharov and Bonner's friends had criticized them for failing to attend Tverdokhlebov's trial.

45. According to Bonner, a police post on the road warned drivers not to pick up passengers.

on August 15 at 3 A.M. they arrived at Tverdokhlebov's. In their talk with
Tverdokhlebov, they repeatedly expressed their anger that the local people
had refused to take them to Tverdokhlebov's house. The conversations between the Sakharovs and Tverdokhlebov were mostly on themes of everyday life.

While walking in the taiga, Sakharov hurt his leg and returned to Moscow on crutches. His injured leg is now in a plaster cast.

Lately Sakharov has been traveling rather often to various towns of the
Soviet Union, where he usually takes part in antisocial actions. During
these excursions, unexpected occurrences, accidents, etc., can happen, and
they might be portrayed by the enemy as a premeditated action against
Sakharov.

Given the above, the Committee for State Security would consider it expedient, through the Department of Science and Education Institutions of
the CPSU Central Committee, to instruct the Presidium of the USSR Academy of Sciences to speak to Sakharov and point out to him the undesirability of doing things that might jeopardize his health. . . .

---

The issue of human rights was about to gain an enormous boost in
visibility and political legitimacy, first with the election of Jimmy
Carter as president of the United States and then with the establishment of Helsinki groups in the Soviet Union. In August 1975, thirty-
five countries, including the United States, had signed the Helsinki
Final Act, which included significant humanitarian provisions. Dissidents throughout the USSR and Eastern Europe saw an opportunity to
use the Helsinki Final Act as a means to monitor Soviet compliance
with its human rights guarantees within a process that the regime itself
had endorsed. After the crackdown surrounding the cases of Yakir and
Krasin, the establishment of Helsinki groups in five Soviet republics
helped to revive the Soviet human rights movement. *A Chronicle of
Current Events* also began to appear regularly again (the editors had
continued to compile information but held back from publishing it)
and continued to challenge the regime's strict control of information.
Sakharov decided not to join the Moscow Helsinki Group, headed by
the physicist Yuri Orlov, but he participated in some of its activities
and signed individual appeals; Elena Bonner did join the Moscow
Helsinki Group.

· DOCUMENT 118 ·

Andropov to Central Committee, November 15, 1976
Establishment of the Moscow Helsinki Watch Group

In recent years the enemy's intelligence services and propaganda organs have attempted to create the appearance of a so-called "domestic opposition" in the Soviet Union. They are taking measures to support the instigators of antisocial manifestations and objectively to assist the participants in various currents of anti-Soviet activities to form a bloc.

Thus, in 1969, antisocial elements led by Yakir and Krasin founded an "Initiative Group" for the purposes of creating an organized association of those who participate in the so-called "democratization movement." In 1970, to stimulate the antisocial activities of hostile elements, Chalidze created the so-called "Human Rights Committee," which was joined by Academician Sakharov and a corresponding member of the Academy of Sciences, Shafarevich. In 1973 the so-called "Russian" section of "Amnesty International," headed by Turchin and Tverdokhlebov, assumed the function of providing an organized association of anti-Soviet individuals. Members of these organizations established contacts with certain foreign anti-Soviet centers and, for purposes of discrediting the Soviet state and public order, collected and assembled libelous materials.

As a result of measures taken by the Committee for State Security, the "Initiative Group" and the "Human Rights Committee" compromised themselves totally and, for all practical purposes, ceased to exist. The activity of the [Amnesty International] "Russian Section" was contained. However, despite all the failures to create a "domestic opposition" in the USSR, the enemy has not abandoned this idea.

On May 12, 1976, at the initiative of Yu. F. Orlov (corresponding member of the Armenian Academy of Sciences; born 1924; unemployed), antisocial elements announced the creation of a "group to help implement the Helsinki Agreements in the USSR."[46]

The "group" includes the following individuals: those who have repeatedly been subjected to criminal prosecution—A. I. Ginzburg (born 1936; Jew; unemployed) and P. G. Grigorenko (born 1907; Ukrainian; pensioner); the professional criminal A. T. Marchenko (born 1938; Russian;

46. Four other Helsinki groups were soon created: the Ukrainian on November 9, 1976; the Lithuanian on November 25, 1976; the Georgian on January 14, 1977; and the Armenian on April 1, 1977.

serving a sentence of exile in Irkutsk Oblast); Jewish extremists—V. A. Rubin (born 1923; Jew; emigrated to Israel); A. B. Shcharansky (born 1948; Jew; unemployed); and V. S. Slepak (born 1927; Jew; unemployed); participants in various hostile activities—the wife of Sakharov, E. G. Bonner (born 1922; Jew; pensioner); M. S. Bernshtam (born 1949; Jew; emigrated to Israel); M. N. Landa (born 1918; Jew; pensioner); L. M. Alexeyeva (born 1927; Russian; unemployed); and A. A. Korchak (born 1922; Ukrainian; researcher at Institute of Terrestrial Magnetism of Ionosphere and Radiowave Distribution at USSR Academy of Sciences).

In creating this "Group," these people pursue the provocative goal of questioning the sincerity of attempts by the USSR to implement the Final Act of the Conference on Security and Cooperation in Europe, and thereby to put pressure on the government of the Soviet Union on questions pertaining to the realization of the Helsinki agreements (above all, in "Basket 3").

The members of the "Group" are collecting information about alleged instances in which the Soviet government has failed to implement the Final Act, in particular through "violations of the fundamental rights of Soviet citizens," "persecution of dissent," etc.

They transmit the information collected on this question through various channels to the governments of countries that signed the Final Act. According to the conception of the "Group's" members, under special circumstances they will appeal to these countries to create an international commission to investigate the facts of a case. Moreover, the "group" is counting on Western public opinion to put pressure on the Soviet government and will not seek, in Orlov's words, "to find support among the [Soviet] people."[47]

Antisocial elements appeal to the heads of states that participated in the Helsinki conference to establish similar unofficial control groups in their own countries. The latter can then all be united in an international committee.[48] During the period of its existence, the "group" has undertaken a

47. For discussion of the history of the Helsinki Watch groups, see Joshua Rubenstein, *Soviet Dissidents: Their Struggle for Human Rights* (Boston, 1985); Paul Goldberg, *The Final Act* (New York, 1988); Ludmilla Alexeyeva, *Soviet Dissent: Contemporary Movements for National, Religious, and Human Rights,* trans. Carol Pearce and John Glad (Middletown, CT, 1985); Daniel Thomas, *The Helsinki Effect: International Norms, Human Rights, and the Demise of Communism* (Princeton, 2001); Yuri Orlov, *Dangerous Thoughts: Memoirs of a Russian Life,* trans. Thomas P. Whitney (New York, 1991); Natan Sharansky, *Fear No Evil,* trans. Stefani Hoffman (New York, 1988); and Petro G. Grigorenko, *Memoirs,* trans. Thomas P. Whitney (New York, 1982).

48. Andropov unwittingly identified the starting point for the international Helsinki movement.

number of attempts to obtain official recognition by governmental agencies in the USA. Thus, Orlov held a discussion with the first secretary of the political section of the U.S. embassy in Moscow, Richard Combs, in September 1976.[49] Orlov insisted that the U.S. Department of State grant official recognition to the "group," and that the Americans use the information from the "group" at the level of governments and heads of state (at the impending conference in Belgrade as well).

The Committee for State Security is taking measures to compromise and interdict hostile activities by the participants of the "group." . . .[50]

---

The following reports by Andropov did not do justice to the drama that was unfolding in the first months of 1977. An unprecedented series of events tested the resolve of both the U.S. government and Andrei Sakharov.

It began on January 8, when a bomb exploded in the Moscow subway, killing seven people and wounding as many as thirty. The regime hinted that a dissident group of some kind had planted the bomb and that the Soviet public demanded retribution. Sakharov had suspicions of his own. He issued a statement on January 12 suggesting that the explosion could have been a provocation by the KGB in order to target dissidents and calling for a public investigation with the assistance of foreign experts. Over the next few days, a friend of Efrem Yankelevich was interrogated about the blast. So was Vladimir Albrekht, who was an active member of Moscow's Amnesty International chapter. And when the veteran dissident Kronid Lubarsky was released from Vladimir Prison on January 22 after serving a five-year term, he was told that had he gotten out two weeks earlier, "he would have had to present an alibi for the day of the explosion." Sakharov's fears seemed to be coming true.

The regime did not relent. Sakharov was summoned to the procurator's office for the second time and officially warned that his slanderous accusation against the Soviet government could lead to prosecution unless he issued a correction. And the next day an angry press campaign began against Sakharov; the opening salvo in *Izvestia* was headed "A Slanderer Is Warned." The Kremlin may well have been preparing a more serious move against him. According to *A Chronicle*

---

49. A year and a half later, in May 1978, the police would not permit Richard Combs to enter the courthouse where Orlov's trial was taking place; see *New York Times*, May 16, 1978, 3.

50. In early January the KGB searched the apartments of Orlov, Ginzburg, and Alexeyeva, and, as usual, claimed to have found incriminating evidence of ties to foreign organizations; see *New York Times*, January 5, 1977, 5.

*of Current Events,* the Novosti press agency was working on the gal-
leys of a pamphlet explaining Sakharov's exile in several languages.[51]

In the midst of these events, Jimmy Carter was inaugurated as president of the United States, promising to make the promotion of human
rights the driving force of U.S. foreign policy. Sakharov wrote to President Carter, urging him to remain steadfast in his defense of human
rights and prisoners of conscience.[52] Carter responded two weeks
later, reaffirming his intentions to make "human rights . . . a central
concern of my administration."[53] Carter's brief correspondence with
Sakharov, coming so soon after his inauguration, stirred a hornet's
nest of controversy, with some observers praising the new president
while others chided him for "an innocent mistake of inexperience."[54]

Soviet leaders did not hesitate to express impatience with Carter's
initiative. The Politburo authorized a toughly worded private letter,
admonishing the president for writing at the same time to Brezhnev
and to "an apostate [Sakharov] who has proclaimed himself the enemy
of the Soviet state and is against normal, good relations between the
Soviet Union and the United States."[55]

Arrests in Moscow immediately took over the headlines. By the middle of March, the regime had arrested Alexander Ginzburg, Yuri
Orlov, and Anatoly Shcharansky of the Moscow Helsinki Group,
while their colleague Ludmilla Alexeyeva was forced to leave the country. Other Helsinki monitors were arrested in Ukraine, Georgia, and
Lithuania. Shcharansky's arrest was particularly provocative for it was
accompanied by a public accusation that he had been working for the
CIA.

51. See *A Chronicle of Current Events,* no. 44, 185 (Amnesty International ed.,
1979). Andrei Sakharov, *Alarm and Hope,* trans. Efrem Yankelevich and Alfred
Friendly Jr. (New York, 1978), 57–80, has a full discussion of the subway bomb
episode.

52. See *New York Times,* January 29, 1977, 2, for the text of his letter along with a
list of fifteen prisoner cases.

53. Sakharov, *Memoirs,* 687.

54. *New York Times,* February 20, 1977, 15.

55. Anatoly Dobrynin, *In Confidence: Moscow's Ambassador to America's Six
Cold War Presidents (1962–1986)* (New York, 1995), 391.

## · DOCUMENT 121 ·

Andropov, Gromyko, and Rudenko to Central Committee, January 18, 1977
A bomb in the Moscow subway and the expulsion of George Krimsky

---

On January 13, 1977, Academician Sakharov, during a meeting with G. Krimsky (the correspondent for the news agency "Associated Press"), made a slanderous statement for the press. He claimed that the explosions that occurred earlier in Moscow were arranged by state security organs, which "with an ever increasing frequency are using exclusively criminal methods that remind one not only of fascist Italy and Germany, but of our own country in the same period." In his opinion, Soviet authorities organized the explosions in the subway in an attempt to place the blame on "dissidents" and lay the basis for a new policy of repression and discrediting dissidents that would be sanctioned from above and would create an atmosphere of "popular fury."[56] To "substantiate" his allegations, Sakharov has been spreading in his circles a rumor that "medical emergency cars had concentrated in the area of the Shchelkovskaya subway station even before the explosion occurred." In his statement, Sakharov urges international public opinion to demand an open investigation of the incident, with the participation of foreign experts and lawyers.

On repeated occasions in the past, Sakharov has made libelous statements against the organs of state security. He has attempted to charge them, among other things, with the murder of the lawyer [Brunov] (who, in an inebriated state, was run over by a freight train);[57] the murder of the poet and translator Bogatyrev (who, while drunk, died from the effects of a brawl with his drinking companions); as well as the murders of the Baptist Petrenko, the Catholic engineer Tomanov, and the preschool teacher Lukshaite, all of whom in fact died in various everyday situations.

Sakharov's provocative statement was picked up by various propaganda organs in capitalist countries and is being actively employed to vilify the domestic and foreign policy of our state.

One cannot help but note that on January 14 Sakharov visited the U.S. embassy in the USSR and for an hour and a half talked with the first secretary of the embassy's political affairs department [name illegible], a regular employee of the CIA (photographs are enclosed).[58]

---

56. Sakharov's suspicions were publicized by the Western press; see, for example, *New York Times,* January 15, 1977, 7.
57. On Yevgeny Brunov, see Sakharov, *Memoirs,* 439–42.
58. Photographs were not included with the declassified document.

Taking into account the fact that the statement about the cause of the explosion was a malicious provocation (which has been actively exploited by Western imperialist propaganda to discredit the Soviet state and public order), it appears expedient to send an official summons to Sakharov to appear at the Office of the Procurator of the USSR to explain his statement to a foreign correspondent. If Sakharov confirms that he made the statement, inform him that such actions contain slander against the government and are punishable by law. He is to be officially warned that such behavior is unacceptable in the future.

As for the correspondent of the agency "Associated Press" G. Krimsky, it is imperative to prepare and implement measures that, once we expose the fact of his connections with the CIA and his violation of customs regulations, would force the American side to recall him from the Soviet Union. If the Americans decline, he is to be expelled from the country.[59]

The measures taken with respect to Sakharov and Krimsky are to be reported in the Soviet press. . . .

· DOCUMENT 122 ·

Andropov to Central Committee, February 9, 1977
Correspondence between Andrei Sakharov and Jimmy Carter

On February 8, after receiving an invitation from the first secretary of the political section of the U.S. embassy in Moscow, Combs, Sakharov visited the embassy. According to information obtained by the Committee of State Security of the USSR Soviet of Ministers, he was given a telegram from U.S. President Carter, bearing the following contents:

Dear Professor Sakharov:
I received your letter of January 21, and I want to express my appreciation to you for bringing your thoughts to my personal attention.[60]

Human rights are a central concern of my administration. In my inaugural address I stated: "Because we are free, we can never be indifferent to the fate of freedom elsewhere." You may rest assured that the Ameri-

59. George Krimsky was expelled from the Soviet Union in February 1977; he was the first American journalist to be expelled in seven years.
60. Sakharov urged the American president to "raise his voice" on behalf of persecuted activists and declare that, the Helsinki Final Act notwithstanding, Soviet officials refused to respect human rights. The letter was published in the *New York Times*, January 29, 1977, 2.

can people and our government will continue our firm commitment to promote respect for human rights not only in our country, but also abroad.

We shall use our good offices to seek the release of prisoners of conscience, and we will continue our efforts to shape a world responsive to human aspirations in which nations of different cultures and histories can live side by side in peace and justice.

I am always glad to hear from you, and I wish you well.

Sincerely,

J. Carter
February 6

Sakharov regards Carter's telegram as an act of support for the illegal activities pursued by himself and his accomplices, and also as a guarantee of his personal immunity. The Committee for State Security is taking these circumstances into account while taking steps to avert and interdict Sakharov's hostile activities. . . .

---

· DOCUMENT 123 ·

Andropov to Central Committee, February 18, 1977
U.S. government activities in defense of human rights

---

The Committee for State Security reports that intelligence services of the USA have been given a definite role in the anti-Soviet campaign "in defense of democratic freedoms in the USSR" that has been unleashed in the USA. Ideological centers and Zionist organizations have involved the new Carter administration and prominent senators in this campaign.

In the past, it was mainly American journalists and foreigners temporarily visiting our country who were drawn into the orbit of this activity. Now, however, diplomats and other representatives of the USA (who have pertinent instructions), with the active participation of resident representatives of the CIA and DIA [Defense Intelligence Agency], are conducting well-targeted work with the so-called "democratic movement," Jewish "refuseniks," and nationalists.

For example, at the end of 1976, the first secretary of the political department of the U.S. embassy, Belousovich, transmitted a large quantity of hostile anti-Soviet literature to the Georgian nationalist Gamsakhurdia.

While visiting the Moscow synagogue in August 1976, embassy coun-
selors Gross and Lobner disseminated Zionist materials.

At a meeting with the well-known "dissident" Orlov in December
1976, the first secretary of the U.S. embassy Combs offered him practical
pointers on stimulating the activity of the anti-Soviet group he heads.
While visiting the Baltic, Combs incited Lithuanian nationalists to increase their activities. Pro-Zionists and other hostile elements consider the
first secretary of the embassy's political department, Pressel, who demonstratively maintains contacts with them, to be an "expert" on issues of the
democratic movement all over the country. They provide him with various
libelous materials, which are then sent abroad through diplomatic channels.

The U.S. embassy in Moscow has begun to maintain regular contact
with Sakharov. On February 8, 1977, the Americans invited Sakharov to
the embassy where the text of a letter from U.S. President Carter was read
to him. At the same meeting Sakharov gave the Americans yet another libelous appeal to the West and agreed to return to the embassy to receive
the original of Carter's letter. On February 17 Sakharov visited the embassy and received the letter.

While making these contacts with Sakharov, the U.S. embassy realizes
that these actions can provoke a sharp reaction from the Soviet side, even
at a very high level. Touching on this question, the same Pressel told his
colleagues that "until the end of the Belgrade conference, one need not
worry about Sakharov's fate, since Soviet authorities will not dare persecute him."[61] In the future, according to him, another outcome is possible,
since "no war is without casualties."

To expose to world public opinion the true aims of those who incite an
anti-Soviet campaign in the West, to unmask the use of "dissidents" and
nationalists from among Soviet citizens by U.S. intelligence services for espionage and subversive activities, and to curb the hostile activities of
American diplomats and journalists who carry out these plans on Soviet
territory, the Committee for State Security deems it necessary to take the
following step: to instruct the Ministry of Foreign Affairs to protest to the
U.S. embassy the provocative role played by American diplomats who receive Sakharov in the embassy and incite him to commit acts hostile to the
Soviet Union and to make libelous statements. . . .

---

61. The Belgrade Conference, the first to review compliance with the Helsinki Final
Act, lasted from the fall of 1977 until March 1978.

· DOCUMENT 124 ·

Andropov to Central Committee, March 29, 1977
The arrest of Anatoly Shcharansky

The Committee for State Security has obtained information that American diplomats and foreign correspondents in Moscow judge the articles and commentaries in the Soviet press and the broadcasts on radio and television (which rebut the Western anti-Soviet campaign about "human rights violations") as showing the firm resolve of the Soviet Union not to tolerate intervention in its internal affairs, particularly on the eve of U.S. Secretary of State [Cyrus] Vance's visit to the USSR.

In their opinion, "the culminating point in Moscow's measures" was the arrest of the "dissident Shcharansky" by Soviet authorities.[62] This shows that the USSR is determined to take measures, as provided by the law, in dealing with such renegades.

According to the statements of the American journalist Axelbank, the publication of compromising materials in *Izvestia* and the subsequent arrest of Shcharansky have left the American side in an awkward position. If this situation is strengthened by new evidence that American intelligence agencies used "dissidents" for espionage, this will significantly impede the West in conducting propaganda in "defense of human rights" in the USSR and will enhance Moscow's position on this issue.

On this question, another American journalist, Rezin, declared that punishment for espionage for a foreign power will not cause doubts in any quarters, including American jurists. There is no reason to fear that Vance will be offended, although he might express his displeasure.

The correspondent of the *Los Angeles Times,* Toth, in an official report from Moscow warned his newspaper's editors that he might be in difficult straits because of Shcharansky's arrest, since the latter helped him to prepare articles with information on secret Soviet installations that use American equipment. In addition, this information was obtained from people who had earlier worked at these installations and who had been provisionally denied permission to emigrate from the USSR.

After Shcharansky's arrest. "dissidents" headed by Sakharov organized an improvised press conference at a private apartment on March 16. Sev-

62. Shcharansky was arrested in Moscow on March 15, 1977. He was released in February 1986. After reaching Israel, he changed his name to Natan Sharansky.

eral American and other Western journalists were invited to this conference, where they were given libelous statements that had been prepared in advance.[63]

According to the information that has been obtained, the U.S. embassy—in its report to the State Department about this press conference—laid particular emphasis on the statements by Sakharov: "Given the current critical state of the Soviet human rights movement, it would be very useful if the American Congress and president somehow reacted to the arrest of Shcharansky. Any reduction in foreign pressure with respect to the human rights question, in such a critical moment, is extremely undesirable."

In response to the question of one foreign correspondent as to whether Sakharov intends to meet with Vance during his visit to the USSR, he said that he does not want such a meeting if it puts the secretary of state in a difficult position, and he himself does not intend to ask for such a meeting.

At a closed press conference for American correspondents held on March 18 in the U.S. embassy, the representative of the embassy made an evasive comment on the appeal from Sakharov and other "dissidents" to give them assistance, declaring that he has not yet been apprised of the U.S. government reaction. In response to a correspondent's query whether Shcharansky's arrest complicates Vance's visit to the USSR, the embassy representative responded that the Carter administration does not link human rights with détente.

According to the available information, the U.S. mass media acknowledge that "concrete, serious accusations of state treason" have been made against Shcharansky, and that this creates a difficult situation for those who attempt to speak on his behalf.

---

A series of Sakharov hearings were held between 1975 and 1985 in Copenhagen (1975), Rome (1977), Washington, D.C. (1979), Lisbon (1983), and London (1985). Initially the conferences reported on human rights in the Soviet Union; later they were broadened to include Eastern Europe. Beginning in 1977, Efrem Yankelevich helped to organize the hearings and in Sakharov's words, "ensured the exclusion of any false, unsubstantiated, or sensational testimony, and a focus on significant issues."[64] The KGB closely observed the first conference in Copenhagen.

63. Reported in *New York Times,* March 17, 1977, 2.
64. Sakharov, *Memoirs,* 474.

## · DOCUMENT 125 ·

Andropov to Central Committee, May 13, 1977
The holding of the first Sakharov hearing in Copenhagen

Our position regarding the provocative campaign of the so-called "Sakharov Committee in Denmark."

1. Agree with the proposal of the Committee for State Security of the USSR Council of Ministers as stated in memorandum no. 989-A of May 13, 1977 (attached).[65]
2. Forward the memorandum of the Committee for State Security regarding this question to the International Department and the Department of Propaganda of the CPSU Central Committee, and to the Ministry of Foreign Affairs for information and practical use.

Our position regarding the provocative campaign of the so-called "Sakharov Committee in Denmark."

According to information in the possession of the Committee for State Security, after an unsuccessful attempt to conduct an anti-Soviet action called "the Sakharov Hearings" in Copenhagen, the so-called "Sakharov Committee in Denmark" (which was created by U.S. intelligence services) has started a new provocative campaign to "exchange" thirteen political prisoners in Chile for thirteen "dissidents" serving sentences in our country for particularly grave state crimes. The "Committee" is primarily using the list of individuals that Sakharov sent to the West last March. Proposed for exchange are: Karavansky, Kovalev, Kuznetsov, Gluzman, Moroz, Shukhevich, and others.

The chairman of the "Sakharov Committee," Andersen, declares that the "exchange" has already been accepted by the Chilean government, which is prepared to release thirteen political prisoners. The USSR embassy in Denmark received the corresponding "message" from the "Committee."

Given the provocative character of this campaign, we consider it expedient to ignore the proposals of the "Committee" completely and to warn Soviet official organs against any contacts with it. . . .

The fall of 1977 marked a major change in Sakharov and Bonner's family. Not only did she receive permission to go to Italy for a second

---

65. The attachment was headed "Decree on the same issue by the Central Committee of the CPSU."

eye operation, but Efrem and Tatiana Yankelevich were given permission to emigrate. "A long period of steadily increasing harassment had convinced them to leave," Sakharov recalled. Efrem, in fact, "was in danger of arrest on political charges."[66] Elena Bonner, Efrem and Tatiana, and their two young children, Matvei and Anya, left for Italy on September 5. After her surgery, Bonner returned to Moscow on November 20; in December the Yankelevich family took up residence in Boston, Massachusetts.

· DOCUMENT 127 ·

Andropov to Central Committee, July 20, 1977
Elena Bonner travels to Italy

In 1975, permission was given for citizen Bonner (wife of Academician Sakharov, who is notorious for his antisocial activities) to travel to Italy. Bonner justified the need for foreign travel by the need for medical treatment for her eyes. In permitting the travel, it was expected that during her stay abroad, Bonner might establish contact with foreign subversive centers and openly express her anti-Soviet views. Account was also taken of the fact that at this time the enemy would stir up a commotion over the award of the Nobel Peace Prize to Sakharov.

In fact, once abroad, Bonner issued a whole series of provocative declarations and made open anti-Soviet attacks, especially when she accepted (at Sakharov's request) the Nobel award.

Such behavior by Bonner, who used the trip abroad for purposes of provocation, nevertheless played a positive role: world and Soviet public opinion saw the true face of Bonner and, through her, Sakharov. In the final analysis, this fact led to further isolation of Sakharov, especially among the Soviet scientific intelligentsia.[67]

At the present time, Bonner is again raising the question of a trip to Italy on a private invitation for a second eye operation. Having weighed all sides of this question, the Committee for State Security finds it expedient on this occasion not to oppose Bonner's trip. One can expect that Bonner will attempt to use her presence abroad for antisocial purposes. However, the very fact that she was permitted to go to Italy will significantly diminish her level

66. Sakharov, *Memoirs*, 472–73.
67. The last phrase alluded to the KGB's attempt to arouse the envy of Sakharov's colleagues; travel abroad was among the most cherished of privileges.

of activity. This decision will put Sakharov himself in a difficult position, since he will find it difficult to explain the authorities' treatment of his wife. One must also take into account the fact that rejection of a trip for medical treatment will entail large costs in terms of propaganda. . . .

The silent vigils in Pushkin Square had begun on December 5, 1965—Soviet Constitution Day—with a call for a fair and open trial for Sinyavsky and Daniel, the writers who had been arrested the previous September. In the fall of 1977, the Soviet Union adopted a new constitution. That December, Moscow activists moved the vigil to December 10, International Human Rights Day, which commemorates the adoption of the Universal Declaration of Human Rights by the U.N. General Assembly in 1948. The KGB took more vigorous action than usual to disrupt the demonstration, placing several of the organizers under brief house arrest. Sakharov had attended several of these vigils, but he "had never been all that enthusiastic about [them]"; they "smacked of 'revolutionary' party rallies, and [he] disliked the role of 'opposition leader' into which [he] was thrust."[68] He did not attend the vigils in 1977, 1978, or 1979.

·  DOCUMENT 128  ·

Andropov to Central Committee, December 11, 1977
Demonstration in Pushkin Square

On December 10, 1977, in connection with Human Rights Day, a group of antisocial elements, who had been incited by foreign anti-Soviet centers, attempted to organize a provocative assembly in Pushkin Square in Moscow.

Preparation for such an action was actively discussed by extremist Zionist elements at the apartments of Sakharov, the wife of Ginzburg (who is under arrest), and in other places. The active Jewish extremist Podrabinek was especially insistent in endeavoring to realize this scheme.[69] It is worth noting that one-third of the "activists" who engineered the gathering are being treated by psychiatrists.

68. Sakharov, *Memoirs*, 476.
69. Alexander Podrabinek is Jewish but was never active in the Jewish emigration movement. He did organize the Working Commission to Investigate the Use of Psychiatry for Political Purposes. He is cited here as a Jewish activist as part of a propaganda attempt to represent any opposition in the USSR as a Jewish-Zionist conspiracy.

The Committee for State Security had taken measures to undermine the antisocial actions being prepared. It established strict control over the most active extremists and individuals who are inclined to participate in mass meetings. As a result, none of the instigators of the provocation appeared at Pushkin Square, and the planned assembly did not take place.[70]

At the time advertised by foreign radio, only seven or eight idle youths from the families of pro-Zionist elements came to the square. Their presence at the square did not arouse the slightest interest in the people around them. Clearly disheartened were the foreign correspondents who gathered there; among them were Kent ("Associated Press"), Shipler (*Washington Post*), Gallagher (*Chicago Tribune*), Coleman (*Newsweek*), Redmond (CBC), Meier and Prede (DPA), Bernard (radio and television corporation BRD), Brenner and Bets (Reuters), Ruane (BBC), Legal (France Presse), Seborg (United Telegraph Agency of the Northern Countries), and Hostad (*Dagens Nyheter*). . . .[71]

---

On March 11, 1978, a PLO commando unit hijacked a busload of tourists in Israel. In the ensuing firefight with Israeli soldiers, thirty-two people were killed and many more were injured. Andropov noted that Sakharov and Bonner joined a group of Jewish refuseniks to express their outrage in front of the PLO office in Moscow. The police broke up the demonstration. The next day the KGB disconnected the telephone in Sakharov's apartment. Until then, he may have been "the only member of the human rights movement in Moscow who retained a working telephone."[72]

·  DOCUMENT 129  ·

Andropov and Rudenko to Central Committee, March 14, 1978
Dissidents protest a PLO attack in Israel

---

According to information obtained by the Committee for State Security, a group of pro-Zionist individuals planned to conduct a provocative action on March 12 at 6 P.M. at the Moscow office of the Palestine Liberation Or-

70. The KGB often intercepted would-be demonstrators and detained them for three or four hours. The disruption of the vigil was widely reported in the Western press; see *New York Times,* December 11, 1977, 1.

71. Andropov referred incorrectly to at least two of the foreign journalists: David Shipler represented the *New York Times* and Bernard Redmont (not Redmond) worked for CBS.

72. See *New York Times,* March 14, 1978, 5.

ganization (PLO) to express their protest against the incident of March 11 near Tel Aviv. The Committee for State Security has taken steps to strengthen the guard near the PLO office and to reinforce surveillance over the organizers of the provocation (Slepak, Nudel, Yelinson, and others).

Meanwhile, it was ascertained that simultaneously nationalists (about twenty people), as well as Sakharov and his wife Bonner, assembled across the street from the building of the Union of Soviet Societies of Friendship and Cultural Ties with Foreign Countries (14 Kalinin Prospekt),where they attempted to unfurl signs ("Shame on Murderers," "Murderers," "Your Weapons Are Killing Our Children") and to chant the word "Murderers." The measures taken served to quell these attempts and to disperse the participants of the gathering.

The presence of five foreign journalists has been established at the place of the provocation.

The most active participants of this action—I. Ya. Nudel, B. M. Chernobylsky, M. Sh. Kremen, and A. D. Sakharov—will be summoned to the Office of the Moscow City Procurator and warned that violation of public order is unacceptable. . . .

---

As the regime continued its assault on the human rights movement, Sakharov grew more assertive in reaching out to foreign diplomats in Moscow. Many activists were now living in the West, while others were in prison, labor camps, psychiatric hospitals, or internal exile. Sakharov understood that his unique stature, inside and outside the country, increased the need for him to represent the movement and the many disaffected groups that were seeking a hearing with a Western journalist or a sympathetic diplomat. Andropov understood this as well.

· DOCUMENT 130 ·

Andropov to Central Committee, March 26, 1978
Sakharov increases his contacts with foreign diplomats in Moscow

---

As information obtained by the Committee for State Security shows, of late one dimension of Academician Sakharov's pernicious activities has become his systematic visits to diplomatic offices of capitalist countries in Moscow. It should be noted that in the past the pretext for such visits was to arrange the emigration of his wife Bonner's children from the USSR, the transmission of libelous materials, and the receipt of mail from abroad.

Now, however, he visits embassies primarily as "the leader of the struggle for human rights." Sakharov champions the cause of Ukrainian and Baltic nationalists, Zionists, reactionary church people and sectarians, and those who wish to emigrate; he also transmits their documents to diplomats. In some cases Sakharov, counting on his "immunity," escorts anti-Soviet individuals who wish to enter the embassies of capitalist countries.

Whereas in 1974–76 Sakharov visited the embassies of capitalist countries only seven times, last year (1977) twenty such visits were recorded (half of which were at the American embassy).

The Committee for State Security regards Sakharov's visits to the embassies of capitalist countries as a convenient opportunity for Western intelligence agencies to obtain information, including state secrets. . . .

---

In the spring of 1978 Sakharov had several public confrontations with Soviet police and security personnel. In March, as we have seen, he participated in a demonstration in front of the PLO's Moscow office, which was summarily dispersed. On May 19 he stood outside the courthouse in the Moscow suburb of Lyublino, where Yuri Orlov was on trial. He argued vehemently that Orlov's friends should be allowed in to hear the verdict. Then a scuffle broke out. When both he and Elena Bonner were dragged to police cars, they struggled with the police and shoved and hit them back. They were quickly released, but they were later fined for hooliganism. Two months later, they wanted to express their solidarity in front of two courthouses: at the trial of Alexander Ginzburg in Kaluga and the trial of Anatoly Shcharansky in Moscow on virtually the same days.

It proved to be impossible for them to get to Kaluga, but they stood in front of the Moscow courthouse every day during Shcharansky's trial. These proceedings attracted tremendous attention. With Shcharansky accused of espionage, Sakharov did not hesitate to issue a warning that the Kremlin was "threatening the Jews," that the trial was "a Soviet version of the Dreyfus case."[73] After Shcharansky's inevitable conviction, Sakharov joined his family and friends in defiantly singing the Israeli national anthem behind a police barrier in an alley next to the court.

Andropov, of course, had little patience for Sakharov's "hooliganism" and forwarded his report with the hope that Sakharov's public and provocative behavior would finally move the Politburo to take de-

73. *Time,* July 24, 1978, 27; Sakharov, *Memoirs,* 483–84.

cisive action. Andropov wanted to change the image of the dignified scientist that Brezhnev remembered.

· DOCUMENT 131 ·

Andropov to Central Committee, May 26, 1978
Confrontations between Sakharov and police

_____

In recent years Sakharov has openly flouted existing laws and taken the path of committing brazen criminal offenses.

In April 1976 Sakharov and his wife Bonner committed acts of hooliganism at the Omsk District Court, which was examining the criminal case of Dzhemilev (who had been indicted for disseminating fabrications, known to be false, that discredited the Soviet state and social system). In response to the demand of police officers (who were performing their duty to maintain public order) to desist from performing acts of hooliganism, Sakharov shouted: "Take this, you puppies, from an academician," slapped two policemen in the face, and unleashed a torrent of insults at them. Bonner also struck the commandant of the courthouse in the face as he tried to restore order. After being taken to the police station, Sakharov and Bonner not only made no attempt to deny what they had done, but confirmed that they had done so deliberately.[74]

In August 1976, Sakharov and Bonner, in the presence of a large number of Soviet citizens and foreigners, committed acts of malicious hooliganism at the Irkutsk airport.[75] In response to the suggestion that they observe the established rules, Sakharov and Bonner started a commotion, insulted the women employees at the airport, . . . [76] and shouted obscene words at them, and made threats.

In October 1977, Sakharov caused a rowdy disturbance in the rector's office at the Lenin Pedagogical Institute in Moscow. As a pretext he used the expulsion from the Institute of his wife's relative Semyonov, who had been dismissed for failing to pass an exam. Sakharov demonstratively ripped from the hands of the deputy rector the documents that served as the basis for the decision to expel Semyonov. Sakharov also hurled insults at other officials of the Institute.

_____

74. Sakharov described this episode differently; see his *Memoirs*, 449–52.

75. The declassified files do not include any KGB report about this episode, if indeed one was submitted to the Central Committee.

76. About thirty characters are deleted from the sentence.

In March 1978, Sakharov was the instigator of a provocative hooligan escapade by a group of pro-Zionist individuals near the building of the Union of Soviet Societies of Friendship and Cultural Ties with Foreign Countries (14 Kalinin Prospekt). As a result, Sakharov was summoned to the office of the Moscow City Procurator and given an official warning about the inadmissibility of illegal conduct in the future.

Ignoring the warning of the authorities, on May 19, 1978, Sakharov committed new brazen acts of hooliganism near the building of the Lyublino District People's Court for the city of Moscow (where the trial of Orlov was under way). Several times he slapped the face of a policeman, who attempted to prevent Sakharov and his wife Bonner from disturbing public order.

Sakharov's acts have been documented. They constitute criminal offenses under Article 206, Part II, and Article 191-1, Part II, of the Criminal Code of the RSFSR (malicious hooliganism and violent resistance to policemen or members of the people's militia while fulfilling their duties to maintain public order). The police organs are deciding the question of Sakharov's accountability.

Given the above facts as well as the extremely negative reaction of the Soviet people to the failure of legal authorities to take legal measures against Sakharov, who has systematically committed acts of hooliganism, we deem it expedient to transmit this information to the Presidium of the USSR Academy of Sciences for a subsequent discussion of his criminal conduct at the Academy of Sciences.

We request your consent.

---

Soon after Sakharov began writing his memoirs, in the spring of 1978, the KGB learned of the manuscript and began seeking ways to disrupt his efforts. But Sakharov and his household tried to avoid leaving the apartment empty; either someone had to stay home or he took his most important papers with him. At that time the KGB had yet to touch Sakharov personally. But in the afternoon of November 29, 1978, the Sakharov family let its guard down for about an hour. The circumstances were altogether mundane. Sakharov and Bonner had just learned that a new Russian translation of *Alice in Wonderland* had appeared and they wanted to buy two copies for their two sets of grandchildren. But Sakharov was sure that if he went alone to the special bookstore that served academicians, he would be permitted to purchase only one copy; so his wife had to come along. At that moment, though, Liza Alexeyeva and Bonner's mother, Ruth, were at the main post office. Ruth Bonner rarely left the apartment because of her age and infirmities. They were due back soon, so Sakharov and his wife left the apartment empty.

We can only imagine how the KGB carried out its operation. One group of agents was watching the apartment, carefully noting everyone's comings and goings; they must have been the first to report to colleagues at a central location that the apartment was empty. Another set of agents could then confirm that Liza Alexeyeva and Ruth Bonner were still downtown and could not possibly return for at least another hour. A third group would have to be dispatched from a standing pool of agents who would actually carry out the search. They ended up stealing the initial pages of Sakharov's manuscript along with appeals and a collection of threatening letters he had received. They failed to find a fairly large sum of money belonging to Solzhenitsyn's Fund for Political Prisoners. The rubles were hidden under the mattress of Ruth Bonner's bed, where she spent most of her time, either resting or doing small household tasks.[77] This report started the process, just one month before KGB agents carried out the operation.

## · DOCUMENT 133 ·

Andropov and Rekunkov to Central Committee, October 31, 1978
The confiscation of Sakharov's personal papers

---

Extract from protocol no. 128 of the meeting of the Politburo of the CPSU Central Committee on November 4, 1978, on measures to stop the activity of A. D. Sakharov that poses a threat to national security

It was decided to agree with the proposal stated in the memorandum of the Committee for State Security of the USSR and the Procurator's Office of the USSR no. 2169-A of October 31, 1978.

Secretary of the Central Committee

For your information
Memorandum: "On Measures to Curb the Activity of
A. D. Sakharov That Harm State Security"

According to information obtained by the Committee for State Security, beginning in June 1978 Sakharov has been actively working on a

---

77. See Sakharov, *Memoirs,* 486–87, and *New York Times,* December 3, 1978, 9, for further information on this incident.

book of an autobiographical nature. In it he describes the years of his childhood and youth as well as the period when he worked at military plants and installations of the Ministry of Medium Machine Building. In one of the main sections of the book titled "Plant—FIAN—Installation, 1942–1968," Sakharov refers to three key problems that he worked on during the creation of thermonuclear weapons. The book contains information about the organization of leading Party and government organs involved in the development of nuclear weapons; it also gives the names and positions of all the main scientists and engineers who participated in their development and testing. Many of these scientists and engineers are currently working in the Ministry of Medium Machine Building.

In addition, the book links the work of the Ministry of Medium Machine Building and its predecessor, the First Main Administration of the Council of Ministers of the USSR, to the development of nuclear weapons, discloses the locations of their installations, and the organization of work; it states outright that nuclear charges are developed at the installation by Zernov and Khariton,[78] decodes the address of its Moscow office, describes how specialists are delivered there, gives a brief account of the tests on August 12, 1953 (with an indication of details and consequences of the explosion), and also refers to operations at the testing ground near Semipalatinsk.

According to the leading specialists of the Ministry of Medium Machine Building, the information contained in the book (taken as a whole)[79] is secret.

Given that the manuscript . . . Sakharov intends to send abroad is detrimental to national security, it is expedient to request that the Committee for State Security and the Office of the Procurator of the USSR conduct a search of Sakharov's apartment and confiscate the manuscript. After the search, it is proposed to summon Sakharov to the Office of the Procurator of the USSR and warn him against divulging state secrets.

The draft of the resolution of the CPSU Central Committee is attached. Submitted for consideration.

Yu. Andropov and A. Rekunkov

---

78. Pavel Zernov was not a scientist but a general chosen by Beria to serve as the first administrative director of Arzamas-16, where Yuli Khariton was the scientific director; see David Holloway, *Stalin and the Bomb: The Soviet Union and Atomic Energy, 1939–1956* (New Haven, 1994), 196–97.

79. In Soviet officialese, "taken as a whole" meant that no single item of information was either classified or top secret, but the sum total of facts represented a "threat to national security."

## · DOCUMENT 134 ·

Andropov to Central Committee, December 14, 1978
Elena Bonner goes to Italy

In 1975 and 1977 the wife of Academician Sakharov, Bonner, visited Italy, where she underwent surgery in a private ophthalmologic clinic in the city of Siena. In both cases, when permission was granted, it was expected that Bonner might use her stay abroad to establish contacts with foreign subversive centers and exhibit openly anti-Soviet views.

In fact, while abroad in 1975, Bonner made a number of anti-Soviet statements, and in 1977 she took an active part in preparing the so-called "Sakharov Hearings" in Rome. As was to be expected, this conduct further compromised Bonner and, through her, Sakharov in the eyes of both the Soviet public and the progressive-minded foreign public.

At this time Bonner is filing an application for a private visit to Italy in order to consult specialists about her eye disease. The Committee for State Security has again decided to allow Bonner the trip to Italy. Such a decision is tactically justified because the fact of permission arouses surprise and envy on the part of her and Sakharov's accomplices, and this leads to greater discord and hostility within their milieu. . . .

More than a year before the XXII Olympic Games were scheduled to open in Moscow, Andropov described the purported plans of a host of subversive and anti-Soviet organizations in the West to disrupt the games and exploit the presence of their followers in the Soviet capital for their own nefarious purposes. Sakharov did in fact, as Andropov noted, support the idea of having "Western teams and individual athletes 'adopt' victims of Soviet repression." But, at least in 1979, he did not advocate a boycott. For Sakharov, "the Olympics were part of the process of détente: the arrival of hundreds of thousands of visitors from the West, even with nothing but sports on their minds, could make a dent in the wall dividing our two worlds."[80] But in April 1979, when Andropov filed this report, it is unlikely that Andrei Sakharov connected a country named Afghanistan to the fate of the Olympics or to his own vulnerable presence in the Soviet capital.

80. Sakharov, *Memoirs*, 496.

· DOCUMENT 135 ·

Andropov to Central Committee, April 25, 1979
Preparations for the Moscow Olympics

―――――――――

. . . Information collected by the Committee for State Security shows that the intelligence agencies of the enemy, ideological sabotage centers, and foreign anti-Soviet organizations (which enjoy the support and protection of reactionary circles in a number of imperialist states) are continuing their campaign to discredit the 1980 Olympic Games.

Moreover, there have been certain changes in their tactics. If in 1977 and in the first half of 1978 their activity was most characterized by appeals to boycott the Moscow Olympics, recently they have put the main emphasis on the idea of using the 1980 Olympic Games to conduct terrorism, sabotage, and other subversive actions of an extremist character on Soviet territory. Particularly active in this regard are the heads of the Narodno-trudovoi soyuz (NTS), Zionist, and other foreign nationalist formations and anti-Soviet organizations. . . .

Foreign nationalist organizations (Ukrainian, Lithuanian, Estonian, Crimean-Tatar, Dashnak,[81] and others) and various "committees" and "unions" that collaborate closely with the intelligence and sabotage services of capitalist states are also conducting an active campaign to prepare emissaries and harbor the intention of including them in a number of national delegations and tourist groups to travel to the USSR before and during the 1980 Olympics. The enemy is giving the emissaries and associated elements from the ranks of Soviet citizens the task of studying the situation and creating conditions to conduct provocative acts. For these purposes, it is recommended that they make a careful study of the places where the Olympic installations are located and the system for passes to them; they are also to establish contacts with the service personnel at the sport installations, to select specific people from the ranks of Soviet citizens for purposes of inspiring, with their assistance, declarations with provocative demands. Nationalist and clerical organizations intend to carry out a massive importation of anti-Soviet literature to the USSR, which, according to their plans, should "inundate Moscow, Kiev, and the Baltics" during the Olympic Games. Simultaneously, clerical centers are

―――――――――

81. Members of the Armenian nationalist party, Dashnaktsutiun, which held power in Armenia from 1918 to 1921; it was overthrown by a Bolshevik-inspired uprising and its members were driven into exile. Today it is a legal political party in Armenia.

endeavoring to unite their efforts to collect slanderous information about the status of believers in the USSR and to encourage religious fanatics in various regions of the country to engage in active illegal activities in the period preceding and during the 1980 Olympics.

The Committee for State Security has obtained information that in December 1978 the Russian Section in the Israeli Ministry of Foreign Affairs sent the government a proposal to use the Olympic Games in Moscow to conduct Zionist propaganda on the territory of the USSR and to inflame nationalist attitudes among citizens of Jewish nationality. For these purposes, it proposes to make maximum use of the Olympic attaché, but also the sports delegation and tourist groups of Israel, which (according to plans) are to include representatives of the Israeli intelligence services and people known for their anti-Soviet activities. They are to organize meetings with nationalist-minded people, collect tendentious information, distribute instructions, money, and literature, and conduct other hostile activities.

For purposes of discrediting the XXII Olympic Games in Moscow, the enemy's intelligence services and foreign anti-Soviet centers, as earlier, are attempting to use various kinds of insinuations about the "violation of human rights in the USSR." In some cases, they succeed in inspiring provocative actions on the part of antisocial elements inside the country and impelling some of them to make irresponsible slanderous declarations that help to inflame anti-Soviet hysteria in the West. Thus, the well-known anti-Soviet Sakharov recommends that each foreign sports delegation make, as a condition for its participation in the 1980 Olympics, the demand that one or two so-called "prisoners of conscience in the USSR" be released. A group of antisocial elements has given the West a declaration about the creation of the so-called "Association of Olympic Guarantees in the USSR," which abound in slanderous fabrications and provocative demands. Some pro-Zionist individuals harbor the intention of organizing a protest demonstration during the days of the Olympics and a number of other extremist actions.

The Committee for State Security is considering this information as it prepares measures to provide for security and public order in the period preceding and during the XXII Olympic Games.

The chairman of the Organizational Committee of the 1980 Olympics, comrade I. T. Novikov, has been informed.

CHAPTER FOUR

# Bitter Air of Exile

ANDREI SAKHAROV was arrested at two o'clock on the afternoon of January 22, 1980. Each Tuesday, Sakharov made a point of attending a seminar at the Physics Institute of the Academy of Sciences. As usual, he ordered a car from the academy's motor pool and "intended to stop first at the Academy commissary to pick up some groceries."[1] But police stopped the car and directed the driver to follow a patrol car to the procurator's office on Pushkin Street.

There Alexander Rekunkov, first deputy procurator general of the USSR, read Sakharov a decree of the Presidium of the Supreme Soviet stripping him of all his state honors. Rekunkov then informed him he was being banished to Gorky, a major industrial city 250 miles east of Moscow. (Its original name, Nizhny Novgorod, has since been restored.) Because it was the home of military factories, the city was officially closed to foreigners. Rekunkov handed Sakharov a copy of the decree with Brezhnev's name typed at the bottom but without his signature. The decree, it later turned out, had been issued on January 8 and would soon appear in the *Gazette of the USSR Supreme Soviet* on January 30. Rekunkov asked Sakharov to sign the decree. He did so, but then added a statement refusing to return the awards "since they

---

1. Andrei Sakharov, *Memoirs* (New York, 1990), 510.

had been granted in recognition of services rendered." Rekunkov made no objection, and he made it clear that Elena Bonner could accompany Sakharov to Gorky. He was allowed to call and tell her to be ready in two hours. Later that afternoon the couple was reunited at Domodedovo airport and flown to Gorky on a special plane supplied with a doctor and gourmet food. Andropov's deputy, Semyon Tsvigun, also came along to ensure that the operation went smoothly.[2]

Sakharov's exile took place within a broader context of foreign and domestic upheaval. In November 1979, "revolutionary students" seized the U.S. embassy in Tehran, taking dozens of diplomats hostage and striking a mortal blow to the administration of President Jimmy Carter. In December the Soviet Union sent its troops into Afghanistan, beginning a devastating war that would drag on for nearly a decade.

Inside the Soviet Union, the regime was carrying out a systematic crackdown on dissent in all its forms. Members of Helsinki Watch groups in Moscow and Ukraine, Christian activists, Crimean Tatar leaders, and editors of samizdat journals were among those arrested and brought to trial. The infamous "Metropol" affair was also unfolding, in which contributors to an unauthorized literary anthology were severely harassed for circulating the typescript in Moscow and abroad. They had meant to issue it openly in January 1979; even in December, the regime was still busy expelling several compilers from the Writers' Union.

Sakharov did not fail to respond to this broadening crisis in domestic and international affairs. In an interview with a German correspondent on January 1 he called for the withdrawal of Soviet troops from Afghanistan, adding that "the Olympic Committee should refuse to hold the games in a country that is waging war." Sakharov's statement marked a shift in his position and enraged Soviet leaders. In a discussion with Anthony Austin of the *New York Times,* Sakharov repeated his denunciation of the Soviet invasion and again called for a boycott of the Moscow Olympics.[3]

Outwardly the regime did not betray its impatience. On January 7, Elena Bonner's elderly mother received permission to visit the United

2. Ibid., 512; *Chronicle of Current Events,* April 30, 1980, no. 56, 74–75 (Amnesty International ed., 1981). Tsvigun and Brezhnev were married to sisters. If Tsvigun was on the flight to Gorky, as Sakharov believed he heard people say at the Gorky airport, it was reasonable to assume that Brezhnev was personally involved in the operation.

3. Sakharov, *Memoirs,* 509; *New York Times,* January 3, 1980, 13.

States to see her grandchildren and great-grandchildren. Perhaps this
was an unexpected humanitarian concession or "perhaps the KGB
wanted to get her out of the way," as Sakharov wondered years later.[4]
The next day the Supreme Soviet secretly passed its decree depriving
Sakharov of his government awards. On January 21 Sakharov joined
the remaining members of the Moscow Helsinki Group in signing a
statement calling for the immediate withdrawal of foreign troops
from Afghanistan. The next day the writer Georgy Vladimov (who
served as head of Moscow's Amnesty International group) called
Sakharov at 1 A.M. (it was now January 22) and alerted him that a
friend had just attended a meeting of political propagandists where a
speaker had announced the decision to send Sakharov away from
Moscow. Sakharov took the warning seriously but saw no point in
trying to leave the capital on his own. Andropov had been arguing for
several years that the Politburo should take decisive action against
him. Ambassador Anatoly Dobrynin was present at a Politburo meeting at a time when Andropov was pressing for Sakharov's removal
from Moscow. "Sakharov and his wife," according to Andropov,
"had turned into a consistent focus of anti-Soviet campaigning abroad
and therefore must be deprived of all access to foreigners through exile to a place closed to foreign reporters."[5] Now Andropov would finally get his wish.

The following memorandum sought to build a case against Sakharov. While asserting the physicist's vulnerability to criminal prosecution for divulging state secrets and active support of anti-Soviet
activity, Andropov and Rudenko opposed an open trial on the grounds
that it would unleash a torrent of Western criticism. Nonetheless, the
administrative kidnapping of Sakharov still provoked an intense international reaction.[6]

4. Sakharov, *Memoirs*, 509.
5. Anatoly Dobrynin, *In Confidence: Moscow's Ambassador to America's Six Cold War Presidents (1962–1986)* (New York, 1995), 513.
6. For significant coverage in the *New York Times*, see January 23, 1980, 1 and 10, and January 24, 1980, 6. The action against Sakharov also provoked criticism from Western Communist parties, including those in France and Italy; see *New York Times*, January 25, 1980, 9.

## · DOCUMENT 136 ·

Andropov and Rudenko to Central Committee, December 26, 1979
The case against Andrei Sakharov

For more than ten years Academician Sakharov, a convinced adversary of the socialist order, has conducted subversive activities against the Soviet state. Having become a staunch enemy of socialism, he incites aggressive circles of capitalist countries to interfere in the domestic affairs of socialist states and to embark on military confrontation with the Soviet Union. He has continually inspired declarations against the Soviet policy of international détente and peaceful coexistence. Sakharov has also undertaken measures to unify anti-Soviet elements inside the country and incites them to engage in extremist acts.

Sakharov has harmed the state interests of the USSR by divulging important defense secrets to representatives of capitalist countries. In particular, during discussions with American, German, and Canadian reporters in 1974, he revealed characteristics of Soviet strategic missiles and launching sites, and information on the number of our warheads; he also named the ministries that participate in their production. In the judgment of experts, the information was "top secret" and represented a state secret. Communication of such information to the adversary comes under the purview of the law on state treason.[7]

In violation of the established rules on work with foreigners, Sakharov has maintained constant contact with the diplomats of capitalist countries stationed in Moscow. Between 1972 and 1979 he visited such diplomatic offices eighty times. His contacts with the U.S. embassy and with American correspondents were particularly close. He systematically tells them about his negative reaction to the political steps taken by our government inside the country and informs them about the provocative activity of antisocial elements. For their part, the diplomats and spies operating under diplomatic cover have used their contact with Sakharov to obtain political information and facts pertaining to his past work at a particularly important defense installation.

Sakharov has established direct contacts with antisocialist elements in the Polish People's Republic and in the Czechoslovak Socialist Republic.

---

7. Andropov was stretching a point in charging Sakharov with treason. The information Sakharov allegedly revealed was discussed during the SALT talks beginning in 1969.

He has expressed solidarity with the Czechoslovak "Chartists" and members of the Polish "Committee of Social Self-Defense." He urges them to unite and coordinate their antisocialist activities.[8]

For purposes of subverting Soviet power, Sakharov has been systematically giving aid to foreign states in conducting their hostile activities against the USSR. He has been very active in anti-Soviet agitation and propaganda. In the period 1968–1979, he wrote and sent abroad a series of anti-Soviet documents that had the character of programs, more than 200 "statements," "appeals," and "protests," in which he has emphatically warned the West against disarmament, asserting that the only acceptable approach for international relations with the USSR would be a situation "where Vance will have forces two or three times stronger than the Soviet side." In these documents he engaged in libelous statements, making assertions about the "totalitarian character of our system," the "global challenge of socialism," the "covert militarization of the Soviet economy," "Communist expansionism," and so forth. Apart from contacts with embassy officials, Sakharov has had over 600 meetings with other foreigners concerning various questions about organizing and conducting anti-Soviet operations; he conducted more than 150 so-called "press conferences" for Western correspondents. Based on his materials, Western radio stations produced and broadcast about 1,200 anti-Soviet programs.

The West has generously compensated Sakharov for his hostile activities. His accounts in foreign banks were credited with tens of thousands of dollars. His diligence was also rewarded with the Nobel Peace Prize and other monetary awards.

In 1970 Sakharov created the so-called "Human Rights Committee." Behind the facade of the "Committee," Sakharov worked vigorously to

8. Sakharov engaged in a dialogue with human rights activists in Eastern Europe in the late 1970s; see his article "The Human Rights Movements in the USSR and Eastern Europe: Its Goals, Significance and Difficulties," *Trialogue,* November 8, 1978. He returned to this topic in "Sakharov Joins Czech Protest," *Daily Telegraph,* August 1, 1979, 17, and this time expressed solidarity not only with Czech dissidents but also with their Polish counterparts. In October 1979, Sakharov again addressed repression against Polish and Czech dissidents; see "Czechoslovak Trials and Moscow Support," in *Chronicle of Human Rights in the USSR,* no. 36, October–December 1979, 19. It was not a one-way street. At the beginning of 1979, the prominent Polish activist Zbigniew Romaszewski visited Sakharov's apartment in Moscow and had a long discussion with him and Tatyana Velikanova. The KGB almost certainly knew about this meeting. Sakharov described it in a short piece, "Vstrecha s Zbignevom Romashevskim" [Meeting Zbigniew Romaszewski]," Andrei Sakharov Archive (Harvard), folder S.IV.2.2.458.

consolidate antisocial elements, established and maintained contact with foreign subversive centers, and directed the realization of extremist and provocative anti-Soviet actions. For criminal activity carried out behind the facade of the "Committee" with Sakharov's direct encouragement, eleven people were put on trial and convicted. The "Committee" gave birth to the so-called "Groups to Assist in the Implementation of the Helsinki Agreements in the USSR," "the Working Commission to Investigate the Use of Psychiatry for Political Purposes," and several other antisocial groups.

Party, Soviet, and public organizations, the Office of the Procurator, and the organs of state security have repeatedly warned Sakharov that his hostile activity was unacceptable. He was also warned by prominent scientists. On behalf of the Soviet government, a deputy chairman of the USSR Council of Ministers talked to him. Three times Sakharov received official warnings from the Office of the Procurator General of the USSR. He has ignored all these warnings.

Hence Sakharov's activity is punishable under criminal law. His conduct comes completely within the purview of Article 64, part "a" (treason to the Motherland) and Article 70, part I (anti-Soviet agitation and propaganda) of the Criminal Code of the RSFSR.[9]

Nevertheless, putting Sakharov on trial can entail serious political costs. It would take at least two or three months to carry out the preliminary investigation and conduct a trial. During this period, the West will undoubtedly organize vociferous anti-Soviet campaigns, which would be difficult to counter because legislation governing the procedure in criminal cases prohibits the use of materials from cases under investigation for the purposes of propaganda before the judicial proceedings have been completed.[10]

As a result, in the Sakharov case it seems expedient to apply administrative measures that would make it possible to halt his contacts with foreigners and seriously limit his ability to conduct hostile activities.

In our opinion, in order to terminate Sakharov's anti-Soviet activity, it is essential to do the following:

• Consider the question of stripping Sakharov of the high titles of Hero

9. These articles stipulated maximum punishments of (a) death and (b) seven years in a labor camp and five years of exile, respectively.

10. In political and even criminal cases the KGB usually declared the indicted person guilty long before the trial through the mass media. A classic example was Shcharansky's case, when *Izvestia* published materials explaining that Shcharansky had been a spy for the CIA.

of Socialist Labor, Laureate of the Lenin and State Prizes of the USSR, and other state awards (drafts for a decree of the Presidium of the Supreme Soviet of the USSR and of a resolution of the Council of Ministers of the USSR are enclosed).

• Adopt a decree of the Presidium of the Supreme Soviet of the USSR that, as an exceptional preventive measure, would order his expulsion from Moscow to a part of the country closed to foreigners (the draft of a decree of the Presidium of the Supreme Soviet of the USSR is enclosed).

• At an expanded meeting of the Presidium (or at another representative meeting of scientists), the Academy of Sciences should discuss the antisocial conduct of Academician Sakharov. The Committee for State Security of the USSR is to forward the necessary information to the Presidium of the USSR Academy of Sciences (draft statement enclosed).

• An appropriate notice in the press should report the measures taken in regard to Sakharov (draft enclosed).

The draft of a Communist Party Central Committee Resolution is enclosed.

We are submitting this for your consideration.

Yu. Andropov
R. Rudenko

Extract from Protocol no. 177 of the Politburo session
of January 3, 1980
No. 1177/X Absolutely Secret. Special Dossier
Copies sent to: Comrades Brezhnev, Andropov, Grishin, Gromyko,
Kirilenko, Kosygin, Kunaev, Pelshe, Romanov, Suslov, Tikhonov,
Ustinov, Chernenko, Shcherbitsky, Aliyev, Gorbachev, Demichev,
Kuznetsov, Masherov, Ponomarev, Rashidov, Solomentsev,
Shevardnadze, Dolgikh, Zimyanin, Kapitonov, Rusakov, Rudenko,
Savinkin, Trapeznikov, Tyazhelnikov, Georgadze, Smirtyukov
(entire file); Alexandrov (p. 1), Alexeyev (p. 3).

On the question of the Committee for State Security and the Office of the Procurator of the USSR:

1. Agree with the proposals of the Committee for State Security of the USSR and the Office of the Procurator of the USSR as presented in the memorandum of December 26, 1979 no. 2484-A (attached).

2. Approve the draft decrees of the Presidium of the Supreme Soviet of the USSR and the decree of the Council of Ministers of the USSR on this question (attached).

3. The editors of the newspaper *Izvestia* are to prepare and publish an announcement on this question, after collaborating with the Committee for State Security in preparing the text (attached).

Politburo meeting of January 3, 1980
Presiding chair: Comrade L. I. Brezhnev
Present: Comrades Yu. V. Andropov, A. A. Gromyko, A. P. Kirilenko,
A. Yu. Pelshe, M. A. Suslov, N. A. Tikhonov, D. F. Ustinov,
K. U. Chernenko, M. S. Gorbachev, P. N. Demichev, V. V. Kuznetsov,
B. N. Ponomarev, I. V. Kapitonov, V. I. Dolgikh,
M. V. Zimyanin, K. V. Rusakov
12. On Sakharov

*Brezhnev:* Comrades Tikhonov and Rudenko have presented proposals regarding Sakharov. He is conducting considerable work that is harmful for our state.

*Andropov:* Sakharov is the initiator of all the anti-Soviet undertakings. Of course, it is necessary to deprive him of the title of Hero of Socialist Labor, his stars, and his Lenin and State prizes.

*Gromyko:* The question of Sakharov has ceased to be a purely domestic question. He finds an enormous number of responses abroad. All the anti-Soviet scum, all this rabble revolves around Sakharov. It is impossible to ignore this situation any longer.

*Ustinov:* I completely and totally support these proposals that have been presented by Comrades Andropov and Rudenko. After all, Sakharov's actions have a bad influence on other scientists. It is necessary to resolve the problem as Comrades Andropov and Rudenko propose.

*Suslov:* I think that, in general, this question has been correctly posed. However, perhaps one should not seek to resolve all these questions at once, but in stages. At first strip him of the title of Hero of Socialist Labor, but he has three stars. Then one should decide the other questions that are attached here.

*Andropov:* We must resolve immediately the following question—namely, that of expelling him from Moscow. I propose to relocate him to Gorky Oblast. If this is not done, then things will be very bad.

*All:* One must adopt the resolution as proposed by Comrades Andropov and Rudenko.

· DOCUMENT 137 ·

Andropov and Rudenko to Central Committee, January 7, 1980
Soviet government decrees on the Sakharov case

We request that the decrees of the Presidium of the USSR Supreme So-viet and the report of the Telegraph Agency of the Soviet Union (TASS) be replaced, after taking into account the comments of the Presidium of the Supreme Soviet of the USSR.

Yu. Andropov and R. Rudenko

Decree of the Presidium of the Supreme Soviet of the USSR (Draft)
On depriving A. D. Sakharov of all government awards of the USSR

In view of A. D. Sakharov's systematic activity, which discredits him as a recipient of awards and in consideration of numerous suggestions of So-viet public opinion, the Presidium of the USSR Supreme Council (on the basis of article 40 of the "General Regulations on Orders, Medals and Honorary Titles of the USSR") decrees:
Deprive Andrei Dmitrievich Sakharov of the title of Hero of Socialist Labor and of all state awards of the USSR.

Chairman, Presidium of the USSR Supreme Council
Secretary, Presidium of the USSR Supreme Council
Moscow, Kremlin
January 8, 1980

Decree of the Presidium of the Supreme Soviet of the USSR [Draft]
On the Administrative Expulsion of A. D. Sakharov
from the City of Moscow

Considering the written representation submitted by the Procurator General of the USSR and the Committee for State Security concerning Sakharov's actions that constitute a criminal offense under point "a" of Article 64 and part I of article 70 of the Criminal Code of the RSFSR and the possibility of initiating criminal proceedings against Sakharov, the Pre-sidium of the Supreme Council of the USSR decrees:
    1. In order to prevent Sakharov's hostile activity, his criminal contacts with citizens of capitalist countries, and the possibility that his conduct could harm the interests of the Soviet state, at the present time it is deemed necessary to go no further than administrative expulsion of Andrei

Dmitrievich Sakharov from the city of Moscow to a region of the country closed to foreigners.

2. Prescribe a regimen of residence for Sakharov that would preclude contact with foreigners and antisocial elements and trips to other regions of the country unless given special permission by the appropriate authority in the Ministry of Internal Affairs of the USSR. The Committee for State Security of the USSR and the Ministry of Internal Affairs of the USSR are to assume control in order to ensure that the rules prescribed for Sakharov's residence are observed.

Chairman, Presidium of the USSR Supreme Soviet
Secretary, Presidium of the USSR Supreme Council
Moscow, Kremlin
January 8, 1980

To item X of protocol no. 177
Decree of the Council of Ministers of the USSR (draft)
January ___ 1980
Moscow, Kremlin
On Depriving A. D. Sakharov of the Titles of
Winner of the Lenin and State Prizes

The Council of Ministers of the USSR decrees:
Deprive Andrei Dmitrievich Sakharov of the titles of Laureate of the Lenin and State Prizes for acts unworthy of the high name of a Soviet scientist.

A. Kosygin, Chairman, Council of Ministers of the USSR
M. Smirtyukov, Administrator, Council of Ministers of the USSR

On A. D. Sakharov (draft)

In the course of several years, A. D. Sakharov has conducted subversive work against the Soviet state. As a result, he has repeatedly been warned about the inadmissibility of such activity by representatives of the appropriate state organs, public organizations, and prominent Soviet scholars.

Ignoring these warnings, Sakharov has recently taken the path of open appeals to reactionary circles of imperialist states to interfere in the internal affairs of the USSR.

Taking into account the numerous proposals from Soviet public opinion, the Presidium of the Supreme Soviet of the USSR has deprived Sakharov of his title as Hero of Socialist Labor and all his state awards, and the Council of Ministers of the USSR has deprived him of the title of laureate of the prizes of the USSR previously awarded to him.

    TASS

---

Andropov's summary of Western responses to Sakharov's banishment to Gorky provides a vivid example of how the KGB twisted the facts in its reports to the country's political leadership. It is hard to believe that the Politburo did not have more reliable sources of information about Western coverage of Soviet affairs—if, that is, Politburo members wanted to know it.

### · DOCUMENT 139 ·

Andropov to Central Committee, January 24, 1980
Responses in the West to Sakharov's banishment

---

According to information obtained by the Committee for State Security, the TASS report on stripping A. D. Sakharov of the title of Hero of Socialist Labor, laureate of USSR prizes, and all state awards caused genuine interest among foreigners, especially among journalists accredited in Moscow.

Referring to the lack of sufficient information, Western journalists nevertheless expressed their views of the measures that the Soviet authorities took with respect to Sakharov.

For instance, a correspondent of the English newspaper *Times* declared: "Soviet authorities chose a good time to put things in order in their country, insofar as the USA has frozen détente. It was time to do this long ago."[11]

The BBC correspondent in Moscow said: "What has happened to Sakharov evidently shows that the Soviet elite has taken a decision not to waste more time on the Americans, to renounce them as a thankless job, to ignore Western criticism, and to emphasize quite plainly the main problem—the security of the Soviet Union."

A correspondent of the American agency "United Press International," while regarding Sakharov as an authoritative figure among Soviet "dissidents," observed that "with Sakharov removed from the scene, the Soviets have deprived the whole dissident organization in the USSR of the opportunity to communicate with Western public opinion."

---

11. The names of all the correspondents and other persons whose work was cited were deleted from the photocopy released to the Sakharov Archive (Harvard).

"The decision of Soviet authorities about Sakharov," observed a correspondent of the American magazine *Time,* "is rather mild, [for] it could be harsher. He himself is to blame for what has happened, because he indulged in too much rhetoric. And the fact that he will live in Gorky is not such an awful thing."

The press attaché of the embassy of the FRG [Federal Republic of Germany] in Moscow, in a conversation with a *New York Times* correspondent, suggested that "it could be a political gesture meant to show Carter that the Soviet authorities are firm in resolving internal problems. Besides, they are so tired of Sakharov that in a critical situation they wanted to get rid of him like some kind of ballast."

The counselor of the Finnish embassy in the USSR claimed: "The actions of the Soviet government regarding Sakharov are legitimate because Sakharov's conduct and his public addresses had a certain detrimental effect on the normalization of East-West relations within the context of the Helsinki agreements on human rights." Considering Sakharov's expulsion from Moscow to be a logical reaction of the Soviet government to his hostile activity, he added: "Now Sakharov will live far from the capital and will no longer be the center of attention for Western journalists. There was a similar story with Solzhenitsyn, who was deported from the USSR and whom no one remembers now."

According to the opinion of the counselor-envoy of the Japanese embassy in Moscow, "measures regarding Sakharov were taken by the Soviet government not just because of his criticism of the USSR for bringing troops into Afghanistan, but also to make Carter understand that the USSR is taking a firm stand and will not make any compromises that inflict harm on its security."

Chinese diplomats and journalists viewed the measures taken against Sakharov as "an internal affair of the Soviet side" and refrained from commentaries on the subject because they had as yet received no instructions from Beijing. . . .

---

· DOCUMENT 140 ·

Andropov to Central Committee, February 7, 1980
Sakharov's first days in Gorky

---

Summary: Sakharov refused to surrender state awards; through his wife, he is making an attempt to gain access to foreign correspondents.

In accordance with the decision of January 22, 1980, Sakharov was delivered to the Office of the Procurator of the USSR, where he was informed of the announcement about the decrees of the Presidium of the Supreme Soviet of the USSR and the resolution of the Council of Ministers of the USSR, which deprive him of the titles of Hero of Socialist Labor, laureate of the Lenin and State prizes of the USSR, and other state awards, and which contain the administrative order for his expulsion from Moscow.

After the decrees of the Presidium of the Supreme Soviet of the USSR were announced, it was suggested that Sakharov surrender the awards and certificates. In response, Sakharov refused, claiming that "the awards are a memento of his past scientific work."

On the same day, Sakharov, accompanied by his wife, was delivered to the city of Gorky (which is closed to foreigners) and settled in a comfortable four-room apartment.

On his arrival in Gorky, he was notified of his residence regimen, which precludes contacts with foreigners and antisocial elements and trips to other regions of the country.

While analyzing steps taken in regard to him, Sakharov declared that in his own milieu,[12] considering his "public activity," they could have been harsher.

Surveillance over Sakharov in Gorky shows that he is trying to maintain contacts with his sympathizers and to find ways to get in touch with foreign journalists. As attempts of this kind are resolutely foiled, he is endeavoring to establish contact with foreigners through his wife Bonner.

On January 28, after returning from Gorky, Bonner conducted a so-called press conference for foreign journalists in her Moscow apartment, where she circulated a so-called "appeal" on behalf of her husband. It declares that Sakharov has been put in a "gilded cage," "isolated from the outer world so as to make his public activity absolutely impossible."[13] It is worth noting that foreign journalists were obviously disappointed that the information came from Bonner, not Sakharov. That is why their reports did not emphasize the "problems" raised in the "appeal," but questions pertaining to Sakharov's stay in Gorky—which are of no fundamental significance.

On February 4, after a second return from Gorky, Bonner again gathered foreign journalists at her apartment and tried to foist on them "infor-

12. The "milieu" was Elena Bonner, since no one else was in contact with Sakharov.
13. *New York Times,* January 28, 1980, 8.

mation from Sakharov."[14] As the information contained nothing new, the so-called "press conference" was rather dull and evoked practically no response.

An analysis of available materials shows that secret services and propagandistic agencies of the West have lost a valuable source of information in Sakharov. Trying to keep alive the flame of anti-Soviet passions created by the "Sakharov case," they have been attempting to find a new figure who could somehow compensate for this loss.

The Committee for State Security is taking steps to frustrate these plans of the enemy, to ensure observance of the regimen set for Sakharov, and to interdict the intermediary hostile activity of Bonner.

· DOCUMENT 142 ·

Andropov to Central Committee, April 2, 1980
Attempts to visit Sakharov in Gorky

After Sakharov's administrative banishment from Moscow, measures were taken to interdict his contact with antisocial elements. To a significant degree, this was successfully accomplished by establishing an appropriate regimen for his residence in Gorky.

During this period, persistent attempts to reach Sakharov were undertaken by his close associates—Shikhanovich, Podyapolskaya, Babyonysheva, Bukharina, and also by Khailo, Pomazov, and others who had earlier been convicted of anti-Soviet activities. Some of them resorted to deception and various tricks. Altogether, about thirty such persons were expelled from Gorky, which finally convinced these antisocial elements of the futility of such actions.

The termination of Sakharov's contacts with foreigners has also brought a positive change in the situation surrounding him. This has not only limited his opportunities to send hostile libelous attacks, "statements," "appeals," "protests," etc. to the West, but has also significantly decreased the agitation around his name conducted earlier by foreign propaganda centers.

Whereas Sakharov's isolation produced a certain sense of perplexity and disorientation in him, his wife's behavior, especially at the beginning,

14. For the text of the interview, see "The Exile of Sakharov," *Chronicle of Current Events*, no. 56, 81–82 (Amnesty International ed., 1981).

was marked by an increase in hostile activity. She visited Moscow several times, arranged meetings with foreign journalists in her apartment, spread provocative rumors about her husband's situation, and transmitted libelous documents to be smuggled abroad. Bonner incited foreign journalists to organize protests against the "abuses committed against Sakharov."

Because of such behavior, Bonner was summoned to the Office of the USSR Procurator, where she received an official warning. This, along with other measures, had a certain effect.

At the present time, we have collected documentary proof of Bonner's anti-Soviet activity, and under current law she can be put on trial. We intend to do this if Bonner resumes her antisocial activity. We think that she might resume this, with the excuse that she needs to go to Italy for treatment of her eyes (we confiscated an invitation to this effect).

In deciding measures against Bonner, we have also taken into account that the thirty-fifth anniversary of Victory Day is approaching (Bonner is an invalid of the Great Patriotic War). . . .

---

Seven months after sending Sakharov to Gorky, Andropov cautiously suggested a further move: confining Sakharov to a psychiatric ward under KGB control. Andropov continued to emphasize the "harmful" influence of Bonner and portrayed her as the moving force behind Sakharov's behavior.

· DOCUMENT 144 ·

Andropov to Central Committee, August 26, 1980
The mental stability of Andrei Sakharov

---

In the course of maintaining surveillance over Sakharov, the Committee for State Security has come to the conclusion that, especially of late, his psychological state has clearly taken a turn for the worse. Sakharov's behavior often does not conform to accepted norms; it is excessively susceptible to the influence of those around him—above all, his wife; his behavior is patently contrary to common sense. Abnormality can also be observed in Sakharov's mood, which is subject to sharp changes, from being withdrawn and reclusive to businesslike and sociable.

According to the opinion of leading Soviet psychiatrists, he is characterized by deep mental changes, which allow us to regard him as "a pathological personality, which is common in families with hereditary schizophrenia": Sakharov's brother and daughter are registered as suffering from schizophrenia, and his son was treated for neurasthenia.

With each passing year, Sakharov's behavior becomes less and less amenable to an objective, logical assessment. On the one hand, he is obsessed with delusions of grandeur, which increase in proportion to the efforts of Western intelligence services to advertise him as a "universal champion of civil rights"; on the other hand, he harbors the intention of drafting a testament about his burial in Oslo. In our opinion, the metamorphosis in Sakharov's behavior does not preclude new hostile outbursts in the future (which are difficult to predict). This is taken into account by the Committee for State Security in its dealings with Sakharov. It also pays heed to the circumstance that for many years Sakharov has been under his wife's psychological pressure, and that at her urging he is constantly committing criminal acts that inflict moral damage on the Soviet state.

At present, acting on Bonner's initiative and with Sakharov's consent, hostile circles in the West are preparing to launch a massive provocative campaign to award him the Nobel Prize in physics. Another of Bonner's schemes is to spur her husband to write and publish in the West scientific articles[15] and all sorts of anti-Soviet "statements," "appeals," and "protests," which in her opinion will improve the financial situation of her children in the USA and will also create favorable conditions for her personally to live abroad in the future.

It has been established that Bonner's activities, which fan her husband's anti-Sovietism, not only are based on her hostile attitude toward the Soviet system but also conform to the recommendations of intelligence services in the USA and foreign anti-Soviet centers. Her links with them are demonstrated by the following fact. In 1979, the Americans, taking advantage of Bonner's travel to Italy for medical treatment, brought her to the USA under an assumed name and without filing documents under the established procedure.[16] There she established contact with anti-Soviet in-

15. Andropov was probably referring to Sakharov's *Collected Scientific Works*, ed. D. ter Haar, D. V. Chudnovsky, and G. V. Chudnovsky (New York, 1982).

16. Bonner visited the United States in order to be examined by a prominent ophthalmologist, Dr. Charles Schepens. She used her Soviet passport, but at her request the visa for entry into the United States was not stamped in it. The American ambassador in Rome told her this was "her responsibility." In Boston she visited for a month with family and a handful of friends, but otherwise maintained a low profile and did her best to avoid being recognized by other émigrés. Sakharov knew about this visit, as did Soviet officials, on the basis of their surveillance of her children's house in Newton, Massachusetts. Nonetheless, they never spoke with her about this discreet visit to the United States; as they well knew, there was nothing illegal about her trip to America. It

dividuals and met with people suspected of having ties to the CIA. From that trip Bonner brought back the idea, which she foisted on Sakharov, of uniting antisocialist elements in the USSR, the People's Republic of Poland, and the Czechoslovak Socialist Republic. Only his banishment from Moscow made it possible to forestall this subversive act.

Western propaganda still exploits the subject of his banishment for the purpose of increasing tensions both inside the country and abroad. Sakharov declares that since the decree of the Presidium of the Supreme Soviet presented to him had facsimile signatures, he does not consider it legally binding and demands its annulment. Such insinuations are enthusiastically taken up by Sakharov's Soviet sympathizers and also by hostile circles in the West. That is demonstrated by the letter from his closest friends, Kopelev, Chukovskaya, Vladimov, and others, that they addressed to the USSR Presidium of the Supreme Soviet in May. The antisocial activities of those who signed this letter are being monitored by state security organs.

Further measures regarding Sakharov and Bonner will be determined by the Committee for State Security on the basis of the newly disclosed circumstances of their hostile activity described above. . . .

· DOCUMENT 145 ·

Andropov to Central Committee, March 11, 1981
To isolate and harass Sakharov and Bonner

. . . State security organs have interdicted more than one hundred attempts by antisocial elements to establish contact with Sakharov. Recently, hostile elements have reduced such attempts to a minimum insofar as they have become convinced that restoring contact with Sakharov is hopeless. Prophylactic measures taken against Sakharov's sympathizers, together with instituting criminal proceedings against some of them, has contributed to this. Simultaneously, these measures succeeded in eliminating any kind of contact between Sakharov and foreigners.

With the agreement of party organs, a complex propaganda campaign has been conducted to expose the essence of Sakharov's anti-Soviet activ-

---

is also worth noting that Dr. Charles Schepens was a human rights hero. During World War II he was a prominent member of the Belgian resistance; see Meg Ostrum, *The Surgeon and the Shepherd: Two Resistance Heroes in Vichy France* (Lincoln, NE, 2004), and a profile of Dr. Schepens in the *Boston Globe*, April 15, 2004, D1.

ity. A series of publications about this appeared in central newspapers as well as in the newspapers of Gorky Oblast; massive explanatory work was conducted among worker collectives in the city of Gorky. These activities helped public opinion to gain a correct evaluation of the measures taken with respect to Sakharov; this is apparent, in particular, from the massive flow of letters from citizens to the editors of newspapers, sharply condemning the renegade's actions.

To exert a positive influence on Sakharov, scientists and representatives of workers' collectives were sent to visit him. While condemning his actions, they demonstrated to him his break with real life and his lack of competence in political matters. At the same time, measures were undertaken to redirect Sakharov's attention to the solution of scientific problems; this was greatly facilitated by his contacts with employees of the Institute of Physics and the regular arrival of scientific literature, including foreign publications. The result of these contacts was a revival of his interest in scientific activity. During his residence in Gorky, Sakharov has prepared three scientific works, which have been published in the journals of the USSR Academy of Sciences.[17]

Thus, the administrative exile of Sakharov from Moscow made it possible to contain his hostile activity. The measures chosen have deprived the propaganda centers of the West of one of their important sources of libelous information, and the so-called "human rights movement" lost its active leader.

However, the positive changes emerging in Sakharov's behavior and his readiness "not to enter into conflict with the authorities" elicited sharp resistance from his wife Bonner, who, exercising boundless influence over her husband, incites him to resume his hostile activity.

Bonner made Sakharov issue a series of statements about the "illegality" of the measures taken against him and the regimen set for his residence. She has also inspired campaigns in her husband's defense in the West. Moreover, she does not conceal the fact that the honoraria for such statements, which are published in the press of capitalist countries, constitute one of the important sources of material support for her children, who live in the USA.[18] At Bonner's initiative, Sakharov prepared twenty-seven malicious anti-Soviet documents, which, as a rule, were timed to coincide with very important political events. Many of these materials inter-

17. Sakharov's scientific work is represented here as a credit to the KGB.
18. The mainstream Western press does not pay for interviews or for the right to print public statements.

pret the events in the People's Republic of Poland and Afghanistan from an intentionally libelous perspective.

Bonner systematically "delivers" to Sakharov questions that serve as the basis for interviews with Western correspondents, and at their request she tapes his slanderous statements. Bonner transmits the prepared materials to foreign correspondents as well as to the U.S. embassy in Moscow. During this period, Western radio stations made over two hundred broadcasts using these materials. The West also organized a mass mailing of letters to Sakharov expressing moral support.

Bonner's activities reveal an effort to organize the nomination of Sakharov for a Nobel prize in science, which, in her opinion, will become an important additional factor in the campaign for his "defense." Simultaneously, Bonner has systematically prodded Sakharov to break off relations with the USSR Academy of Sciences. Upon her insistence, in September 1980 Sakharov refused contact with the employees of the Institute of Physics, since, in his words, "such controlled trips of employees from the Institute to Gorky could, in the long run, undermine all the international campaigns in my defense."[19] In November 1980, Sakharov dispatched a so-called "Open letter to A. P. Alexandrov, President of the USSR Academy of Sciences," which announced that he was terminating contact with Soviet scientific institutions. Commenting on his letter, Sakharov declared: "We have initiated serious pressuring of the Academy, blackmail, if you wish. . . . We are beginning a new stage of struggle, which may last a long time."

Sakharov and Bonner do not conceal the fact that their activities are directed at exacerbating international relations between the USSR and Western countries. In particular, their appeals to curtail scholarly contacts with Soviet scientists and to heighten the arms race testify to this. "I believe," declares Sakharov, "that the Americans should not begrudge money for conventional types of arms and for technical means for a precise thermonuclear strike against military targets, as they endeavor to achieve definite strategic parity. . . . The balance of power is nearly gone; it is disappearing. The West should be very firm on the question of Soviet interference in the fate of developing countries."

The Committee for State Security continues to apply measures directed at limiting and averting Sakharov's hostile activity. . . .

---

19. All the quotations in this document are supplied by KGB surveillance.

## · DOCUMENT 146 ·

Andropov to Central Committee, May 2, 1981
Sakharov's sixtieth birthday

. . . Western propaganda centers intend to use Sakharov's forthcoming sixtieth birthday on May 21 as a pretext for a new anti-Soviet campaign.

In Washington, D.C., a special "committee" was created to prepare and implement "anniversary celebrations." At the beginning of May, the New York Institute of Physics, the Physics Society, and the U.S. Academy of Sciences plan a so-called "international conference in honor of Sakharov," and Georgetown University is preparing a student demonstration.

On May 19 the "committee" is proposing to hold a special "anniversary" meeting in Washington, featuring [Arthur] Goldberg (former head of the U.S. delegation at the Belgrade Conference for Security and Cooperation in Europe), Congressman [Jack] Kemp, Senator [Samuel I.] Hayakawa, and several Nobel Prize laureates. It is planned to have a screening of the film on Sakharov made in France as well as a concert with the participation of Rostropovich and Vishnevskaya.

On May 21 they plan to hold a so-called "protest demonstration" in front of the Soviet embassy in Washington. The organizers of the "anniversary celebrations" are actively putting pressure on congressmen, senators, and public figures in the USA, with the goal of persuading them to push through Congress a resolution "in defense of Sakharov" and forwarding letters of protest to the leaders of the USSR and Soviet organizations located in the USA.

Similar provocative actions are planned in France, the Netherlands, and a number of other countries in the West.

Antisocial elements in Moscow have created the so-called "commission for organizing Sakharov's anniversary celebrations," which is preparing a book of his scientific and "public" articles.[20] The members of the "commission" have started a mass production of Sakharov's picture for distribution throughout the territory of the country.

The Committee for State Security is taking steps to contain anti-Soviet

20. Two books, in Russian and in English translation, later appeared as part of the commemoration of Sakharov's sixtieth birthday: Aleksandr Babionyshev, Raisa Lert, and Evgeniia Pechuro, eds., *Sakharovskii sbornik* (New York, 1981); and Alexander Babyonyshev, ed., *On Sakharov*, trans. Guy Daniels (New York, 1982). They contained tributes to Sakharov for his work in science and in defense of human rights.

actions in the West and to interdict the hostile activities of antisocial elements on the territory of this country. . . .

## · DOCUMENT 147 ·

Andropov to Central Committee, June 26, 1981
The effectiveness of banishing Sakharov to Gorky

Summary: After his administrative expulsion from Moscow, Sakharov, in an effort to make himself known, is undertaking attempts to increase his hostile activities. The Committee for State Security is taking measures to contain this.

An analysis of the available materials shows that Sakharov's administrative expulsion from Moscow and the establishment of a regimen precluding contact with foreigners and antisocial elements have made it possible to curb his hostile activity and deprive Western propaganda centers of an important source of libelous information.

Understanding that the measures taken against Sakharov have deprived the so-called "human rights movement" of its leader, the West is gradually dismantling its propaganda campaign in his "defense." That is evident from the sharp decrease in articles about Sakharov in the pages of newspapers and journals in the capitalist countries, as well as in the number of broadcasts produced on the basis of slanderous information that Sakharov had supplied. Believing that the "Sakharov problem" is no longer of current interest, many foreign correspondents have reduced to a minimum their visits to the Moscow apartment of his wife, Bonner. To a significant degree, this results from the fact that Sakharov, having lost his sources of slanderous information, has been forced to resort to repeating empty verbiage about "general issues of world politics" and also about his personal problems. . . .

However, unreconciled to his loss of status and seeking to reassert himself, Sakharov continues to fabricate documents of a libelous and often provocative character, which he transmits through his wife for publication abroad. Thus, this May, in response to questions that a *Washington Post* correspondent sent to him in Gorky (via Bonner), Sakharov declared that "the intensification of Soviet expansion, especially the invasion of Afghanistan, together with repressive actions inside the country, call for decisive actions in response. It is necessary to increase diplomatic pressure, to find new forms of pressure, and, if necessary, to supplement these with other measures, including the delivery of defensive weapons to the [Afghan] partisans."[21] Repeating the fabrications of Western propaganda, Sakharov asserted that "the USSR is frightened by the situation in Poland and fears that pluralistic changes in the structure of Polish society may continue to develop and spread to the USSR and other socialist countries." He declared that he is convinced "about the desirability and necessity of similar changes for our people and for the entire world."[22]

. . . The Committee for State Security is taking measures to contain the anti-Soviet commotion caused by Sakharov's provocative statements and documents. Simultaneously, measures are being taken to ensure that the regimen established for him in Gorky is strictly observed. . . .

---

The following documents relate to Sakharov and Bonner's first major confrontation with Soviet officials since his forced removal to Gorky: the struggle to gain an exit visa for Liza Alexeyeva, the fiancée and then wife of Bonner's son, Alexei Semyonov. Andropov's reports fail to convey the drama and determination of this elderly, physically fragile couple to help a young woman who had become a "hostage . . . to [Sakharov's] public activities." Alexei had left the country on March 1, 1978, with the hope that Liza would soon be able to join him in America. But fate and Soviet officialdom were not so kind. After Alexei's departure, Liza began living as part of the Sakharov household on Chkalov Street. The regime responded in its usual hamhanded way. First she was denied the opportunity to take her final examinations in the spring of 1978, thereby losing her chance for a diploma. Then the next summer she lost her job as a computer operator, "clearly on instructions from above, since she was well regarded at her place of work."[23] And her initial request for a visa was denied.

Liza's difficulties grew complicated and dispiriting. Her parents, as Sakharov observed, were vulnerable to "distorted notions of life abroad," viewing emigration "as tantamount to treason."[24] They re-

---

21. Andropov was referring to an interview given on February 22, 1980, and published in the *Washington Post,* March 9, 1980. Sakharov also gave an interview on May 4, 1980, that was published in the *New York Times Magazine,* August 6, 1980, 31–39.

22. Soviet fears over Poland and the transmission of the "Polish disease" to the USSR were hardly a fabrication; see the text of Politburo discussions in Mark Kramer, ed., *Soviet Deliberations during the Polish Crisis, 1980–1981* (Washington, DC, 1999).

23. Sakharov, *Memoirs,* 556, 552; see 552–75 for a comprehensive account of this episode.

24. Ibid., 552.

fused to consent to her departure, although she had turned eighteen in
1974 and was an adult in the eyes of Soviet law. Elena Bonner made a
desperate, albeit creative, attempt to approach a group of political
prisoners who were released in April 1979 and permitted to emigrate,
to see if one of them might claim Liza as his fiancée.[25] But the idea led
nowhere. Sakharov even tried to interest relatives of another well-
known prisoner, the pastor Georgy Vins, who also gained his release
that spring, to see if his son would "adopt" Liza as a fiancée and if they
would then take her with them when they joined Vins in the West. But
the KGB intercepted Sakharov's letter. The continued failure unnerved
Liza. In despair, she swallowed a potentially lethal dose of pills. Fortunately, Elena Bonner recognized her symptoms and immediately summoned an ambulance, saving her life.

The regime continued its efforts to intimidate Liza and use her tragic
situation to compromise Sakharov and Bonner. Articles were planted
in the Soviet and Italian press with insinuations about Liza's attempted
suicide and about Elena Bonner's previous relationships. By the late
spring and summer of 1980, Liza was no longer allowed to visit Gorky,
and KGB agents threatened to arrest her for slandering the Soviet system; one even threatened to kill her.

Sakharov sent repeated appeals to Brezhnev and leaders of the
Academy of Sciences. Liza was still denied a visa. By the spring of
1981, Sakharov was discussing with his wife the need to force the issue
by declaring a hunger strike; the KGB's listening devices performed
flawlessly. That June, Alexei arranged to marry Liza by proxy in Butte,
Montana; a family friend, Edward Kline, stood in for her, armed with
her power of attorney.[26]

Sakharov and Bonner began their hunger strike on November 22,
the day before Brezhnev was due to begin a state visit to West Germany. Alerted, the Western press increased pressure on the Kremlin.
After thirteen days during which they drank only mineral water to sustain their strength, the KGB took Sakharov and Bonner to separate
hospitals, hoping to exploit their fears for each other's safety and bring
an end to the protest; but they refused to give in. After a hunger strike

25. They had been involved in the ill-fated Leningrad hijacking case. That April,
Anatoly Altman, Hillel Butman, Aryeh (Leyb) Knokh, Boris Penson, and Wolf Zalmanson were released fourteen months early and permitted to leave for Israel.

26. The power of attorney required Liza's notarized signature. "No Soviet notary
public would notarize such a document," Elena Bonner wrote in *Alone Together* (New
York, 1986), 129. So Bonner was compelled to ask the U.S. embassy for assistance.

of seventeen days, they were assured that Liza would be permitted to leave the Soviet Union. She was able to visit them in Gorky before she left for America.

In his memoirs Sakharov recalls that one of the most difficult aspects of the hunger strike was the response of dissidents who disapproved of the decision to risk their lives "for such a trivial purpose as [his] daughter-in-law's happiness." Such august figures as Pyotr Grigorenko and Lidia Chukovskaya voiced their explicit objection. Another friend, Revolt Pimenov, went so far as to dismiss the significance of Liza's case, arguing that Alexei and Liza's ability "to argue, to make up, to fall into bed . . . should not be bought at the cost 'of a great man's suffering.'" But Sakharov and Bonner understood that the hunger strike was the culmination of a two-year struggle to help Liza rejoin Alexei. It was also, as Sakharov makes clear in his memoirs, "the consequence of all that had happened to us, including exile in Gorky and a continuation of my struggle for human rights and the freedom to choose one's country of residence—not in the abstract, but in a situation in which Lusia and I had from the beginning felt a direct responsibility."[27] For the Sakharov family it was a difficult victory. Bonner's kidneys were badly affected, and Sakharov suffered a heart spasm and then a heart attack after the hunger strike. In the broader world, troubling events overtook their personal drama; on December 13 martial law was declared in Poland, followed by the arrest of thousands of Solidarity activists.

· DOCUMENT 148 ·

Chebrikov to Central Committee, September 2, 1981
The struggle to unite Liza Alexeyeva and Alexei Semyonov begins

The Committee for State Security has received information that Sakharov and Bonner, disturbed that Western interest in them has declined, are planning to exploit the presence of well-known Soviet and foreign scientists at the Tenth European Conference on Controlled Synthesis and Plasma Physics (to be held in Moscow this September) for yet another provocative scheme and for settling their private affairs.

For these purposes, in June Sakharov prepared and sent letters to Soviet Academicians E. P. Velikhov, B. B. Kadomtsev, P. L. Kapitsa, the American

27. Sakharov, *Memoirs*, 560–61.

scientists Gell[28] and Ionis, and the Frenchmen Brefault and Stonnon, with a request to put pressure on the authorities of the USSR and force them to annul their earlier decision ordering his administrative exile from Moscow. In addition, Sakharov plans to circulate his own report among the participants at the conference in the hope that someone will read it aloud at official sessions and demand that the author be allowed to participate in its work.

However, uncertain that these actions will have the needed provocative effect, Sakharov and his wife are ready to announce a hunger strike during the conference in Moscow.

The Committee for State Security is taking steps to foil the escapade planned by Sakharov and Bonner. These steps include preventing Sakharov from leaving Gorky and also preventing the delivery of his report at the conference. If, as a result of the hunger strike contemplated by Sakharov, his life is put in jeopardy, the measures foreseen for such circumstances will be taken. . . .

· DOCUMENT 149 ·

Andropov to Central Committee, November 5, 1981
How Elena Bonner continues to incite Sakharov

Summary: Bonner tries to persuade Sakharov to declare a hunger strike on November 22. The Committee for State Security takes measures to thwart the planned provocation.

. . . Under Bonner's influence, Sakharov decided to declare a hunger strike on the eve of the state visit by the Soviet head of state to the Federal Republic of Germany (as a sign of protest against the authorities' negative answer concerning the reunion of Alexeyeva, whom they pass off as their daughter-in-law, with Bonner's son Semyonov, who lives in the USA). Bonner transmitted this information to the West; in addition, in a letter to the chancellor of the Federal Republic of Germany, Schmidt, she asked him to provide assistance in Alexeyeva's case.

There are reasons to believe that in provoking Sakharov (who suffers from heart disease) to begin a hunger strike, Bonner is aware of a possible tragic outcome. To all appearances, she wishes such an outcome, since the erosion of Sakharov's "status of a fighter" is becoming more and more apparent. She would also like to appear before public opinion "as a victim of

28. Murray Gell-Mann, who was awarded the Nobel Prize for physics in 1969.

the regime." Pursuant to her propagandistic goal, Bonner announced that she is joining Sakharov's hunger strike. However, during the period of Sakharov's hunger strike, she left for Moscow, raising serious doubts about the sincerity of her intentions. The pretext used by Sakharov and Bonner to declare the hunger strike is groundless and, from beginning to end, is a total fiction.

E. K. Alexeyeva, born in 1955, has lived in Sakharov's family since 1978 as domestic help. At one point, Bonner's son Semyonov cohabited with her. In 1979 she applied to the Department of Visas and Registrations of the Ministry of Internal Affairs (under the Moscow Oblast Executive Committee) for permission to emigrate for permanent residence abroad.

In accordance with current law, Alexeyeva's request was denied. Among other things taken into consideration, the invitation to Israel that she submitted was fabricated abroad in the name of an alleged Aunt Feigin, who in fact does not exist.[29] Also taken into account is the fact that Alexeyeva's disabled parents categorically object to their daughter's emigrating and deny her permission to do so (a copy of their statement with a synopsis of the parents' position is attached). Semyonov, to whom Sakharov and Bonner want to send Alexeyeva, is registered as married to a foreign citizen, Levshina.[30] He did not file any documents necessary for Alexeyeva's departure from the USSR. The only connection between Alexeyeva and Semyonov is her past relationship as his lover. The refusal to grant Alexeyeva an exit visa for permanent residence abroad is therefore justified. As for Sakharov and Bonner, they are using the decision to deny an exit visa for purposes of staging a provocation. The Committee for State Security is taking measures to thwart the new provocation by Sakharov and Bonner. . . .

---

· DOCUMENT 150 ·

Andropov to Central Committee, November 19, 1981
The impending hunger strike

---

. . . The pretext chosen by Sakharov for this next hunger strike is so contrived that it cannot be taken seriously by broad circles of public opinion. The refusal to permit Alexeyeva to emigrate for permanent residence

---

29. Tamar Feigin did indeed exist. She was the mother of Efrem Yankelevich and was living in Israel.

30. Olga Levshina emigrated with Alexei Semyonov in February 1980; they were divorced on July 15, 1980.

abroad is well justified, because the invitation to Israel was issued by a fictitious person, and because her disabled parents categorically object to their daughter's emigration.[31] The indicated circumstances have been taken into account in carrying out measures to deal with the intended hunger strike.

Moreover, if the additional measures prove ineffective in forcing Sakharov to renounce the hunger strike, and if Western mass media launch yet another anti-Soviet campaign, it may be advisable to publicize the matter appropriately in the Soviet press.

If Sakharov undertakes a hunger strike and it becomes evident that it is life threatening, he will be hospitalized and force-fed. . . .

· DOCUMENT 151 ·

Andropov to Central Committee, December 1981
The hunger strike continues

The Committee for State Security of the USSR has earlier reported (no. 2735-A of November 19, 1981) on Sakharov's intention to begin a hunger strike to protest the refusal to grant Alexeyeva an exit visa to the USA.

Despite preventive measures, on November 22 Sakharov and his wife Bonner began to carry out this provocative step. Simultaneously, hostile circles in the West, with whom Bonner had earlier coordinated both the hunger strike and the date of its beginning, set about unleashing an anti-Soviet clamor, involving in their propaganda campaign governmental and political figures, broad circles of public opinion, prominent representatives of the artistic and scientific intelligentsia, and Nobel prize laureates.[32]

Information collected by agents of the Committee for State Security shows that since the beginning of the hunger strike, Sakharov's and Bonner's interest in foreign broadcasts to the Soviet Union—which carry reports about their provocative step—has increased significantly. According to this information, the hunger strike has been conducted in conformity with medical instructions for fasting and under the supervision of their

31. After Alexei arranged to marry Liza by proxy, her parents relented and expressed their willingness to support her application for an exit visa; see Sakharov, *Memoirs,* 557–58.

32. President Reagan publicly expressed his concern for the Sakharovs' health; see *New York Times,* December 5, 1981, 6.

personal doctor; as of December 4, the hunger strike has not affected any vital body functions.[33]

However, given that continuation of the hunger strike could cause a serious deterioration in their health, Sakharov and Bonner were hospitalized on December 4. At present, they are being provided with prophylactic medical assistance to prevent any possible complications to their health.

These measures have been taken in consultation with the Procurator's Office of the USSR (Comrade A. M. Rekunkov) and the Ministry of Health of the USSR (Comrade S. P. Burenkov). The Committee for State Security continues to control the situation surrounding Sakharov and Bonner. . . .

---

The declassified archival record contains no document on the Soviet decision to capitulate. We know only that on December 10 the visa office informed Alexeyeva that she was invited to come to get her exit visa. Two days later, the *New York Times* reported that the Soviet Union conceded, albeit obliquely, that it had bowed to Sakharov's demand.[34] Further documents have not been declassified. At the same time, Andropov's report failed to anticipate what would actually happen to Sakharov's health. On the same day as this report, Sakharov suffered a heart spasm. A cardiogram was taken on December 23 and he was discharged from the hospital the next day. Then on December 26, when he was back in the Gorky apartment, he suffered a heart attack. Andropov may be reassuring the Politburo that Sakharov will not manage to participate in a forthcoming meeting of the Academy of Sciences. But he also wanted to be sure that Sakharov would not die while he was in the hospital. Andropov did not want responsibility for his death; such a tragedy would have compelled the Kremlin to do more explaining than it preferred to do.

---

33. At approximately this time, the Fifth Main Directorate of the KGB issued a directive for KGB officials abroad to provide the Western media with disinformation that Sakharov himself caused the deterioration in his health by ignoring the advice of physicians. This cable was later described by Konstantin Preobrazhensky at a conference in February 1995 and published in *KGB: Vchera, segodnia, zavtra* [The KGB: Yesterday, today, tomorrow] (Moscow, 1996), 98. This operation was part of a broad plan comprising a total of thirty-two operations, including thirteen outside the USSR; see Christopher Andrew and Vasili Mitrokhin, *The Sword and the Shield: The Mitrokhin Archive and the Secret History of the KGB* (New York, 1999), 325–27.

34. *New York Times*, December 11, 1981, 3, and December 13, 1981, 11.

· DOCUMENT 153 ·

KGB to Central Committee, December 22[?], 1981[35]
Permission to travel for Liza Alexeyeva and the health of Andrei Sakharov

On December 19, E. K. Alexeyeva, whose departure from the USSR had been demanded by Sakharov and his wife Bonner, flew from Moscow to the USA.

Bonner came from Gorky to say goodbye to Alexeyeva. To do this, Bonner managed to have herself discharged from the hospital, where she had been under treatment for seven days after ending her hunger strike. Sakharov is still in the hospital but also demands to be discharged in the next day or two. This is apparently due to his desire to obtain access to a meeting at a session of the Academy of Sciences of the USSR, which will take place on December 28–29.

The Committee for State Security of the USSR continues to monitor Sakharov's and Bonner's behavior. Particular attention is being paid to discovering the character of Bonner's contact with employees of the U.S. embassy and foreign correspondents during her visits to Moscow. Measures have been taken to interdict Sakharov's contacts with foreigners and antisocial elements and to enforce the ban on his travel outside Gorky.

Given the undesirability of Sakharov's participation in the work of the session of the USSR Academy of Sciences, it is planned not to discharge him from the hospital during the next few days. . . .

· DOCUMENT 155 ·

Andropov and Rekunkov to Central Committee, March 31, 1982
Contacts between Elena Bonner and the American embassy

After Academician Sakharov's administrative expulsion from Moscow, his wife Bonner has maintained regular contact with personnel from the American embassy. During the last two years, she has visited the embassy thirty-five times.

According to our . . .[36] information, embassy staff are attempting to

35. The photocopy poorly reproduces the date (too close to the binding). The date was probably after December 19, when Alexeyeva left Moscow.
36. The word "operational"—i.e., through agents or listening devices—was probably deleted.

stir up an anti-Soviet furor about the "Sakharov problem" and to incite Bonner to make her husband fabricate various kinds of anti-Soviet and provocative "statements" and "appeals."

During his stay in Gorky, Sakharov—at Bonner's insistence—has concocted over thirty malicious anti-Soviet documents, including: "An Appeal to the Governments of Western Countries in Connection with the Madrid Conference,"[37] "A Statement Regarding the Situation in Afghanistan,"[38] "Some Thoughts on the Threshold of the Eighties,"[39] "What the USA and the USSR Should Do to Preserve World Peace,"[40] and "A Statement about Events in Poland."[41]

. . . Bonner takes Sakharov's anti-Soviet and libelous articles to Moscow and transmits them to the American embassy and foreign correspondents for further dissemination. The documents are subsequently used widely by the mass media in capitalist countries to harm the political interests of the USSR.

Bonner's involvement in disseminating Sakharov's anti-Soviet articles makes her liable to criminal punishment. However, to institute criminal proceedings against her now is not deemed expedient, since it would give the adversary additional material for speculation about the "persecution" of Sakharov. . . .

---

The KGB was now about to renew its efforts to steal the manuscript of Sakharov's memoirs. After the first theft of hundreds of pages in November 1978, Sakharov rewrote what had been stolen. But in March 1981, while Sakharov was at a dental clinic, they succeeded in stealing the bag in which he carried sensitive material. Against his better judgment, Sakharov left the bag in the waiting room, and it disappeared while he was having a set of dentures fitted.

A year and a half later, on October 11, 1982, the manuscript was stolen again—500 typewritten pages that his wife had brought back

37. See "World Security, Human Rights Linked," *Los Angeles Times,* September 9, 1980, II, 5.
38. For the complete text, see Sakharov, *Memoirs,* 657–59.
39. Interview given on February 22 and published in *Washington Post,* March 9, 1980, C1, C4; reprinted in Babyonyshev, *On Sakharov,* 241–43.
40. This text, written March 31, 1981, was first published in *Parade,* August 16, 1981, 4–7.
41. Probably a reference to "Obrashchenie k Polskomu mezhzavodskomu komitetu" [Message to the Polish Interfactory Committee], co-authored with Lert, Bogoraz, I. Kovalev, Marchenko, Bonner, Serebrov, Sorokina, Sorokin, and Petrenko-Podiapolskaia. It was published in "Materialy samizdata," 35/80 (October 13, 1980), AS #4092.

from Moscow, where a typist had copied his handwritten pages, and another 900 pages he had completed himself. This time, as Sakharov recalled, "the theft was staged in more spectacular fashion, employing what can only be called gangster methods." While he was sitting behind the wheel of his car, someone smashed the window in the rear, stunned him with some kind of narcotic, and stole his bag from the floor behind the driver's seat. As Sakharov wrote to Fedorchuk, "a policeman is stationed at my door around the clock, and during trips and walks around town, KGB agents always follow me by car (sometimes in two cars) or on foot. They take note of everyone who approaches me, and I suspect that they would quickly apprehend a common thief who tried to steal my bag."[42] It did not matter to the KGB that its methods were so transparent. Harassing Sakharov and disrupting the publication of his memoirs were more important than any adverse publicity their actions could provoke. Its threshold of embarrassment, after all, was very high.

· DOCUMENT 157 ·

Fedorchuk[43] to Central Committee, August 13, 1982
The need to confiscate Sakharov's memoirs

The Committee for State Security of the USSR has received information on attempts of American intelligence services and ideological centers to stir up an anti-Soviet campaign around the "Sakharov problem."

For this purpose, American diplomats and journalists in Moscow have intensified their contact with his wife, Bonner, and through her are inciting Sakharov to prepare various kinds of anti-Soviet and libelous materials. Of special significance is the manuscript of his autobiography, which describes different stages of Sakharov's life and activities. Of late Sakharov has been working intensively on this. Bonner is constantly driving her husband to complete the work on his "autobiography" in the shortest possible time; under her influence, Sakharov is describing certain episodes in an exaggerated form, tendentiously emphasizes his own "hu-

---

42. Sakharov, *Memoirs,* 531–32, 681–82.
43. Vitaly Fedorchuk, former KGB chief in Ukraine, became the new KGB USSR chairman in the spring of 1982, after Andropov replaced Suslov as the Politburo member responsible for ideology in April 1982. Fedorchuk was an interim chairman; when Andropov became general secretary, he appointed Viktor Chebrikov to head the KGB.

man rights activities," and assesses Soviet reality and the domestic and foreign policy of the Soviet Union from a hostile point of view.

According to available information, on August 26 Bonner intends to bring some chapters of the "Autobiography" from Gorky to Moscow and pass them on to the Americans. To curb Bonner's hostile activities involving the transfer of Sakharov's anti-Soviet documents to the West, the Committee for State Security has decided to conduct a personal search of Bonner, with the sanction of the Procurator, and to confiscate the above materials. The matter has been coordinated with the Office of the Procurator of the USSR (Comrade A. M. Rekunkov). . . .

· DOCUMENT 158 ·

Fedorchuk to Central Committee, August 31, 1982
Sakharov's appeal to the Pugwash Conference

In May 1982, Academician A. D. Sakharov wrote an "Appeal" to the "Participants of the Pugwash Conference,"[44] which contains a strident anti-Soviet assessment of the domestic and foreign policy of the CPSU and the Soviet government. . . . He accuses the participants of the Pugwash movement of "blindly following" the policy of the USSR,[45] incites scientists to interfere in the internal affairs of our country, and appeals to them to speak out in defense of persons convicted of committing especially dangerous state crimes.

According to information at our disposal, this "Appeal" was sent to the West by Sakharov's wife, Bonner.

For anti-Soviet purposes, the Americans attempted to use this libelous attack at the next session of the Pugwash Conference in Warsaw to offset the "Declaration of Ninety-seven Nobel Laureates," which reflects the basic principles of the international movement of scientists for peace. On August 28, the Americans illegally[46] circulated Sakharov's "Appeal"

44. First published in *New York Times*, September 10, 1982, 6; for the full text, see "The Sakharov Letter," *Bulletin of the Atomic Scientists*, November 1982, 61–62.
45. Sakharov was not alone in his criticism of the Pugwash Conference; see the column by Flora Lewis in *New York Times*, September 7, 1982, 23, where she wrote that "after some confusion and a charge of censorship, the letter was distributed privately with no chance for debate." A week later, officials of the Pugwash Conference replied, contending that Sakharov's letter and other material critical of the Soviet and Polish governments also circulated during the conference.
46. I.e., in defiance of Soviet controls.

among some of the delegates, while the Canadian scientist Sommers intended to read it aloud and to put it on the agenda for discussion by conference participants. . . .

One goal of the crackdown that began in 1979 was to eliminate dissident groups whose members were publicly known. The Helsinki
Watch groups, the Working Commission against the Abuse of Psychiatry for Political Purposes, and the Christian Committee for the Defense of Believers' Rights all demonstrated the dissidents' ability to attract attention inside the country and in the West. According to their
particular agendas, they collected information and distributed signed
documents. But by 1982 the regime had achieved its objective: all the
members of the Working Commission were either in prison or in exile.
As Fedorchuk announced to the Politburo, the Moscow Helsinki
Watch Group was also closing. One of its members, the lawyer Sofia
Kalistratova, was being threatened with arrest. The regime had initiated a case against her based on 120 Helsinki Group documents. Hoping to forestall her arrest, the group, which formally included only
three veteran activists still at large in the country—Bonner, Kalistratova, and the refusenik Naum Meiman—hastily announced its dis-
banding that September. Contrary to Fedorchuk's assertion, Kalistratova was not arrested or brought to trial.

· DOCUMENT 159 ·

Fedorchuk to Central Committee, September 12, 1982
The closing of the Moscow Helsinki Watch Group

According to information obtained by the Committee for State Security,
Sakharov and his wife, Bonner, are trying to increase their anti-Soviet activity. . . .

On September 5–7, Bonner (together with her closest allies) . . . [47] produced a so-called "Appeal to World Public Opinion"[48] calling for statements to speak out in defense of a "Helsinki Group" member, S. V. Kalistratova, who has been put on trial for violating Article 190-1 of the

47. Three-quarters of a line are deleted in the copy of the declassified document.
48. Fedorchuk was probably referring to the collective letter in defense of Sofia
Kalistratova that was issued in September 1982; this letter and others signed by
Sakharov in defense of Kalistratova have been published in *Zastupnitsa: Advokat Sofia
Kalistratova* [The defender: Attorney Sofia Kalistratova], ed. E. Pechuro (Moscow,
1997), 117–21.

Criminal Code of the RSFSR (dissemination of consciously false fabrications that defame the Soviet state and social system). Simultaneously, Bonner and Kalistratova prepared a statement about the dissolution of the "Helsinki Group," which made libelous assertions that they took this step allegedly because of the "continual persecution of the Group's members in the Soviet Union."[49]

On September 8, Bonner gave these provocative materials to foreign correspondents, with the request they be widely publicized.

In addition, Bonner forced Sakharov to prepare and notarize at the Gorky Notary Office his will and power of attorney (the texts of the documents are attached).[50]

As is evident from the contents of the will, Bonner becomes the sole executor of his copyrights and his monetary accounts in foreign banks; in the event of her death, all rights go to her daughter, T. I. Yankelevich, who now lives in the USA.

While registering his will, Sakharov insisted that the following provisions be inserted: "In the event of my death, I ask that my body be cremated in the USSR and the ashes sent abroad for burial, where my children live (the reference is to Bonner's children, who reside in the USA). I ask the Soviet Government not to prevent the removal of my remains. I entrust everything to my wife. . . . In leaving the copyrights to my wife, I entrust her with the right to edit my memoirs and political articles, as well as my scientific and popular writings." The notary rejected these requests by Sakharov.[51]

It is noteworthy that the power of attorney gives Bonner the right not only to manage all of Sakharov's property but also to conduct in her husband's name "business with all state institutions and cooperative and public organizations, as well as civil and criminal cases in all courts."

According to information at the disposal of the KGB of the USSR, Bon-

49. The statement, signed by Sofia Kalistratova, Elena Bonner, and Naum Meiman, was issued on September 6, 1982; see "Helsinki Group Disbands," *Chronicle of Human Rights in the USSR*, no. 47 (July–September 1982), 30.

50. These documents, in fact, were not released.

51. The format of a legal will in the USSR generally included only information about beneficiaries. After a discussion with Sakharov, the notary accepted the provisions relating to the assignment of author's rights, but refused to accept how and where Sakharov wished to be buried, a provision that was not a customary part of a will. Sakharov was trying to ensure that he would be buried where he expected Elena Bonner to be living—with her children in the United States. Alternatively, he wished to be buried near her brother, Igor. In fact, Sakharov was interred next to Elena Bonner's mother and brother in Vostryakovskoe Cemetery in Moscow.

ner (after obtaining the above documents) soon plans to apply to the USSR Ministry of Internal Affairs for a visa to travel to Italy for treatment of her eye disease.

Surveillance over the behavior of Sakharov and Bonner is continuing. . . .

------

· DOCUMENT 160 ·

Fedorchuk to Central Committee, November 1, 1982
The seizure of Sakharov's memoirs

------

In the process of conducting operations, the Committee for State Security of the USSR covertly procured "Pages of Reminiscences" (autobiography) and a diary handwritten by Sakharov himself.[52] Also seized were some originals of provocative "addresses" and "appeals" that he prepared for world public opinion, and his correspondence with sympathizers who live abroad and collaborate with subversive anti-Soviet organizations.

The autobiography covers Sakharov's life as a scientist and the period of his so-called "public activities," from his childhood to the present. It contains information, in a concentrated form, that in particular shows the causes that led him to assume a hostile position. Depicting himself as a "fighter for civil rights," Sakharov defames the Soviet government and system as well as the domestic and foreign policies of the Soviet state. He makes assertions about the "totalitarianism and aggressiveness" of the socialist system, about the genocide of Crimean Tatars and Germans of the Volga region, and about the "annexation" of the Baltic republics, Ukraine, and Armenia. He falsifies the history of the development of the Soviet state and the practice of communist construction, appeals to the West to intervene in the domestic affairs of socialist countries, urges a military confrontation with the Soviet Union, and makes a libelous assessment of the USSR's efforts to reduce international tensions. . . .

Sakharov has been keeping his diary since March 1980. It records Sakharov and Bonner's attitude toward various events inside and outside the country, their joint work in composing libelous and provocative "appeals," "letters," "statements," and their intercession on behalf of people convicted of especially dangerous crimes against the state.

From Bonner's and Sakharov's correspondence it is clear that they maintain illegal contacts with sympathizers abroad by using the diplo-

52. Sakharov started to keep his diary, at Bonner's insistence, on January 1, 1977.

matic mail[53] of the American embassy in Moscow as well as foreigners who come to the Soviet Union on scientific and cultural exchange and as tourists. Through them, Bonner sends to the West the anti-Soviet and provocative materials produced by her husband, information for various hostile campaigns organized abroad and associated with Sakharov's name, and his taped "addresses" to foreign public opinion. Through the same channels, they receive Sakharov's "works" and other materials printed abroad and coordinate anti-Soviet campaigns planned abroad, in particular the so-called "Sakharov Hearings." In August of this year Sakharov illegally dispatched a document to the West, which gives his consent to launch a provocative campaign in support of his travel to Switzerland, allegedly for medical treatment.

The contents of his autobiography, diary, and correspondence provide documentary proof that for ten years Sakharov's anti-Soviet activity has been fomented and directed by his wife. It is also she who sends abroad his libelous attacks through American diplomats and journalists from various capitalist countries.

Characteristically, after the above materials disappeared, Sakharov and Bonner did not claim that violence or any other physical measures had been used against them, but only reported to the police the circumstances of the theft. However, for propaganda purposes, they are now disseminating all kinds of fantasies, in particular that Sakharov was allegedly drugged.[54]

We intend to use this situation to issue another warning to Sakharov about the inadmissibility of disseminating libelous fabrications. As to the materials obtained during the operation, they will be used . . . to expose the hostile activities of Sakharov and Bonner. . . .

· DOCUMENT 162 ·

Fedorchuk to Central Committee, December 4, 1982
A plan to search Elena Bonner

The Committee for State Security of the USSR reports that on September 26 Bonner asked the Department of Visas and Registrations of the

53. The diplomatic pouch, which was secure from Soviet inspection and, as the KGB suspected, was used to transmit sensitive materials abroad.
54. Sakharov informed police about the violence against him. He also transmitted his statement to Western correspondents; see *New York Times,* October 31, 1982, 1. Sakharov later included the story in his *Memoirs,* 532–33.

Ministry of Internal Affairs (the branch at the Zhdanov District Executive Committee of Moscow) to grant her permission to travel to Italy for treatment of her eye disease.

Bonner has traveled to Italy three times (1975, 1977, and 1979) under the same contrived pretext. The basis for such a statement is her way of life and behavior in recent years. Bonner drives her car with assurance and, before receiving her driver's license, passed the examination of a special medical commission. She works at her typewriter daily; she reads and writes a lot; she very rarely complains about her eye disease; she practically never goes to doctors for help. The last circumstance provides the most objective evidence that the pretext for travel abroad is fictitious, for there are highly qualified ophthalmologists working in Moscow, and she could use their services if she so wished.

An analysis of Bonner's previous trips to Italy and her behavior abroad provides grounds to state that their real purpose is to stir up interest in Sakharov (which has periodically flagged in the West); enemy intelligence agencies and propaganda organs regularly try to use his name and behavior in subversive actions against the Soviet Union. Bonner's behavior was most hostile in 1979, when, according to information at our disposal, the Americans brought her illegally from Italy to the USA. While abroad, she participated in various kinds of anti-Soviet gatherings and gave interviews of a provocative character. Among her circle in Moscow, Bonner repeatedly emphasized that she considered the founding of the so-called "American Helsinki Group" to be the main achievement of her stay in the USA. . . .

Recently Bonner and (under her influence) Sakharov have been hastily restoring the lost portions of his "Autobiography," without which it cannot be published abroad. Bonner intends to take the restored parts of the text to Moscow on December 7 and send them through illegal channels to the United States.

To contain Bonner's hostile activities (associated with the transmission of Sakharov's anti-Soviet materials to the West), the Committee for State Security has decided to search Bonner, with the sanction of the Procurator, and to confiscate the above items. The matter has been coordinated with the Office of the Procurator of the USSR (Comrade A. M. Rekunkov).

As for Bonner's trip to Italy, permission will be denied. A statement will be issued by the Department of Visas and Registrations of the Main Administration of Internal Affairs (through the branch at the Moscow City Executive Committee) that this decision resulted from her violation of the rules governing Soviet citizens abroad—in particular, the trip from Italy to the USA in 1979 without appropriate permission.

· DOCUMENT 163 ·

Fedorchuk to Central Committee, December 8, 1982
Confiscation of Sakharov's papers from Elena Bonner

---

The Committee for State Security of the USSR reports that Sakharov has recently taken steps to resume his antisocial activity in order to sustain foreign interest in him. Bonner, acting on instructions from representatives of the American embassy in Moscow, systematically pushes him in this direction.

One such action by Bonner and Sakharov is their preparation of the so-called memoirs of an academician for publication in the West. . . .

The KGB organs have repeatedly thwarted Sakharov's intentions to send the final draft of this manuscript abroad. Nevertheless, he and Bonner continue their systematic work to restore it. After information was received that Bonner left from Gorky for Moscow on December 6 to hand over the manuscript to the Americans, the decision was made to subject her to an official search. As a result of this measure, 240 pages of the manuscript of the memoirs were confiscated from Bonner. In particular, this included a chapter titled "The Year 1965," which provides, along with libel of the Soviet state and social system, a detailed description of his work in the Ministry of Medium Machine Building. In addition, in writing about his participation in developing thermonuclear weapons, Sakharov includes some classified information that cannot be made public.

The search confirmed Bonner's intention to send all this abroad through illegal channels for publication in the United States.

In addition, Bonner had a video camera given her by foreign correspondents to videotape an interview with Sakharov. The videotape with Sakharov's statement, probably intended for American television, was confiscated. Among other things, Sakharov said in the interview that his administrative exile "is related to everything—to the domestic and foreign policy of our country, to the repression of other dissidents, such as Shcharansky, Orlov, and others, to such events as Afghanistan, Poland, the missiles aimed at Europe, to questions of domestic policy, to the needed liberalization of our country. . . . Therefore, all these matters are related and covered up by the lies of our official representatives as well as by those who go abroad allegedly representing the Soviet intelligentsia. It is necessary to expose these lies and to understand the true state of affairs."

As Bonner's behavior shows, after recovering from the shock of the unexpected search, she still intends to continue her anti-Soviet activity. She informed employees of the American embassy and foreign correspondents of what had happened.

It is also known that she harbors plans to carry out other antisocial actions. In particular, she is planning to make a row over her desire to go abroad under the pretext of receiving medical treatment. The decision has been made not to allow such a trip.

Considering the type of anti-Soviet activity that Bonner has been engaged in for so long and her participation in many antisocial actions, we think it expedient to stop her from coming to Moscow. It is possible to do this by indicting her on criminal charges in the city of Gorky; there are more than sufficient legal grounds to do this. The investigation will be conducted without subjecting Bonner to arrest; she could be sentenced to exile. This has been coordinated with the Office of the Procurator of the USSR (Comrade Rekunkov). We request your consent.

·  DOCUMENT 164  ·

Chebrikov to Central Committee, December 22, 1982[55]
More on the search of Elena Bonner

The Committee for State Security of the USSR reported (no. 2367-F of December 8, 1982) about a personal search of Bonner and the confiscation of Sakharov's hostile writings, which were intended for illegal transmission to the USA.

This measure left Bonner confused, perplexed, and frightened. She is especially upset over the fact that the authorities have foiled her husband's and her own attempt to send to the West Sakharov's recent work (on which he recently expended so much energy and without which it will be difficult to publish his memoirs abroad any time soon). The following day Bonner informed American diplomats about what had happened and invited them to her place to discuss the situation.

According to information at the disposal of the Committee for State Security, the Americans, concerned no less than Bonner by the search, are now trying to work out measures to maintain contact with her and to continue using her as the only link between Sakharov and the American em-

55. In December 1982, Viktor Chebrikov replaced Vitaly Fedorchuk as chairman of the KGB.

bassy in Moscow. Their greatest worry, of course, is that such measures could lead to Sakharov's total isolation, which would limit opportunities for the West to use his name, actions, and activities to fuel anti-Soviet campaigns. For this reason, the Americans are planning, among other things, to organize protests by Western scientists, officials, and public figures to protest the restrictive measures already taken, or that may be taken, with respect to Sakharov and his wife, Bonner.

Fearing more searches yet unwilling to abandon attempts to bring Sakharov's anti-Soviet writings from Gorky, Bonner and her closest associates are discussing various ways to deliver these materials to Moscow. They all share the opinion that the safest way to do this, under present circumstances, is through an illegal multistage channel using their most reliable acquaintances.

The Committee for State Security continues to monitor the behavior of Sakharov and Bonner and is taking measures to interdict their attempts to supply the West with anti-Soviet materials. . . .

· DOCUMENT 167 ·

Chebrikov to Central Committee, January 23, 1984
Appeal from Sakharov to permit Elena Bonner to travel to the West

Academician Sakharov has addressed an appeal to the Presidium of the Supreme Soviet of the USSR to permit his wife to travel as a private citizen to Italy for medical treatment and to visit her mother, children, grandchildren, and other relatives, who emigrated to the West and now live in the USA. . . .

Bonner has previously been abroad three times (1975, 1977, and 1979). She justified each trip by the need for medical treatment. However, she used her stays abroad to participate in anti-Soviet campaigns unleashed by our enemy and timed for her arrival. Thus, in 1975, she delivered a slanderous speech at the award ceremony for the Nobel Peace Prize, which had been awarded to Sakharov as a provocation. At the same time, the "Cultural Center" of the Italian Neo-Fascist party awarded her a prize to express its appreciation for her "vigorous social activism."[56] In 1977

56. This was a nonmonetary award given to Bonner by the Italian Adelaide Ristori Society. Adelaide Ristori (1822–1906) was a celebrated actress who was also famous for asking Queen Isabel II, after a performance in Spain, to commute the death sentence for all prisoners. In Italy her name became a symbol of social activism.

Bonner participated in arranging and conducting anti-Soviet gatherings in
Florence: the "conference of dissidents" and the "Sakharov Hearings." In
1979 she took part in a conference, "The Dissident Movement and
Democracy in the Countries of Eastern Europe." Then, without obtaining
permission from the Soviet embassy in Rome, Bonner traveled to the USA,
where Americans involved her in resolving problems associated with increasing anti-Soviet activity in the West. Bonner's journey to the USA was
organized by American intelligence agencies and carried out through illegal channels. . . .

Given the above circumstances, it is deemed expedient to reject Sakharov's request that Bonner be allowed to travel abroad.

However, one should not exclude the possibility that Bonner may use
such a decision to goad Sakharov into committing new provocations, such
as a "hunger strike." In case of such behavior, it will be necessary to take
the appropriate measures through medical agencies.

The decision to refuse Bonner permission to travel abroad should be announced to Sakharov through the Department of Visas and Registrations
of the Ministry of Internal Affairs (the branch at the Executive Committee
of the Gorky Oblast Council of People's Deputies). The refusal should be
explained by citing Bonner's repeated violation of the rules of behavior for
Soviet citizens abroad.

· DOCUMENT 168 ·

Chebrikov to Central Committee, March 5, 1984
Efforts to isolate Sakharov more effectively

In 1983 the USSR Committee for State Security carried out a series of
prophylactic, propaganda, and operational measures that somewhat
curbed the anti-Soviet activities of Academician A. D. Sakharov, his wife
E. G. Bonner, and a number of their ideological allies.

For all practical purposes, in the past year Sakharov remained the only
prominent figure who is closely linked to the subversive schemes of Western intelligence services, centers of ideological sabotage, and foreign anti-
Soviet organizations. His name, his deeds, and his activities continue to be
used for various purposes hostile to the Soviet state, but most actively in
propaganda campaigns to secure the deployment of nuclear missiles in Europe. For this purpose, the Americans, for example, made widespread use
of Sakharov's so-called "Open Letter" to the U.S. scientist S. Drell. The

appearance of this letter was preceded by Bonner's meeting with Drell, which was arranged by members of the staff of the American embassy in Moscow. During that meeting, Drell gave copies of his own statements on nuclear weapons for delivery to Sakharov. While working on his response to Drell, Sakharov was continually subjected to pressure by his wife, who insisted, in particular, that he should incorporate in the letter the thesis about the necessity for the U.S. to build MX missiles.

The attempts of the American administration to use Sakharov's "Open Letter" as a propaganda shield to disguise its militaristic policies has been convincingly rebuffed by Soviet scientists in the article "When Honor and Conscience Are Lost" (*Izvestia*, July 2, 1983).[57] According to operational information at the disposal of the KGB, about 3,500 Soviet citizens from 438 cities sent Sakharov letters in which they angrily denounced him as a hatemonger for his stand on the questions of war and peace, and have accused him of "treason to the Motherland." In this connection Sakharov made the following entry in his diary: "It should be kept in mind that as many as half of those letters are collective letters; hence the total number of those who signed those letters runs into tens of thousands. . . . Sad as it is, one has to admit that this time the campaign against me proved more effective than in earlier years."[58]

Sakharov's open support for Reagan's militaristic course has resulted in his estrangement from a number of progressive-thinking individuals abroad. Of particular significance among the measures designed to discredit Sakharov and Bonner in the eyes of Soviet and foreign public opinion was the publication of *CIA Target—USSR*, a book by the well-known Soviet historian N. Yakovlev,[59] and the publication of excerpts from this book in the journals *Chelovek i zakon* [Man and the Law] and *Smena* [Change].

The prevention of hostile activities by certain extremists from Sakharov and Bonner's circle, the removal of some politically unstable persons from their anti-Soviet influence, and the above publications—all these things

57. An English translation of this text is in Sakharov, *Memoirs*, 670–72.

58. Once again the KGB report confirmed that the diaries were stolen and used against Sakharov. Since the stolen manuscripts were never returned either to Sakharov or to Bonner after his death, it is impossible to verify the accuracy of this quotation.

59. This was Nikolai N. Iakovlev, author of *CIA Target—USSR*, rev. ed. (Moscow, 1983). Sakharov sued Iakovlev for libel, but a Soviet court refused to hear the case. Iakovlev had the temerity to visit Sakharov in Gorky on July 14, 1983. Elena Bonner was out at the time. Sakharov slapped Iakovlev for the way he had slandered his wife, then threw him out of the apartment. In a dismaying development, Yakovlev's book was reissued in Moscow in 2003.

have forced the enemy to seek new tactics for working with Bonner and
Sakharov. At present, the Americans are evidently trying to involve government and political figures as well as representatives of the intelligentsia
from Norway, Switzerland, and Holland in a provocative campaign on
their behalf. Upon instructions from Washington, a vociferous campaign
has been unleashed in these countries, making demagogic demands that
Sakharov be permitted to leave the USSR or at least that Bonner be allowed to go to the West, where it is proposed to use her as a leader of the
anti-Soviet emigration. In discussing with Sakharov the question of emigration, Bonner declared: "If they summon us, I am ready to exchange my
own motherland if you go too, without thinking about it. I have no use
whatsoever for the Russian people or our 'Motherland.' My homeland is
the earth."

The Committee for State Security is taking into account the above and
the enemy's other schemes to intensify the anti-Soviet activities of
Sakharov and Bonner. . . .

---

The following set of reports provided a slanted account of Sakharov
and Bonner's thwarted attempt to compel the regime to grant her permission to visit the West for health and family reasons. Ever since their
joint hunger strike in 1981 on behalf of Liza Alexeyeva, both experienced persistent and substantial medical difficulties. Her glaucoma
continued to grow worse, but she was not allowed to return to Italy,
where she had received treatment on three occasions. She also suffered
from severe heart problems, including a massive heart attack in April
1983, but the regime refused to relent. Sakharov felt compelled to act
decisively on his wife's behalf. In the fall of 1983 he was considering
another hunger strike. Bonner, however, dissuaded him, understanding how such an ordeal would undermine his health.

But on March 30, 1984, in response to Sakharov's direct appeals to
Andropov and then to Chernenko, he was told to wait until May 1 for
an answer. Unwilling to permit the regime to manipulate them further,
Sakharov and Bonner agreed that he would declare a hunger strike in
Gorky, while she would seek temporary refuge in the U.S. embassy. The
KGB, though, learned about the plan in mid-April, when Sakharov's
papers were again stolen during a brief stay in the hospital to treat an
infected abscess on his leg. On May 2 Bonner was to travel either by
train or by air to Moscow. (She had actually sent a telegram to a friend,
asking him to meet her at the train station, but this was meant to
confuse the KGB.) Sakharov accompanied her to the Gorky airport.

"I watched through the airport window as she was detained by the aircraft and taken away in a police car. I immediately returned to the apartment and took a laxative," Sakharov later recalled, "thereby beginning my hunger strike for my wife to be able to travel."[60]

The ensuing confrontation between them and the regime lasted four months. Bonner was officially charged with Article 190–1, which forbids making deliberately false statements against the regime. Allowed to return to their apartment, she was summoned to repeated interrogations until her two-day trial opened on August 9. Convicted of the charge, she was sentenced to five years of internal exile, with Gorky designated as her place of exile; she could remain with Sakharov, "creating a semblance of humanity."

Sakharov, meanwhile, endured far harsher treatment. They were forcibly separated on May 7, when he was seized by KGB officers "disguised in doctors' white coats" and taken to Gorky Regional Hospital. That summer and fall, their family and supporters, whether in Moscow or abroad, had no clear or reliable idea of their fate. When Elena Bonner failed to reach Moscow on May 2, it was assumed that Sakharov had begun a hunger strike. Then an extraordinary thing happened. Their friend Irina Kristi, a forty-seven-year-old mathematician, traveled to Gorky by train on May 6. She saw them on the balcony of their apartment and managed to speak with them for three minutes before police seized her and took her to a cell. She was kept overnight and fined 15 rubles (about $20 at the official exchange rate at that time) for resisting the police. The next day she returned to Moscow and contacted two Western journalists, passing along the news that Sakharov had begun a hunger strike and Bonner was being indicted. But Kristi was then herself placed under house arrest; police barricaded her and her family in their apartment. This was the last reliable information to reach the West for several months. Sakharov and Bonner, in fact, were separated and unable to contact each other from May 7 until September 7—"isolated from each other and the outside world." Sakharov "was subjected to the excruciating and degrading process of force-feeding." At first with intravenous feedings and then with a tube inserted through his nose, the KGB compelled him to accept nourishment. Then on May 25

the most excruciating, degrading and barbarous method was used. I was again pushed down onto the bed without a pillow and my hands

60. From a letter to Anatoly Alexandrov, president of the Academy of Sciences, in Sakharov, *Memoirs*, 700.

and feet were tied. A tight clamp was placed on my nose so that I could breathe only through my mouth. Whenever I opened my mouth to take a breath, a spoonful of nutriment or a broth containing strained meat would be poured into my mouth. Sometimes my jaws were pried open by a lever. They would hold my mouth shut until I swallowed so that I could not spit out the food. When I managed to do so, it only prolonged the agony. I experienced a continuing feeling of suffocation, aggravated by the position of my body and head. I had to gasp for breath. I could feel the veins bulging on my forehead. They seemed on the verge of bursting.[61]

None of this was known at the time. Not until Sakharov and Bonner were reunited and permitted to have a photograph taken together at a studio could they confirm to her mother and children in America that they were again together and alive. But she could not send the photograph until the end of October. We now understand how the physical torture and the brain spasms and possible stroke brought on by the trauma of force-feeding caused Sakharov to suspend his hunger strike.

· DOCUMENT 169 ·

Chebrikov to Central Committee, April 13, 1984
A long and dangerous hunger strike is about to begin

. . . While exploiting the question of Sakharov's health, Bonner at the same time forces him to spurn medical assistance on the false pretext that it allegedly "poses a threat to his life."

On April 9, as a result of Bonner's psychological pressure, Sakharov—under unsanitary conditions—used ordinary scissors to open the abscesses on his leg, which caused an outbreak of phlegmon,[62] a high fever, and deterioration of his general condition. That same day he was forced to seek medical assistance, and the doctors recommended surgical intervention under hospital conditions. On April 12 Sakharov was admitted to the Semashko Hospital of Gorky Oblast.

Bonner was in Moscow from April 8 to April 12; she returned to Gorky

61. Ibid., 698–706.
62. According to Bonner (interview with author, Brookline, MA, 2003), Sakharov had a carbuncle, not a phlegmon.

on April 12 at 8:10 P.M. While in Moscow, she held a secret forty-five-minute meeting with two American diplomats. In addition, using a telephone installed in the apartment of the former wife of the poet [Yevgeny] Yevtushenko,[63] she spoke with her children and mother, who reside in the USA. During this conversation, her relatives informed her that a feature film about Sakharov and Bonner was being produced in the West.[64] The Committee for State Security continues to monitor the behavior of Sakharov and Bonner. . . .

· DOCUMENT 170 ·

Gromyko, Chebrikov, and Rekunkov to Central Committee, April 26, 1984
How the KGB will handle the hunger strike

. . . The Committee for State Security now has reliable operative information showing that our enemy has prepared a range of special measures to achieve Bonner's departure from the USSR and, in the event things take a favorable turn, Sakharov's departure as well. The idea of this provocation, which they have planned jointly, is as follows. To exert psychological pressure on the Soviet government, Sakharov is to declare a "hunger strike with no fixed time limit," and his wife will meanwhile take refuge in the American embassy in Moscow, where she will remain until their demand that Bonner be permitted to go abroad is satisfied. In the embassy, she will conduct a press conference for foreign correspondents and will officially declare that she is joining her husband's hunger strike. This extreme action was intended to take place in the middle of April, but was temporarily postponed because of Sakharov's illness and measures taken by the Committee for State Security.

In order to generate international publicity about this action and to involve foreign statesmen and politicians, scientists, and the general public, Sakharov (under pressure from Bonner) wrote a number of provocative statements urging intervention on their behalf. In one of them, titled "An Appeal to Friends Everywhere,"[65] he points out in particular that "I have

63. Galina Yevtushenko, a close friend of Elena Bonner's.
64. The TV movie *Sakharov*, starring Jason Robards and Glenda Jackson, came out in 1984.
65. Published as "Appeal on Beginning a Hunger Strike" in Edward D. Lozansky, ed., *Andrei Sakharov and Peace* (New York, 1985), 281–82, and in Bonner, *Alone Together*, 240–41. The first news about the hunger strike reached the Western public

appealed to the U.S. Department of State and the American ambassador in the USSR with a request that, during my hunger strike, they grant Elena Bonner temporary asylum in the embassy." These appeals are designed to stir up an anti-Soviet uproar in the West that is, in particular, linked with his impending birthday (May 21), which Reagan has proclaimed "National Sakharov Day."

Given what has been described above, it is necessary to take measures to prevent Bonner from traveling to Moscow and contacting foreigners. This could be accomplished if the Procurator's Office of Gorky Oblast were to institute criminal proceedings against Bonner by charging her under Article 190–1 of the Criminal Code of the RSFSR . . . and, without resorting to her arrest, as a means to prevent her [activities], have her sign a pledge not to leave the city of Gorky. . . .

At the same time, one must also take into account that the proposed measure does not exclude the possibility that Bonner and Sakharov will conduct a hunger strike. In this case, it will be necessary to take appropriate measures through the USSR Ministry of Public Health.

Simultaneously, we deem it imperative to address a verbal note to the Americans in Washington about the intolerable activity of embassy personnel, who are inciting Bonner and Sakharov to commit anticonstitutional acts. We request that this be considered.

Attached: Excerpt from Politburo Protocol no. 156 (April 28, 1984)[66]
On the antisocial activity of Bonner and Sakharov,
and the measures taken to curtail it.

1. Approve the proposals contained in the memorandum from Comrades A. A. Gromyko, V. M. Chebrikov, and A. M. Rekunkov of April 26, 1984 (attached).

2. Approve the draft instructions to the Soviet ambassador in Washington (attached).

[Marginal note: To be returned in seven days to the Central Committee of the CPSU (General Department, Sector 1)]
[Addition] to point 20 of Protocol no. 156

With the detention of Elena Bonner in Gorky, the leaders of the KGB

---

through a statement made by Efrem and Tatiana Yankelevich (see *New York Times*, May 9, 1984, 1 and 7); their source was Irina Kristi.

66. This addition to the Protocol was addressed "to Comrades Chernenko, Tikhonov, Gromyko, Chebrikov, Rekunkov, Savinkin."

and the Soviet Foreign Ministry reported on the expected international protests. Both Gromyko and Chebrikov warned that the West would soon launch a major campaign against the Soviet Union. To preempt this criticism, the memorandum advanced a proposal (approved by the Politburo) to publish an official account of the scheme for a hunger strike and Sakharov's plan to ask the U.S. embassy in Moscow to grant Bonner temporary refuge.[67]

· DOCUMENT 171 ·

Gromyko and Chebrikov to Central Committee, May 3, 1984
The hunger strike and official measures to thwart the plans
of Sakharov and Bonner

In accordance with the decision of April 28 (P[rotocol] 156-[pt.]20), measures were taken to thwart the provocation planned by American intelligence services, which had the goal of arranging for E. G. Bonner, the wife of Academician A. D. Sakharov, to travel abroad.

The note of protest submitted to the State Department via the Soviet embassy in Washington, citing the direct collusion of the American embassy in Moscow in preparing this provocation, clearly upset the calculations of the Americans.

At the same time, the Americans probably have prepared another course of action in case the plan to grant Bonner "temporary political asylum" in the U.S. embassy in Moscow goes awry. One should expect that it will be activated once they learn of the measures taken to prevent Bonner from leaving Gorky for Moscow. . . .

The U.S. administration may issue its own version of events related to Sakharov and Bonner, using the materials they had received earlier from them. All this will be accompanied by attempts to put pressure on us, including such means as a massive anti-Soviet campaign. According to information received from the Soviet embassy in Washington, one can already see signs that such a campaign is being prepared.

Under these circumstances, it appears expedient to forestall the actions of the Americans and to publicize facts that expose Washington's objectives in pursuing this provocation. The emphasis should be on the un-

67. The TASS account was reported in the *New York Times*, May 5, 1984, 7, and the *Washington Post*, May 5, 1984, 1. Bonner gave her account of the events in *Alone Together*, 57–58.

seemly role played by personnel of the American embassy in Moscow (by using the facts outlined in the representations made to the State Department).

Appropriate articles should be published in the Soviet press in the form of a TASS release, which should then be widely distributed abroad by TASS, the Novosti Agency, and State Radio and Television. We ask that this be given consideration.


Resolution of the Central Committee CPSU [Draft]
On making public new facts about the provocative activity of
Sakharov and Bonner and the involvement of Americans

1. Accept the suggestions contained in the memorandum by Comrades A. A. Gromyko and V. M. Chebrikov of May 3, 1984 (attached).

2. Approve the draft TASS materials on this subject (attached). Transmit this material via radio and television and publish it in the central press. Disseminate it abroad through TASS, APN [Novosti Press Agency], and the State Television and Radio of the USSR.

3. Instruct the KGB to prepare an article about the antisocial, criminal behavior of E. G. Bonner for publication in the newspaper *Izvestia*.

Secretary of the Central Committee


Draft: Appendix "The Real Cause of the Provocation"

It has long been known that whenever reactionary circles in the West want to complicate the international situation and divert public attention from their own dangerous plans and actions, they resort to crude and frenzied anti-Soviet campaigns. To achieve their goals they stop at nothing, including the use of all sorts of renegades who have sold out their conscience and renounced their own people.

A special place in such dirty machinations has been reserved by our adversaries for the well-known anti-Soviet Sakharov, whose antisocial behavior was condemned by the Soviet people long ago.

Mention should be made of Sakharov's wife, E. G. Bonner, who regularly goads her husband into actions hostile to the Soviet state and society, and also commits such actions herself as reported on numerous occasions in the press. She also acts as intermediary between reactionary Western circles and Sakharov. For a number of years, Bonner has made a business of delivering to Western anti-Soviet centers shameless slanders and malicious libels, which blacken our country, our political system, and our people.

For this purpose, as has been irrefutably established, she used the services of the staff of the American Embassy in Moscow, who, through diplomatic channels, sent abroad materials obtained from Bonner. Lately such assistance was rendered to her by, among others, First Secretary E. MacWilliams and Second Secretaries G. Glass and J. Purnell.[68]

As has recently become known to the appropriate Soviet organs, in accordance with a thoroughly worked-out scenario and with the participation of American diplomats, an operation with far-reaching goals was devised: Sakharov was supposed to declare his next "hunger strike," while Bonner was to receive "asylum" in the U.S. embassy in Moscow. According to this plan, it was assumed that Bonner's stay in the embassy would be used by her to meet with foreign correspondents and pass libelous falsehoods abroad about the Soviet Union as well as all kinds of fabrications about the situation of her husband, Sakharov.

These coordinated actions were to serve as a signal for the beginning of an anti-Soviet campaign in the West, primarily in the USA.

Simultaneously, on a false pretext—the state of her health—an attempt was to be made to arrange Bonner's travel abroad, where she was to become one of the leaders of the anti-Soviet scum, supported by Western intelligence services.

As a result of measures implemented in good time by Soviet law enforcement organs, this operation was thwarted. The American side was presented with a note of protest, which contained facts testifying to the direct involvement of employees of the U.S. embassy in Moscow in this provocation, and which demanded the termination of such impermissible actions. The organizers of this provocation appeared to be caught unawares. Nevertheless, they are attempting to dodge responsibility. They proclaim hypocritically that they are motivated solely by humanitarian considerations.

Nothing can be further from the truth. They count on naive people who are able to believe in the humanitarian motives of a malefactor caught red-handed.

Those who shed crocodile tears over Sakharov's "difficult fate" fail to mention that they are trying to put on a pedestal a man who besmirches his own people, who openly calls for war, for the use of nuclear weapons against his own country, and who preaches hate-mongering ideas. They also fail to mention that the Soviet state has demonstrated generosity

---

68. George Glass and Jon Purnell , second secretaries at the U.S. embassy in Moscow, were detained for two hours; see *New York Times*, July 5, 1984, 6.

and patience toward this man, that it has given him a chance to leave his dangerous road and to restore his good name in the eyes of his countrymen.

Oh no, those who want to start a new propaganda commotion about Sakharov and Bonner are not motivated by humanitarian considerations: they are blinded by vicious anti-Sovietism, they would like to poison the international atmosphere even further, to sow venomous seeds of distrust among nations.

It is time, however, for each and every organizer of such "crusades," of ideological and other subversions against the Soviet land to understand that this will not bring them glory. It never did so in the past; it never will in the future. (TASS)

## · DOCUMENT 172 ·

Chebrikov and Rekunkov to Central Committee, May 12, 1984
The hunger strike continues

The measures implemented by the Committee for State Security and the Office of the Chief Procurator of the USSR to thwart a provocation planned by Sakharov and Bonner, together with employees from the American embassy in Moscow, have left Sakharov and Bonner confused and perplexed.

On May 3, Bonner was summoned to the Office of the Procurator of Gorky Oblast, where she was informed of the resolution to institute criminal proceedings against her. She signed the resolution, but she declared that she does not admit to being guilty and she refused to participate further in the investigation, citing her poor state of health. Under these circumstances and at the investigator's request, she was examined by two cardiologists, who confirmed that Bonner's state of health does permit her to participate in the investigation.[69]

On May 7, accompanied by Sakharov, Bonner appeared for her next interrogation. Sakharov then informed the investigator about his hunger strike. As a result, the investigator from the Procurator's office invited doctors to examine Sakharov; on their recommendation, he was put into the Semashko Hospital for Gorky Oblast. Bonner was also offered med-

---

69. No cardiologists examined Bonner (Elena Bonner, interview with author, Brookline, MA, 2003). To cover themselves, KGB officials may have obtained a letter from the Academy of Sciences hospital.

ical treatment in the hospital; however, she categorically rejected this offer, declaring that she would be treated only abroad.

On May 8, a search was conducted in Sakharov and Bonner's apartment in Gorky. During this search, the following were confiscated: a portable radio of foreign manufacture, which they used every day to listen to foreign broadcasts, and copies of the anti-Soviet publications *Kontinent, Russkaya Mysl, Posev,* and *Grani.* Altogether 318 items were confiscated, including printed matter and other objects. During the search, Bonner declared demagogically that she used only two rooms in the apartment and that Sakharov occupies the places where anti-Soviet and libelous materials were found, and that the confiscated items were his property.

The mass media in the capitalist countries, in the USA in particular, are paying a good deal of attention to the TASS report exposing the actions of American intelligence services involved in the organization of a new anti-Soviet campaign focused on Sakharov and Bonner. In particular, the newspapers *Washington Post, New York Times,* and *Sun* mentioned in their articles Bonner's ties with the American embassy in Moscow and published the names of the American diplomats with whom she had maintained contacts.

Simultaneously, in replies to the correspondents of foreign news agencies, senior officials at the American embassy in Moscow decline to provide any explanation with respect to the TASS release. Without denying that meetings took place between diplomats and Bonner, they try to justify them by the need to obtain information about the health of Sakharov and his wife.

Official representatives of the U.S. State Department, several embassy staff members, and correspondents from the capitalist countries have expressed serious concern that if Bonner is barred from coming to Moscow, the West will lose its main channel for obtaining libelous anti-Soviet materials from Sakharov.

Sakharov remains in the hospital and refuses to eat. Medical agencies are preparing measures to force-feed Sakharov. For this purpose, the USSR Ministry of Health has dispatched A. P. Golikov and M. A. Samsonov (corresponding members of the Academy of Medical Sciences of the USSR) to Gorky.

The investigation of Bonner is continuing.

According to our information, the unmasking of the provocative action by Sakharov and Bonner and their American benefactors was welcomed by wide circles of Soviet public opinion. Reported for purposes of information.

Three weeks into the episode, the KGB chief felt the need to rebuff international concerns about Sakharov and Bonner and to reaffirm his claims about Bonner's collusion with the U.S. embassy. As Western newspapers gave prominence to the Sakharov story,[70] Chebrikov made clear that Soviet agencies had not been idle, arranging for appropriate materials in the press and mobilizing a letter-writing campaign that even included Sakharov's children by his first marriage.

· DOCUMENT 173 ·

Chebrikov to Central Committee, May 20, 1984
How the KGB is handling the hunger strike

According to information received by the KGB of the USSR, reactionary circles in the USA and several other capitalist states are seeking to organize an anti-Soviet campaign in the West based on the provocations of Sakharov and Bonner. To do this, they are using deliberately falsified, slanderous assertions about their health; it has even been alleged that the two are in critical condition because of the hunger strike.[71] Our enemies need all this in order to gloss over, at least in part, the negative impression that ensued when the provocation prepared by the Americans (with the collusion of Sakharov and Bonner) was foiled and exposed to world opinion.

---

70. Ironically, much of the story revolved around the very inaccessibility of Sakharov and Bonner; even while the KGB continued to boast of its success in isolating the couple, this very fact made it impossible to verify their physical condition and inspired the most lurid suspicions. See, for example, an article about the "mysterious" condition of Sakharov's health in *Washington Post*, May 17, 1984, 33. Such fears inspired widespread concern; see, for example, an appeal on Sakharov's behalf by the presidents of six leading American universities, ibid., 15. Soviet authorities successfully kept Sakharov and Bonner incommunicado until August, a policy that provoked continued criticism in the West. See, for example, the Senate resolution demanding that the Soviet Union provide "specific information" on the health and legal status of Sakharov and Bonner (*New York Times*, July 25, 1984, 8). Nonetheless, some people in the West blamed Elena Bonner for Sakharov's decision to undertake another hunger strike. Jeremy Stone, director of the Federation of American Scientists and a long-time supporter of independent-minded Soviet scientists, wrote that "when KGB-inspired articles attack Mr. Sakharov as having been 'captured' by a Zionist agent, Yelena Bonner, there is, amidst the anti-Semitic smear, a grain of truth. . . . It is no accident that two of the three Sakharov hunger strikes have been in defense of her interests" (*Los Angeles Times*, May 27, 1984, IV, 5).
71. See *New York Times*, May 16, 1984, 9.

In reality, according to the conclusion of medical experts, at the present time Sakharov's and Bonner's health status does not constitute a cause for any concern.[72] Sakharov is still in Semashko Hospital for Gorky Oblast, where he is force-fed with the help of a tube but without the use of narcotics or sedatives. This method of feeding is harmless and does not produce any medical consequences or complications. Moreover, although Sakharov insists that he has not abandoned his hunger strike, in fact he is eating voluntarily. The attending doctors, including experts from the USSR Ministry of Health, have noted a general improvement in the functioning of Sakharov's heart, liver, and other vital organs. He enjoys his daily massage, has begun asking for consultations with specialists, and is more sociable with the medical staff.

Bonner's health, according to the doctors' findings, likewise shows no cause for concern and does not prevent her from participating in the investigation of the criminal case initiated against her. She takes food regularly, is quite mobile, actively performs household chores, in Sakharov's absence has repaired her own car, and drives it around the city.

Since Sakharov's hospitalization, Bonner regularly comes to the investigator's office for interrogations. She still refuses to give formal depositions, but during conversations with the investigator insists that she acted only as a courier in passing her husband's materials to the West. She does not deny having contacts with employees of the American embassy. She pushed Sakharov to initiate this hunger strike, but constantly repeats that he made this decision on his own.

An analysis of the materials obtained and Sakharov's and Bonner's behavior demonstrates that they had a carefully prepared plan for Bonner's trip abroad. They set the time and regimen of the hunger strike; they also prepared and passed the appropriate statements to the American embassy in Moscow in advance. Sakharov and Bonner are still hoping that they will be able to obtain permission for Bonner to go to the West.

The materials confiscated during the search of Sakharov and Bonner's apartment in Gorky clearly indicate their direct contact with intelligence agencies and anti-Soviet organizations in the West (through Bonner's children and other close relatives residing in the USA). The following confiscated items are particularly noteworthy:

- A "voice mail" sent from abroad by Bonner's daughter and son-in-law through illegal channels in which they talk about their meeting

72. The same day Sakharov suffered a slight stroke, almost certainly brought on by the force-feeding.

with Reagan, the anti-Soviet campaigns they plan to organize, and their editing (jointly with American "experts in Russian language and disarmament") of Sakharov's provocative letter to Drell.

• Suggestions by Yankelevich, Bonner's son-in-law, "on the principles and practice of broadcasts by 'Radio Liberty' and 'the Voice of America' to the Soviet Union."

It is our intention to use these materials to expose the U.S. administration and intelligence services.

The measures taken by the KGB to isolate Sakharov and Bonner from foreigners, from their allies, and from each other, and to put an end to their ability to listen to foreign broadcasts, have been fully justified.

Appropriate information is delivered to Sakharov and Bonner through KGB channels. Simultaneously, TASS and the State Radio and Television of the USSR have distributed abroad information refuting the insinuations of subversive centers of the West about the state of Sakharov's and Bonner's health; they also report the reluctant admission by the American ambassador in Moscow, [Arthur A.] Hartman, that employees of the embassy illegally[73] received Sakharov's letters from Bonner, which raise the question of giving Bonner asylum in the U.S. embassy.

In compliance with the Central Committee decision of May 3, 1984 (P[rotocol no.] 156, [pt.] 77), the Committee for State Security—together with the Departments of Propaganda and International Information of the Central Committee and the Ministry of Foreign Affairs—has prepared and published an article exposing Bonner's criminal activity in *Izvestia* on May 20.

Law enforcement agencies, as well as Bonner, continue to receive letters from representatives of various strata of Soviet society and from Sakharov's children condemning Bonner's criminal activity.

Reported for purposes of information.

[attachment]

Meeting of the Politburo
May 31, 1984
Chairman: Comrade K. U. Chernenko
Present: Comrades G. A. Aliyev, V. I. Vorotnikov, M. S. Gorbachev,
V. V. Grishin, A. A. Gromyko, G. V. Romanov, M. S. Solomentsev,
N. A. Tikhonov, D. F. Ustinov, P. N. Demichev, V. N. Dolgikh,

---

73. I.e., despite the KGB blockade around Sakharov and Bonner.

V. V. Kuznetsov, B. N. Ponomarev, V. M. Chebrikov, M. V. Zimyanin,
I. V. Kapitonov, K. V. Rusakov, N. I. Ryzhkov

*Gromyko:* In addition to the agenda, I want to report that a telegram has been received from Paris. Our ambassador reports that he was invited to lunch with Mitterrand. Apparently, it will concern the impending visit of the president of France to the Soviet Union and possibly about a delay in this trip. It is not excluded that Mitterrand will again start a conversation about Sakharov and Bonner. Here our ambassador has to give him a calm response.

*Ustinov:* Calm, but firm.

*Gromyko:* Yes, calm but firm. Apparently, Mitterrand nevertheless senses that, in the course of his visit to the USSR, we do not intend to bestow on him any gifts. After all, in terms of proposals, all he has is absolutely nothing. I do not think this visit will give us anything worthwhile.

*Ponomarev:* Absolutely nothing.

*Gromyko:* As far as I know, the French Communists share that view.

*Chebrikov:* As for the so-called "case" of Sakharov and Bonner, the Western press is now raising a great hue and cry about this. In general, bourgeois propaganda asserts that both of these people are practically on their deathbed. In fact, Sakharov, after fasting for three to four days, has actively been eating for almost two weeks now, to be sure, while declaring that he "continues his hunger strike." His pressure is 120 over 80, and his pulse is 64.

*Gromyko:* A Napoleonic pulse.

*Chebrikov:* Sakharov is in the care of the best doctors in Gorky.[74] He goes on strolls and generally feels entirely normal. As for Bonner, who allegedly suffers from eye disease, she drives her automobile, goes to the market, walks around, and at the same time visits the investigator in charge of her case.

*Ponomarev:* Georges Marchais asked us to inform him about the status of Sakharov's and Bonner's health. We gave him this information. It satisfied him completely and this has been published in France.[75]

*Ustinov:* Thus we have every basis for making a calm and firm reply.

The members of the Politburo support this opinion.

---

74. Despite attempts to find Sakharov's medical records in Gorky, no documentation of his treatment by "the best doctors" could be located.

75. Such optimism about the French Communist Party chief was somewhat premature; the *New York Times* reported on June 4, 1984, 7, that Marchais warned that his party might break with the CPSU over the Sakharov case.

## · DOCUMENT 174 ·

Leonid Zamyatin to Central Committee, June 5, 1984
A rumor that Sakharov has died

In connection with the telegram from the Soviet ambassador in France (sh/t special no. 1611, from Paris on June 4, 1984), which reports rumors about the "death of Sakharov," the KGB of the USSR and the Department of Foreign Political Propaganda of the Central Committee prepared an operational commentary. On June 5, 1984, the commentary was disseminated through TASS channels to all countries of the world. The operational dissemination of the commentary evoked a positive response.

The text of the commentary is attached.

### "Once More on the Health of Sakharov and Bonner"

The special services of the USA and their patrons absolutely refuse to accept the fact that their provocation with Sakharov and Bonner has failed. They continue to disseminate new false reports based on conjecture and nothing else. Whoever whips up rumors about "Sakharov's death," as a certain Italian "journalist" is doing, is simply burying him alive.

We do not intend to defend Sakharov and Bonner, but we cannot allow all this to be exploited for false anti-Soviet propaganda. Provocateurs are thirsting after sensations. The true sensation is that the filthy role of the intelligence services of the USA (and the official American circles that stand behind them) has been on full public view. They, and no one else, prepared plans for Sakharov's "hunger strike," Bonner's attempts to seek "political asylum" in the American embassy in Moscow, and her provocative ties with Western correspondents.

All these plans have crashed. And here the quite unseemly role of certain employees of the American embassy in Moscow has been exposed. After all, it was not from the kindness of their hearts that they were forced to admit that they had orchestrated this anti-Soviet campaign. A number of organs of the Western press nevertheless continue to shout about the health of Sakharov and Bonner. They are healthy and are not starving! The "concern" of American intelligence services about their health is perfectly clear: they are needed only for the purpose of defaming the Soviet Union. And indeed the American administration spares nothing to achieve this. Washington has long since based its policy on the premise that the worse relations are with the Soviet Union, the better they are for the American administration: international tensions are a major boon to the arms race. So they stir up tensions, sparing nothing in the process.

We note, incidentally, that certain gullible people have joined this anti-Soviet campaign in the West that the White House has stirred up. Unfortunately, they believe lies, not facts. The facts, we repeat, are as follows: Sakharov and Bonner are healthy. Perhaps, in the centers of Western psychological warfare, they would like to hear different news, but we cannot report anything else.

· DOCUMENT 175 ·

Chebrikov to Central Committee, July 6, 1984
The manipulation of international concern over Sakharov

The Committee for State Security is taking measures to thwart the hostile actions of American intelligence services, which attempted to organize a major provocation with the participation of Sakharov and Bonner.

In order to expose the unseemly actions of the U.S. administration and reactionary circles in other NATO countries, TASS and the State Television and Radio of the USSR have distributed documented reports abroad. These reports, which are based on materials supplied by the Committee for State Security, refute the insinuations of foreign propaganda about Sakharov's and Bonner's health.[76]

The Committee has brought to the attention of world public opinion the fact that the West prepared obituaries for Sakharov for purposes of provocation. Simultaneously, on the eve of Mitterrand's arrival in the USSR, photographs of Sakharov and Bonner (taken during their walks on June 12 and 15 of this year) were released abroad and appeared in the newspaper *Bild Zeitung* (Federal Republic of Germany).[77] These materials attracted widespread attention from foreign mass media and came as a surprise to the organizers of the anti-Soviet campaign.

The Committee has also forestalled persistent attempts by intelligence services, other subversive centers in capitalist countries, and individual antisocial elements to contact Sakharov and Bonner and to obtain libelous information.

76. See, for example, the TASS declaration in *New York Times*, June 5, 1984, 11, and assurance from the Soviet biochemist Academician Yuri Ovchinnikov in *New York Times*, June 7, 1984, 8. For Bonner's account, see *Alone Together*, 206–15.
77. See *New York Times*, August 23, 1984, 4.

Sakharov and Bonner continue to receive letters and telegrams from So-viet citizens denouncing them for their anti-Soviet activity. Even some American correspondents—Schmemann, Kimmelman, Dusko[78]—sta-tioned in Moscow, as well as some Soviet citizens with hostile attitudes, have expressed sharply negative views of Bonner. For example, Schme-mann said in a private conversation: "I don't think anyone has a high opinion of her. . . . This story with the hunger strike antagonized many people. Now, no one believes her stories of the difficult living conditions that she talks about. . . . She behaves provocatively. . . . People are begin-ning to detest her."

As for Sakharov's behavior at present, he is eating normally, and the state of his health, according to attending physicians, is entirely satisfac-tory. He takes strolls in the hospital garden, is active, follows the press, watches television broadcasts, and takes an interest in international events. He had high hopes that Mitterrand would help resolve the ques-tion of Bonner's trip abroad. On June 26 he declared to his attending physician: "I thought my French friends would assist me through Mitter-rand. I see now that this did not work, or else Mitterrand's intercession was ignored."[79]

In response to Sakharov's threat to start a new hunger strike, the hospi-tal administrators warned him that "the doctors will not permit a hunger strike."

After the investigation of Bonner and her trial have been completed, the plan is to discharge Sakharov from the hospital. . . .[80]

---

This report summarizes the trial, conviction, and sentence of Elena Bonner. News of the trial did not become known until two weeks later.[81]

78. The KGB mistakenly used the given name of Dusko Doder, a Moscow corre-spondent for the *Washington Post*. Serge Schmemann was a correspondent for the *New York Times*.

79. In fact, at a summit in Moscow in June, President Mitterrand abandoned diplo-matic conventions to raise the issue of Sakharov, though the Soviet side had warned him not to do so; see *New York Times,* June 22, 1984, 1.

80. Several words in this line were obviously deleted from the declassified copy. The report, however, makes it clear that the KGB planned to keep Sakharov in the hospital until after his wife's trial.

81. See *New York Times,* August 24, 1984, 4.

## · DOCUMENT 176 ·

Chebrikov, Terebilov, and Bazhenov to Central Committee, August 13, 1984
The trial of Elena Bonner

On August 9–10, 1984, the Criminal Court of Gorky Oblast, after hearing in open court sessions the criminal case against E. G. Bonner, found her guilty of committing a crime under Article 190-1 of the Criminal Code of the RSFSR. . . .

Bonner is found guilty of systematically disseminating libelous materials, including sound recordings and videotapes, throughout the years 1975–84 on the territory of the USSR and during her trips abroad.

In particular, during her trips abroad, she spoke at press conferences attended by West European journalists and media representatives, and knowingly made libelous statements to the effect that the Soviet people allegedly live in fear, are deprived of protection by the courts and trade unions, and are subjected to repression for their convictions.

In both oral and written form, Bonner systematically transmitted to diplomats and correspondents of capitalist states slanderous information about the rights and freedoms of Soviet citizens and other questions. Among close associates and in conversations with foreigners, she has demagogically asserted that "the violation of the rights of Soviet citizens and baseless repression constitutes governmental policy."

These and other slanderous fabrications by Bonner have been used by the intelligence services and propaganda organs of the USA and other NATO countries to stir up anti-Soviet campaigns.

Bonner committed the above acts despite repeated warnings by law enforcement organs that this type of behavior is intolerable. Bonner's guilt was irrefutably confirmed by the testimony of witnesses and by a large body of material evidence. However, although Bonner confirmed the factual side of the charge, she did not admit to being guilty. The court collegium, considering the crimes but also taking into account the age of the defendant (62), sentenced Bonner to five years' exile. . . .

· DOCUMENT 177 ·

Tsinev to Central Committee, September 12, 1984
More effective isolation of Elena Bonner

In the city of Gorky on September 7, 1984, an assize session of the Supreme Court of the RSFSR heard the appeal in the criminal case of E. G. Bonner, who was charged with violating Article 190-1 of the Criminal Code of the RSFSR (dissemination of knowingly false fabrications that defame the Soviet state and social system). The appeals court found that Bonner's guilt had been proved and on this basis upheld the sentence of the Gorky Oblast Court (five years' exile). As an exception to ordinary practice, Gorky was designated as her place of exile.

On September 8, after the completion of a full course of treatment, Sakharov was discharged from the Semashko Hospital of Gorky Oblast. In the doctors' opinion, his health is now satisfactory, and in the future it will depend on his following their recommendations concerning his regimen and medication, but mainly on the behavior of Bonner, who constantly drives her husband to commit actions that have a deleterious effect on his health. . . .

· DOCUMENT 178 ·

Chebrikov to Central Committee, February 14, 1985
Sakharov's letter to the president of the Academy of Sciences

According to information received by the Committee for State Security, Bonner (who is serving her sentence of exile in Gorky) persists in her overtly hostile attitude and tries to involve A. D. Sakharov in new schemes to obtain permission, by whatever means possible, to go abroad. In December 1984 she forced Sakharov to address a provocative and libelous appeal to the Presidium of the USSR Academy of Sciences, insisting that his wife should be given permission to travel abroad "for medical treatment and for a family visit."

In this letter Sakharov issues a kind of ultimatum:

If you and the Presidium of the Academy of Sciences do not find it possible to support my request in this tragic matter (which is most important for me) of my wife's trip abroad, or, in case your intervention and other efforts do not lead to the resolution of this problem before

March 1, 1985, I ask that you regard this letter as a resignation from the USSR Academy of Sciences. I renounce the title of full member of the USSR Academy of Sciences, in which, under different circumstances, I could take great pride. I renounce all rights and privileges associated with that title, including my salary as an Academician. . . . If my wife is not given permission to travel abroad, I cannot remain a member of the USSR Academy of Sciences. I cannot and should not participate in a colossal lie, which in part includes my membership in the Academy.[82]

. . . At the present time we plan to limit our actions to informing members of the USSR Academy of Sciences about Sakharov's statement. The matter has been coordinated with Comrade A. P. Alexandrov. . . .

---

The old and ailing Konstantin Chernenko died on March 10, 1985. Mikhail Gorbachev, his successor as general secretary, would soon have to deal with the Sakharov problem. A month after Chernenko's death, Chebrikov sent Gorbachev a comprehensive briefing about Sakharov and Bonner. The KGB understood that Sakharov was considering another hunger strike, which was set to begin April 16. But now the ultimate responsibility for Sakharov's fate would be in the hands of Mikhail Gorbachev.

## · DOCUMENT 179 ·

Chebrikov to Central Committee, April 13, 1985
A report for Gorbachev on the possibility of another hunger strike

---

For many years the Committee for State Security has been working to contain and eliminate the antisocial activity of Academician A. D. Sakharov and his wife, E. G. Bonner. [Chebrikov then summarizes Sakharov's statements on disarmament and describes his removal to Gorky and the behavior of Elena Bonner in the same tendentious manner seen in the KGB's earlier reports.]

. . . At present, Sakharov, at his wife's instigation, is again preparing another hunger strike, which he intends to announce on April 16. The couple wants to avoid making the same "errors" that they made during their

82. Sakharov, "Letter to Anatoly Alexandrov," in his *Memoirs,* 698–706. Despite his isolation in Gorky, news of the letter was reported in the West a few months later; see *New York Times,* March 27, 1985, 12.

past hunger strikes. Sakharov is trying to prepare himself to endure artificial feeding with less difficulty. To make it impossible for Sakharov to take solid food, Bonner has secretly hidden his dentures.

In the event that Sakharov declares another hunger strike, he will be hospitalized, isolated from Bonner, and supervised by experienced doctors familiar with his medical history and constitution. One must take into account the fact that, given his age and the general condition of his health, it will be more difficult for Sakharov to survive his third lengthy hunger strike in the last few years. Reported for purposes of information.

---

Five days after beginning his hunger strike, Sakharov was forcibly taken to a hospital by a team of seven men and two women. After entering the apartment, they isolated Elena Bonner in a separate room while doctors (or were they security personnel, or both?) pinned Sakharov onto a couch and administered an injection. An elderly neighbor later told Bonner that she had seen Sakharov removed on a stretcher.

Chebrikov claims in this report that Sakharov "broke off his hunger strike" on April 24. The doctors, in fact, force-fed him in the same painful, degrading way he had experienced in 1984. At the same time, the KGB employed its tried and true methods of disinformation. Bonner had no contact with Sakharov, in spite of repeated attempts to see him in the hospital. His postcards to the children in America were doctored to confuse the dates and seasons of the year. But even in the hospital, Sakharov could sense a change in the Kremlin. He caught Gorbachev speaking on television and was impressed by his obvious intelligence. On June 20 he decided to offer a compromise, to make a gesture of good faith toward the regime after a visit by his KGB case officer, Sergei Sokolov. Sakharov wrote to Gorbachev with an offer to end the hunger strike if Bonner were permitted to travel. If he did not receive an answer within two weeks, he would resume his protest. There was no word from Gorbachev. Nonetheless, on July 11, "no longer able to bear the torture of my isolation from Lusia and the thought that she was ill and alone," Sakharov declared an end to the hunger strike.[83] They brought him home that same day, but not without a final sleight of hand. Bonner was persuaded to wait for him on the sidewalk, so that when Sakharov arrived and they embraced, a clandestine camera could film their reunion. These scenes, along with unremarkable images from

---

83. Sakharov, *Memoirs,* 599.

the hospital, were also recorded and sold to the West, all part of the KGB's efforts to camouflage the true state of affairs.

## · DOCUMENT 180 ·

Chebrikov to Central Committee, July 20, 1985
Sakharov leaves the hospital

---

The Committee for State Security earlier reported (no. 6341-Ch., dated April 13, 1985) on yet another provocation—Sakharov's intention to begin a hunger strike. According to Sakharov and Bonner, this action should put pressure on the Soviet authorities to grant permission for Bonner to travel abroad.

In accordance with the scenario designed by Sakharov and his wife, on April 16 he stopped taking food, and as a result was hospitalized on April 21. Three days after he was placed in the Gorky Oblast hospital, Sakharov broke off his hunger strike. He began eating three times a day according to a diet that was specially devised for him by medically trained dieticians and that took into consideration his age and his constitution. Sakharov's state of health has been constantly monitored by attending doctors; he has willingly undergone a daily medical examination and followed all the prescribed procedures, including those aimed at restoring his strength. During his stay in the hospital, no deviations from the norm in Sakharov's state of health were observed. At the same time, Sakharov insisted that he should be viewed as being on a hunger strike since, he says, he is accepting food in the hospital under medical supervision, which he regards as coercion.

Bonner has followed her daily routine during this period. She drives around the city in her car, puts her apartment in order (purchasing a bookcase and wall shelves in a furniture store), reads a lot, and goes to the movies. It is worth noting that she did visit her husband once.

On July 11, Sakharov, seeing the futility of his provocative maneuver and after a conversation with a high-ranking official from the KGB, asked the chief physician to discharge him without delay. In particular, in his declaration he pointed out: "I have made a difficult decision—I am leaving the hospital without achieving my goal. . . . Let me go home immediately. . . . I assume full responsibility." In addition, he emphasized demagogically that he "retains the right to resume his hunger strike if it is needed to achieve his objective."

That same day, Sakharov's request was granted. While being discharged, he listened attentively to his doctors' recommendations concerning medications, agreed to appear regularly for routine physical checkups, and thanked the attending doctors for their attention and care.

Immediately after her husband returned home, Bonner subjected him to an intense psychological barrage and, in harsh terms, accused him of checking out of the hospital prematurely, saying that she had expected him to stay in the hospital for "half a year or even a year."

In order to unmask insinuations about Sakharov circulating in the West, the Committee for State Security, through operational methods, has made a documentary video film that objectively records Sakharov's stay in the hospital; it shows Sakharov eating food on his own, working with scientific literature, undergoing regular medical tests, watching television broadcasts, reading the Soviet and foreign press, and conducting lively discussions with his roommate in his semiprivate hospital ward.[84] The film also contains objective information about Sakharov's health (cerebral arteriosclerosis with damage to the vessels of the brain; Parkinson's syndrome; arteriosclerosis of the aorta and the coronary vessels; chronic ischemic disease of the heart). . . .

---

That July, Sakharov and Bonner enjoyed a relaxed, leisurely two weeks together, "hunting for mushrooms, going to the movies and the market, watching TV at night." But without word from the regime, Sakharov was determined to resume his protest. On July 25 he declared an indefinite hunger strike; two days later, he was again taken by force to the hospital. Sakharov wrote to both Gorbachev and Gromyko soon after, reiterating his demand that Elena Bonner be allowed to travel. But he also offered to limit his public activities and acknowledged the Kremlin's right to "regulate" his travel abroad.[85] The force-feeding continued. By August, his weight had dropped to 138 pounds, almost 40 pounds below his normal weight of 175. To supplement the force-feedings, the doctors administered painful subcutaneous feedings in both thighs, as well as intravenous infusions.

In spite of the Soviet disinformation effort, the West was aware that Sakharov was in trouble. Bonner's son declared a hunger strike of his own on August 30, sitting near the Soviet embassy in Washington during the day and holding to it for two weeks until both Congress and the State Department pledged to renew their efforts on behalf of Sakharov and Bonner.

Unbeknownst to the West, Gorbachev was now eager to resolve the

---

84. Elena Bonner discusses the clandestine film in *Alone Together,* 204–15.
85. Sakharov, *Memoirs,* 599–600.

entire affair. On August 10 he sent a brief note to the heads of the Foreign Ministry (Eduard Shevardnadze) and the KGB (Viktor Chebrikov) asking for a review of the matter. Their response on August 28 expressed their readiness to permit Bonner to travel to America, as long as it remained clear that Sakharov could not be permitted out of the country.

According to Anatoly Dobrynin, on the very next day, August 29, the Politburo faced the question of her travel abroad. At times the discussion assumed a crude tone. Chebrikov invoked the standard line that "Sakharov's behavior is shaped by his wife's influence." Gorbachev then responded, "There, that's what Zionism is like!" In his memoirs, Dobrynin explained that "Bonner was only half-Jewish. But because most of the dissidents were Jewish—Sakharov was not— . . . Bonner's case seemed an extension of Zionist influence in the mind of Gorbachev and much of the Politburo."[86] They did agree to let her go.

Nonetheless, the KGB prolonged the process. On September 5, Sergei Sokolov again visited Sakharov in the hospital to discuss the terms he had offered in his letter to Gorbachev. That same afternoon, Sakharov was taken to the apartment for a three-hour meeting with his wife; she was able to type their statements for the KGB (and for Gorbachev). Sakharov returned to the hospital and it was not until October 18 that, upon receiving a postcard with the agreed-upon signal from his wife, he ended the hunger strike. Bonner was permitted to leave Gorky on November 25 and soon after flew to Italy on her way to the United States. On January 13, 1986, doctors at Massachusetts General Hospital performed open-heart surgery, including six bypass procedures, to repair the damage to her heart. Before returning to Moscow on June 2, she wrote her memoir, *Alone Together.*

· DOCUMENT 181 ·

Chebrikov to Central Committee, August 3, 1985
Sakharov resumes his hunger strike

───────────────

As the Committee for State Security has earlier reported (no. 1291-Ch., dated July 20, 1985), on July 11 A. D. Sakharov was discharged, at his own request, from Semashko Hospital of Gorky Oblast.

Sakharov's discharge from the hospital was totally unexpected for Bon-

───────────────

86. Dobrynin, *In Confidence,* 553. Dobrynin was wrong to claim that most human rights activists were Jewish.

ner and evoked an extremely negative reaction on her part. With her characteristic aggressiveness and stubbornness, in a crude and derisive manner she criticized her husband, saying that his decision to return home was ruining her plans to obtain permission to travel abroad—at any price. She also tried to convince him that his decision was hasty and premature, that the campaign in their defense was supposedly still being waged abroad. Insisting that the so-called "hunger strike" be continued, Bonner emphasized that it was especially necessary because of the forthcoming meeting of foreign ministers in Helsinki (to mark the tenth anniversary of the signing of the Final Act of the Conference on Security and Cooperation in Europe). She sought to convince Sakharov that, again in Helsinki, delegations from capitalist countries would supposedly raise questions about Sakharov and Bonner's fate, and that they had to bolster the démarche of the West.[87]

Bonner's psychological harassment caused Sakharov to experience cardiac pain, and he was repeatedly forced to take nitroglycerin. Knowing her husband's condition, Bonner nevertheless forbade him to take the medication prescribed by the doctors and once again drove him into resuming his "hunger strike."

On July 27, Sakharov was again admitted to the Semashko Hospital of Gorky Oblast, where he told the chief physician that, in order to obtain permission for Bonner to travel to the USA, he was declaring "an unrestricted hunger strike and will take food only when forced to do so." In fact, just as before, it was not necessary to force-feed Sakharov. A member of the hospital staff has to give him the first two or three spoonfuls, but he eats the rest of the food quite voluntarily and with the appetite that he usually has in the hospital. . . .

· DOCUMENT 182 ·

Chebrikov and Shevardnadze to Gorbachev, August 28, 1985
The KGB and Foreign Ministry recommend that Bonner be allowed to travel

[Marginal note:] I ask that, with the present situation in mind, you give careful thought to everything once again and present your own thoughts on the matter.

M. Gorbachev (August 10, 1985)[88]

87. Sakharov described the end of his last hunger strike in the book *Gorky, Moskva, dalee vezde* (New York, 1990), 5–11. This is the original version of *Moscow and Beyond,* which differs in some respects.
88. Shortly after Gorbachev came to power, Ronald Reagan personally appealed to

In accordance with instructions, we report on A. D. Sakharov:

The use of Sakharov's name for anti-Soviet purposes by our adversaries has been going on for almost twenty years. They play on him both as an author of anti-Soviet publications and as "a human rights activist in the USSR" and have portrayed him as the most prominent representative of an opposition that purportedly exists in the USSR. A great deal of effort was put into making him not only the "banner" but also the organizer and leader of antisocial elements.

Systematic work directed at foiling the enemy's machinations produced results. The chief of these was Sakharov's refusal to engage in organizational activities (he had earlier headed a group "for the defense of human rights"). Sakharov's authority and influence have dropped significantly among negatively oriented people; many antisocial elements distanced themselves from him.

Aware of this, the enemy is constantly seeking ways to renew Sakharov's activity—that is, exploit his name to influence Western public opinion in a manner politically unfavorable to us. Sakharov is important for the enemy for another reason: at present, there is no one like him in our society. His wife, E. G. Bonner, who closely cooperates with official representatives of the USA, plays an active role in inspiring Sakharov's antisocial activities. It is through her that Sakharov has been drawn into antisocial actions that galvanize interest in his person. . . .

In recent months, seeing the futility of his efforts as well as an abatement of Western interest in him, Sakharov has timidly begun to declare his readiness to renounce antisocial activities. At the same time, however, he categorically demands that his wife be allowed to travel abroad, and not just for medical treatment, but for a reunion with her relatives as well. In response to one appeal that had been addressed to the chairman of the KGB, in May 1985 a high-ranking officer of the KGB had a talk with Sakharov and Bonner in order, once again, to make Sakharov understand that we will not accept his ultimatums and that his actions did not accord with his statements about abandoning antisocial activities. This conversation neutralized Sakharov during the period when the meeting in Helsinki was being actively prepared and conducted, and it also yielded additional impressions about both Bonner and Sakharov.

---

him to release Sakharov and permit Bonner to leave the country for medical treatment; see *New York Times*, May 16, 1985, 14. Gorbachev was writing in response to Sakharov's letter to him. The note is now in the Archive of the President of the Russian Federation (APRF), no. 140, f. 3, op. 108, d. B.6.9.4.1/2, l. 40; a copy is in the Sakharov Archive (Harvard), folder S.II.2.4.164.

One gains the impression that Sakharov himself is tired of his situation and would apparently be ready to renounce his antisocial activities if it were not for the pressure of his spouse. The conversation did not produce a negative effect on him, but the same cannot be said of Bonner. She behaved in a provocative manner and was two-faced even with respect to Sakharov. Later, when Bonner came to understand that, to some extent, this conversation had induced Sakharov to end his "hunger strike," Bonner tried to do everything in her power to make Sakharov resume the "hunger strike." Not without relief, he signed into the hospital and made no attempt to go on a "hunger strike" again.

It was from the hospital that he sent a letter on July 29 to the general secretary of the Central Committee of the CPSU, again requesting permission for Bonner to go abroad.

Considering all the circumstances and taking into account Sakharov's age and the state of his health (although normal right now, it will definitely deteriorate) as well as his statement that he is abandoning antisocial activities, the KGB and the Ministry of Foreign Affairs consider it possible to allow Bonner to travel to Italy for a period of three months. As an exception, it is possible to permit Bonner to leave her place of exile (per Article 82 of the Corrective Labor Code of the RSFSR) during this period.

If such a decision is made, Sakharov could then be informed that, in making this decision, the relevant competent organs were guided exclusively by humanitarian considerations and that his former services to the state were taken into account.

In making this decision about Bonner's travel to Italy, one must be prepared for the fact that, once she is abroad, she will intensify her hostile activities, that she may make anti-Soviet statements, spread slander about the situation in our country and about Sakharov, and meet with state officials and political figures of bourgeois countries and parties. It is possible that she will be awarded all kinds of prizes, diplomas, and other awards and decorations.

Finally, since all of Bonner's close relatives live in the USA, she may refuse to return to the USSR. This circumstance is fraught with the danger that, at some point, she may demand family reunification—i.e., that Sakharov join her. In that event, one must expect the onset of another campaign, which will inevitably be joined by the leaders of some countries, deputies of parliaments, public figures, and representatives of science and culture, who would either succumb to this provocation or even act as its organizers. A few Communist parties may also become involved in this type of campaign.

Despite the possibility of a broad campaign in support of Sakharov, the question of his going abroad should be decided negatively. We think that, in Bonner's absence, it will be easier to persuade Sakharov himself of this. In addition, in his statement he has written that he understands that he cannot travel abroad because of the secret nature of his work in the past.

· DOCUMENT 183 ·

Chebrikov to Gorbachev, October 12, 1985
Pledges to Gorbachev from Sakharov and Bonner

As an addendum to the memorandum of the KGB and the Ministry of Foreign Affairs (no. 1560-Ch), we report that one more conversation was held with Sakharov. As he confirmed in the course of that conversation, he understands that his own travel abroad is impossible, and he said that he will never raise this question. In a letter addressed to the general secretary of the Central Committee of the CPSU, Sakharov acknowledges the validity of the refusal to permit him to depart from the USSR, since in the past he had access to particularly important secret information (a copy is attached).

At the same time, Bonner also wrote a letter, in which she certifies that her trip abroad is for purely personal reasons, and she pledges that she will not meet with representatives of the press, radio, or television while abroad and that she will not participate in anti-Soviet actions (a copy is also attached).

Sakharov's letter gives complete grounds to deny him an exit visa even if the question of family reunification arises (on the assumption that Bonner may not return to the USSR). Bonner's pledge, however, does not inspire trust, and one must presume that her participation in anti-Soviet acts in the West is by no means excluded. Nevertheless, for the reasons given in the above memorandum, it is deemed possible to grant her permission to travel abroad.

To: Mikhail Sergeevich Gorbachev, General Secretary
of the Central Committee of the CPSU
To: Viktor Mikhailovich Chebrikov, Chairman of the USSR KGB
Declaration

In connection with the question about the travel abroad of my wife, E. G. Bonner, to see her family and for medical treatment, I consider it nec-

essary to affirm that I recognize that the refusal to grant me an exit visa for
the purpose of traveling outside the USSR is well founded, since in the past
I had access to particularly important secret information of a military
character, some of which may still preserve its significance at the present
time.

A. Sakharov

To: Mikhail Sergeevich Gorbachev, General Secretary
of the Central Committee of the CPSU
To: Viktor Mikhailovich Chebrikov, Chairman of the USSR KGB
From: Elena Georgievna Bonner

With respect to the question of my travel abroad to see my mother, children, and grandchildren, as well as for medical treatment, I affirm that
this trip is for strictly personal reasons and has no other purposes. I pledge
that I will not meet with representatives of the press, radio, or television,
that I will not grant any interviews, and that I will not participate in any
press conferences during my stay abroad.

E. G. Bonner
September 1985

· DOCUMENT 184 ·

Chebrikov to Gorbachev, November 26, 1985
Bonner's travel to the West

As an addendum to the memorandum of the KGB (no. 1881-Ch, dated
October 12, 1985), we report that on October 23 Sakharov was discharged from Semashko Hospital of Gorky Oblast, where he had been
hospitalized since July in connection with yet another of his provocative
"hunger strikes." Upon leaving the hospital, he assured the head physician
of his intention to follow the recommendations given to him, regularly
take his medications, and have periodic physical exams. He thanked the
medical staff for their attention and care for him.

On October 24, the Department of Internal Affairs (the branch at the
Gorky Oblast Executive Committee) notified Bonner that permission was
granted to her to travel for three months to Italy for medical treatment and
to the United States to see her relatives. In a conversation with an employee of the Department of Internal Affairs, she emphasized that she

wants to leave the Soviet Union after the Soviet-American summit meeting in Geneva is over.[89]

Sakharov informed Comrade A. P. Alexandrov, president of the USSR Academy of Sciences, that his wife had been granted permission and, in this regard, asked that his declaration of May 10, 1985 (about resignation from the Academy), be disregarded.

Since Bonner received permission to go abroad, there has been no positive change of any kind in her behavior. As before, she tells Sakharov that his "exile" in Gorky was unlawful. Without any proof, she blames the doctors for causing a deterioration in his health, and she declares that her trip became possible only because of Sakharov's "self-sacrifice," the pressure applied by state officials and public figures of capitalist countries, and protests by her children and her son-in-law, Yankelevich. Bonner urges Sakharov to use his status as the "victor" to continue the "struggle." In conversations with her husband, she persists in making negative references to Soviet peace initiatives, asserting that the USA will never be the first to start a nuclear war, and declaring that Reagan is "absolutely right" in linking disarmament problems to the prior solution of so-called "regional issues." At the same time, Bonner constantly stresses that she has pledged not to participate in political activity and intends to keep her word. However, this does not preclude the possibility that she will become involved in these matters, as is clear from the actions of the enemy's intelligence agencies.

Bonner informed her relatives in the USA, and close acquaintances in Moscow, about her impending trip abroad. This left the latter extremely bewildered and, in a number of cases, even aroused hostile feelings toward her.

The press in several capitalist countries regards Bonner's permission to go abroad as a step that demonstrates goodwill on the part of the Soviet leadership.

In order to neutralize a possible campaign of slander over Bonner's impending trip abroad, information has been sent to the West (through the channels of the Committee for State Security) reflecting the humanitarian character of this decision and the fact that Sakharov and Bonner have given written statements with appropriate pledges.

---

89. Bonner stated that she would leave the country only after staying a month with her husband, since Sakharov needed her attention after the hunger strike. The connection with the meeting in Geneva was invented by the KGB. For Sakharov's account of his final hunger strike in Gorky, see his *Memoirs*, 600–604.

Elena Bonner was originally permitted to leave on a three-month visa, but after her surgery she requested permission to remain abroad for three additional months. The KGB had feared that she would refuse to return altogether and might wage a campaign to have Sakharov join her in the West. Nonetheless, she returned to Moscow in May 1986, "to the old world of unfreedom, familiar and joyless."[90]

·  DOCUMENT 186  ·

Chebrikov to Central Committee, February 7, 1986
Bonner extends her visit to the United States

In accordance with a decision adopted earlier (memorandum of the KGB and Ministry of Foreign Affairs, no. 1560-Ch, dated August 28, 1985), Bonner has been abroad since December 2, 1985. In January 1986 she asked the USSR embassy in Washington to extend her stay in the USA for another three months for postoperative treatment.

The Committee for State Security believes it expedient to satisfy Bonner's request.

Coordinated with the Ministry of Foreign Affairs (Comrade G. M. Kornienko). . . .

After her surgery in January, Elena Bonner met with a number of political leaders in the West. Her activity did not please the KGB, which regarded such visits as a violation of her pledge that her trip was strictly for personal reasons. Nonetheless, she did not regard her visit to the Reagan White House as successful. She met with the president's national security adviser, Admiral John Poindexter. She had "the impression that [he] was not well informed on the concrete work of Sakharov." She had put off having an angioplasty procedure for three days just to go to Washington, but then was disappointed that Poindexter was not "planning to tell me something important, or at least something new."[91]

In his memorandum, Chebrikov reported on a propaganda film that had been produced in order to give the impression that Sakharov was living a normal life in Gorky. The KGB, in fact, produced and distrib-

90. Bonner, *Alone Together*, Foreword.
91. Ibid., 128–32.

uted a series of photographs and videos that were distributed through the German mass-circulation magazine *Bild* between 1984 and 1986.[92]

· DOCUMENT 187 ·

Chebrikov to Central Committee, May 11, 1986
The impact of Bonner's stay in the United States

———————————————

The Committee for State Security continues to take measures to expose the anti-Soviet campaigns whipped up by the West around Sakharov. Thus, in March 1986,[93] another video film, "Sakharov Speaks," was made. The film objectively shows Sakharov's living conditions in Gorky. Its centerpiece is a conversation between Sakharov and the chief physician of the Semashko Hospital in Gorky, where Sakharov criticized the American "Star Wars" program and spoke approvingly about the peace initiatives of the Soviet leadership. The video film was telecast in the USA,[94] the Federal Republic of Germany, and France. The mass media in Canada, Switzerland, Spain, the USA, the Federal Republic of Germany, France, and Japan displayed great interest. Some, especially the influential West German newspaper *Frankfurter Allgemeine* [*Zeitung*], underscored the importance of Sakharov's criticism of the "Star Wars" program.

Sakharov's comments aroused the displeasure of the American administration. As a result, according to reports in the West, Reagan spurned the insistent recommendation of the State Department that he officially receive Bonner at the White House.

Information received indicates that the film had a favorable effect on public opinion in the USA and a number of countries in Western Europe.

At the same time, Bonner, who is now in the USA, is making every effort to revive the interest of Western public opinion, scientists, and government officials in the so-called "Sakharov problem." For this purpose, she has taken steps to publish her husband's "autobiography" under the provisional title "Memoirs." The Committee for State Security has reported earlier to the Central Committee about Sakharov's work on this book. . . .

———————————————

92. See ibid., 263–64, for a list of the photographs and videos.

93. Several words have been deleted from the declassified copy.

94. For reports that ABC television paid $25,000 for an eighteen-minute videotape of Sakharov, see *New York Times,* March 25, 1986, 22.

Bonner transmitted Sakharov's manuscript to the West while visiting the U.S. embassy in Moscow. The Americans have agreed to assist in the publication of the "Memoirs" on the condition that sensational materials of a political character be added, and Bonner is now trying to do this. . . .[95]

---

95. The contract regarding Sakharov's *Memoirs* was signed two years before Bonner's open heart surgery in January 1986. She did not and could not bring any additional materials for Sakharov's book. KGB officials may have obtained information that Bonner had begun to write her own book (*Alone Together*), which was published the same year, and confused the two books.

# CHAPTER FIVE

# New Rules of Engagement

A YEAR AFTER Gorbachev came to power, he was finally ready to address issues that Andrei Sakharov had so stubbornly raised for so long: the arrest of prisoners of conscience and the general lack of freedom and democracy in the country. By the end of 1986, Sakharov would be welcomed back to Moscow. For the remaining three years of his life, he was fully engaged in the political life of the Soviet Union, this time not as a dissident on the margins of society but as "one of the leaders of a legal opposition" (in the words of KGB Chairman Vladimir Kryuchkov),[1] able to travel around the country, visit parts of Europe, Asia, and North America, and make speeches critical of the Kremlin as an elected member of the Congress of People's Deputies.

The archival record that has been declassified is clearly incomplete. The KGB continued to monitor Sakharov's activities and it is inconceivable that it failed to report on his involvement in numerous political events, among them his attempt to mediate the conflict between Armenia and Azerbaijan in December 1988 and his visit to Tbilisi, Georgia, in April 1989, when he sharply criticized the brutal suppression of Georgian nationalist demonstrators. At his death the KGB found it necessary to monitor the behavior of tens of thousands of peo-

---

1. See Document 199, December 8, 1989.

ple who demonstrated support for his ideas and used the occasion of his funeral to call for an end to the Communist Party's monopoly of power.

Viktor Chebrikov's report to the Central Committee of May 11, 1986, began, "The Committee for State Security continues to take measures to expose the anti-Soviet campaigns whipped up by the West around Sakharov." His next report, dated June 17, 1986, addressed directly to General Secretary Mikhail Gorbachev, is dramatically different in tone and content. In May Chebrikov communicated to the Party leadership on the assumption that the initiative belonged to the KGB. In June Chebrikov was obviously on the defensive, and we understand that he must have had instructions from Gorbachev to respond to a letter from Sakharov. Sakharov's letter dealt with the core problem that had been the fundamental reason for his opposition to the regime: the violation of human rights. And for the first time Sakharov was able to compel the KGB to enter a discussion on this theme.

## · DOCUMENT 188 ·

Chebrikov to Gorbachev, June 17, 1986
The KGB reports to Gorbachev on Sakharov and other prisoners of conscience

In accordance with your instruction, the Committee for State Security has considered the letter by A. D. Sakharov.[2]

In effect, Sakharov repeats in his letter the familiar fabrications of reactionary circles in the West about alleged "human rights violations" in the Soviet Union, about criminal prosecutions for opinions, and about the presence of so-called "political prisoners" in the USSR.

He asserts that there are cases of conviction for anti-Soviet agitation and propaganda (under Article 70 of the Criminal Code of the RSFSR) even though any intention to subvert or weaken the Soviet system is absent, and also convictions for the dissemination of knowingly false fabrications that defame the Soviet state and its social system (under Article 190-1 of the Criminal Code of the RSFSR), but without proof that it is "knowingly false." He also discusses wrongful convictions (under Article 142 of the Criminal Code of the RSFSR) for violating the laws on separa-

2. Sakharov's letter was written and mailed to Gorbachev on February 19, 1986. The original is in APRF; a copy is in the Andrei Sakharov Archive (Harvard), folder S.II.2.4.17. The letter was reported in the *New York Times*, September 4, 1986, 10.

tion of church and state and separation of school and church. All these assertions by Sakharov are manifestly unfounded.

Preliminary investigation of crimes under Article 70 of the Criminal Code
of the RSFSR falls within the competence of the KGB, while crimes under
Articles 190-1 and 142 fall within the authority of the Procurator's office.

During the preliminary investigation and court proceedings, all the circumstances surrounding unlawful actions and, in particular, the degree of
guilt (intent) are fully clarified. While investigating criminal cases of anti-
Soviet agitation and propaganda, one must—in keeping with the law—
investigate the presence of a specific goal (subversion or weakening of the
Soviet system, or the commission of especially dangerous state crimes).

It should be noted that the number of individuals prosecuted under the
criminal code for these types of crimes is insignificant, and that there is a
trend showing its decrease. At the present time, in corrective labor camps
and exile, there are 172 individuals serving sentences for anti-Soviet agitation and propaganda, 179 for the dissemination of knowingly false fabrications that defame the Soviet state and its social system, and 4 for violating the laws on separation of church and state and the separation of school
and church.

The twelve people cited in Sakharov's letter (Marchenko, Osipova,
[Ivan] Kovalev, Orlov, Nekipelov, Shikhanovich, and others) were convicted of committing concrete criminal acts as stipulated in current law
and in strict keeping with those norms. Their guilt was fully proved by the
materials of the preliminary investigations and court proceedings, by
abundant testimony of witnesses, and by material evidence. Through the
system of cassation and through the department of public prosecution,
these criminal cases were reviewed by appellate courts and the Procurator's office, which found the charges to be substantiated.

It is necessary to note that these individuals had been involved in unlawful activities for a long time. Prior to their criminal prosecution, a great
deal of prophylactic and admonitory work was carried out by workers'
collectives, public representatives, and law enforcement agencies. A number of these people had been prosecuted for other crimes. For example,
Marchenko (whom Sakharov calls "my friend"), prior to being convicted
under Article 70 of the Criminal Code of the RSFSR, was tried for hooliganism, for attempting to cross the USSR state frontier illegally, and for
the systematic violation of passport regulations;[3] Shcharansky served a
term for treason (espionage) and was deported in 1986.

3. Anatoly Marchenko (1938–86) was a worker, writer, and activist in the human

Certain individuals now in detention, among them Kovalev, Osipova, and Shikhanovich, who were mentioned in the letter, as a result of systematic educational work conducted with them, have condemned their activities, repented, and declared that they will refrain from unlawful activities in the future.

In his letter, Sakharov points to the allegedly unlawful practice of trying prisoners for a second time in their places of detention. Here one can easily discern an attempt to present, in a tendentious manner, facts regarding justifiable indictments under Article 188-3 of the Criminal Code of the RSFSR (malicious refusal to obey the demands of the administration in a corrective labor facility). Four persons previously convicted under Article 70 were prosecuted under Article 188-3 and two persons previously convicted were tried under Article 190-1.

The reason Sakharov has raised these questions is probably related to his misconceptions, compounded by the constant negative influence of his wife, Bonner.[4]

Sakharov has been informed that his letter was received by the Central Committee of the CPSU.

Appendix: 5 pages, unclassified, no. 315-op. (to addressee only)[5]

---

Soon after Elena Bonner returned to the Soviet Union, the KGB provided a highly misleading report, both of her stay in the West and of Sakharov's activities in Gorky during her absence. The Chernobyl nuclear accident had taken place that spring and the KGB was eager to claim that Sakharov's remarks about the accident were now properly "objective" (as the regime liked to say of opinions that suited its purposes), as if it only required the absence of Elena Bonner for him to come to his senses. Sakharov, in fact, "pretended . . . that nothing much had happened [and adopted] far too sanguine an approach to the accident," as he later admitted. He trusted the initial reports in the

---

rights movement. After his initial arrest for participating in a brawl, he was sentenced five more times for political and literary activity. He began his writing career with *My Testimony* (New York, 1969), the most vivid and authoritative account of the labor camps in the post-Stalin era. Marchenko protested the Soviet invasion of Czechoslovakia, the attacks on Sakharov and Solzhenitsyn, and the political abuse of psychiatry. He was arrested for the last time in 1980 and sentenced to ten years in a labor camp and five years of exile. He died in prison after a long hunger strike in December 1986. His second book, *From Tarusa to Siberia* (Royal Oak, MI, 1980), describes his fifty-three-day hunger strike in 1975. His final book, *To Live Like Everyone* (New York, 1989), was published posthumously.

4. Several lines were deleted from the declassified copy of the document.

5. These pages were not released.

Soviet press and reassured "people pretending to be chance passers-by [who] would stop me on the street to ask about Chernobyl, . . . although I always cautioned them that my information was limited." The regime was quick to exploit his lapse of judgment and even produced a film with a severely edited version of what he had been saying.[6]

· DOCUMENT 189 ·

Chebrikov to Central Committee, June 18, 1986
Bonner in the West; Sakharov on the Chernobyl accident

───────────────

In October 1985, E. G. Bonner, the wife of Academician Sakharov, was permitted to travel to Italy and the USA. Bonner had argued the necessity of a trip abroad to obtain treatment for her cardiovascular and eye diseases, and to see her relatives.

According to mass media in the West, Bonner was examined by doctors while abroad and on January 13 supposedly had heart surgery in a hospital in Boston (USA). However, doctors at this hospital, who examined her on December 18, 1985, had concluded that her health was satisfactory and that she did not need surgery; instead, they suggested that she stop smoking, take medications, and change her diet.[7]

During her first days abroad, Bonner demonstratively refused to give interviews and make any statements, referring to her "pledge to Soviet authorities" not to have contact with representatives of the mass media in the West.

However, starting in February, Bonner became actively involved in various anti-Soviet gatherings (as an "honorary guest" and "leader of the Soviet human rights movement") that included participation by the leaders of Zionist organizations, Jewish religious activists, heads of anti-Soviet émigré groups, and representatives of the press, radio, and television. As something unprecedented for such an individual, she had widely advertised meetings with Thatcher, Mitterrand, Chirac, Craxi, John Paul II, and Poindexter (the national security adviser to the U.S. president). These meetings had a demonstratively provocative character; their obvious aim was to push Bonner and other renegades toward anti-Soviet activities. Re-

6. Andrei Sakharov, *Memoirs* (New York, 1990), 608.
7. In January 1986, Elena Bonner had multiple coronary bypass surgery and surgical procedures to relieve atherosclerosis in her right leg.

actionary circles and the intelligence agencies of the imperialist countries made use of Sakharov's sixty-fifth birthday (May 21) to whip up an anti-Soviet propaganda campaign around his name. Bonner took an active part in "banquets," "receptions," and "manifestations" timed for this date. One such gathering was attended by members of Afghan counterrevolutionary bands; on their behalf, the ringleader of the anti-Soviet and anti-socialist Afghan community in the USA, Khabib Meir, presented Bonner with a Dushman headdress,[8] saying that "it symbolizes the resolution to continue the struggle against the Soviets on Afghanistan's territory to a victorious conclusion."

In keeping with a resolution of the American Congress, Reagan proclaimed May 21 "Andrei Sakharov Day," which was marked in the USA by "appropriate ceremonies and activities." Speaking to Congress on the eve of this date, Bonner made an appeal "to intercede for Sakharov," who, in her words, "is one of the spiritual leaders of our time." At a meeting with members of the National Academy [of Sciences] of the United States, she said: "What Sakharov has suffered at the hands of the Soviet leaders is worthy of the same sort of investigation as the events in Chile and the Philippines." She blasphemously compared the medical help rendered to Sakharov in Gorky to the experiments that the Nazi executioner Mengele conducted on prisoners in concentration camps.

. . . It must be said that during Bonner's absence from Gorky, efforts to exert a positive influence on Sakharov have had some success. In particular, scientists and representatives of workers' collectives met with him and showed him the error of his views and his lack of competence in political matters. Simultaneously, measures were also taken to redirect his attention to the solution of scientific problems. As a result, Sakharov showed a renewed interest in scientific work and prepared an article for publication in a journal of the USSR Academy of Sciences.

The next pretext for an outburst of anti-Soviet campaigns in the West over Sakharov and Bonner was her return to the USSR on June 2, 1986. On behalf of the U.S. Congress, she was accompanied by two members of Congress under the pretext of safeguarding her security.[9] At the airport she was met by the first secretaries of the embassies of the United States, Canada, Great Britain, and other countries, along with more than forty foreign correspondents, to whom she said: "If my husband were not in the USSR, I would never have returned."

8. "Dushman" was a derogatory term for members of the Afghan resistance.
9. They were Rep. Barney Frank (D-MA) and Rep. Dan Lungren (R-CA). Frank represented the suburban Boston district in which her children lived.

Bonner arrived in Gorky on June 4. On the platform at the railway station, without even inquiring about Sakharov's health, she immediately began reprimanding him for the interview he gave about events at the Chernobyl nuclear power station. Without concealing her irritation, Bonner declared that he "lacked information" and did not know that, according to the data of Western doctors, "100,000 gravely ill people will die from radiation within three months, and that, according to modest estimates by Western specialists, the radiation fallout is equal to five Hiroshimas." While inquiring about the circumstances under which he talked with residents of Gorky about disarmament questions and the Chernobyl accident, Bonner made the following slip: "The world is very frightened by the nonsense you are babbling. Your 'representative' [Bonner's son-in-law, Yankelevich] said: 'Oh, Elena Georgievna, go home before he says something else.'" In her conversation with Sakharov, Bonner told him that while she was in the USA, she wrote a book about her life, which she sold to Bernstein, a famous American publisher, for $250,000.[10] Her book will be a best seller, and she received more money for this than Sakharov did for his "Memoirs."

Materials obtained by the Committee for State Security about the first days after Bonner's return to the USSR show that she subjected Sakharov to massive psychological brainwashing. She is seeking to foist on him the idea that he should repudiate everything he said in conversations with residents of Gorky about the American "Star Wars program," and about the accident at the Chernobyl nuclear power plant. In an emphatically provocative manner, Bonner makes hostile statements about Soviet reality.

An analysis of all this information about Bonner's activities shows that she will continue to incite Sakharov to participate in antisocial activities, without in the least caring about his fate and health.

The Committee for State Security continues to monitor the situation around Sakharov and Bonner. Reported for your information.


Appendix: On Sakharov's statements about Chernobyl.[11]

The West learned of Sakharov's telephone conversation with Bonner on May 15, while she was in the USA, during which he touched on events in

---

10. Robert Bernstein was then president and CEO of Random House.

11. The attachment included remarks Sakharov allegedly made to local residents in Gorky. He did not make these remarks to his wife and they differ markedly from five documents that Sakharov wrote after the Chernobyl disaster. These texts are in the Sakharov Archive (Harvard), folders S.III.1.1.117; S.II.2.9.45.1; S.II.2.1.133.1.1; S.II.2.1.95.2; S.III.1.1.116.2.

Chernobyl and said: "The accident is terrible, of course. Only they have blown it out of proportion over there. . . . One can say they exaggerated things by a factor of ten. Well, you know how they can exaggerate things. . . . One can eat everything. In general, on the border of the zone over there, the level of radiation is already low. There is absolutely no danger."

In private conversations with residents on the streets of Gorky, Sakharov said: "Everything necessary is being done to minimize any consequences; the announced radiation level, 10–15 milliroentgens, is minuscule and poses no health threat." With respect to food products from Ukraine, Sakharov remarked that they "will all be carefully checked for radiation" and therefore one can buy and consume them without fear. Answering a question about the comparative reliability of Soviet and foreign reactors, Sakharov said that they are approximately the same. He referred to accidents that took place at atomic power plants in the USA and England. Atomic power plants, in his opinion, are safer than thermal power stations, which pollute the air with sulfur. During the period when thermal power stations were introduced, there were more human victims. He expressed his firm opinion that atomic power should continue to be developed. He also emphasized: "The Twenty-seventh [Party] Congress has taken this decision. So be it."

---

The following documents record the decision to allow Sakharov and Bonner to return to Moscow. The memorandum prepared by Yegor Ligachev (a hard-line Central Committee secretary) together with the head of the KGB and the president of the Academy of Sciences proposed to permit their return. It is a peculiar document; after condemning both for years of anti-Soviet activity, it nonetheless proposed to rescind the banishment of Sakharov and to grant amnesty to Bonner. Although the archival record is incomplete, Gorbachev clearly favored their release, as is evident from the Politburo discussion on November 10, which is appended to this memorandum. His more conservative colleagues remained opposed. So it was to be expected that Ligachev and Chebrikov would describe reasons to oppose Sakharov's return to Moscow and recall how he had attached qualifications to his promise to "make no more public statements" when he appealed to Gorbachev in October, even as they concluded, as they had to do, that it was time to permit Sakharov to return to Moscow.

Eight years later, an adviser to Gorbachev named Andrei Grachev described how he had been approached by Alexander Yakovlev in late

1986 and asked to devise a suitable argument to present to the Polit-buro in favor of allowing Sakharov to return to Moscow. According to Grachev, Yakovlev explained that the Politburo was divided and it was important not to "break the delicate and quite obviously temporary balance between the two parts of this political centaur." The discussion in Grachev's office, as he described it in his memoir, echoes the tone of the following document.[12]

## ·  DOCUMENT 190  ·

Ligachev, Chebrikov, and Marchuk to Central Committee, December 9, 1986
A proposal to allow Sakharov and Bonner to return to Moscow

---

On January 8, 1980, the Presidium of the Supreme Soviet of the USSR adopted a decree that declared that "to prevent Sakharov's hostile activity, his criminal contacts with citizens of capitalist countries, and the possibility that his conduct could hurt the interests of the Soviet state, at the present time it is deemed necessary to go no further than the administrative expulsion of Andrei Dmitrievich Sakharov from the city of Moscow to one of the regions in the country that is closed to foreigners." The same decree established a regimen for Sakharov's residence that precluded communication with antisocial elements as well as travel to other regions of the country without special permission from the appropriate organ of the USSR Ministry of Internal Affairs.

That same year, Sakharov was resettled in Gorky, where he was allotted a well-furnished apartment and where all the necessary conditions for life and scientific activity were created.

The decision to interrupt Sakharov's hostile activity was occasioned by the fact that, for of an extended period of time, he had conducted subversive work against the Soviet state. He incited aggressive circles in capitalist countries to interfere in the domestic affairs of socialist countries and to engage in military confrontation with the Soviet Union; he inspired demonstrations against the policies of the Soviet state, which were directed toward peaceful coexistence and the relaxation of international tensions. At the same time, Sakharov took steps to organize and unite anti-Soviet elements inside the country and incite extremist activities on their part.

---

12. See Andrei Grachev, *Kremlevskaia khronika* [Kremlin chronicle] (Moscow, 1994), 94–100.

He established contacts with antisocialist elements in the People's Republic of Poland and the Czechoslovak Soviet Socialist Republic, expressed his solidarity with members of Poland's so-called "Workers' Defense Committee" and with the Czechoslovak "Chartists," and appealed to them to unite for purposes of carrying out antisocialist activity.

Before the Presidium of the USSR Supreme Soviet adopted its decree, Sakharov had been repeatedly warned—by representatives of Party and Soviet organs, by the state procurator's office, and by the USSR Committee for State Security—that his hostile activity was intolerable. He also received warnings from eminent Soviet scientists. He ignored all these warnings.

To a large degree, the preventive measures applied to Sakharov have justified themselves. They isolated him from the agents of Western intelligence agencies, from subversive ideological centers, and from foreign anti-Soviet organizations; they also prevented his contact with antisocial elements inside the country. The fact that Sakharov's wife, Bonner, was prosecuted for criminal activity and sentenced to serve her term of exile in her husband's place of residence helped to neutralize his unlawful activity.

Moreover, while living in Gorky, Sakharov again returned to his scientific work. As a result, he has lately developed some new ideas. Thus, for example, he has been expressing his ideas on the further development of atomic power, on questions related to controlled fusion reactions (the "Tokamak" system),[13] and on other scientific topics. Characteristically, during Bonner's absence (when she was spending some time in the USA), he became more sociable and willingly conversed with residents of Gorky; in his discussions with them, he criticized the American "Star Wars" program, commented favorably on the peace initiatives of the Soviet leadership, and made an objective assessment of the events at the Chernobyl Atomic Power Station.

As before, Bonner adamantly opposes these changes in Sakharov's behavior and way of life. In essence, she induces her husband to abandon his scientific work, directs all his efforts toward the preparation of provocative documents, and forces him to keep a diary (with the prospect of publishing it abroad). However, despite this, it is deemed expedient to continue trying to involve Sakharov in scientific work, which is advantageous by itself and can also restrain him from participating in antisocial activities.

13. "Tokamak" is an acronym for *toroidalnaia kamera s magnitnimi katushkami* (toroidal chamber with magnetic induction coils). It was developed primarily by Sakharov and Igor Tamm.

For these purposes, at the present time it is deemed possible to address the question of Sakharov's return to Moscow, since his further residence in Gorky might again impel him to increase his anti-Soviet activity, especially if one takes into account his wife's pernicious influence and the West's continuing interest in the so-called "Sakharov problem."

Furthermore, we would like to believe in Sakharov's statement that, upon his return to Moscow, he is prepared to give up his "public activism."

Sakharov's return to Moscow may entail some negative consequences, given Bonner's anti-Soviet orientation, her constant attempt to provoke a confrontation between Sakharov and the authorities, and her patent desire to collaborate with Western circles that oppose Soviet policy. Their apartment once again might become the center of all kinds of press conferences with the participation of foreign correspondents; it might become the place where antisocial elements will meet to work on statements and demands of a negative character. Sakharov himself is hardly likely to refrain from participating in the so-called "defense of human rights." But even so, Sakharov's return to Moscow will mean fewer political costs than his continued isolation in Gorky.[14] At the same time Bonner should be pardoned and released from exile.

Draft resolutions of the Central Committee of the CPSU and draft decrees of the Presidium of the USSR Supreme Soviet are attached.

This matter has been coordinated with the Office of the Chief Procurator of the USSR (Comrade A. M. Rekunkov).

We ask that this be given consideration.


Appendix [1]
Draft: "Decree of the Presidium of the USSR Supreme Soviet on annulling the decree of the Presidium of the Supreme Soviet of January 8, 1980 concerning the banishment of A. D. Sakharov"

The Presidium of the Supreme Soviet decrees:
The decree of the Presidium of the Supreme Soviet of the USSR on January 8, 1980, "Concerning the administrative banishment of A. D. Sakharov from the city of Moscow" is annulled, together with the measures taken to forestall his hostile activity and criminal contacts with citizens of capitalist countries, which might cause harm to the interests of the Soviet state.

Chairman of the Presidium of the USSR Supreme Soviet
Secretary of the Presidium of the USSR Supreme Soviet

14. Two lines have been deleted from the declassified copy.

Appendix [2]
Draft: "Decree of the Presidium of the Supreme Soviet
of the USSR on the pardon of E. G. Bonner"

The Presidium of the Supreme Soviet decrees:
Elena Georgievna Bonner, born in 1922, is pardoned from serving the re-
mainder of the term to which she was sentenced by the court for committing a crime covered under Article 190–1 of the Criminal Code of the RS-
FSR.

Chairman of the Presidium of the USSR Supreme Soviet
Secretary of the Presidium of the USSR Supreme Soviet


Appendix [3]
Draft: "Resolution of the Central Committee of the CPSU
on proposals pertaining to A. D. Sakharov"

1. Agree with the proposals contained in the memorandum by comrades
E. K. Ligachev, V. M. Chebrikov, and G. I. Marchuk of December 9, 1986.
2. Approve the draft decrees of the Presidium of the USSR Supreme Soviet
on this question (attached).

Secretary of the Central Committee


Transcript of Politburo meeting[15]
Presiding chair: Comrade M. S. Gorbachev
Present: Comrades G. A. Aliyev, V. I. Vorotnikov, A. A. Gromyko,
L. N. Zaikov, E. K. Ligachev, N. I. Ryzhkov, M. S. Solomentsev,
V. M. Chebrikov, E. A. Shevardnadze, A. F. Dobrynin,
V. A. Medvedev, A. N. Yakovlev
V. On Sakharov and Bonner

*Gorbachev:* Now about Sakharov and Bonner. I have the following
document (he reads the document aloud). It looks as if his head knows
how to think and does so, it seems, in the interests of the country. This
factor interested me most of all. Let's go on. (He continues reading.)
He wants to return to Moscow. We should use this and talk to him.
Provide an apartment here.
*Ligachev:* As a beginning shall we let [Academician Guri I.] Marchuk visit him?
*Gorbachev:* Yes, we should send Comrade Marchuk to visit him and

15. The date of the meeting, November 10, 1986, was omitted from the declassified
copy.

tell him that the academicians had a talk with the Soviet leadership, and that they were asked to speak with him so that he might resume a normal life. Tell him to let bygones be bygones; our country has become engaged in a gigantic creative effort. Ask him how he feels about putting his knowledge, his energy at the service of his Motherland and the people.

*Gromyko:* That's good—it's a matter of principle.

*Gorbachev:* If there are good inclinations there, they should be used. Well, Viktor Mikhailovich [Chebrikov], do you see any complications?

*Chebrikov:* We'll work on it. With respect to an apartment, he has a good two-room apartment on Chkalov Street. The two of them lived there. It's fully equipped.[16] There is another apartment, where he used to live with his first wife. That one is a four-room apartment. His children lived in it at the beginning, then they moved out. But Bonner doesn't want to live there.[17]

*Gorbachev:* Well, that's their affair.

*Chebrikov:* There is a dacha in Zhukovka; you know, the academicians live there—Alexandrov, Zeldovich, and the rest of the atomic crowd. There is also a government dacha. It too is vacant.[18] So the apartment question is solved.

*Gorbachev:* So tell him: Your apartment has been kept for you, the dacha as well. If you have any other problems, let us know. But go to work. The entire country is now energetically at work, and you too should get busy.

*Chebrikov:* But in one of the letters he said: I promise to behave better but I cannot keep silent when it is impossible to do so.

*Gorbachev:* Let him speak. But if he speaks against the people, then let him get himself out of it. Well, comrades, does anyone have any problems with this?

*Gorbachev:* Then we authorize Comrades Ligachev and Chebrikov to invite Academician Marchuk and tell him that he is to act.[19]

*Chebrikov:* But we have to adopt a decree of the Presidium of the USSR Supreme Soviet on this question.

*Gorbachev:* Yes. Maybe we shall improvise for now, and later you,

16. Chebrikov was referring to the listening devices installed in Sakharov's apartment in 1970 (see Document 13, April 20, 1970).

17. Sakharov's daughter Lyubov was living in this apartment with her husband and son. Sakharov's son, Dmitri, was also registered to live in the apartment, but he was actually staying at Sakharov's dacha in Zhukovka.

18. Sakharov had only one dacha—the house in Zhukovka.

19. Since Gorbachev is noted as the speaker two times in a row, it is reasonable to assume that the declassified text was spliced together from a longer transcription—in other words, this transcript was edited.

together with Comrade Ligachev, will work all this out, and then invite Comrade Marchuk and tell him what has to be done. Had we talked with Sakharov before, perhaps this whole situation wouldn't have arisen. Well, in short, we have to invite him.

*Members of the Politburo:* Correct.

*Gorbachev:* Let the correspondents gather, and let them talk.

*Chebrikov:* We have some experience working with them.

*Gorbachev:* But just don't let them discuss inappropriate topics.

*Chebrikov:* I must say that we have never had any reason to charge Sakharov for divulging secrets. He understands that.

*Gorbachev:* Victor Mikhailovich, Comrade Marchuk should be told that everything must be done in such a way that it doesn't come as a surprise for the public. Perhaps one should convene the Presidium of the Academy of Sciences and tell them about this. Have Comrade Marchuk tell them that he was at the Central Committee and discussed this subject. Otherwise, look what happens: at one point, the scientists supported his departure from Moscow, and now they're not even notified that a different approach is being taken on this question.

*Gromyko:* I think the scientists will act properly.

*Gorbachev:* Have we finished with this topic?

*Members of the Politburo:* Yes.

The resolution is approved.

---

This report by four ranking party leaders emphasizes the overwhelmingly positive response that Sakharov's return to Moscow received in the West. It also outlines a plan to repair the Kremlin's relationship with Sakharov and even attempt to use him as a tool of Soviet propaganda. As part of its effort at reconciliation, Soviet officials allowed Elena Bonner's son, Alexei Semyonov, to visit Moscow that January.[20]

· DOCUMENT 191 ·

Shevardnadze, Chebrikov, Yakovlev, and Dobrynin to
Central Committee, January 15, 1987
How to exploit Sakharov's return to Moscow

---

In accordance with the instruction (sh/t spets. no. 4055,[21] from Paris on December 24, 1986), we report the following:

20. See *New York Times*, January 24, 1987, 7.
21. Russian acronyms translate: "coded cable, special no. . . ." We do not have the

The return of Academician A. D. Sakharov to Moscow has generally elicited a favorable response abroad. The dominant theme is that this decision demonstrates the depth and seriousness of the changes in the Soviet Union, and the firm commitment of the Soviet leadership to a further expansion of democracy, glasnost, and the just resolution of humanitarian problems. Naturally, there were also some tendentious responses. In particular, it is asserted that the return of A. D. Sakharov from Gorky was due to "pressure from the West," and that this fact alone does not fundamentally change the unsatisfactory situation of human rights in the USSR, etc.

Westerners are actively working on Sakharov and seek to induce him to make sharply critical statements about various aspects of foreign and domestic policies of the CPSU. Sakharov has been restrained in his pronouncements; on the whole, his judgments concerning military and strategic questions have been balanced. One can also notice the tendency of Western media to distort some of Sakharov's statements concerning SDI[22] and his attitude toward perestroika. In their commentaries, the organs of Western propaganda introduce him as the "key" figure among Soviet dissenters.

Under these conditions, it would be justified to undertake additional steps so as to bring about the necessary political and propa[ganda advantages].[23]

It would be expedient to implement the following:

1. The USSR Academy of Sciences should show the necessary attention to Sakharov's scientific work and also help him resolve any problems in everyday life that he may have.

At a high level, it should be suggested to Academician Sakharov that he describe his attitude on disarmament, the use of nuclear energy, SDI, and the peaceful use of space so that his time free from scientific work should be devoted to work on this document.

2. Publish an article in the newspaper *Izvestia* describing the general approach of the Soviet Union toward humanitarian questions and, within this framework, explain the decision to allow Sakharov's return to Moscow.

3. Suggest to Sakharov that he give an interview to *Literaturnaya Gazeta*, which would emphasize his views on questions of war and peace,

text of that cable, and we do not know who signed it. It seems likely that it was sent in response to an instruction from Gorbachev.

22. Strategic Defense Initiative, the system of missile defenses promoted by Reagan, popularly known as "Star Wars."

23. Probably through carelessness, the rest of this page was omitted from the declassified photocopy.

nuclear disarmament, and the danger of extending the arms race into outer space. Do not attempt to avoid sensitive questions connected with his attitude toward the process of perestroika in Soviet society after the Twenty-seventh Party Congress.[24]

4. If things take a favorable turn, consider the possibility of organizing a meeting between Sakharov and Soviet and foreign journalists at the Press Center of the USSR Ministry of Foreign Affairs, an account of which might be reported on Soviet television.

5. The USSR Ministry of Foreign Affairs, jointly with the Department of Propaganda of the CPSU Central Committee, should prepare additional briefing materials for Soviet embassies on Sakharov's life in Moscow and his activities [in general].

With the passage of time, it may well be possible to take additional steps with regard to working with Academician Sakharov, including a reconsideration and possible revocation of the decision to strip Sakharov of his state awards and honorary titles, as well as inviting him to participate in the forthcoming international forum "For a Nonnuclear World, For the Survival of Mankind."[25]

We ask that this be given consideration.

---

Chebrikov sent Gorbachev fragments of a recorded conversation between Sakharov and two leaders of the Federation of American Scientists, Jeremy Stone and Frank von Hippel ("obtained through operational means").

· DOCUMENT 192 ·

Chebrikov to Gorbachev, June 19, 1987
Sakharov and two American physicists discuss disarmament

---

. . . *Sakharov:* I know there was a discussion as to whether Reagan's strategic [defense] initiative violates the agreement on antimissile defense. If so, at which stage? I think the American side always recog-

---

24. Such an interview actually took place: on December 30, 1986, two journalists from *Literaturnaya Gazeta*, Oleg Moroz and Yuri Rost, approached Sakharov for an interview. They met with him in early January 1987, but the interview was never published. See details in Andrei Sakharov, *Moscow and Beyond, 1986–1989* (New York, 1991), 7–8, and the account by Oleg Moroz in *Andrei Dmitrievich: Vospominaniia o Sakharove* [Andrei Dmitrievich: Recollections of Sakharov] (Moscow, 1990), 271–366.

25. Several of their recommendations were adopted. In February 1987, Sakharov participated in the international forum and the press conference that followed. On October 13, 1988, the government annulled the withdrawal of his state prizes and awards.

nized that the development and expansion of military systems into space is a violation of the agreement on antimissile defense.

*Stone:* I want to give you a letter from Senator Edward Kennedy.

*Sakharov:* Here is a kind invitation from Edward Kennedy to come to the USA. This is always a complicated question for me. I have a fixed position toward all the invitations I have recently received. The representatives of Soviet authorities have repeatedly and officially declared that I have no opportunity to leave the USSR for any kind of trip. I had access to secret work. Therefore, I myself am not undertaking any steps with respect to my departure. I think that for this to have any point, it is necessary that Soviet authorities change their position on this question. This can happen in two cases: if this is needed by the authorities for political considerations, or if foreign political figures and organizations exert very powerful pressure that could force a change in policy here. With respect to the second avenue, I think that here one needs such powerful, concentrated efforts that they are no longer commensurate with the goal. There are many other important tasks with respect to putting pressure on Soviet authorities. I think that, on my part, I cannot be the initiator of such campaigns and bring about a change in respect to my security status.

---

That October, Sakharov helped to organize Moscow Tribune, an independent political club that was intended to provide a forum for liberal figures such as he to express their views on the country's ongoing problems. The KGB could not help but monitor its activities.

This document was signed by Vladimir Kryuchkov, who had recently succeeded Chebrikov as chairman of the KGB.

## · DOCUMENT 194 ·

Kryuchkov to Central Committee, October 15, 1988
The establishment of Moscow Tribune

---

The Committee for State Security of the USSR reports for your information that on October 12, 1988, in a building at the Moscow Historical-Archival Institute, a founding meeting of a public discussion club, "Moscow Tribune," was convened, with the participation of more than 130 people. The founders of the club, Yu. N. Afanasiev, A. D. Sakharov, L. M. Batkin, Yu. G. Burtin, Yu. F. Karyakin, L. V. Karpinsky, A. M. Adamovich, M. M. Gefter, and A. V. Migdal,[26] sent invitations to persons who—

---

26. This list is inaccurate; neither Mikhail Gefter nor Arkady Migdal took part in

in their opinion—are "members of the elite, well protected, with status, and wielding influence."

At the beginning of the meeting, L. M. Batkin read a statement concerning the founding of "Moscow Tribune." The statement, among other things, asserts that "the club unites fragmented intellectual and creative forces in order to promote the transformation of our society into one with a modern, highly efficient economy, with genuine democracy and the rule of law, and with responsible foreign, military, and ecological policies under the control of democratic institutions. We believe that we can help implement the present political course of the CPSU leadership only if we succeed in preserving the capacity to exercise independent, sober, and critical judgments of that course."

According to the ideas of the club's founders, it should function as an "Academy of Political Sciences." Its main activity, as announced, will be to hold regular discussions on the most important problems in economics, nationality issues, law, international politics, and culture. To study these problems, there are plans to organize study groups (as part of the club) and to publish a weekly bulletin, the *Moscow Tribune,* as a cooperative, self-financing enterprise. To handle everyday business, a bureau with a technical secretary will be elected for one year; to secure financial independence for the work of the club and to acquire photocopying equipment, a membership fee of 100 rubles has been established.

Twenty-two people participated in the discussions. They include: Yu. P. Lisovsky (Institute of the International Workers' Movement), E. L. Feinberg (Lebedev Institute of Physics of the USSR Academy of Sciences), S. G. Dzarasov (USSR Academy of Sciences), V. M. Volkenshtein (a corresponding member of the USSR Academy of Sciences), V. L. Sheinis (Institute of World Economy), G. G. Guseinov (Institute of World Literature), A. M. Adamovich (a member of the USSR Union of Writers), G. O. Pavlovsky (of the journal "Twentieth Century and the World"), B. I. Chernykh (resident of Irkutsk; earlier convicted of anti-Soviet activities), Yu. F. Karyakin and L. A. Gordon (Institute of the International Workers' Movement), S. V. Kalistratova (a retired attorney and an active participant in antisocial actions), L. V. Altshuler (Doctor of Physics), A. D. Sakharov, and his wife, E. G. Bonner.

The speakers supported the idea of creating "Moscow Tribune" in or-

the first meeting of Moscow Tribune. Among those who discussed the creation of this forum was Academician S. Shatalin, but he soon withdrew from the group; see details in Sakharov, *Moscow and Beyond,* 56–57, 78–80.

der to make a critical analysis of government decision making, and they agreed to establish a provisional administrative bureau.

At the end of the meeting, the participants discussed two draft documents: "An Open Letter to the USSR Supreme Soviet Concerning Twenty Political Prisoners and the Rehabilitation of Those Freed Earlier" and "An Appeal to the USSR Supreme Soviet and the CPSU Party Commission on Meetings, Demonstrations, and Parades."

During the discussion of an appeal, "Toward Peace in Our Home" (on the events in the Nagorno-Karabakh Autonomous Region), participants differed in their opinions. It was decided to continue working on this appeal and adopt it at the next meeting of the club.

Appendix: Draft statement "On the Founding of a Political-Cultural Club, "Moscow Tribune," three pages, not classified.[27]

Sakharov was also involved in the initial efforts to organize the Memorial Society, one of the few organizations that emerged in the first years of perestroika that is still functioning today. He was among its original honorary chairmen. It works to document and commemorate the victims of seven decades of Communist rule in the Soviet Union and to campaign in defense of human rights in contemporary Russia.

· DOCUMENT 195 ·

Kryuchkov to Central Committee, November 16, 1988
The establishment of Memorial

On October 29–30, 1988, the conference of the so-called All-Union Voluntary Historical-Educational Society "Memorial" was held in Moscow (at the Central House of Cinematographers).

According to the available information, about 600 people participated in its work. The Credentials Commission registered 338 representatives from 58 cities in the country; 220 of them came from Moscow and Moscow Region. The presidium, among others, included: Academician A. D. Sakharov; the writers A. N. Rybakov, B. Sh. Okudzhava, and R. A. Medvedev; and the secretaries of cultural unions Yu. P. Platonov, Yu. B. Solovev, T. T. Salakhov, and A. F. Yermakov.

27. This document was not accepted because no agreement had been reached on the issue of membership in Moscow Tribune. The appended text was not included.

As a whole, the organizing committee and advisory council failed to channel the work of the conference into a constructive exchange of opinions on the draft version of the organization's founding charter and on the main directions of its activity. Only a few speeches, mainly by representatives of societies and groups from other cities in the country, touched upon these questions.

The work of the conference, along with its overtly political and at times anti-Party orientation, was defined by the speeches of representatives from the "Moscow initiative group 'Memorial,'" the "Democratic Union," the "Moscow People's Front," the nonofficial journals *Glasnost* and *Express Chronicle,* as well as in speeches by a number of persons known for their antisocial statements.

It is worth noting that while some of the conference participants tried to introduce a healthy note into the proceedings, they failed to influence the whole process of the discussion.[28] On the whole, it was evident that the organizers were disorganized and not prepared to run the conference. Had they made minimal prior preparation for active and constructive participation, the entire character of the discussion could have taken a different, positive direction.

The speakers, Bogoraz-Brukhman, Bonner, Krivenko, Skubko, Timofeev, Roginsky, Aksiuchits, and several others, promoted the idea of a detailed study of all the periods of repressions, from 1917 until the present time, as one of the main directions of the society's research activity. That is because, in their opinion, "the repression continues today." "We are responsible for all the terror in the history of our country, both for the 'red' terror, and the 'white' terror," declared Bonner.

In Skubko's words, "Despite perestroika, the political system of our country remains essentially a political system of Stalinism." He proposed the adoption of a resolution that would declare that "destalinization cannot be realized as long as there is a one-party system operating in the country."

The writer and columnist Volkov, who called himself "a prisoner of the Solovetsky camp," declared in his speech that "he could not draw a clear line of demarcation between the repressions that preceded Stalin and the Stalinist repressions." In his words, "those whom the Germans brought in a sealed railroad car conducted an experiment on the country in 1917."[29]

---

28. Approximately three-quarters of a line was deleted from the declassified photocopy.

29. This is an allusion to Lenin and his fellow Bolsheviks.

According to him, "they should have thought about what this experiment would cost." The speaker then emphasized that "if the experiment began to fail, the leader's hand would not have trembled during executions."

A member of the so called "Democratic Union," Roginsky, suggested that the list of victims should include all the victims, including Trotskyites, Banderites,[30] participants of nationalist military groups in the Baltics, and others. In his opinion, the "Memorial" Society should become the political successor to the so-called "Helsinki Watch Group" that used to function in the USSR, and it should actively defend human rights both in our country and abroad. As a model of a historically accurate work, he cited "A Chronicle of Current Events," which had been illegally issued at an earlier time. As collaborators in the production of this journal, he named several people who had served terms under criminal charges: Velikanova, Kovalev, Podrabinek, Svetov, Kalistratova, and Bonner. The introduction of these persons to the audience led to a stormy ovation.

Aksiuchits read a resolution calling for the "restoration of historical justice to Solzhenitsyn," which was adopted by an overwhelming majority of votes.

An economist, Krivenko, declared that "the Soviet Union is 'an evil empire' not only for Americans, but for our friends from socialist countries as well," since "all the tragic events in those countries were orchestrated from Moscow."

Academician Sakharov proposed to make an addition to the procedure for the forthcoming census, namely, by preparing a supplementary questionnaire to collect full statistical information about persons who were repressed during the years of Stalin's personality cult. Zedin, Kotlyar, and Dobroshtan (speakers who had been repressed earlier) proposed that Academician Sakharov be nominated as "Memorial's" candidate for deputy in the Supreme Soviet of the USSR. They and some others demanded that pensions be established for persons who suffered during the period of the personality cult, that these people be treated the same as participants in the Great Patriotic War, and that an honorary title, "Victim of Stalinist Repressions," be established.

Dryubin, who introduced himself as a freelance journalist and also as

30. The followers of Stepan Bandera (1909–59), a Ukrainian nationalist who helped to proclaim the establishment of an independent Ukrainian state on June 30, 1941, a week after the Nazi invasion. Because he refused to withdraw this proclamation, he was arrested by the Germans and interned at the Sachsenhausen concentration camp. He survived the war but was assassinated by a KGB agent in Munich on October 15, 1959.

someone who had been repressed in the past, declared that the main task of "Memorial" is to unite all the forces for the political struggle [against the Communist Party]. At the end of his speech he turned to the audience with a provocative question: "What will you do if the Stalinist times return?" In response to this question, cries were heard from the audience: "We will take up arms and fight."

The representative of the Crimean Tatars, Adelseitov, appealed to the organizing committee of "Memorial" to join the struggle for the fastest possible return of the Crimean Tatars to their historic motherland. One of the leaders of the so-called "Jewish Cultural Organization," Chlenov, appealed to "Memorial" to assist in defending the interests of the Jewish people, who are still, to this day, allegedly being subjected to "racial and cultural genocide."

There was practically no discussion during the conference of the draft charter of the All-Union Voluntary Historical-Educational Society "Memorial." Each speaker considered himself obliged either to speak about himself or to advance his own political platform. It is worth noting that representatives of the so-called "Democratic Union" attempted to turn the society into an opposition political party and to use the podium of "Memorial" for the promotion of their extremist ideas. These statements by members of this "Union" did not receive a proper rebuff from the audience.

The following incident shows the extreme tension in the hall. Skubko, in response to someone's critical comment about his unseemly conduct at the podium, started a fight in the foyer by striking Yermakov, the organizational secretary of the USSR Union of Cinematographers.

American and West German television journalists were in the hall and taped the conference. Reported for purposes of information.

· DOCUMENT 196 ·

Kryuchkov to Gorbachev, June 30, 1989
More on Moscow Tribune

In the fall of 1988, at the initiative of a group of representatives of science and culture (Yu. Afanasiev, A. Sakharov, L. Batkin, Yu. Burtin, L. Karpinsky, Yu. Karyakin, and others), a public politico-cultural discussion club, "Moscow Tribune," was founded. . . . At present "Moscow

Tribune" has about 200 members, of whom 30 are USSR people's deputies.[31] A bureau of fifteen people provides general leadership.[32]

To judge from the club's activities, its main effort is directed at having the intelligentsia exert influence on the Party-state apparatus in resolving political, economic, and social questions. Another goal is to "use the intellectual potential of the club to unite and coordinate an informal movement." Individual club members propagate the idea that it is necessary to counterpoise grassroots social groups and associations (including those of a nationalist and separatist persuasion) against the Party and state bodies on the subject of implementing perestroika. They challenge the leading role of the CPSU.

"Moscow Tribune" gives considerable attention to social and economic reform in the country. Along with constructive suggestions on the implementation of changes, they make appeals "to defer reforms until we have an effective government" and to adopt the slogans "All Power to the Soviets" and "Restore capitalism through constitutional means." As some members of the club maintain, "The official doctrine—the concept of communism—lacks any scientific foundation and is a bogus idea; what is needed is private property and complete freedom of expression, not just glasnost."

During the period when the Congress of People's Deputies of the USSR was being prepared and conducted, "Moscow Tribune" made an attempt to create a "faction of left-radical independent deputies." It prepared the faction's political platform and alternative draft proposals for various aspects of perestroika; the purpose was to oppose what the club members regarded as the "administrative-Party system" that the majority of deputies represented at the Congress. The essential tenets of "Moscow Tribune" are reflected in the speeches made by club members—People's Deputies A. Adamovich, Yu. Afanasiev, Yu. Karyakin, G. Popov, A. Sakharov, and others. Simultaneously, in order to compile a social and political portrait of the Congress, the club organized a sociological study of the deputies

31. Elected members of the Congress of People's Deputies. Created in November 1988 by a special session of the Supreme Soviet, this body of 2,250 members was to elect the president of the Soviet Union by secret ballot and choose a newly restructured Supreme Soviet of 422 members to review legislative and administrative acts. The Congress was elected on March 26, 1989. The Communist Party was the only legal party and won 87 percent of the seats. Among the few outsiders to be elected was Sakharov, who, after a bitter fight, was elected to represent the Academy of Sciences.

32. Notice the change of tone in Kryuchkov's reports; now he is dealing with a legally recognized opposition.

and their platforms. In the future, the club plans to use the data from this study for work targeted at deputies who "lean toward the left radicals" and, in the long run, to create a "democratic majority."

On June 16, 1989, at the club's last meeting before the "summer holiday," it analyzed the results of the Congress of People's Deputies of the USSR and the tasks of "Moscow Tribune" for the period preceding the Second Congress.

Together with some positive evaluations of the Congress, the members of the "Tribune" insisted that "it did not justify expectations, since a political opposition was not created; the speeches by Gorbachev and Ryzhkov demonstrated that the CPSU is unable to change or improve anything." They declared that "the CPSU is losing its power and authority; one must demonstrate to the people that only the intelligentsia can provide leadership for society; perestroika from above has reached its maximum limits; the intelligentsia should take the fate of the country into its hands; it is impossible to be oriented solely toward Gorbachev."

A member of the club's bureau, Batkin, declared: "We are on the eve of unprecedented riots, and therefore, in practical terms, openness has become advantageous. At the Congress we discovered that the intra-Party struggle has reached the point of no return. People have become disillusioned with Gorbachev. A dual power system is dangerous. Power must be taken from the Party. This is possible only under a parliamentary democracy."

"Moscow Tribune" set for itself the task of "uniting and politicizing the elements of an emerging civil society." The club should become "the intellectual bridge between the deputies, public opinion, and scientific experts." It proposed to prepare, before the Second Congress of People's Deputies (and taking into account the experience of the First Congress), a solid alternative statement that presents an alternative platform." This is to be based on the following fundamental principles:

- Equal rights for Communists and noncommunists.
- Independence of the mass media.
- Equality of all peoples and nations, with a new treaty of the [Soviet] Union.
- New laws on elections, land, and the press.
- Complete openness in government policies.
- Transfer of power from the CPSU to the soviets.
- Elimination of the Party apparatus.
- Creation of an open opposition based on the Interregional Group of Deputies.

At the club's meeting, some recommended that "in its work the Congress must take into account the social psychology of the masses and especially their low level," and therefore it must not inflame passions with unorthodox slogans about "the restoration of capitalism" and the like. It is better to stir up emotions through the press, not from the podium of the Congress. One should be oriented toward "independent" support of Gorbachev; one should support, not fight, the "centrists," and seek an alliance with the "agrarians." Before the Second Congress begins, it is necessary to strengthen ties with the corps of deputies and with voters, to organize talks at factory clubs and "roundtables," and to discuss publicly Sakharov's "Decree on Power" and a new draft for a Union treaty, and so forth.[33]

It was announced at the meeting that a "Leningrad Tribune," an organization analogous to "Moscow Tribune," had been set up in Leningrad. . . .

---

Sakharov was now extending his contacts within the country to striking miners in far-off Vorkuta, a thousand miles northeast of Moscow, above the Arctic Circle. Such efforts echoed the work of the Polish Committee for the Defense of Workers (KOR), an organization of intellectuals and workers who found ways to cooperate in opposition to Communist rule. And the Vorkuta miners were not only looking to invoke Sakharov's prestige on behalf of their cause; they understood that he was someone they could trust.

### · DOCUMENT 197 ·

Kryuchkov to Gorbachev, November 14, 1989
Sakharov's influence on the labor movement in the Vorkuta mining region

---

According to information at the disposal of the KGB, the Vorkuta Strike Committee is widely distributing information about Academician A. D. Sakharov's support for the strike movement among the miners. Great significance is attached to his endorsement of the miners' political demands as well as the decisiveness and purposefulness of their actions. Sakharov is very disturbed by "the unhealthy atmosphere that is being artificially cre-

---

33. The text of Sakharov's "Decree on Power" can be found in his *Moscow and Beyond*, 152–53. As Sakharov explains, it was designed to reinforce the power of the Congress of People's Deputies.

ated around the striking miners" and intends to do everything possible to provide them with qualified legal counsel when the legality of the strike is reviewed by the Supreme Court of the RSFSR. He also supports the efforts of the city strike committee to obtain help from American trade unions and to establish an independent trade union of Vorkuta miners.

On November 13, the internal radio network of the mine, Khalmer-Yu, broadcast the contents of Academician Sakharov's response to the appeal sent to him from the strike committee. In his reply, Sakharov declared: "You are doing something important. I personally support your strike and your demands, and I believe that they contribute to the general workers' movement and to the entire country's struggle against the Stalinist bureaucratic apparatus. This is especially important in our difficult economic and political situation." Sakharov does not rule out visiting Vorkuta and speaking before the miners. . . .

---

Sakharov was prepared to move beyond support for a localized strike by disgruntled miners in Vorkuta. By December, he and four other members of the Congress of People's Deputies were issuing a call for a general warning strike to demand immediate substantive reform, including repeal of Article 6 of the Soviet Constitution.[34] The announcement was widely broadcast and reported in the Western press.[35]

· DOCUMENT 198 ·

Kryuchkov to Central Committee, December 4, 1989
Sakharov's call for a general strike

---

According to information received, USSR People's Deputies A. D. Sakharov, A. N. Murashov, G. Kh. Popov, V. A. Tikhonov, and Yu. D. Chernichenko prepared and are now circulating in our country and abroad an "Appeal to Our Fellow Countrymen" (the text is attached). The authors of the document negatively assess the results of the legislative activity of the Supreme Soviet of the USSR and assert that "perestroika is encountering organized resistance."[36] They are appealing to all workers

---

34. This was the 1977 Brezhnev Constitution of the USSR, whose Article 6 stated: "The Communist Party of the Soviet Union is the leading and guiding force of Soviet society, the nucleus of its political system of state and public organizations. The CPSU exists for the people and serves the people."

35. *New York Times*, December 6, 1989, 24.

36. The Communist Party's dominance at the Congress of People's Deputies (and by

in the country to conduct, on December 11, 1989, between 10 A.M. and 12 noon (Moscow time), "a general political warning strike to demand that discussion of the laws on land, property, enterprises, and Article 6 of the Constitution be included in the agenda of the Second Congress of USSR People's Deputies." They also propose to set up "strike committees" in places where people work and study.

On December 2, 1989, the text of the "Appeal" was publicly read and endorsed at meetings of "Moscow Tribune" and "the All-Union Conference of Voters' Alliances and Democratic Organizations." Speaking to the participants of the "conference," A. D. Sakharov declared that "the strike is meant to accelerate perestroika and may become its turning point; given the political character of the strike, it cannot be judged unlawful, and its brevity guarantees that it poses no threat to the economy." In his opinion, the orientation of the strike "will promote the success of the political course of the country's leadership and will help M. S. Gorbachev, during his negotiations with [President George H. W.] Bush, demonstrate the strength of the democratization process in the Soviet Union. We should not fall behind the countries of Eastern Europe, where the entire population went on strike for several days." In conclusion, Sakharov appealed to all those present "to provide the initial jolt, to mobilize people for this strike."

In order to realize the call for a strike, "Moscow Tribune" activists—L. M. Batkin, G. Ya. Kovalskaya, and others—intend to set up an organizing committee including people's deputies and members of grassroots associations, and also to launch an active propaganda "campaign of support" among the population. For these purposes, they plan to duplicate the "Appeal" and circulate it widely in the streets and squares, at the entrances to factories and plants, at subway stations and other densely populated points in Moscow, Leningrad, and other cities in the country. Reported for purposes of information.

## Appendix
## Appeal

Dear fellow countrymen!

Perestroika in our country is encountering organized resistance. There are persistent delays in adopting fundamental economic laws "on property," "on enterprises," and (most important of all) "on land," which

---

extension in the Supreme Soviet) created strong resistance to further economic and political reform.

would finally give the peasant the right to become his own master. The Supreme Soviet of the USSR has not included in the agenda of the Congress [of People's Deputies] Article 6 of the Constitution of the USSR.

If the law on land is not adopted, yet another agricultural year will be lost. If the laws on property and enterprises are not adopted, the ministries and state agencies will continue, as before, to command and ruin the country. If Article 6 is not removed from the Constitution, the crisis of trust in the leadership of the state and Party will increase.

We urge all the toilers of the country—workers, peasants, intelligentsia, students—to express their will and, on December 11, 1989, between 10 and 12 noon (Moscow time), conduct a general political warning strike, with a demand that the Second Congress of People's Deputies of the USSR include on its agenda the laws on land, property, enterprises, and Article 6 of the Constitution.

Establish committees to conduct this strike in enterprises, organizations, collective and state farms, and educational institutions.

Property to the people!
Land to the peasants!
Factories to the workers!
All power to the soviets!
Moscow, December 1, 1989

People's Deputies of the USSR: A. D. Sakharov, V. A. Tikhonov, G. Kh. Popov, A. N. Murashov, Yu. D. Chernichenko

Ever since Sakharov's return to Moscow, his stature with the public had only grown. Now that he was an elected member of the country's newly established Congress of People's Deputies, he was becoming known to broader circles of people. His ideas and advocacy of systemic reform were finding support, a development that concerned the KGB and Gorbachev himself.

· DOCUMENT 199 ·

Kryuchkov to Gorbachev, December 8, 1989
Sakharov's radical ideas and his growing support

In their practical activities and theoretical models, many radical grassroots organizations frequently make use of Academician Sakharov's assessment of the processes transpiring in the USSR. Propaganda support from abroad, the opportunity to make his views public, and the uncritical coverage of Sakharov's activity by Soviet mass media have allowed him to strengthen significantly his standing among certain circles of the scientific and cultural intelligentsia.

Although he regards the idea of perestroika itself positively, he has not changed his overall negative attitude toward the experience of socialist construction in our country.

His election as a people's deputy of the USSR was perceived by his followers in our country and abroad as a change in his status from "an individual human rights activist" to becoming one of the leaders of a legal opposition. This circumstance, in particular, has given him the opportunity not only to propagate personally his ideological blueprints but also to endeavor to implement them through other deputies of the Interregional Group.[37] With some variations, he expounds his views on the situation in the country and the development of perestroika in the Supreme Soviet as well as in numerous interviews and public statements at public meetings.

In his opinion, the current crisis in the USSR "was predetermined by the October Revolution and the entire subsequent history of the country." At present, according to Sakharov, power belongs to a "two-headed force"— the Party and the administrative-economic apparatus—which are supported by the army and the KGB. As a result, he proposes to introduce a multiparty system in the country and to transfer power to soviets freed from the influence of the CPSU. Believing that the Supreme Soviet cannot represent the interests of the whole nation (given the predominance there of the apparatchiks), Sakharov insistently advocates the idea of transferring its functions to the Congress of People's Deputies.

With respect to the nationality question, A. D. Sakharov begins with the premise that it is necessary to destroy what he calls the "imperial constitutional structure of the USSR," which is an "instrument for the oppression of other peoples." In lieu of this structure, he proposes an association of independent republics based on a new Union treaty. In keeping with this approach, Sakharov assesses positively the activity of separatist groups in a number of Union republics, regarding them as national liberation movements. At the same time, he considers the CPSU platform on the national

37. The Interregional Group was a loose alliance of people's deputies who opposed the Communist Party and demanded more radical reforms than Gorbachev was willing to accept.

question to be "absolute insanity," and believes that its realization would inevitably lead to some of the republics' leaving the USSR.

A. D. Sakharov propagates the idea that there is a growing crisis of confidence in the present leadership, which is due (in his words) "to lack of consistency on the part of the supreme leadership of the Party and state." In his public pronouncements he asserts that the First Congress of People's Deputies was followed by a "retreat" in the process of democratizing society and that total power has been concentrated in the hands of the chairman of the Supreme Soviet, and that this has led to limits on glasnost in the mass media and to attempts by the "apparatus" to set workers and peasants against the intelligentsia. A. D. Sakharov claims that the driving force of perestroika is an oppositionist intelligentsia and that it is capable of leading the working class. In this connection, despite his positive evaluation of the strike movement in the summer and fall of 1989, he condemns the creation of the "United Workers Front."

A. D. Sakharov has repeatedly declared that perestroika realizes the ideas of the so-called "human rights activists" who were earlier persecuted and whom the authorities are in no hurry to rehabilitate. In order to prevent a further "drift of the country to the right," he appeals to the West to make economic aid to the Soviet Union directly dependent on "the observance of legality with respect to human rights" in our country.

Although A. D. Sakharov himself is not an organizer of the activities of radically oriented deputies and members of unofficial associations, he has become their banner, a unique moral symbol and the author of many political initiatives. Thus, he was one of the first to suggest the need for repeal of Article 6 of the USSR Constitution, which later became a key demand of the radicals. His "Decree on Power" served as a political platform both for the Interregional Group of deputies and for many voters' clubs. His idea about the need for a radical change in the structure of the USSR, through the efforts of People's Deputies Yu. N. Afanasiev and G. V. Starovoitova, was adopted by the conferences of "democratic movements and organizations" in Leningrad and Chelyabinsk.

Recently A. D. Sakharov has demonstrated a marked disdain for any suggestions emanating from our country's top authorities, and he often tries to block them or to counter them with his own initiatives, such as his alternative draft for a USSR constitution.

Doing everything possible to aggravate the situation in the country, he was one of the sponsors of the appeal to conduct a general political warning strike on December 11, 1989. In his interview with French radio on

December 2, Sakharov did not exclude the possibility of embarking on still more radical actions.

Taking into account Sakharov's ambitious nature and the excessive attention accorded him by the news media, it is to be expected that he will continue his attempts to play the role of "generator of ideas for the opposition." The activists surrounding him, employees of various institutes of the USSR Academy of Sciences (who earlier participated in his election campaign), are also encouraging him to do this. . . .

Kryuchkov described attempts by Sakharov and others to mobilize support for a general strike on December 11. The report reflects the regime's growing anxiety about domestic opposition and political stability in the country.

· DOCUMENT 200 ·

Kryuchkov to Central Committee, December 8, 1989
The impending general strike

Supplement to no. 2451-K/ov of December 4, 1989.

According to information received, the "Appeal to Citizens" prepared on December 1 by a group of USSR people's deputies is being circulated throughout the Soviet Union by various grassroots organizations. The tone of this campaign has been set by the people's deputies themselves. Thus, A. Sakharov personally handed the text of the "Appeal" to Agence France-Presse. The "Appeal," together with commentaries by Sakharov and Afanasiev, has been aired repeatedly by foreign radio stations broadcasting to the USSR.

At present, the circulation of this document has been reported in Moscow, Kharkov, Krasnoyarsk, Ussuriisk, Smolensk, and a number of other cities around the country as well as among workers' collectives in the coal fields of Donbass, Vorkuta, and Kemerovo. The workers' reaction to this "Appeal" is primarily negative. Thus, the Council of Workers' Committees in Kemerovo Oblast considers the strike pointless, and in Vorkuta the appeal was supported only by the Strike Committee at the "Vorgashorskaya" mine. Participants in the so- called All-Union Conference of Voters' Associations and Democratic Organizations, with representatives of 42 cities of the RSFSR and of several Union republics, which convened in Moscow on December 2–3, supported Sakharov's speech calling for a strike.

Sensing the vulnerability of their position, the authors of the "Appeal"

are obliged to maneuver and justify their actions in order to minimize its
negative effect. Thus, on December 6, during a meeting with representatives of workers' collectives of Moscow, Afanasiev declared: "The warning strike is necessary in order to obtain substantive results at the Congress. This strike is a way of involving the masses in political activity. Our appeal is not a binding demand to start a strike. This appeal will help everyone to determine his or her position. Our appeal is meant to be advice, a recommendation. From an economic point of view, the strike will cause no harm, but it will be an effective way of exerting influence."

In his interview with the BBC, A. Sakharov echoed Afanasiev and stated that the "two-hour strike does not endanger the economy of the country."

The Committee for State Security continues to monitor the situation created by the appeal for a strike. . . .

---

Sakharov died suddenly at home on the evening of December 14. He was in the midst of a difficult debate in the Congress of People's Deputies over Article 6 of the Constitution, which granted the Communist Party a monopoly of political control. He had also completed a draft of a new constitution that was designed to address the need for democratic accountability and to establish a new federal structure for the Soviet Union in order to preserve the unity of the country. Sakharov's death set off a wave of demonstrations in his memory.

· DOCUMENT 201 ·

Kryuchkov to Central Committee, December 18, 1989
The funeral of Andrei Sakharov

---

On December 17, between 1 and 11 P.M., the farewell ceremony for USSR People's Deputy Academician A. D. Sakharov was held in Moscow's Palace of Youth. About 50,000 residents and visitors to the capital, among them over one hundred USSR people's deputies and diplomatic representatives from the embassies of Great Britain, the USA, the Federal Republic of Germany, Canada, France, Belgium, and Poland participated in the ceremony. Some of the numerous wreaths in the funeral hall came from the Popular Workers' Union [NTS], "Citizens of Israel," "Democratic Union," "Russian People's Front." There was also a floral arrangement from A. Solzhenitsyn.

About 150 representatives of foreign mass media were present; they actively interviewed people and took video films and photographs.

Several Soviet citizens carried signs reading: "Andrei Dmitrievich, we vow to be faithful to your banner," "We will carry on Sakharov's work, the struggle for democracy," and so on. A group of citizens from the town of Zelenograd carried signs with the slogan: "Down with Article 6 of the USSR Constitution"; some wore badges on their clothing symbolizing its abrogation. A delegation of twelve people from the Ukrainian National Movement ("Rukh") arrived with a yellow and blue flag[38] to bid farewell to Academician A. D. Sakharov.

Funeral services were conducted in the Church of the Assumption in the Novodevichy Convent and the Patriarch's Church of the Epiphany.

On the same day, meetings to commemorate Sakharov's death took place in Novosibirsk, Vorkuta, Yaroslavl, Kalinin, Kiev, Odessa, Kharkov, Lvov, Ivano-Frankovsk, and other cities around the country. They were organized by various unofficial associations, and negative sentiments were sometimes voiced at them. Thus, in Lvov and Ivano-Frankovsk, the crowd displayed nationalist symbols and called for a work stoppage of 5 to 10 minutes at industrial enterprises on December 18. A representative of the Strike Committee of the "Vorgashorskaya" mine in Vorkuta, Pimenov, declared publicly that "for 72 years the Party has strangled everything that is alive. . . ."

· DOCUMENT 202 ·

Kryuchkov to Central Committee, December 20, 1989
More on the funeral of Andrei Sakharov

On December 18, 1989, the funeral ceremonies for Academician A. D. Sakharov were completed. After the farewell ceremonies at the building of the Presidium of the USSR Academy of Sciences and at the Lebedev Physics Institute of the USSR Academy of Sciences,[39] the funeral cortege proceeded toward the Luzhniki sports complex. The bus with Sakharov's coffin was accompanied on its final stage by a crowd of about 20,000 people, some of whom, organized beforehand by representatives of grassroots public associations, carried Russian, Ukrainian, Moldavian, and Latvian national flags, and also banners with these inscriptions: "You were a ray

38. Two years later these colors adorned the national flag of an independent Ukraine.
39. Gorbachev was joined by Alexander Yakovlev and other members of the Politburo during the service at the Lebedev Institute.

of light in the kingdom of darkness amidst an aggressive-submissive majority," and "Even dead you terrify them,"[40] and others.

Approximately 40,000 people (including 300 people's deputies of the USSR) took part in the memorial service, which started in Luzhniki at 2 P.M. Twenty-six people spoke: fourteen people's deputies of the USSR, Deputy Prime Minister Martelli of Italy, Senator Romaszewski of the People's Republic of Poland,[41] Metropolitan Pitirim, the priest Gleb Yakunin, and representatives of grassroots associations.

In their speeches they talked about Sakharov's contributions to the world community, about his tireless struggle for human rights, and expressed their support for his activity. Some of the speakers tried, in effect, to canonize the late academician, to turn him into a unique symbol of the struggle to realize the goals of groups that oppose the CPSU.

A member of the Interregional Group, Murashov, declared that following Sakharov's behest the group is ready to declare itself a parliamentary opposition group. People's Deputy of the USSR Yu. N. Afanasiev sharply criticized the work of the Second Congress and appealed [to the deputies] "to unite into a single 'Sakharov Democratic Bloc.'" The representative of the coordinating council of the association "Shield," Major Moskovchenko, insisted that "the decisive battle against Stalinist-Brezhnevite bastards still lies ahead."

At 4 P.M., after the official part of the memorial service was over, the majority of the gathering left the site. However, for another forty minutes, representatives of grassroots associations attempted to conduct what was in fact an independent meeting of a provocative character.

At the entrance to Vostryakovskoe Cemetery, starting at 5 P.M. and lasting for thirty minutes, the farewell to the deceased took place. The following people participated: the leader of Polish "Solidarity," Lech Walesa;[42] the U.S. ambassador in Moscow, [Jack] Matlock; other representatives of

40. The KGB continued to gather information on Sakharov and his family even after his death. A sample of Bonner's secretly and illegally recorded conversations was published in V. Stepankov and E. Lisov, *Kremlevskii zagovor: Versiia sledstviia* [A Kremlin plot: A version of the investigation] (Perm, 1993), 196.

41. This was the same Zbigniew Romaszewski who visited Sakharov in Moscow in January 1979, when Romaszewski was active in the Polish opposition group KOR (Committee for the Defense of Workers). Romaszewski would be arrested in 1981 during the crackdown on Solidarity. He returned to Moscow for Sakharov's funeral as a democratically elected senator.

42. Walesa could not attend the ceremony at the cemetery because his airplane inexplicably landed in Leningrad rather than Moscow. Walesa eventually arrived in time for the dinner ceremony. The burial itself took place later than scheduled because the police escort drove the procession around for an hour before heading for the cemetery.

the diplomatic corps, foreign correspondents, and members of the Interregional Group of People's Deputies.

After the burial a funeral banquet for 510 persons was held at the restaurant of the Hotel "Rossiya."

The funeral ceremonies demonstrated that the intentions of certain circles to exploit Sakharov's death for political purposes were not borne out. Contrary to their plans, the ceremonies failed to attract hundreds of thousands of people. That is why all the funeral ceremonies were deliberately prolonged, and attempts were made to ensure that as many people as possible (especially students) participated in the funeral ceremonies. Nor did appeals in some regions of the country—for mass demonstrations, for work stoppages, for naming streets, squares, and residential areas after Sakharov—elicit any kind of broad support. . . .

· DOCUMENT 203 ·

Kryuchkov to Central Committee, December 23, 1989
The political consequences of Sakharov's death

Dealing with this event [Sakharov's death],[43] American diplomats comment that A. Sakharov was "a major influential representative of social thought in the second half of the twentieth century; both in the USSR and in the West, he symbolized the democratic liberal opposition movement." According to their statements, "A. Sakharov was more a unifying symbol for the diverse mass of democratic forces in the USSR than a real political figure." He enjoyed great confidence in the West, the trust of many people's deputies and representatives of the intelligentsia, and the admiration of university students. Despite the fact that Sakharov "had lately been prone to idealism in his political moods and in a number of cases preached a destructive radicalism, he enjoyed the respect of his political opponents, including the CPSU leadership."

According to the American assessment, with Sakharov's death "the democratic opposition movement, as represented by the Interregional Group of People's Deputies and other political associations, find themselves in a difficult position." "The leaders of this movement do not enjoy any special trust of the people, since they unabashedly seek power and popularity, pursuing their selfish political goals and often resorting to un-

43. Several words have been deleted from the declassified text.

seemly means to achieve them." In addition, with the exception of B. Yeltsin, they are unknown in the West.

Discussing the causes of Sakharov's death, American diplomats believe that it was precipitated by great emotional and physical overexertion. To some degree, the academician's widow, E. Bonner, contributed to this by fanning her husband's political ambitions and by attempting to play on his pride.[44]

According to the words of embassy employees, E. Bonner did not behave properly when they offered her their assistance and expressed their condolences. She told the American correspondents who participated in Sakharov's funeral that, "through their intrusive attention and pestering on every pretext, they had hastened the death of A. Sakharov."[45]

E. Bonner intends to dedicate her activity to propagating widely, through the mass media of the USSR and the West, A. Sakharov's image as "the greatest humanist and leader." She plans to prepare for publication in the Soviet Union a number of A. Sakharov's books, and also to organize the showing of a documentary film on central television about her husband's activity. The academician's widow asked representatives of the U.S. embassy and American correspondents to assist her to send to the United States some valuable personal possessions, both Sakharov's and hers, as well as materials from his archive.[46] Reported for purposes of information.

---

44. Note that the criticism of Sakharov and Bonner that Kryuchkov attributes to unknown American diplomats and journalists is undistinguishable from the attacks the KGB had been making for years.

45. Approximately half a line is deleted from the declassified photocopy.

46. According to Bonner, she did not ask for any help in transporting archives or "valuable" possessions. Elena Bonner, interview with author, Brookline, MA 2003.

# Annotated List of KGB Documents

## Compiled by Alexander Gribanov

What follows is a comprehensive list of the secret police files of Academician Andrei Sakharov that were provided to his family after his death. The 146 documents included in this volume are drawn from this larger collection of KGB reports, which are stored in The Andrei Sakharov Archive at Houghton Library, Harvard University (SA). The entire set of documents, in Russian and in English translation, can be found at the following Web site: www.yale.edu/annals/sakharov/

The information in this list is structured in the following way:

1. The date the document was issued by the KGB.
2. The name of the person who signed it.
3. The title of the report. (The editors chose a title for each report; most of them were sent without a title.)
4. The number of folios.
5. The code of the document as issued by the KGB.
6. The archive that declassified the document and its reference marking in official Russian archives if provided in the process of declassification.
7. The code of the document in the Andrei Sakharov Archive (SA). A code beginning with *S* indicates that it can be found in the Andrei Sakharov Collection.
8. An asterisk indicates that the document is not included in this volume.

1. May 22, 1968. Andropov to Central Committee. The appearance of "Progress, Coexistence, and Intellectual Freedom." 3 folios. #1169-A/ov. APRF, #3, f. 3, op. 80, d. 637, ll. 20–23. SA, S.II.2.4.27. The coding suffix "ov" means *osobo vazhnyi* (especially important). Reports with such codes usually stayed in the personal archives of the general secretary of the CPSU, now the Archive of the President of the Russian Federation (APRF).

*2. May 27, 1968. Andropov to Central Committee. On the missing pages from Sakharov's manuscript. 1 folio. #1201-A/ov. APRF, #2, f. 3, op. 80, d. 637, l. 20. SA, S.II.2.4.27. A cover letter accompanied the missing pages. The Sakharov Archive has another, doctored copy from the collection transferred by the Federal Counterintelligence Service (FCS) on November 18, 1994, along with a distribution document signed and dated by several Politburo members. Brezhnev's signature was dated May 29, 1968. SA, S.II.2.6.70.

3. June 13, 1968. Andropov to Central Committee. Sakharov and the activity of other dissidents. 4 folios. #1395-A/ov. APRF, #3, f. 3, op. 80, d. 637, ll. 68–71. SA, S.II.2.4.28. There are marginal notes on the first and last pages.

4. July 18, 1968. Andropov to Central Committee. Moscow dissidents linked to Andrei Sakharov. 3 folios. #1681-A. FCS. SA, S.II.2.5.01.

5. August 4, 1968. Andropov to Central Committee. Sakharov and the dissident historian Roy Medvedev. 2 folios. #2095-A. The same document was later mentioned and mailed again from Bobkov to Lukianov under the code 1985, #1773-B. SA, Vladimir Bukovsky Collection, B.2.

6. August 26, 1968. Tsvigun to Central Committee. Growing Western interest in Soviet dissent. 1 folio. #2016-Ts. FCS. SA, S.II.2.5.03.

7. August 26, 1968. Tsvigun to Central Committee. How should the Kremlin respond to Sakharov's memorandum? 3 folios. #2017-Ts. FCS. SA, S.II.2.5.02.

*8. September 20, 1968. Andropov to Central Committee. The demonstration in Red Square against the Warsaw Pact invasion of Czechoslovakia. 3 folios. #2205-A. SA, Vladimir Bukovsky Collection, B.3.

*9. April 16, 1969. Andropov to Central Committee. The activities of Pyotr Grigorenko and his contacts with Sakharov. 4 folios. #887-A. SA, Vladimir Bukovsky Collection, B.4.

10. September 8, 1969. Andropov to Central Committee. Sakharov and the scientific bureaucracy. 3 folios. #2259-A. FCS. SA, S.II.2.5.04. Andropov was reporting on a memorandum by Chumakov of the Second Main Directorate (counterintelligence). His report was dated July 25, 1969; its code was #2/9–1894.

11. September 15, 1969. Andropov to Central Committee. Sakharov visits the Installation for the last time. 2 folios. #2312-A. FCS. SA, S.II.2.5.05.

12. March 30, 1970. Andropov to Central Committee. The second memorandum. 1 folio. #776-A/ov. APRF, #7, f. 3, op. 80, d. 637, l. 139. SA, S.II.2.4.32.

13. April 20, 1970. Andropov to Central Committee. The placing of eavesdropping equipment in Sakharov's apartment. 1 folio. #1069-A/ov. APRF, #170, f. 3, op. 80, d. 675, l. 152. SA, S.II.2.4.194. Marginal notes of consent are signed by Brezhnev, Kosygin, Podgorny, and other members of the Politburo.

*14. July 10, 1970. Andropov to Central Committee. Incidents during the trial of Natalya Gorbanevskaya and problems related to defense attorneys. 3 folios. #1878-A. SA, Vladimir Bukovsky Collection, B.5. There are signatures of consent by several Politburo members. There is also an enclosure with an excerpt from Central Committee Secretariat decision #102, paragraph 10, of July 17, 1970: "Directive to Moscow City Party Committee to consider issues raised by KGB report #1878-A."

15. October 5, 1970. Andropov to Central Committee. Sakharov and the Human Rights Committee. 2 folios. #2715-A/ov. APRF, #58, f. 3, op. 80, d. 640, ll. 42–43. SA, S.II.2.4.83. The signatures of Suslov, Kosygin, and other members of the Politburo appear in the margins.

16. November 18, 1970. Tsvigun to Central Committee. Sakharov is approaching other scientists to support the Human Rights Committee. 2 folios. #3163-Ts/ov. APRF, #8, f. 3, op. 80, d. 637, ll. 152–53. SA, S.II.2.4.33. There are marginal notes on the document. Sakharov's name was entered by hand in the typed text.

17. December 4, 1970. Andropov to Central Committee. The Human Rights Committee begins its work. 1 folio. #3300-A/ov. APRF, #10, f. 3, op. 80, d. 637, l. 154. SA, S.II.2.4.35. There are marginal notes and signatures on the document. According to the inventory prepared by APRF, additional folios numbered 155–60 were not released.

18. December 16, 1970. Andropov to Central Committee. Alexander Solzhenitsyn and the Human Rights Committee. 2 folios. #3402-A/ov. APRF, #11, f. 3, op. 80, d. 637, ll. 161–62. SA, S.II.2.4.36.

19. December 21, 1970. Andropov to Central Committee. The spread of samizdat. 4 folios. #3461-A. SA, Vladimir Bukovsky Collection, B.6. There are signatures of several Politburo members in the margins of the first page.

20. December 30, 1970. Andropov to Central Committee. Increased pres-

sure on the Human Rights Committee. 2 folios. #3539-A/ov. APRF, #12, f. 3, op. 80, d. 637, ll. 163–64. SA, S.II.2.4.37. Marginal note "Vkrugovuiu" (Circulate [among members of the Politburo]) with only Suslov's signature attached.

*21. January 13, 1971. Andropov to Central Committee. Contacts between foreign journalists and dissidents in Moscow. 2 folios. #77-A. FCS. SA, S.II.2.5.06.

22. January 13, 1971. Andropov to Central Committee. The trial of Angela Davis in the United States and the trial of Jewish would-be airplane hijackers in the Soviet Union. 2 folios. #80-A/ov. APRF, #14, f. 3, op. 80, d. 638, ll. 2–4. SA, S.II.2.4.39. Names were inserted by hand in the typed text. Enclosed was the Russian translation of the cable signed by Martin U. Hillenbrand, assistant secretary of state for European affairs.

23. January 18, 1971. Andropov to Brezhnev. Sakharov, the Human Rights Committee, and the need to meet with him. 3 folios. #130-A. APRF, #15, f. 3, op. 80, d. 638, ll. 5–10. SA, S.II.2.4.40. A brief account of Sakharov's background was attached to the report. Brezhnev's signature appears in the margin along with the phrase "Need to talk," followed by the signatures of Kosygin and Podgorny. Several sentences in the text are underlined.

24. February 12, 1971. Andropov to Central Committee. Recommendation that a party leader meet with Sakharov. 5 folios. #368-A/ov. APRF, #16, f. 3, op. 80, d. 638, ll. 11–15. SA, S.II.2.4.41. This document has marginal notes by Brezhnev, Kosygin, and Podgorny; several sentences are underlined.

25. February 19, 1971. Andropov to Central Committee. Two dissidents discuss the question of violence against the regime. 3 folios. #449-A/ov. APRF, #17, f. 3, op. 80, d. 638, ll. 16–18. SA, S.II.2.4.42. Brezhnev's signature appears in the margin and several sentences are underlined.

*26. March 18, 1971. Andropov to Central Committee. The potential influence of the Human Rights Committee. 2 folios. #703-A/ov. APRF, #20, f. 3, op. 80, d. 638, ll. 78–79. SA, S.II.2.4.45.

27. April 7, 1971. Andropov and Rudenko to Central Committee. The arrest of two Belgian tourists. 3 folios. #890-A. FCS. SA, S.II.2.5.07. Drafts of the decrees by the Central Committee and the USSR Supreme Soviet were enclosed. There are illegible signatures in the margins of the first page.

28. April 17, 1971. Andropov to Central Committee. Sakharov's broadening activity. 2 folios. #981-A/ov. APRF, #21, f. 3, op. 80, d. 638, ll. 80–85. SA, S.II.2.4.46.

29. May 13, 1971. Andropov to Suslov. An update on Sakharov and the Human Rights Committee. 4 folios. #1257-A. APRF, #22, f. 3, op. 80, d. 638, ll. 86–89. SA, S.II.2.4.47. This report on the Human Rights Committee was signed by the chief of the Second Main Directorate (counterintelligence), Major General Grigory Grigorenko, dated May 12, 1971. A handwritten note at the bottom of the first page reads: "Reported to C[omrade]. Suslov."

*30. May 21, 1971. Andropov to Suslov. Sakharov tested about violence against the regime. 1 folio. #1325-A. APRF, #23, f. 3, op. 80, d. 638, ll. 90–94. SA, S.II.2.4.48.

31. May 31, 1971. Andropov to Suslov. Another update on the activities of the Human Rights Committee. 3 folios. #1392-A. APRF, #24, f. 3, op. 80, d. 638, ll. 95–97. SA, S.II.2.4.49. This report was compiled by Major General Grigory Grigorenko on May 27. An inscription at the bottom of the first page reads: "Reported to Comrade Suslov."

*32. June 7, 1971. Andropov to Suslov. A conversation between Sakharov and his son. 1 folio. #1453-A. APRF, #25, f. 3, op. 80, d. 638, ll. 98–100. SA, S.II.2.4.50. A report is enclosed about Sakharov's contacts by the chief of the Second Directorate (counterintelligence), Major General Grigory Grigorenko, dated June 4, 1971, with an inscription at the bottom: "Reported to Comrade Suslov." 2 folios.

*33. July 6, 1971. Andropov to Suslov. A conversation between scientists. 3 folios. #1728-A. APRF, #26, f. 3, op. 80, d. 638, ll. 101–4. SA, S.II.2.4.51.

34. August 23, 1971. Andropov to Suslov, "personally." On the political abuse of psychiatry. 5 folios. #2126-A. APRF, #27, f. 3, op. 80, d. 638, ll. 105–9. SA, S.II.2.4.52.

*35. October 2, 1971. Andropov to Central Committee. On the reported nomination of Sakharov for the Nobel Prize in chemistry. 1 folio. #2491-A. FCS. SA, S.II.2.5.08. There are marginal notes at the bottom with the signatures of Viktor Chebrikov and V. Solovyov. Sakharov's name is also handwritten on the document.

36. October 2, 1971. Andropov to Suslov. The impending marriage of Andrei Sakharov and Elena Bonner. 1 folio. #2493-A. APRF, # 28, f. 3, op. 80, d. 638, ll. 113–16. SA, S.II.2.4.53. According to the inventory of transferred documents from APRF, three pages of a report signed by Seregin, deputy chief of the Fifth Main Directorate, were not released to SA.

*37. October 13, 1971. Andropov to Suslov. Sakharov's statement on the right to emigrate. 4 folios. #2590-A. APRF, #29, f. 3, op. 80, d. 638, ll. 117–20. SA, S.II.2.4.54. SA has another copy from the FCS. The copies bear different marginal notes and signatures. The Russian

translation of the English text of Sakharov's statement, dated September 20, 1971, is enclosed. Andropov's signature is on the cover
letter. Sakharov's name is handwritten on the document. A marginal
note is illegible.

38. December 15, 1971. Andropov to Central Committee. Cooperation
between Moscow activists and Ukrainian nationalists. 4 folios.
#3156-A. FCS. SA, S.II.2.5.10. This communication came from the
Kiev office of the KGB; Bobkov's signature is at the bottom of the first
page.

39. December 20, 1971. Andropov to Central Committee. Sakharov's
criticism of the regime grows harsher. 3 folios. #3188-A. APRF, #31,
f. 3, op. 80, d. 638, ll. 127–29. SA, S.II.2.4.56. A report on Sakharov
was enclosed, signed by Filipp Bobkov and dated December 15,
1971. A note at the bottom of the first page reads: "Keep in archive
by order of Comrade Tsukanov." Tsukanov was a personal assistant
to Brezhnev.

40. December 28, 1971. Pirozhkov to Central Committee. Contacts between the Human Rights Committee and groups in Europe. 1 folio.
#3270-P. FCS. SA, S.II.2.5.11. A note at the top of the first page
reads: "International Department [of the Central Committee]."

*41. January 7, 1972. Andropov and Rudenko to Central Committee.
The trial of Vladimir Bukovsky. 2 folios. #40-A. FCS. SA,
S.II.2.5.161.

42. May 26, 1972. Andropov to Central Committee. Sakharov intervenes
for political prisoners. 3 folios. #1414-A. APRF, #32, f. 3, op. 80, d.
638, ll. 131–33. SA, S.II.2.4.57. The report was signed by Bobkov
and dated May 20, 1972. Politburo members signed their names in
the left margin. A note at the bottom of the first page reads: "Keep in
archives by order of Comrade K. Chernenko." Another copy of the
report is in FCS; it differs only in being addressed to Mikhail Suslov.

43. May 26,1972. Andropov to Central Committee. Sakharov's appeals
to the Supreme Soviet. 1 folio. #1416-A. APRF, #33, f. 3, op. 80, d.
638, l. 135. SA, S.II.2.4.58. The quotations from Sakharov's appeals
were verified by Filipp Bobkov under codes 5/1–8335 and 5/1–
8336, both dated May 24, 1972. An attached report by M. Yasnov
concerned a cable sent by Sakharov and Leontovich protesting a decree of the Presidium of the Supreme Soviet calling for more severe
punishment for attempts to bring food into a labor camp; the text of
the cable is in *Chronicle of Current Events* (Amnesty International
ed., 1972), no. 26, July 5, 1972, 263–64.

44. June 26, 1972. Andropov to Central Committee. Andrei Sakharov
and the case of Pyotr Yakir. 6 folios. #1725-A. APRF, #37, f. 3, op.
80, d. 638, ll. 145–50. SA, S.II.2.4.62. Andropov's cover letter to the

Central Committee, dated July 5, 1972, was enclosed along with drafts of the decree by the Central Committee of the CPSU and excerpts from Politburo minutes reporting on the results of the vote about Sakharov dated June 27 and June 29, 1972.

45. July 10, 1972. Andropov to Central Committee. The dissidents approach other prominent figures. 2 folios. #1867-A. APRF, #35, f. 3, op. 80, d. 638, ll. 142–43. SA, S.II.2.4.60. The initials of several Politburo members are written at the bottom of the first page.

46. September 7, 1972. Tsinev to Central Committee. Moscow demonstration over the attack at the Munich Olympics. 1 folio. #2361-Ts. FCS. SA, S.II.2.5.83. This document was later published in *Izvestia*, May 20, 1992. The SA also has a more detailed report on the same event by Minister of Internal Affairs Nikolai Shchelokov, same date. 1 folio. #1/5507. SA, Vladimir Bukovsky Collection, B.8.

*47. December 7, 1972. Andropov to Central Committee. Sakharov and the vigil in Pushkin Square. 2 folios. #3015-A. FCS. SA, S.II.2.5.162.

*48. December 15, 1972. Andropov to Central Committee. Sakharov and Bonner attend the trial of Vladimir Popov. 1 folio. #3085-A. FCS. SA, S.II.2.5.15.

49. February 18, 1973. Andropov to Central Committee. The first public denunciation of Andrei Sakharov. 1 folio. #320-A. FCS. SA, S.II.2.5.16. Andropov wrote in the margin: "To Com.[rade] Chebrikov—see that it is done." Chebrikov, Bobkov, and Seregin also signed the document. At the top of the first page is a stamp: "Consent of the Central Committee secured; reported by Com.[rade] Myshenkov." This document was published in *Trud*, December 14, 1993.

50. March 1, 1973. Andropov to Central Committee. Measures to compromise the work of the Human Rights Committee. 1 folio. #459-A. APRF, #39, f. 3, op. 80, d., 639, l. 4. SA, S.II.2.4.64. A copy of the report was released by the FCS; they differ in various marginal notes.

51. March 13, 1973. Andropov to Central Committee. Sakharov and increased contact with the West. 2 folios. #567-A. FCS. SA, S.II.2.5.17. A marginal note by Andropov, "To Comrade Bobkov," is accompanied by Bobkov's signature.

52. March 28, 1973. Andropov to Central Committee. The case of Yuri Shikhanovich. 2 folios. #700-A. FCS. SA, S.II.2.5.18.

53. April 12, 1973. Andropov to Central Committee. Sakharov tries to help the children of Elena Bonner. 1 folio. #843-A. FCS. SA, S.II.2.5.19.

*54. July 5, 1973. Andropov to Central Committee. Sakharov's interview with the Swedish correspondent Olle Stenholm. 1 folio. #1585-A.

FCS. SA, S.II.2.5.82. Eleven folios of the transcript were enclosed but were not released to Bonner. The cover letter bears the signatures of Chebrikov and Bobkov.

55. August 2, 1973. Andropov and Rudenko to Central Committee. A sustained public campaign against Sakharov. 1 folio. #1837-A. FCS. SA, S.II.2.5.21. SA has a second copy of the same document from the APRF; the two copies bear different marginal notes and signatures.

56. August 14, 1973. Andropov to Central Committee. Sakharov's call for democratization. 3 folios. #1931-A. FCS. SA, S.II.2.5.22.

57. August 21, 1973. Andropov and Rudenko to Central Committee. Sakharov is summoned to meet with a prosecutor. 4 folios. #1985-A. FCS. SA, S.II.2.5.23.

*58. August 31, 1973. Andropov to Central Committee. Cover letter to accompany a research paper by the U. S. Library of Congress about samizdat. 1 folio. #2091-A. FCS. SA, S.II.2.5.84. The enclosure contained an 11-page transcript of a shortened version of the research paper.

*59. September 4, 1973. Andropov to Kosygin. Cover letter to accompany a transcript of the conversation between Malyarov and Sakharov, along with information on Sakharov. Sakharov's interview with Stenholm. Sakharov's interview with Dillon. Two issues of the émigré journal *Posev* and an issue of the émigré newspaper *Russkaya Mysl* dated July 19, 1973. 1 folio. #2124-A. FCS. SA, S.II.2.5.85. Only the cover letter was released.

60. September 8, 1973. Chebrikov to Central Committee. A meeting between Sakharov and Solzhenitsyn. 1 folio. #2176-Ch. APRF, #171, f. 3, op. 80, d. 646, l. 45. SA, S.II.2.4.195. This report has several signatures and marginal notes.

61. September 9, 1973. Chebrikov to Central Committee. Sakharov holds a press conference. 3 folios. #2177-Ch. FCS. SA, S.II.2.5.24. This document, signed by Andropov, was published in *Izvestia*, May 20, 1992, and in *Trud*, December 14, 1993.

62. September 17, 1973. Andropov to Central Committee. Détente and the need to neutralize Sakharov and Solzhenitsyn. 6 folios. #2239-A. APRF, #172, f. 3, op. 80, d. 646, ll. 85–91. SA, S.II.2.4.196. The signatures of several Politburo members and several notes are written in the margins of the first page. This document was published in Michael Scammell, ed., *The Solzhenitsyn Files: Secret Soviet Documents Reveal One Man's Fight against the Monolith* (Chicago, 1995), document 92, pp. 259–63.

63. September 18, 1973. Tsvigun to Central Committee. Sakharov on the right to emigrate and the Jackson-Vanik amendment. 2 folios. #2244-

Ts. FCS. SA, S.II.2.5.25. Chebrikov's signature is at the bottom of the first page. This document was published in *Izvestia*, May 20, 1992. A similar report from Chebrikov, #2176/Ch, appeared in Scammell, *Solzhenitsyn Files*, 251.

64. September 28, 1973. Chebrikov and Rudenko to Kosygin. Proposals on how to deal with Sakharov and Solzhenitsyn. 7 folios. #2260-Ch. FCS. SA, S.II.2.5.164. Excerpts from Sakharov's texts were enclosed. See also the Politburo's decree on establishing a special commission to deal with Sakharov and Solzhenitsyn, in Scammell, *Solzhenitsyn Files*, document 104, pp. 330–31.

65. October 19, 1973. Andropov to Central Committee. Sakharov is growing harsher in his criticism. 3 folios. #2487-A. FCS. SA, S.II.2.5.165. This document can also be found in Scammell, *Solzhenitsyn Files*, 264–66.

66. October 21, 1973. Andropov to Central Committee. The World Congress of Peace-Loving Forces comes to Moscow. 3 folios. #2508-A. FCS. SA, S.II.2.5.86.

67. November 11, 1973. Andropov to Central Committee. Sakharov meets with a foreign delegate to the World Congress of Peace-Loving Forces. 3 folios. #2736-A. APRF, #62, f. 3, op. 80, d. 640, ll. 53–55. SA, S.II.2.4.87. The APRF copy bears the signatures of Suslov, Kosygin, Podgorny, and Brezhnev. The same report was released by the FCS, bearing the signatures of Andropov and Bobkov.

*68. November 14, 1973. Andropov to Central Committee. On Lidia Chukovskaya. 3 folios. #2790-A. FCS. SA, S.II.2.5.87.

*69. November 20, 1973. Andropov to Central Committee. An academic honor from the United States. 3 folios. #2850-A. APRF, #63, f. 3, op. 80, d. 640, ll. 56–58. SA, S.II.2.4.88.

*70. December 29, 1973. Andropov to Brezhnev. A cover letter to accompany the transcript of a conversation between Sakharov and Solzhenitsyn. 1 folio. #3231-A. FCS. SA, S.II.2.5.88. According to a Central Committee note attached to the document, the enclosed transcript had 6 pages and was sent only to Brezhnev, but the transcript has not been released.

*71. December 30, 1973. Andropov to Central Committee. Sakharov honored by an American human rights organization. 2 folios. #3245-A. FCS. SA, S.II.2.5.28.

*72. January 25, 1974. Andropov to Central Committee. On Sakharov's election to the New York Academy of Sciences. 1 folio. #234-A. APRF, #64, f. 3, op. 80, d. 640, ll. 66–70. SA, S.II.2.4.89. The APRF copy bears the signatures of Andropov, Brezhnev, Podgorny, and Kosygin. The SA has another copy of the same document from the

FCS. Photocopies of the diploma and translations on 4 folios (with the name of the translator) were enclosed.

73. January 29, 1974. Andropov to Central Committee. Leaflets in support of Alexander Solzhenitsyn and Andrei Sakharov. 1 folio. #266-A. FCS. SA, S.II.2.5.30. This document appears in Scammell, *Solzhenitsyn Files*, 335, where it is described as coded in APRF as f. 3, op. 80, d. 647, l. 64. It bears the signatures of Chebrikov, deputy chairman of the KGB, and Bobkov, head of the Fifth Directorate.

*74. February 20, 1974. Andropov to Central Committee. On Western reaction to the expulsion of Solzhenitsyn. 4 folios. #511-A. RGASPI, #7, f. 5, op. 67, d. 960. SA, S.II.2.6.1.08. The signatures of several Politburo members are barely legible on the photocopy released to SA.

*75. February 22, 1974. Andropov to Central Committee. Reaction of the Italian ambassador to Solzhenitsyn's expulsion. 2 folios. 542-A. RGASPI, #8. SA, S.II.2.6.1.09. There are remnants of several signatures in the left margin of the first page.

*76. February 25, 1974. Tsvigun to Central Committee. On the investigation and arrest of people for distributing leaflets in Leningrad in defense of Solzhenitsyn and Sakharov. 1 folio. #565-Ts. FCS. SA, S.II.2.5.31.

77. March 7, 1974. Andropov to Central Committee. Proposals on how to handle Sakharov. 2 folios. #663-A. FCS. SA, S.II.2.5.32. On the first page Andropov has written "To Chebrikov and Bobkov." At the top of the first page there is a stamp of consent by the Central Committee of the CPSU and another stamp: "Personally to C.[omrade] Chernenko." Sakharov's introduction to *Sakharov Speaks* was enclosed.

*78. June 7, 1974. Andropov to Central Committee. Cover letter to accompany Sakharov's stolen manuscript "Mir cherez polveka" [The world in fifty years]. 1 folio. #1481-A. FCS. SA, S.II.2.5.89.

*79. June 17, 1974. Andropov to Central Committee. Sakharov participates in a seminar for Jewish refusenik scientists. 2 folios. #1586-A. FCS. SA, S.II.2.5.90.

80. July 1, 1974. Andropov to Central Committee. Sakharov declares a hunger strike in support of Vladimir Bukovsky and other political prisoners. 1 folio. #1797-A. FCS. SA, S.II.2.5.34.

*81. July 10, 1974. Andropov to Central Committee. On the award of the Cino del Duca Prize to Sakharov. 1 folio. #1875-A. FCS. SA, S.II.2.5.35. The signatures of Chebrikov and others appear at the bottom of the page. The enclosure contains copies of financial documents from the Rothschild Bank in Paris, with a translation of the material. 5 folios.

*82. July 24, 1974. Andropov to Central Committee. On Solzhenitsyn's assessment of Sakharov and other dissidents. 2 folios. #2035-A. FCS. SA, S.II.2.5.166. This is document 140 in Scammell, *Solzhenitsyn Files*, 388–89.

83. October 10, 1974. Andropov to Central Committee. Elena Bonner invited to Italy for medical treatment. 1 folio. #2928-A. FCS. SA, S.II.2.5.91.

*84. November 11, 1974. Andropov to Gromyko. Protesting the behavior of Senator James Buckley. 1 folio. #3184-A. SA, S.II.2.5.92.

85. November 19, 1974. Andropov to Central Committee. Sakharov's contacts with the U.S. embassy. 1 folio. #3283-A. APRF, #65, f. 3, op. 80, d. 647, l. 119. SA, S.II.2.4.90.

*86. November 30, 1974. Andropov to Central Committee. The search of Andrei Tverdokhlebov's apartment. 2 folios. #3384-A. RGASPI, #13, f. 5, op. 67, d. 960. SA, S.II.2.6.1.14.

87. January 11, 1975. Andropov to Central Committee. Continuing concern over Sakharov's contacts with American officials. 2 folios. #71-A. FCS. SA, S.II.2.5.94. The Politburo decree on this matter and the text of the note to the U.S. embassy were enclosed; the latter was identical to the KGB draft.

88. February 27, 1975. Andropov to Central Committee. Invitations to Elena Bonner for medical treatment in Europe. 2 folios. #463-A. FCS. SA, S.II.2.5.95. The signatures of Andropov, Chebrikov, and Bobkov appear in the margins.

89. March 29, 1975. Andropov to Central Committee. Sakharov insists on his wife's right to seek medical treatment in the West. 2 folios. #716-A. FCS. SA, S.II.2.5.96. Sakharov's letter to Keldysh is attached.

*90. April 5, 1975. Andropov to Central Committee. The attempt to establish an independent branch of the International PEN Club in Moscow. 3 folios.. #784-A. SA, Vladimir Bukovsky Collection, B.9.

*91. April 12, 1975. Andropov and Rudenko to Central Committee. To arrest and punish Andrei Tverdokhlebov. 3 folios. #878-A. SA, Vladimir Bukovsky Collection, B.10.

92. April 30, 1975. Andropov to Central Committee. On the right to leave one's country. 4 folios. #1070-A. FCS. SA, S.II.2.5.97. The signatures of Chebrikov and other KGB officials appear at the bottom of the first page.

*93. June 12, 1975. Andropov to Central Committee. On the activities of the ethnic German minority in the USSR. 2 folios. #1482-A. SA, Vladimir Bukovsky Collection, B.11. There are illegible signatures on the first page.

94. June 22, 1975. Andropov to Central Committee. Nobel laureates appeal on behalf of Elena Bonner. 4 folios. #1596-A. APRF, #69, f. 3, op. 80, d. 640, ll. 150–53. SA, S.II.2.4.94. A photocopy of the cable with a Russian translation was attached, with the signatures of Politburo members in the margins of the translation.

*95. June 22, 1975. Andropov to Central Committee. On Sakharov's collection of essays *O strane i mire* [My country and the world]. 5 folios.. #1597-A. FCS. SA, S.II.2.5.152. The signatures of Bobkov and Chebrikov appear.

96. July 9, 1975. Andropov to Central Committee. Sakharov continues to insist on his wife's right to seek medical treatment in Italy. 3 folios. #1780-A. APRF, # 70, f. 3, op. 80, d. 641, ll. 2–4. SA, S.II.2.4.95. The enclosure contains a copy of Sakharov's letter to Brezhnev with verification by Bobkov. The APRF document bears the signatures of several Politburo members. The SA has a copy of the same document from the FCS.

*97. July 18, 1975. Andropov to Central Committee. Sakharov's statement to the Pugwash Conference. 4 folios. #1889-A. FCS. SA, S.II.2.5.100.

98. July 18, 1975. Andropov to Central Committee. Bonner receives permission to travel abroad. 2 folios. #1899-A. FCS. SA, S.II.2.5.101. The signatures of Andropov, Chebrikov, and Bobkov are in the margins of the first page.

*99. July 21, 1975. Andropov to Central Committee. Sakharov's reaction to permission for Bonner to go to Italy. 2 folios. #1982-A. FCS. SA, S.II.2.5.102.

100. September 27, 1975. Chebrikov to Central Committee. The appearance of Sakharov's *O strane i mire* [My country and the world]. 2 folios. #2486-Ch. APRF, #71, f. 3, op. 80, d. 641, ll. 25–26. SA, S.II.2.4.96. There are marginal notes on the first page.

101. October 10, 1975. Andropov to Central Committee. Sakharov receives the Nobel Prize for peace. 2 folios. #2754-A. SA, Vladimir Bukovsky Collection, B.18. This document appeared in English in Yevgenia Albats, *The State within a State* (New York, 1994), 30–31.

102. October 28, 1975. Andropov to Central Committee. Response to the Nobel award. 4 folios. #2715-A. FCS. SA, S.II.2.5.104. Some lines have been deleted from l. 4 of the copy released to SA.

103. November 12, 1975. Andropov to Central Committee. Sakharov is not permitted to travel to Oslo for the Nobel ceremony. 1 folio. #2841-A. APRF, #79, f. 3, op. 80, d. 641, l. 63. SA, S.II.2.4.103. There are marginal notes on the first page.

104. November 13, 1975. Andropov to Central Committee. Press conference by Elena Bonner in Italy. 3 folios. #2845-A. FCS. SA, S.II.2.5.106.

105. November 16, 1975. Andropov, Ustinov, and Rudenko to Central Committee. The broad challenge posed by Sakharov and a proposal to expel him and his wife from Moscow. 5 folios. #2869-A. APRF, #81, f. 3, op. 80, d. 641, ll. 68–76. SA, S.II.2.4.105.

106. November 30, 1975. Andropov to Central Committee. Sakharov's speech for the Nobel ceremony. 1 folio. #2975-A. FCS. SA, S.II.2.5.107.

107. December 8, 1975. Andropov to Central Committee. Demonstration in Moscow's Pushkin Square. 1 folio. #3039-A. FCS. SA, S.II.2.5.108.

108. December 29, 1975. Andropov to Central Committee. Appeals to Western Communist parties and the need for continuing internal repression. 5 folios. #3213-A. SA, Vladimir Bukovsky Collection, B.12.

*109. January 11, 1976. Andropov to Central Committee. Leningrad demonstration to commemorate the Decembrist uprising of 1825. 1 folio. #81-A. FCS. SA, S.II.2.5.109.

*110. February 16, 1976. Andropov to Central Committee. The challenge posed by ongoing dissent. 3 folios. #394-A. FCS. SA, S.II.2.5.110. There is a marginal note on the first page.

111. February 21, 1976. Andropov to Central Committee. Sakharov appeals on behalf of prisoners of conscience. 2 folios. #443-A. FCS. SA, S.II.2.5.111.

112. April 15, 1976. Andropov to Central Committee. The trials of Andrei Tverdokhlebov and Mustafa Dzhemilev. 1 folio. #847-A. FCS. SA, S.II.2.5.112.

113. April 16, 1976. Andropov to Central Committee. More on the trials of Tverdokhlebov and Dzhemilev. 2 folios. #876-A. FCS. SA, S.II.2.5.46.

*114. June 21, 1976. Tsvigun to Central Committee. The funeral of Konstantin Bogatyrev. 3 folios. #1390-Ts. RGASPI, #22, f. 5, op. 69, d. 2890, ll. 46–48. SA, S.II.2.6.1.23. There is a one-page attachment with a stamp, "To inform Central Committee secretaries and C.[omrade] V. F. Shauro," above the signatures of several secretaries and Shauro.

115. August 26, 1976. Andropov to Central Committee. Sakharov and Bonner visit Andrei Tverdokhlebov in his place of exile. 2 folios. #1924-A. FCS. SA, S.II.2.5.47.

*116. September 4, 1976. Andropov to Central Committee. Sakharov's conversations with visiting Dutch parliamentarians. 2 folios. #1998-A. FCS. SA, S.II.2.5.113.

*117. September 19, 1976. Andropov to Central Committee. Sakharov's letters to Gerald Ford and Jimmy Carter during the presidential campaign. 2 folios. #2152-A. FCS. SA, S.II.2.5.114.

118. November 15, 1976. Andropov to Central Committee. Establishment of the Moscow Helsinki Watch Group. 3 folios. #2577-A. SA, Vladimir Bukovsky Collection, B.13. Several signatures appear on the first page.

*119. December 6, 1976. Andropov to Central Committee. Demonstration in Pushkin Square. 2 folios. #2755-A. RGASPI, #23, f. 5, op. 69, d. 2890, ll. 95–96. SA, S.II.2.6.1.24.

*120. December 23, 1976. Andropov to Central Committee. On Sakharov's alleged reaction to an increase in the prices of basic goods. 2 folios. #2882-A. FCS. SA, S.II.2.5.115.

121. January 18, 1977. Andropov, Gromyko, and Rudenko to Central Committee. A bomb in the Moscow subway and the expulsion of George Krimsky. 2 folios. #110-A. FCS. SA, S.II.2.5.48. The signatures of Chebrikov, Bobkov, and several other officials appear in the margins.

122. February 9, 1977. Andropov to Central Committee. Correspondence between Andrei Sakharov and Jimmy Carter. 2 folios. #261-A. FCS. SA, S.II.2.5.153.

123. February 18, 1977. Andropov to Central Committee. U.S. government activities in defense of human rights. 3 folios. #330-A. FCS. SA, S.II.2.5.168.

124. March 29, 1977. Andropov to Central Committee. The arrest of Anatoly Shcharansky. 3 folios. #674-A. SA, Vladimir Bukovsky Collection, B.14.

125. May 13, 1977. Andropov to Central Committee. The holding of the first Sakharov hearing in Copenhagen. 2 folios. #989-A. APRF, #93, f. 3, op. 80, d. 642, ll. 19–20. SA, S.II.2.5.154.

*126. June 4, 1977. Andropov to Central Committee. Sakharov's statement on the new Soviet constitution. 2 folios. #1164-A. FCS. SA, S.II.2.5.116.

127. July 20, 1977. Andropov to Central Committee. Elena Bonner travels to Italy. 2 folios. #1541-A. RGASPI, f. 5, op. 73, d. 1877, ll. 68–69. SA, S.II.2.6.1.26.

128. December 11, 1977. Andropov to Central Committee. Demonstration in Pushkin Square. 3 folios. #2631-A. RGASPI, #26. f. 5, op. 73,

d. 1877, ll. 141–43. SA, S.II.2.6.1.27. An additional page bears the inscription "To communicate to the secretaries of the CC of the CPSU" and the secretaries' signatures. The code 5665-s at the bottom of the first page probably indicates that the report originated in the Fifth Main Directorate of the KGB. It is dated December 11, 1977.

129. March 14, 1978. Andropov and Rudenko to Central Committee. Dissidents protest a PLO attack in Israel. 2 folios. #476-A. FCS. SA, S.II.2.5.117.

130. March 26, 1978. Andropov to Central Committee. Sakharov increases his contacts with foreign diplomats in Moscow. 2 folios. #566-A. FCS. SA, S.II.2.5.118.

131. May 26, 1978. Andropov to Central Committee. Confrontations between Sakharov and police. 3 folios. #1051-A. FCS. SA, S.II.2.5.119. There are marginal notes on the first page.

*132. August 1978. Andropov to Central Committee. On Western proposals to award the Nobel Peace Prize to Soviet human rights activists. 2 folios. SA, Vladimir Bukovsky Collection, B.15. The full date is not legible on the photocopy; the date of registration in the General Department of the Central Committee was September 13, 1978. There is an illegible signature on the first page.

133. October 31, 1978. Andropov and Rekunkov to Central Committee. The confiscation of Sakharov's personal papers. 3 folios. #2169-A. APRF, #97, f. 3, op. 80, d. 642, ll. 38–40. SA, S.II.2.4.121

134. December 14, 1978. Andropov to Central Committee. Elena Bonner goes to Italy. 2 folios. #2449-A. APRF, #98, f. 3, op. 80, d. 642, ll. 41–42. SA, S.II.2.4.122. Of four signatures in the left margin of the first page, those of Suslov and Brezhnev are legible. Marginal notes appear on both pages. The FCS released an incomplete copy to the SA.

135. April 25, 1979. Andropov to Central Committee. Preparations for the Moscow Olympics. 4 folios. #819-A. SA, Vladimir Bukovsky Collection, B.16. Several fragments from this document were published by Vladimir Bukovsky in *Moskovsky protsess (Moscow, 1996)*, 332–33.

136. December 26, 1979. Andropov and Rudenko to Central Committee. The case against Andrei Sakharov. 6 folios. #2484-A. APRF, #99, f. 3, op. 80, d. 642, ll. 52, 59–67. SA, S.II.2.5.49. A slightly different version of this document was published in Diane P. Koenker and Ronald D. Bachman, eds., *Revelations from the Russian Archives* (Washington, DC, 1997), 305–7. The copy here has various stamps at the top of the first page: (1) "Decree by CC of CPSU #P177/X-op"; (2) "Decree by Presidium of Supreme Soviet #1389.1390-X dated January 8,

1980"; (3) "Decree by Council of Ministers #22 dated January 8, 1980." Chebrikov's signature is at the bottom of the first page, dated December 26, 1979.

137. January 7, 1980. Andropov and Rudenko to Central Committee. Soviet government decrees on the Sakharov case. 1 folio. #68-A. FCS. SA, S.II.2.5.122.

*138. January 18, 1980. Andropov to Central Committee. Cover letter to accompany the transcript of Sakharov's interview with Charles Bierbauer of ABC News. 1 folio. #156-A. APRF, #100, f. 3, op. 80, d. 642, ll. 68–73. SA, S.II.2.4.124. There are signatures of Politburo members on the cover letter. The attachment, 5 folios with the text of the transcript, was not released.

139. January 24, 1980. Andropov to Central Committee. Responses in the West to Sakharov's banishment. 3 folios. #192-A. FCS. SA, S.II.2.4.125. Of five signatures at the top of the first page, only Suslov's and Brezhnev's are legible.

140. February 7, 1980. Andropov to Central Committee. Sakharov's first days in Gorky. 3 folios. #280-A. FCS. SA, S.II.2.4.129.

*141. February 12, 1980. Andropov to Central Committee. Sakharov and a meeting of the Academy of Sciences in Moscow. 3 folios. #315-A. FCS. SA, S.II.2.5.50.

142. April 2, 1980. Andropov to Central Committee. Attempts to visit Sakharov in Gorky. 2 folios. #634-A. FCS. SA, S.II.2.5.58. The signatures of Chebrikov and Bobkov appear at the bottom of the first page, along with marginal notes.

*143. April 24, 1980. Andropov to Central Committee. On Bonner's unsuccessful attempt to meet with KGB chairman Yuri Andropov. #797-A. 2 folios. RGASPI, #29, f. 5, op. 77, d. 994, ll. 41–42. SA, S.II.2.6.1.30.

144. August 26, 1980. Andropov to Central Committee. The mental stability of Andrei Sakharov. 4 folios. #1805-A. FCS. SA, S.II.2.5.55.

145. March 11, 1981. Andropov to Central Committee. To isolate and harass Sakharov and Bonner. 4 folios. #679-A. FCS. SA, S.II.2.5.54. The signatures of Bobkov and Chebrikov are at the bottom of the first page.

146. May 2, 1981. Andropov to Central Committee. Sakharov's sixtieth birthday. 2 folios. #1201-A. FCS. SA, S.II.2.5.125. This document appeared in *Izvestia*, May 20, 1992.

147. June 26, 1981. Andropov to Central Committee. The effectiveness of banishing Sakharov to Gorky. 3 folios. #1637-A. FCS. SA, S.II.2.5.126.

148. September 2, 1981. Chebrikov to Central Committee. The struggle

to unite Liza Alexeyeva and Alexei Semyonov begins. 2 folios. #2204-Ch. FCS. SA, S.II.2.5.53.

149. November 5, 1981. Andropov to Central Committee. How Elena Bonner continues to incite Sakharov. 3 folios. #2625-A. FCS. SA, S.II.2.5.56. There are several signatures at the bottom of the first page.

150. November 19, 1981. Andropov to Central Committee. The impending hunger strike. 2 folios. #2735-A. FCS. SA, S.II.2.5.52.

151. December 1981. Andropov to Central Committee. The hunger strike continues. 2 folios. #2859-A. FCS. SA, S.II.2.5.57. Only month and year are legible. This document was issued after December 4 (a date mentioned in the document) and before December 9 (the date of the next document). Two documents related to this report are in SA: an excerpt from the Politburo proceedings concerning the refusal to grant entrance visas for Tatiana Yankelevich and Alexei Semyonov and the cable from the Politburo to Ambassador Dobrynin in Washington, D.C., with the same directive.

*152. December 9, 1981. Andropov to Central Committee. The need to involve the Academy of Sciences. 2 folios. #2892-A. FCS. SA, S.II.2.5.59.

153. December 22[?], 1981. KGB to Central Committee. Permission to travel for Liza Alexeyeva and the health of Andrei Sakharov. 1 folio. #2965-A. FCS. SA, S.II.2.5.60. The document was doctored before it was copied and released; the last page was retyped to exclude some information. The folio indicating who sent the document is omitted from the photocopy. The code markings of the report, #2965-A, show that it was issued under the name of Andropov, but his name does not appear at the top of the report, as one would expect.

*154. March 28, 1982. Andropov to Central Committee. Questions about Sakharov's health. 2 folios. #592-A. FCS. SA, S.II.2.5.61.

155. March 31, 1982. Andropov and Rekunkov to Central Committee. Contacts between Elena Bonner and the American embassy. 2 folios. #632-A. APRF, #118, f. 3, op. 108, d. B.6.9.4.1/1, ll. 105–6. SA, S.II.2.4.142. Another copy of the report was released by the FCS with the signatures of both authors on the first page.

*156. April 2, 1982. Andropov to Central Committee. Sakharov's "Open Letter to Soviet Scientists." 3 folios. #656-A. FCS. SA, S.II.2.5.62. A draft decree by the Central Committee of the CPSU had been attached to this report, but it was not released.

157. August 13, 1982. Fedorchuk to Central Committee. The need to confiscate Sakharov's memoirs. 2 folios. #1668-F. FCS. SA, S.II.2.5.127.

158. August 31, 1982. Fedorchuk to Central Committee. Sakharov's ap-

peal to the Pugwash Conference. 2 folios. #1789-F. FCS. SA, S.II.2.5.128. This document appeared in Diane P. Koenker and Ronald D. Bachman, eds., *Revelations from the Russian Archives* (Washington, DC, 1997), 304–5.

159. September 12, 1982. Fedorchuk to Central Committee. The closing of the Moscow Helsinki Watch Group. 3 folios. #1866-F. FCS. SA, S.II.2.5.129.

160. November 1, 1982. Fedorchuk to Central Committee. The seizure of Sakharov's memoirs. 3 folios. #2139-F. FCS. SA, S.II.2.5.64. The bottom of the first page is signed by Chebrikov and Bobkov, who probably was in charge of the operation.

*161. November 15, 1982. Fedorchuk to Central Committee. An incident during a performance at the Moscow Art Theater. 1 folio. #2219-F. RGASPI, #34, f. 5, op. 88, d. 1083, ll. 167–69. SA, S.II.2.6.1.35.

162. December 4, 1982. Fedorchuk to Central Committee. A plan to search Elena Bonner. 3 folios. #2351-F. FCS. SA, S.II.2.5.130.

163. December 8, 1982. Fedorchuk to Central Committee. Confiscation of Sakharov's papers from Elena Bonner. 3 folios. #2367-F. APRF, #120, f. 3, op. 108, d. B.6.9.4.1/1, ll. 115–17. SA, S.II.2.4.144. The signatures of several Politburo members appear at the top of the first page.

164. December 22, 1982. Chebrikov to Central Committee. More on the search of Elena Bonner. 2 folios. #2463-Ch. FCS. SA, S.II.2.5.132. The signatures of several Politburo members appear at the top of the first page.

*165. April 19, 1983. Chebrikov to Anatoly Alexandrov, president of Soviet Academy of Sciences. Cover letter to accompany the text of Sakharov's "Open Letter to Sidney Drell." 1 folio. #824-Ch. FCS. SA, S.II.2.5.133.

*166. May 19, 1983. Tsinev to Central Committee. On attempts by Sakharov to challenge his isolation in Gorky. 2 folios. #1061-Ts. APRF, #125, f. 3, op. 108, d. B.6.9.4.1/1, ll. 149–50. SA, S.II.2.4.149. There is a marginal inscription at the bottom of the second page.

167. January 23, 1984. Chebrikov to Central Committee. Appeal from Sakharov to permit Elena Bonner to travel to the West. 3 folios. #115-Ch. APRF, #126, f. 3, op. 108, d. B.6.9.4.1/1, ll. 152–54. SA, S.II.2.4.150. Handwritten notes on this document: "We are requesting your consent" and "The KGB has been notified that consent is given (Com[rade] Sidorenko A. T.). January 26, 1984." The signatures of several Politburo members appear on the first page.

168. March 5, 1984. Chebrikov to Central Committee. Efforts to isolate Sakharov more effectively. 3 folios. #343-Ch. FCS. SA, S.II.2.5.65.

Annotated List of KGB Documents

There are three signatures, dated February 2, 1984, at the bottom of the first page; only Bobkov's is legible.

169. April 13, 1984. Chebrikov to Central Committee. A long and dangerous hunger strike is about to begin. 2 folios. #594-Ch. FCS. SA, S.II.2.5.66. There are several signatures at the bottom of the first page; one of them is Bobkov's.

170. April 26, 1984. Gromyko, Chebrikov, and Rekunkov to Central Committee. How the KGB will handle the hunger strike. 4 folios. #686-Ch. APRF, #127, f. 3, op. 108, d. B.6.9.4.1/1, ll. 162–68. SA, S.II.2.5.156. This message was the background report for a Politburo decision ("point 20 of protocol #156").

171. May 3, 1984. Gromyko and Chebrikov to Central Committee. The hunger strike and official measures to thwart the plans of Sakharov and Bonner. 3 folios. #460/gs. APRF, #128, f. 3, op. 108, d. B.6.9.4.1/1, ll. 169–71. SA, S.II.2.4.152. This is not the customary KGB coding. It probably refers to Gromyko and the Ministry of Foreign Affairs, which will have to deal directly with the U.S. embassy.

172. May 12, 1984. Chebrikov and Rekunkov to Central Committee. The hunger strike continues. 3 folios. #787-Ch. FCS. SA, S.II.2.5.68. Bobkov's signature is at the bottom of the first page.

173. May 20, 1984. Chebrikov to Central Committee. How the KGB is handling the hunger strike. 4 folios. #833-Ch. FCS. SA, S.II.2.5.157.

174. June 5, 1984. Leonid Zamyatin to Central Committee. A rumor that Sakharov has died. 3 folios [This is one of only two documents in this collection that was not generated by the KGB.] #19-3-71. APRF, #134, f. 3, op. 108, d. B.6.9.4.1/2, ll. 2–4. SA, S.II.2.4.158. The digits #19–3-71 are coding issued most likely by the Department of Foreign Political Propaganda, a department of the Central Committee responsible for counterpropaganda; it worked to maintain a favorable image of the Communist regime. A note at the bottom of the first page reads: "To archives. M. Sokolov. June 19, 1984." There is an illegible signature on the last page.

175. July 6, 1984. Chebrikov to Central Committee. The manipulation of international concern over Sakharov. 2 folios. #1103-Ch. FCS. SA, S.II.2.5.69.

176. August 13, 1984. Chebrikov, Terebilov, and Bazhenov to Central Committee. The trial of Elena Bonner. 2 folios. #1297-Ch. APRF, #135, f. 3, op. 108, d. B.6.9.4.1/2, ll. 14–15. SA, S.II.2.4.159. There are three signatures at the end of the document and a marginal note at the bottom of the last page.

177. September 12, 1984. Tsinev to Central Committee. More effective isolation of Elena Bonner. 2 folios. #1448-Ts. FCS. SA, S.II.2.5.137.

178. February 14, 1985. Chebrikov to Central Committee. Sakharov's letter to the president of the Academy of Sciences. 2 folios. #246-Ch. APRF, #137, f. 3, op. 108, d. B.6.9.4.1/2, ll. 28–29. SA, S.II.2.4.161.

179. April 13, 1985. Chebrikov to Central Committee. A report for Gorbachev on the possibility of another hunger strike. 4 folios. #631-A. APRF, #138, f. 3, op. 108, d. B.6.9.4.1/2, ll. 31–34. SA, S.II.2.4.162.

180. July 20, 1985. Chebrikov to Central Committee. Sakharov leaves the hospital. 3 folios. #1291-Ch. APRF, #139, f. 3, op. 108, d. B.6.9.4.1/2, ll. 36–38. SA, S.II.2.4.163.

181. August 3, 1985. Chebrikov to Central Committee. Sakharov resumes his hunger strike. 2 folios. #1393-Ch. FCS. SA, S.II.2.5.141.

182. August 28, 1985. Chebrikov and Shevardnadze to Gorbachev. The KGB and Foreign Ministry recommend that Bonner be allowed to travel. 5 folios. #1560-Ch. FCS. SA, S.II.2.5.142.

183. October 12, 1985. Chebrikov to Gorbachev. Pledges to Gorbachev from Sakharov and Bonner. 1 folio. #1881-Ch. FCS. SA, S.II.2.5.143. The report included copies of Sakharov's letters to Gorbachev and Chebrikov, dated September 5, 1985, and Bonner's letters to Gorbachev and Chebrikov of the same date.

184. November 26, 1985. Chebrikov to Gorbachev. Bonner's travel to the West. 3 folios. #2180-Ch. FCS. SA, S.II.2.5.144.

*185. [Sometime in] 1985. Bobkov to Lukyanov. Cover letter to accompany two enclosed documents in response to a request from Lukyanov: (a) fragments from Sakharov's memoirs, which had been stolen from his apartment; (b) a copy of Andropov's report about Roy Medvedev, dated August 4, 1968. 1 folio. #1773-B. SA, Vladimir Bukovsky Collection, B.17. Neither document was released. They were mailed in 1970 and 1968 respectively.

186. February 7, 1986. Chebrikov to Central Committee. Bonner extends her visit to the United States. 1 folio. #225-Ch. APRF, #145, f. 3, op. 108, d. B.6.9.4.1/2, l. 63. SA, S.II.2.4.169. The signatures of several Politburo members appear on the top of the first page.

187. May 11, 1986. Chebrikov to Central Committee. The impact of Bonner's stay in the United States. 2 folios. #874-Ch. APRF, #146, f. 3, op. 108, d. B.6.9.4.1/2, ll. 71–72. SA, S.II.2.4.170.

188. June 17, 1986. Chebrikov to Gorbachev. The KGB reports to Gorbachev on Sakharov and other prisoners of conscience. 3 folios. #1163-Ch. FCS. SA, S.II.2.5.146.

189. June 18, 1986. Chebrikov to Central Committee. Bonner in the West; Sakharov on the Chernobyl accident. 6 folios. #1172-Ch. APRF, #149, f. 3, op. 108, d. B.6.9.4.1/2, ll. 85–90. S.II.2.4.173. The signatures of all Politburo members appear on the first page.

190. December 9, 1986. Ligachev, Chebrikov, and Marchuk to Central Committee. A proposal to allow Sakharov and Bonner to return to Moscow. 4 folios. #2407-Ch. FCS. SA, S.II.2.5.147. Attached documents are in RGASPI, f. 89, op. 25, d. 9, ll. 1–3. SA, S.II.2.6.1.85.

191. January 15, 1987. Shevardnadze, Chebrikov, Yakovlev, and Dobrynin to Central Committee. How to exploit Sakharov's return to Moscow. 3 folios. #84-Ch. FCS. SA, S.II.2.5.70. Below the authors' signatures is a date: December 31, 1986. So the date at the beginning (January 15, 1987) must be the mailing date, and that explains the exceptional coding of the document: Usl #84Ch. The letter *Ch* means that the final version of the document was issued by Viktor Chebrikov. The reasons for the delay from December 31 to January 15 are not clear.

192. June 19, 1987. Chebrikov to Gorbachev. Sakharov and two American physicists discuss disarmament. 1 folio. APRF, f. 89, op. 18, d. 114. SA, S.II.2.5.71. Chebrikov did not give the date of the conversation. The cover letter of this document and a shortened version of it were published by Iu. Krivonosov in *Voprosy istorii estestvoznaniia i tekhniki* [Problems in the history of science and technology], no. 3 (1993), 131–32. The copy in SA bears an archivist's note: "Declassified for Kovalev. Extracts from text for quotation only."

*193. October 13, 1988. Politburo meeting. The decision to restore Sakharov's prizes and awards. 2 folios. APRF, #158, f. 3, op. 108, d. B.6.9.4.1/2, ll. 239–40. SA, S.II.2.4.182. The declassified copy was spliced together from the transcript of the meeting on October 13, 1988. It appears to include the text of point 8 (on the restoration of Sakharov's awards) in its entirety. Vladimir Kryuchkov was not included in the list of participants, but he had just been nominated as KGB chairman and took part in the discussion. (This is the second document in the collection that was not generated by the KGB.)

194. October 15, 1988. Kryuchkov to Central Committee. The establishment of Moscow Tribune. 3 folios. #1791-K. FCS. SA, S.II.2.5.148.

195. November 16, 1988. Kryuchkov to Central Committee. The establishment of Memorial. 5 folios. 1979-K. FCS. SA, S.II.2.5.149.

196. June 30, 1989. Kryuchkov to Gorbachev. More on Moscow Tribune. 4 folios. #1342-K/ov. FCS. SA, S.II.2.5.73. Bobkov's signature appears at the bottom of the first page.

197. November 14, 1989. Kryuchkov to Gorbachev. Sakharov's influence on the labor movement in the Vorkuta mining region. 2 folios. #2292-K/ov. FCS. SA, S.II.2.5.74. Bobkov's signature appears on the document.

198. December 4, 1989. Kryuchkov to Central Committee. Sakharov's

call for a general strike. 2 folios. #2451-K/ov. FCS. SA, S.II.2.5.169. According to the code 2451-K/ov, this report, though addressed to the Central Committee, was issued and registered in the *osobaya papka* (or special archive) of the general secretary.

199. December 8, 1989. Kryuchkov to Gorbachev. Sakharov's radical ideas and his growing support. 4 folios. #2482-K/ov. FCS. SA, S.II.2.5.75. Bobkov's signature appears at the bottom of the first page.

200. December 8, 1989. Kryuchkov to Central Committee. The impending general strike. 2 folios. #2483-K/ov. FCS. SA, S.II.2.5.76. Bobkov's signature appears at the bottom of the first page.

201. December 18, 1989. Kryuchkov to Central Committee. The funeral of Andrei Sakharov. 2 folios. #2551-K. FCS. SA, S.II.2.5.77.

202. December 20, 1989. Kryuchkov to Central Committee. More on the funeral of Andrei Sakharov. 3 folios. #2568-K. FCS. SA, S.II.2.5.78. Bobkov's signature appears at the bottom of the first page.

203. December 23, 1989. Kryuchkov to Central Committee. The political consequences of Sakharov's death. 2 folios. #2588-K. FCS. SA, S.II.2.5.150.

*204. August 10, 1991. Kryuchkov to Elena Bonner and Yuri Samodurov. Letter concerning preparations for the First International Sakharov Congress. 3 folios. #1565-K. FCS. SA, S.II.2.5.79.

# Glossary of Names

**Abakumov, Viktor**  Head of military counterintelligence, 1943–46; minister of the interior, 1946–51

**Adamovich, Alexander**  Writer, literary scholar; co-chairman of Memorial; founding member of Moscow Tribune

**Afanasiev, Yuri**  Historian, co-chairman of Memorial Society; closely collaborated with Sakharov

**Albrekht, Vladimir**  Mathematician, human rights activist, political prisoner

**Alexandrov, Anatoly**  Nuclear physicist, president of Academy of Sciences, 1975–86

**Alexeyeva, Elizaveta (Liza)**  wife of Elena Bonner's son, Alexei Semyonov

**Alexeyeva, Ludmilla**  Historian, member of Helsinki Watch Group

**Aliyev, Geidar**  Chairman of Azerbaijan Communist Party from 1969; member of Central Committee from 1971; member of Politburo, 1982–87

**Altman, Anatoly**  Leningrad skyjacker; emigrated 1979

**Altshuler, Lev**  Physicist at the Installation

**Amalrik, Andrei**  Historian, dissident; emigrated 1976

**Andropov, Yuri**  Chairman of KGB, 1967–82; general secretary of Communist Party, 1982–1984

**Artsimovich, Lev**  Nuclear physicist, academician

**Astaurov, Boris**  Biologist, professor

**Avtorkhanov, Abdurakhman**  Chechen Party official; scholar, escaped during World War II
**Azbel, Mark**  Physicist, Jewish emigration activist

**Baklanov, Oleg**  Communist Party official, secretary of Central Committee of CPSU in 1988
**Barabanov, Yevgeny**  Art historian, religious activist
**Basov, Nikolai**  Physicist, academician
**Batkin, Leonid**  Historian, collaborated with Sakharov in Moscow Tribune in 1989
**Bazhenov, N.**  First deputy prosecutor of USSR in 1984
**Belinkov, Arkady**  Literary scholar, dissident; emigrated 1968
**Biryukova, Alexandra**  Chairman of trade unions, 1968–86; secretary of Central Committee for light industry and consumer goods production, 1986–88; deputy prime minister, 1988–89
**Blinov, P. V.**  Head of Leningrad mental hospital in 1971
**Bobkov, Filipp**  Chief of Fifth Directorate of KGB, 1971–85; deputy chairman of KGB from 1985
**Bogatyrev, Konstantin**  Poet and translator
**Bogoraz, Larisa**  Linguist, human rights activist; took part in demonstration in Red Square against invasion of Czechoslovakia, August 1968
**Bolonkin, Alexander**  Mathematician, human rights activist
**Bonner, Elena**  Pediatrician, second wife of Andrei Sakharov, human rights activist
**Borisov, Vladimir**  Worker, dissident
**Brezhnev, Leonid**  General secretary of Communist Party, 1964–82
**Brodsky, Joseph**  Poet; awarded Nobel Prize in literature, 1987; emigrated 1972
**Brunov, Yevgeny**  Sought Sakharov's support against KGB persecution
**Bukovskaya, Nina**  Radio journalist, mother of Vladimir Bukovsky, dissident
**Bukovsky, Vladimir**  Writer and human rights activist; released from prison in 1976 in exchange for Luis Corvalán, head of Communist Party of Chile
**Burenkov, S. P.**  Official of Ministry of Health in 1981
**Burtin, Yuri**  Literary critic

**Chakovsky, Alexander**  Writer, editor in chief of *Literaturnaya Gazeta*
**Chalidze, Valery**  Physicist, human rights activist, writer, publisher
**Chebrikov, Viktor**  Chairman of KGB, 1982–88; member of Politburo from 1985
**Chernenko, Konstantin**  General secretary of Communist Party, 1984–85

**Chernichenko, Yuri**   Journalist, member of Congress of People's Deputies

**Chernovil, Vyacheslav**   Ukrainian journalist, dissident

**Chernykh, Vasily**   Baptist, dissident

**Chlenov, Mikhail**   Anthropologist, Jewish activist

**Chukovskaya, Lidia**   Writer, human rights activist

**Chukovsky, Kornei**   Writer, literary critic

**Daniel, Yuli [pseud. Nikolai Arzhak]**   Writer, dissident

**Davidovich, Yefim**   Decorated World War II fighter pilot, Jewish refusenik

**Delone, Vadim**   Poet, dissident; emigrated 1975

**Demichev, Pyotr**   Secretary of Central Committee in charge of ideology, 1961–74; minister of culture, 1974–86

**Dobroshtan, Igor**   Political prisoner under Stalin; speaker at Memorial conference, November 1987

**Dobrynin, Anatoly**   Soviet ambassador to United States, 1962–86

**Dolgikh, Vladimir**   Secretary of Central Committee in charge of heavy industry and energy, 1976–83

**Dymshits, Mark**   Jewish emigration activist, pilot in Leningrad skyjacking case; sent to America as part of a prisoner exchange in 1979

**Dzarasov, S. G.**   Researcher at Academy of Sciences; participant in Moscow Tribune in 1988

**Dzhemilev, Mustafa**   Worker, Crimean Tatar activist, political prisoner

**Dzyuba, Ivan**   Ukrainian literary critic, dissident

**Esenin-Volpin, Alexander**   Poet, mathematician, dissident; emigrated 1972

**Fainberg, Viktor**   Mechanic, dissident; emigrated 1974

**Fedorchuk, Vitaly**   Chairman of Ukrainian KGB from 1970; chairman of KGB, 1982; minister of interior, 1982–86

**Feinberg, Yevgeny**   Nuclear physicist, academician

**Feldman, Alexander**   Jewish emigration activist

**Fyodorov, Yuri**   Worker, dissident, Leningrad skyjacker

**Gabai, Ilya**   Teacher, poet, dissident

**Galanskov, Yuri**   Poet, dissident; died in labor camp

**Galich, Alexander**   Poet, playwright, balladeer; emigrated 1974

**Gamsakhurdia, Zviad**   Georgian dissident and literary scholar

**Gastev, Yuri**   Mathematician, philosopher, dissident

**Gefter, M. M.**   Historian; founding member of Moscow Tribune, 1988

**Genkin, Sergei**   Mathematician, dissident

**Ginzburg, Alexander** Editor and journalist, human rights activist, prisoner; sent to America as part of a prisoner exchange in 1979

**Ginzburg, Vitaly** Physicist, academician; awarded Nobel Prize in physics, 2003

**Glazov, Yuri** Linguist, dissident; emigrated 1972

**Gluzman, Semyon** Psychiatrist, human rights activist

**Golikov, A. P.** Corresponding member of Academy of Medical Science; sent to Gorky with Samsonov to supervise force-feeding of Sakharov in May 1984

**Gorbachev, Mikhail** General secretary of Communist Party, 1985–91

**Gorbanevskaya, Natalya** Poet, first editor of *A Chronicle of Current Events;* emigrated 1975

**Gordon, L. A.** Researcher, Institute of International Workers Movement; participated in founding meeting of Moscow Tribune

**Graver, Petter** Norwegian ambassador to USSR in 1975

**Grechko, Andrei** Marshal; minister of defense, 1967–76

**Grigorenko, Pyotr** General, writer, human rights activist; emigrated 1977

**Grishin, Viktor** Member of Politburo; first secretary of Moscow Committee of the Communist Party, 1967–85

**Gromyko, Andrei** Foreign minister, 1957–85

**Guseinov, Gasan** Researcher at Institute of World Literature; participated in founding meeting of Moscow Tribune

**Handler, Philip** Biochemist; president of National Academy of Sciences, 1969–81

**Henry, Ernst** Pseudonym of Leonid Khentov, alias Semyon Rostovsky; intelligence agent, journalist

**Ilin, Anatoly** Army officer, attempted to assassinate Brezhnev

**Ivanov, Vyacheslav** Linguist, literary critic, dissident

**Izgoev, Alexander** Philosopher; emigrated 1922

**Kadomtsev, Boris** Physicist, academician

**Kalistratova, Sofia** Attorney, human rights activist

**Kantorovich, Leonid** Mathematician; Nobel laureate in economics, 1975

**Kapitonov, Ivan** Secretary of Central Committee in charge of organizational party work, 1965–86

**Kapitsa, Pyotr** Physicist; Nobel laureate in physics, 1978

**Karavansky, Sviatoslav** Writer, translator, dissident

**Karpinsky, Len** Journalist and publisher, wrote for samizdat; expelled from Communist Party, 1975

**Karyakin, Yuri** Writer, sociologist, editor; expelled from Communist Party, 1968

**Kaverin, Veniamin** Writer and literary scholar

**Keldysh, Mstislav** Mathematician; president of Academy of Sciences, 1961–75

**Khalif, Lev** Writer, dissident

**Khantsis, Yankel** Worker, dissident; emigrated 1974

**Khariton, Yuli** Physicist, academician, research director of Installation

**Khaustov, Viktor** Worker, dissident

**Kheifets, Mikhail** Writer, dissident

**Khenkin, Kirill** Journalist, Jewish emigration activist

**Khodorovich, Tatyana** Linguist, human rights activist; emigrated 1975

**Khrushchev, Nikita** General secretary of Communist Party, 1953–64

**Kim, Yuli** Poet, singer, composer, dissident

**Kirilenko, Andrei** Member of Politburo; secretary of Central Committee; supervised party organization and Soviet industry in Secretariat, 1964–82

**Kirillin, Vladimir** Physicist; chairman, State Committee on Science and Technology

**Knuniants, Ivan** Organic chemist, defended academic freedom against Lysenkoism

**Kopelev, Lev** Writer and critic; dissident, stripped of Soviet citizenship in 1980

**Korchak, A. A.** Physicist, member of Helsinki Watch Group in 1976

**Kornienko, Georgy** Deputy Minister of Foreign Affairs in 1986

**Kornilov, Lavr** General; leader of failed counterrevolutionary uprising in Russia, 1917

**Korzhavin, Naum** Poet, dissident; emigrated 1973

**Kosygin, Alexei** Prime minister, 1964–80

**Kotelnikov, Vladimir** Vice president of Academy of Sciences; protested award of Nobel Peace Prize to Sakharov, 1975

**Kovalev, Sergei** Biologist, human rights activist

**Kovalskaya, Galina** Activist in Moscow Tribune, 1989

**Krasin, Viktor** Economist, dissident; emigrated 1975

**Krasnov, M. M.** Ophthalmologist

**Krasnov-Levitin, Anatoly** Writer, religious philosopher, dissident; emigrated 1974

**Kristi, Irina** Mathematician, dissident; emigrated 1985

**Kryuchkov, Vladimir** Chairman of KGB, 1988–91

**Kulakov, Fyodor** Head of Department of Agriculture of Central Committee from 1964; member Politburo, 1971–78

**Kunaev, Dinmukhamed** Member of Politburo; first secretary of Kazakh Communist Party

**Kurchatov, Igor**  Nuclear physicist, academician, director of Atomic Energy Institute

**Kuznetsov, Eduard**  Writer, dissident, Leningrad skyjacker; sent to America as part of a prisoner exchange in 1979

**Landa, Malva**  Geologist, human rights activist

**Leontovich, Mikhail**  Physicist, academician

**Lerner, Alexander**  Computer scientist, Jewish emigration activist; emigrated 1987

**Levshina, Olga**  Mathematician, first wife of Alexei Semyonov; emigrated 1980

**Ligachev, Yegor**  Secretary of Central Committee in charge of ideology and party organization, then of agriculture, 1985–88; member of Politburo

**Lisovsky, Yuri**  Physicist; participant in Moscow Tribune, 1988

**Litvinov, Pavel**  Physicist, dissident; emigrated 1974

**Litvinova, Tatyana**  Translator, human rights activist; emigrated 1974

**Lukin, Vladimir**  Politician and dissident

**Lukyanov, Anatoly**  Lawyer, member of Central Committee from 1987; chairman of Supreme Soviet, 1988–91

**Lunts, Alexander**  Jewish emigration activist

**Lyubimov, Yuri**  Actor, stage director; emigrated 1983

**MacWilliams, E.**  First secretary of U.S. embassy, 1984

**Maisky, Ivan**  Diplomat, historian, academician

**Maltsev, Yuri**  Dissident

**Malyarov, Mikhail**  Deputy procurator general of USSR

**Marchenko, Anatoly**  Writer, dissident, prisoner

**Marchuk, Guri**  Physicist, president of Academy of Sciences

**Maximov, Vladimir E.**  Novelist, editor in chief of *Kontinent;* emigrated 1974

**Mazurov, Kirill**  First secretary of Belorussian Communist Party, 1956–65; member of Politburo, 1964–78

**Medvedev, Roy**  Historian, writer, dissident

**Medvedev, Vadim**  Member of Politburo and secretary of Central Committee overseeing ideology, 1988–90

**Mendelevich, Iosif**  Leningrad skyjacker

**Meshko, Oksana**  Ukrainian human rights activist

**Migdal, Arkady**  Physicist, academician

**Mikheev, Dmitri**  Physicist, arrested for attempting to flee to West; emigrated 1978

**Millionshchikov, Mikhail**  Physicist, academician, administrator

**Moroz, Valentin** Historian, Ukrainian dissident

**Moskovchenko, Nikolai** Representative of military association Shield at memorial service for Sakharov

**Murashov, Arkady** Member of Congress of People's Deputies

**Murzhenko, Alexei** Writer, Leningrad skyjacker, political prisoner

**Nashpits, Mark** Dentist, Jewish emigration activist

**Nazarov, Anatoly** Dissident

**Nekipelov, Viktor** Pharmacist, poet, human rights activist

**Nekrasov, Viktor** Writer; emigrated 1974

**Nekrich, Alexander** Historian; expelled from Communist Party, 1967; emigrated 1976

**Nikonov, Viktor** Minister of agriculture of Russian Federation. 1983–85, then secretary of Central Committee in charge of agriculture; member of Politburo, 1987–89

**Novikov, Ignaty** Chairman of State Committee for Construction, 1962–83

**Novikov, Sergei** Mathematician, academician

**Nudel, Ida** Jewish emigration activist; emigrated 1987

**Okudzhava, Bulat** Poet, novelist, balladeer

**Orlov, Yuri** Physicist, chairman of Moscow Helsinki Watch Group, political prisoner; exiled 1986

**Osipova, Tatiana** Human rights activist; emigrated 1987

**Palatnik, Raisa** Librarian, dissident; emigrated 1972

**Pavlovsky, Gleb** Staff member of *Dvadtsatyi vek i mir* (Twentieth century and peace); participant in Moscow Tribune, 1988

**Pelshe, Arvid** Member of Politburo and chairman of Committee for Party Control, 1966–83

**Perutz, Max** Biochemist, Nobel laureate in chemistry, 1962

**Petrovsky, Leonid** Historian, dissident

**Pimenov, Revolt** Mathematician, writer, dissident

**Pirozhkov, Vladimir** Deputy chairman of KGB, 1971

**Pitirim [Konstantin Nechaev]** Head of Publishing Department of Moscow Patriarchate of Russian Orthodox Church, 1963–74; metropolitan of Volokolamsk and Yurev, 1986–2003

**Platonov, Yuri** Memorial official, 1988

**Plyushch, Leonid** Mathematician, dissident, writer, confined in psychiatric hospital; emigrated 1976

**Podgorny, Nikolai** Chairman of Presidium of Supreme Soviet and member of Politburo, 1965–77

**Podrabinek, Alexander**  Writer, human rights activist

**Podyapolskaya, Maria**  Human rights activist

**Podyapolsky, Grigory**  Geophysicist, writer, human rights activist

**Poindexter, John**  Admiral; national security adviser to Reagan, 1981–88

**Polyansky, Dmitri**  Member of Politburo, 1960–76; minister of agriculture, 1973–76

**Ponomarev, Boris**  Candidate member of Politburo, 1972–86

**Popov, Gavriil**  Economist and politician, member of Congress of People's Deputies

**Pressel, Joseph**  First secretary, Political Department, U.S. embassy, 1977

**Purnell, Jon**  Second secretary, U.S. embassy, 1984

**Rekunkov, Alexander**  Procurator general of USSR from 1981

**Rigerman, Leonid**  Chemist, human rights activist; emigrated 1971

**Roginsky, Arseny**  Historian, founding member of Memorial

**Romanov, Grigory**  First secretary of Leningrad Communist Party, 1973–76; member of Politburo from 1976; secretary of Central Committee in charge of armed forces and defense industry, 1983–85

**Romaszewski, Zbigniew**  Polish dissident, member of Polish Committee for Defense of Workers

**Romm, Mikhail**  Film director and scriptwriter

**Rosario, Romeo**  Professor in Rome; participated in Bonner press conference in Italy, November 1975

**Rostropovich, Mstislav**  Cellist, conductor; emigrated 1974

**Rubin, Vitaly**  scholar of ancient Chinese philosophy, Jewish emigration activist; emigrated 1976

**Rudakov, Ivan**  Human rights activist

**Rudenko, Mykola**  Ukrainian dissident, writer

**Rudenko, Roman**  Procurator general of USSR, 1953–81

**Runov, Georgy**  Physician in Gorky during Sakharov's compulsory confinement in hospital and hunger strike, winter 1981–82

**Rusakov, Konstantin**  Aide to Brezhnev, 1972–77; secretary of Central Committee, 1977–86

**Rybakov, Anatoly**  Writer

**Rybkin**  Official of Ministry of Interior, 1971

**Ryzhkov, Nikolai**  Secretary of Central Committee from 1982; member of Politburo from 1985; chairman of Council of Ministers, 1985–91

**Salakhov, Timur**  Painter; participant in establishment of Memorial, 1988

**Salova, Galina**  Dissident; participant in demonstration in Pushkin Square, December 5, 1975

**Samodurov, Yuri**   Geologist; director of Andrei Sakharov Museum, Moscow

**Samsonov, M. A.**   Corresponding member, Academy of Medical Sciences; sent to Gorky with Golikov to oversee force-feeding of Sakharov during hunger strike, May 1984

**Sanger, Frederick**   Twice recipient of Nobel Prize in chemistry, 1958 and 1980

**Schmemann, Serge**   Moscow bureau chief of *New York Times*, 1980–86, 1991–94

**Schmidt, Helmut**   Chancellor of Federal Republic of Germany, 1974–82

**Sebreghts, Hugo**   Belgian tourist arrested by KGB, March 1971

**Semyonov, Alexei**   Mathematician, Elena Bonner's son; emigrated 1978

**Semyonova [Yankelevich], Tatiana**   Daughter of Elena Bonner; emigrated 1977

**Sergienko, Alexander [Olexander]**   Ukrainian dissident

**Shafarevich, Igor**   Mathematician, corresponding member of the Academy of Sciences, dissident, Russian nationalist

**Shakhovskaya, Zinaida**   Russian émigré writer

**Shatunovskaya, Nadezhda**   Dissident, participant in demonstration in Pushkin Square, December 5, 1975

**Shcharansky, Anatoly [Natan Sharansky]**   Human rights activist; prisoner, exchanged 1986

**Shchelokov, Nikolai**   Minister of interior, 1968–82

**Shcherbitsky, Vladimir**   Member of Politburo, 1971–89; first secretary of Ukrainian Communist Party, 1972–89

**Sheinis, Viktor**   Researcher, Institute of World Economy; participant in Moscow Tribune, 1988

**Shelepin, Alexander**   Chairman of KGB, 1958–61; member of Politburo, 1964–75; chairman of trade unions, 1967

**Shenfeld, Ignaty**   Polish émigré writer

**Shevardnadze, Eduard**   Minister of interior, Georgia, 1968–72; first secretary of Georgian Communist Party, 1972–85; foreign minister of USSR, 1985–91

**Shikhanovich, Yuri**   Mathematician, human rights activist, prisoner

**Shipler, David K.**   *New York Times* correspondent in Moscow, 1975

**Short, Philip**   BBC correspondent in Moscow, 1974–76

**Shtern, Mikhail**   Physician, Jewish emigration activist

**Simonov, Konstantin**   Writer

**Sinyavsky, Andrei [pseud. Abram Tertz]**   Writer and literary critic; political prisoner; emigrated 1973

**Skobeltsyn, Dmitri**   Physicist, academician

**Skryabin, Georgy**   Biologist, secretary of Academy of Sciences

**Skubko, Yuri**   Speaker at Memorial conference, October 1988

**Slepak, Vladimir**　Electronics engineer, refusenik

**Slyunkov, Nikolai**　First secretary of Belorussian Communist Party; member of Politburo and secretary of Central Committee in charge of economy, 1987–90

**Smith, Hedrick**　*New York Times* correspondent; interviewed Sakharov, March 1973

**Solomentsev, Mikhail**　Chairman of Council of Ministers of Russian Federation from 1971; member of Politburo and chairman of Party Control Committee, 1983–88

**Solzhenitsyn, Alexander**　Writer; awarded Nobel Prize in literature, 1970

**Solzhenitsyna, Natalya**　Mathematician; second wife of Alexander Solzhenitsyn

**Stalin, Joseph**　Longtime dictator of the Soviet Union

**Starovoitova, Galina**　Social anthropologist; member of Congress of People's Deputies; member of Russian Parliament from 1990

**Stenholm, Olle**　Correspondent of Swedish Radio and Television; interviewed Sakharov, 1973

**Stone, Jeremy**　Physicist; president of Federation of American Scientists

**Stroeva, Yelena**　Dissident; emigrated 1972

**Strokatova [Strokataya], Nina**　Microbiologist, Ukrainian dissident

**Superfin, Gabriel**　Literary scholar, dissident

**Suslov, Mikhail**　Member of Politburo from 1955; secretary of Central Committee in charge of ideology, 1955–82

**Terebilov, Vladimir**　Minister of Justice from 1970

**Thant, U**　Secretary General of United Nations, 1962–72

**Thatcher, Margaret**　Prime Minister of United Kingdom, 1979–90

**Tikhonov, Nikolai**　Member of Politburo from 1979; chairman of Council of Ministers, 1980–85

**Tikhonov, Vladimir**　Member of Congress of People's Deputies, political ally of Sakharov

**Timofeev, Lev**　Journalist, political prisoner; speaker at Memorial conference, October 1988

**Toth, Robert C.**　*Los Angeles Times* correspondent, 1977

**Trapeznikov, Sergei**　Head of Department of Science and Education Institutions, Central Committee, 1965–83

**Trutnev, Yuri**　Nuclear physicist, academician

**Tsinev, Georgy**　Deputy chairman of KGB from 1970; member of Central Committee

**Tsitlyonok, Boris**　Jewish emigration activist

**Tsukerman, Boris**　Physicist, human rights activist

**Tsvigun, Semyon**　Chairman of Tadzhik KGB, 1957–63; chairman of

Azerbaijan KGB, 1963–67; first deputy chairman of USSR KGB, 1967–82

**Turchin, Valentin**   Mathematician, physicist, writer, human rights activist; emigrated 1977

**Tvardovsky, Alexander**   Poet; editor of *Novy Mir*

**Tverdokhlebov, Andrei**   Physicist, dissident; emigrated 1980

**Ustinov, Dmitri**   Marshal; minister of defense, 1976–84

**Vail, Boris**   Puppeteer, political prisoner

**Vance, Cyrus**   U.S. secretary of state; visited Moscow, March 1977

**Velikanova, Tatyana**   Mathematician, human rights activist

**Velikhov, Yevgeny**   Vice president of Academy of Sciences from 1978; director of Kurchatov Institute of Atomic Energy from 1988

**Verdi, L. L.**   Distributed leaflets in defense of Sakharov and Solzhenitsyn, Leningrad, January 1974

**Vishnevskaya, Galina**   Soprano, wife of Mstislav Rostropovich; emigrated 1974

**Vladimov, Georgy**   Writer; emigrated 1975

**Vlasov, Alexander**   Chairman of Council of Ministers of RSFSR, 1988–90

**Vlasov, Andrei**   Russian general captured by Germans, 1942; head of anti-Soviet military units, 1943–45

**Voinovich, Vladimir**   Writer and playwright, human rights activist; emigrated 1980

**Volkenshtein, Mikhail**   Biophysicist, corresponding member of Academy of Sciences

**Volkov, Oleg**   Writer, political prisoner

**Vorotnikov, Vitaly**   Member of Politburo, 1983–90; chairman of Council of Ministers of Russian Federation, 1983–88

**Walesa, Lech**   Chairman of Solidarity trade union; awarded Nobel Peace Prize, 1983; president of Poland, 1989–96

**Weizsäcker, Richard von**   Mayor of West Berlin, 1981–84; president of Federal Republic of Germany, 1984–94

**Worsnip, Patrick**   Reuters correspondent in Moscow, 1975

**Wren, Christopher**   U.S. correspondent, covered demonstration in Pushkin Square, December 5, 1975

**Yakhimovich, Ivan**   Teacher, kolkhoz chairman, dissident

**Yakir, Pyotr**   Historian, dissident

**Yakobson, Sergius**   Library of Congress specialist, co-author of *Aspects of Intellectual Ferment in the USSR*

**Yakovlev, Alexander**   Head of Propaganda Department of Central Committee, 1985–86; member of Politburo, 1987–90

**Yakovlev, Nikolai**   Historian, writer

**Yakunin, Gleb**   Russian Orthodox priest, religious activist

**Yankelevich, Efrem**   Electronic engineer, son-in-law of Elena Bonner, representative of Sakharov abroad; emigrated 1977

**Yazov, Dmitri**   Marshal; minister of defense, 1987–91

**Yeltsin, Boris**   Member of Central Committee from 1981; first secretary of Moscow Communist Party Committee, 1985–87; president of Russian Federation, 1991–99

**Yermakov, A. F.**   Secretary of Cinematographers' Union

**Yevtushenko, Galina**   Friend of Andrei Sakharov and Elena Bonner


**Zaikov, Lev**   First secretary of Leningrad Communist Party Committee, 1983–85; secretary of Central Committee in charge of defense industry, 1985–87; first secretary of Moscow Communist Party Committee, 1987–89

**Zalmanson, Wolf**   Leningrad skyjacker; emigrated 1979

**Zamyatin, Leonid**   Member of Central Committee, 1976–90; director general of TASS, 1970–78; head of International Information Department, Central Committee, 1978–86

**Zeldovich, Yakov**   Nuclear physicist, Sakharov's friend and colleague

**Zheludkov, Sergei**   Theologian, Russian Orthodox priest; religious activist

**Zhivlyuk, Yuri**   Physicist

**Zimyanin, Mikhail**   Deputy foreign minister, 1960–65; editor in chief, *Pravda*, 1965–78; member of Politburo from 1980; head of Propaganda Department of Central Committee, 1978–85

**Zolotukhin, V. T.**   Deputy director of Moscow Office of Visas and Registrations, 1975

# Selected Bibliography

WORKS BY ANDREI SAKHAROV

*Alarm and Hope.* Trans. Efrem Yankelevich and Alfred Friendly Jr. New York: Knopf, 1978.
*Collected Scientific Works.* Ed. D. ter Haar, D. V. Chudnovsky, and G. V. Chudnovsky. New York: Marcel Dekker, 1982.
*Memoirs.* New York: Knopf, 1990.
*Moscow and Beyond, 1986–1989.* New York: Knopf, 1991.
*My Country and the World.* New York: Knopf, 1975.
*Progress, Coexistence, and Intellectual Freedom.* New York: Norton, 1968.
*Sakharov Speaks.* Trans. and ed. Harrison E. Salisbury. New York: Knopf, 1974.

WORKS BY ELENA BONNER

*Alone Together.* New York: Knopf, 1986.
*Mothers and Daughters.* New York: Knopf, 1992.

SELECTIONS OF MATERIALS BY AND ABOUT SAKHAROV

*Andrei Sakharov and Peace.* Ed. Edward Lozansky. New York: Avon, 1985.
*On Sakharov.* Ed. Alexander Babyonyshev. New York: Knopf, 1982.

BIOGRAPHIES

Bailey, George. *The Making of Andrei Sakharov*. New York: Penguin, 1990.

Lourie, Richard. *Sakharov*. Hanover, NH: Brandeis University Press and University Press of New England, 2002.

# Index

Academy of Sciences: appeal for travel abroad, 300–301; appeal from Sakharov, 180–181; Congress of People's Deputies, 65; denunciations, 190, 193; membership, 9; mental illness accusations, 41; Moscow Tribune, 332; official warnings on anti-Soviet behavior, 161–162; participation in meetings, 268; protest against awarding Nobel Peace Prize to Sakharov, 194–196; resignation threat, 301, 311; termination of contact with, 258; unauthorized meeting with foreign scientist, 106

Adamovich, A. M., 331, 332, 337

Afanasiev, Yu. N., 331, 336, 337, 344–346, 348

Afghanistan invasion, 36–37, 65–66, 241–242, 260–261, 320

Aksyonov, Vasily, 28

Albrekht, Vladimir, 192, 219

Alexandrov, Anatoly, 41, 246, 258, 283, 301, 311

Alexeyeva, Liza, 234–235, 261–268, 282

Alexeyeva, Ludmilla: comment on KGB language, 3; emigration, 28, 220; Helsinki Watch Groups, 34, 218; human rights movement, 21; KGB surveillance, 219

Aliyev, Geidar, 246, 294, 326

Allende, Salvador, 32, 164

All-Union Research Institute of Experimental Physics, 87, 89, 95–97

*Alone Together* (Bonner), 305, 314

Amalrik, Andrei: amnesty appeals, 213; dissident activities, 4, 17, 21, 26, 59; emigration, 28; human rights activism, 34; Soviet collapse, 69, 149

amnesty appeals, 134–138, 212–213

Amnesty International, 6, 141, 170, 217, 242

Andrei Sakharov Museum and Public Center, 75

Andropov, Yuri: and Bonner, 143–144, 176, 198–204, 237, 264–265, 268–269; and Carter, Jimmy, 222–223; confiscation of personal documents, 234–236; death of, 26, 43–44; decision to exile Sakharov, 197, 198–204, 243–254; disparagement of Sakharov, 33, 40–41, 71–72, 88; Eurocommunism, 205–212; Helsinki Watch Groups, 217–219; Human Rights Committee, 101–102, 104–106, 110–111, 132–133, 140; hunger strikes, 175, 265–267; importance of internal repression, 207–212; isolation efforts, 256–258, 260–261; as KGB chairman, 2, 18, 47; as member of Politburo, 38; mental health of Sakharov, 254–256; Nobel Peace Prize, 191–197, 204–205; Olympic Games (Moscow, 1980), 237–239; political prisoners, 134–135, 212–213; popularity of Sakharov and Solzhenitsyn, 173–174; press campaign against Sakharov, 139–140, 144–146; and "Progress, Coexistence, and Intellectual Freedom," 86–88, 98; Pushkin